The Oneiric in the Films of David Lynch

The Oneiric in the Films of David Lynch

A Phenomenological Approach

Raphael Morschett

BLOOMSBURY ACADEMIC
NEW YORK • LONDON • OXFORD • NEW DELHI • SYDNEY

BLOOMSBURY ACADEMIC

Bloomsbury Publishing Inc, 1359 Broadway, New York, NY 10018, USA
Bloomsbury Publishing Plc, 50 Bedford Square, London, WC1B 3DP, UK
Bloomsbury Publishing Ireland, 29 Earlsfort Terrace, Dublin 2, D02 AY28, Ireland

BLOOMSBURY, BLOOMSBURY ACADEMIC and the Diana logo are trademarks of
Bloomsbury Publishing Plc

First published in the United States of America 2024
Paperback edition published 2026

Copyright © Raphael Morschett, 2024

For legal purposes the Acknowledgments on p. ix constitute an extension of this
copyright page.

Cover design: Eleanor Rose
Cover photograph: Laura Harring in *Mulholland Drive*; Dir. David Lynch; 2001 © Les Films
Alain Sarde / Asymmetrical Productions / Collection Christophel /
ArenaPAL www.arenapal.com

All rights reserved. No part of this publication may be: i) reproduced or transmitted in
any form, electronic or mechanical, including photocopying, recording or by means of
any information storage or retrieval system without prior permission in writing from
the publishers; or ii) used or reproduced in any way for the training, development or
operation of artificial intelligence (AI) technologies, including generative AI technologies.
The rights holders expressly reserve this publication from the text and data mining
exception as per Article 4(3) of the Digital Single Market Directive (EU) 2019/790.

Bloomsbury Publishing Inc does not have any control over, or responsibility for, any
third-party websites referred to or in this book. All internet addresses given in this
book were correct at the time of going to press. The author and publisher regret any
inconvenience caused if addresses have changed or sites have ceased to exist,
but can accept no responsibility for any such changes.

Library of Congress Cataloging-in-Publication Data

Names: Morschett, Raphael, author.
Title: The oneiric in the films of David Lynch : a phenomenological approach /
Raphael Morschett.
Description: New York : Bloomsbury Academic, 2024. | Includes bibliographical
references and index.
Identifiers: LCCN 2023055194 (print) | LCCN 2023055195 (ebook) | ISBN 9798765107041
(hardback) | ISBN 9798765107058 (paperback) | ISBN 9798765107089 (ebook) |
ISBN 9798765107072 (pdf)
Subjects: LCSH: Lynch, David, 1946–Criticism and interpretation. |
Dreams in motion pictures.
Classification: LCC PN1998.3.L96 M67 2024 (print) | LCC PN1998.3.L96 (ebook) |
DDC 791.4302/33092–dc23/eng/20240220
LC record available at https://lccn.loc.gov/2023055194
LC ebook record available at https://lccn.loc.gov/2023055195

ISBN: HB: 979-8-7651-0704-1
PB: 979-8-7651-0705-8
ePDF: 979-8-7651-0707-2
eBook: 979-8-7651-0708-9

Typeset by Deanta Global Publishing Services, Chennai, India

For product safety related questions contact productsafety@bloomsbury.com.

To find out more about our authors and books visit www.bloomsbury.com and sign up
for our newsletters.

Für Vivianna Indira

Contents

Acknowledgments ix

Introduction: Directing the Lynchian Dream 1

Part I Methodology and Concepts

1 Film Phenomenology 13
   The Role of Subjectivity in Film Analysis 15
   Auditory Perception in the Film Experience 20

2 Phenomenology and the Oneiric Film 23
   Framing the Object of Investigation 23
   The Implicit Phenomenological Basis of the Film/Dream Analogy 25
   Explicitly Phenomenological Studies on Oneiric Film 29
   The Lynchian Oneiric and Phenomenology 33
   Dream Phenomenology and Freudian Psychoanalysis 37
   Systematic Approach 42

Part II The Oneiric in the Films of David Lynch: A Phenomenological Approach

3 Three Early Short Films (1967–70) 49
   Absurd Encounter with Fear (1967) 49
   The Alphabet (1968) 53
   The Grandmother (1970) 64

4 *Eraserhead* (1977) 82
   Audio-Viewing *Eraserhead* 82
   Dream Experience in *Eraserhead* 84
   The Dream as the Meta-Medium of Lynch's Films? 110

5 *Twin Peaks* (1990–1; 1992; 2017) 113
   Proper (Spatio-)temporality in Cooper's Dream (Season One of *Twin Peaks*) 113
   Oneiricity and Temporality in Season Three of *Twin Peaks* 121

6 *Lost Highway* (1997) 153
   Audio-Viewing *Lost Highway* 153
   The Dream between Loss of Reality and Dissociative (Identity) Disorder 158
   Oneiric Self-Reflexivity and Meta-Mediality 169

7	*Mulholland Drive* (2001)	174
	Audio-Viewing *Mulholland Drive*	174
	The Interconnection of Dream and Film	179
	Club Silencio—A Cinematic Reflection on the Bodily Nature of Film Viewing/Dreaming and on the Dreamlike Ontology of Film	196
	Conclusion: The "Twin Peak" of the Lynchian Oneiric	210
	Pre-reflective Sensory Address	211
	Reflective Medialization	213
	"Watch and Listen to the Dream of Time and Space"	217
	Notes	223
	Works Cited	250
	Index	262

Acknowledgments

A big thank you goes out to many people who have contributed to this work in a variety of ways. First of all to my supervisors, Professor Astrid Fellner and Professor Stephanie Catani, whose encouragement, trust, and commentaries were of great importance to the initiation and continuous development of this project; to my colleagues from the DFG-funded Research Training Group "European Dream-Cultures" at Saarland University for a pleasant and open atmosphere, and to the professors who created the research training group for bringing something special to life; to Professor Engel and Professor Miedema for their critical commentary on two chapters and the structure of this work; to Dr. Simon Dickson who supported me at an early stage of research; to my mother, Anna, and my father, Mario, my brothers, Roman and Robert, and my sister, Giannina, for their kind and supportive words in the years before and during this work; to my meticulous proofreaders Manon Preußner, Leoni Ziemen, Philipp König, Nils Fischer, Lukas Motsch, Max Paulus, Johannes Rudolph, Ipek Atila, Tristan Piotrowski, and Milena Fichtner; to Max Holl for designing a cover for an earlier version of this book; to Lukas Motsch for introducing me to the "wonderfully strange" world of *Twin Peaks*; and to Manon for her oneiric way of being.

Introduction

Directing the Lynchian Dream

There is hardly a contemporary film director whose name is as closely linked to the dream(-like) as that of David Lynch.[1] Yet at the same time, the dream has never been placed at the center of a book-length study on his films—a fact that is all the more surprising given that his films, which are among the most studied in film history, are frequently identified by their dreamlike atmosphere. The dream researcher Kelly Bulkeley, for example, attributes to Lynch "the uncanny skill in using cinema as a means of conveying the moods, mysteries, and carnivalesque wildness of our dreams" ("Dreaming" 49). Embodying a unique aesthetics, Lynch's cinema defies easy classification, as neologisms such as "Lynchland," "Lynchville," and "Lynchism" suggest (Kaul and Palmier 7; Schmidt 9–10; Rodley 125). The name of the American director, whom *The Guardian* called "the most important film-maker of the current era," has even been turned into an adjective recently, as an entry in the *Oxford English Dictionary* acknowledges. "Lynchian," it is suggested, refers to the "juxtapos[ition of] surreal and sinister elements with mundane, everyday environments, and [the usage of] compelling visual images to emphasize a *dreamlike quality* of mystery or menace" (my italicization).[2] The Lynchian seems to be closely related to the dreamlike—but what exactly does "dreamlike" mean in this characterization? A definition of "Lynchian" is unsatisfactory, too, if it relies on a second term that remains unclear in meaning.

Lynch's recent memoir/biography is titled *Room to Dream* (2018), a phrase he uses himself in an interview with Chris Rodley (228). Lynch's cinema, as a whole, may be termed a "room to dream," both as a metaphor for the underlying creative act bringing it into being and because of its potentially "dreamlike" effect on the viewers. There are countless descriptions of Lynch's films as "dreamlike," to the extent that the word risks losing its meaning in regard to them. After all, if his cinema is dreamlike by nature (cf. Lahde 95),[3] then it is impossible to distinguish between *more* dreamlike and *less* dreamlike sequences; that is, the characterization is not specific enough to be meaningful.[4] Arguably, a certain fuzziness may be implied by the word "dreamlike" itself. It is often used as a word for that which cannot be fully grasped, thus becoming a word that *really* expresses a gap or void, the inability of language to signify. And yet, because it describes something important about Lynch's films, this study seeks to draw closer to the dreamlike, to make it a bit more tangible, even if, in the end, it will not simply be nameable or definable by a fixed set of characteristics. Approaching the dreamlike requires a thorough exploration of the aesthetics, structure, and function of the depicted dream experiences. In a certain sense, the dreamlike in this work functions as the notion of verification does in Karl Popper's philosophy of science. A statement is scientific only as long as there is the possibility that it could be false (Popper 10).[5] This reflects the aspiration for truth of the scientific endeavor, which structurally shapes scientific discourse, acts as its motor, so to speak, but, by definition, never stands as fully realized (for then, the statement would no longer be falsifiable and thus unscientific). If the question for truth structures scientific discourse in general, the question for the "oneiric," analogously, structures this work. To be clear, the primary focus in this book is not on working out the *concept* of the Lynchian oneiric but on "measuring the scope of experience" provided by the dream(-like) sequences (cf. Morsch 9–10; my translation).[6] This work is phenomenological rather than philological in nature. While the notion of the Lynchian oneiric does give a common thread to this study, it is continually sharpened at the same time.

The main argument of this book is that the Lynchian oneiric exhausts the full spectrum of the film experience between the poles of pre-reflective sensory address and reflective medialization. It is in the dynamic interplay between sensory and reflective oneiricity that Lynch's cinema unfolds its full potential. Through the oneiric mode (understood as indicated by the four "dimensions" later in the text), Lynch's films both involve the viewer sensorially and challenge her[7] perceptual patterns, on the one hand, while also reflecting on their own status as films, on the other. In the former respect, the sensory potential of Lynch's films is discussed both on the character level and on the level of film–viewer interaction. In the latter respect, the focus is on the psychological and media-aesthetic potential of the dream. I will show how the experiences represented in and presented by Lynch's dream(-like) sequences are crucial for understanding (1) the role that immersion and disruption play in the viewer's sensory experience of the films and (2) the way in which Lynch's films conceive of themselves as films. For one, the oneiric brings out film's inherent fascination with the material world, with what immediately appears to the senses and how it appears. As I move through Lynch's filmography, it will become clear that the Lynchian oneiric also increasingly manifests the reflective potential of the medium, a capacity that Robert Sinnerbrink calls "cinematic thinking," that is, a "non-conceptual affective thinking in images that resists cognitive closure or theoretical subsumption" (*New Philosophies* 139). More specifically, the Lynchian oneiric reflects on cinema's poetic possibilities of representation and perception in making mediality a phenomenological characteristic of dream experience. In a first step, however, it addresses the viewer's senses, vacillating between immersion and disruption, between stabilizing our material relationship to the film world and de-automatizing our perception of it. In equal measures, thus, the films discussed in this book can be understood as a contribution to media theory and to the phenomenology of dreaming. As the subtitle of Tanja Michalsky's paper on *Lost Highway* (1997)—"a filmic contribution to media theory" (397; my translation)[8]— shows, the media-reflexive dimension has been taken into account in the study of individual films. But the significance of the medial dimension in Lynch's pre-1997 and post-1997 films as well as its special relationship to dreams has yet to be explored. This is where this book comes in, showing that it is Lynch's cinema itself—the dream in particular—that reflects on the nature of the medium. Further, I link back Lynch's medial oneiricity to the fundamentally ambivalent material dynamic of the night dream. While dreams frequently involve intense bodily sensations (e.g., dreams of flying), in order for a dream to occur, one needs to "let go of the bodily self of sensation and to let appear an *other*" (Brudzinska 60; my translation and italicization).⁹ So the dream is a bodily and a medial experience at the same time, and the question arises whether or not film—that is, a *medium* predicated on the performance of *embodied* perception—uses this dynamic in its depiction of the oneiric.

Lynch's cinema has invited studies from very diverse theoretical backgrounds, such as psychoanalysis (Žižek and Mc Gowan), narratology (Buckland, Kaul and Palmier, Kuhn, Kreuzer, Laass), genre studies (Sellmann, Schröder), auteur studies (Menarini, Dottorini), semiotics (Basso Fossali), (film-)philosophy (Sinnerbrink, Riches), sound studies (Chion, Kalinak, Heiland, and Van Elferen), and even quantum physics (Nochimson). Why add *phenomenology* to the list? And what does it mean to approach the infamous "oneiricity" of Lynch's films from a phenomenological perspective? Essentially, it means that both viewer and film are conceptualized as subjects for experience that first *perceive* pre-reflectively before taking a stance toward the film images on a reflective level (as "objects" of experience), that is, before "reading" these images "as" something. The extension of the discourse around Lynch's films toward a poetics of experience is not attempted for the sake of theoretical reasons (or as an end in itself) but is demanded by Lynch's films themselves. A cognitive reading of his cinema remains insufficient; the diegetic worlds of *Twin Peaks* (2017) and *Lost Highway* (1997), for example, are systematically designed as ontologically ambiguous (regarding the dream/reality status). Thus, it seems all the more important for the analysis to address a more fundamental level of cinematic communication: namely, before the images and sounds of a film can be conceived as a (diegetic) "world," they present themselves as perception (perceiving–perceived) and experience (experiencing–experienced). In other words, the interest in the dream experience (i.e., the experience *in* the dream, its aesthetic design, and the spectator experience *of* the dream scene) is the direct result of the systematic denial of knowledge constituted by dreams and dream structures. In an exemplary manner, this shift of focus to the pre-reflective level of film experience is put on display by the Club Silencio scene in *Mulholland Drive* (2001; 01:44:46–01:52:53). Naomi Watts's character shows an almost violent physical reaction to a stage show, which reveals the illusory nature of her reality. On the edge of a dream that is about to collapse, sensory intensity is a direct result of the inability to understand.

The idea in this study is to approach the more abstract category of the dreamlike through the more graspable dream sequence, in a first step. This may appear self-evident, given that the meaning of "dreamlike" relies on that of its lemma "dream." What was observed so far could be understood as a warning against the inflationary use of the term "dreamlike" in regard to Lynch's cinema. Wary of overusing the term—but curious about its basis at the same time—one can ask why there are (marked) dreams at all in Lynch's cinema, if it is already dreamlike in nature. In other words, what is the function of a marked unit of dream experience if the experience of the whole film is already dreamlike in itself? To understand this function, one must first get a sense of the *nature* of Lynch's dream sequences. What are they like? How can they be described in terms of their aesthetics and structure? What kind of perception is expressed through a Lynchian dream? And how does the particular perceptual form of the dream relate to its content? As a cinematic form with particular properties, the dream is both an *object of* experience (a sequence as a unit of experience inserted into a stream of waking experience) and a *subject for* experience (embodying an experiential agency with idiosyncratic rules). What role does the dream, understood as both an *object of* and a *subject for* experience, as both content and form of experience, play in the context of a film as a whole?

For Kenneth Godwin, the distinction between content and form is significant when it comes to the question of the particular qualities of Lynchian dreams: "More than any other filmmaker, Luis Buñuel included, Lynch has managed to capture not only the *matter* of dream, but, more importantly, the *manner*, also. His film [. . .] is not only a fantasy related to us and labeled 'dream,' something which we can stand apart from as passive observers. *It is the dream experience itself*" (Godwin qtd. in Lahde 95). Even though Godwin wrote this passage in 1984—that is, long before *Twin Peaks* (1990-1; 1992; 2017), *Lost Highway* (1997), and *Mulholland Drive* (2001) were released—he makes an important point that will often be made about Lynch's oeuvre as a whole: the Lynchian oneiric has a particularly involving quality for the viewer. While critics and fans have frequently commented on the subjective dimension of "experiencing a Lynch movie," much less analytic work has been done on the part of theoretically inflected research. This may be related to the fact that the field of film studies has only recently embraced the subjective dimension of film experience—it is only since the 1990s that film phenomenology has become a "legitimate" subdiscipline. Ever since Vivian Sobchak's landmark study *The Address of the Eye: A Phenomenology of Film Experience* (1992), film phenomenology has grown into a well-respected strand of film studies, making valuable contributions to the practice of film analysis. If Sobchak argues that film has the ability to *express perception* as something that is, in turn, perceived by the viewer (*Address* 3), then it should be stressed that this (former) perception does not necessarily intend the external world but extends to include our dreams, that is, "internal perceptions." The potential of film to depict dreams and dreamlike states has frequently been asserted in film scholarship and criticism since the early days of the cinematic medium but has only rarely led to a distinctively film-phenomenological approach to dream representations (cf. Chapter 2). That is, the dream(-like) on film remains underspecified from the perspective of theories of experience and perception—a gap that this study aims to fill.

From this perspective, the choice of David Lynch's films as the objects of this investigation seems appropriate, not only because they provide a paradigmatic example of contemporary filmic representations of the dream(-like) but also because they combine two forms of cinematic oneiricity. Alongside Andrei Tarkovsky, Ingmar Bergman, and Luis Buñuel, Lynch is one of the few directors whose films both contain marked dream sequences and are said to evoke a broader dreamlike quality (cf. Menarini 16). The exploration of the interplay between these two forms of oneiricity (i.e., between dimension 1, on the one hand, and dimension 2 and 3, on the other; see later in the chapter) will drive much of the analyses. In my approach, the analysis of dream experience paves the way for a deeper understanding of the *oneiric*, that is, a broader, more abstract category comprising four dimensions. For all of these dimensions, I am interested in both the fictional experience that the film characters make *in* a dream and the viewer's experience *of* a dream sequence. First of all, there is experience as it occurs in marked dreams. Second, "oneiric" applies to experiences that can be said to be *like* experience in a marked dream ("dream*like*" in the literal sense, if "dream" refers to the experience in a marked dream sequence). In a third sense of the word, "oneiric" refers to those aspects of specific sequences that aim for an imitation of the nocturnal dream-experience (see the section on *Absurd Encounter with Fear* in Chapter 3, "Oneiricity and the Ambivalence of Sensory Motor Activation" in Chapter 5, and "It [Cinema] is an Illusion . . ." in Chapter 7). To be sure, "(nocturnal) dream-experience" refers to the experience of a nonfictional night dream. A fourth sense of "oneiric" builds upon the way the dream is conceptualized in and by films. Concerning the fourth dimension, it is important to note that, in addition to sequences evoking dream(-like) experience, verbalizations *about* the dream come into play. In this categorization, it is important to note that the proposed four dimensions are not mutually exclusive. A scene may be marked as a dream (and thus assigned to dimension 1) while asking for a conceptualization of the dream (dimension 4) at the same time (e.g., Cole's dream in *Twin Peaks*'s [2017] "Part 14"). This list gives a schematic overview over the main sequences analyzed in this study and how they relate to the oneiric:

Dimension 1: Dream experience (i.e., experience in a marked dream)

- The girl's dream in *The Alphabet* (1968)
- The birth of the grandmother in the boy's dream in *The Grandmother* (1970)[10]
- Henry's (day-)dreams in *Eraserhead* (1977)
- *Twin Peaks* (1990–1; 2017):
  - Cooper's dream ("Episode 2")
  - Cole's dream ("Part 14")
- Fred's dream in *Lost Highway* (1997)
- Diane's dream in *Mulholland Drive* (2001)

Dimension 2: Dreamlike experience ("like" or "in reference to" experience in a marked dream)

- Scenes displaying *haptic visuality* (cf. Marks 178) in *The Grandmother* (1970) (→ the boy's dream)
- *Twin Peaks* (1990–1; 1992; 2017)
  - The room above the purple sea ("Part 3") (→ Cooper's dream)
  - The Convenience Store
    - Phillip Jeffries at the FBI headquarters in *Twin Peaks: Fire Walk with Me* (1992) (→ Cooper's dream)
    - "Part 8" (→ Cooper's dream)

- *Lost Highway* (1997)
  - The dissolution of the protagonist's identity in the finale (→ mysterious face as Fred "wakes up" → upside-down face in *The Alphabet*)
  - Alice/Renée: The ambivalence of personal identity (→ Renée not being herself in Fred's dream)

Dimension 3: Imitation of the night dream ("like" or "in reference to" [the memory of] nocturnal dream-experience)

- *Absurd Encounter with Fear* (1967)
- *Lost Highway* (1997): Ambivalence of personal identity—Alice "is" and Renée, and she "is not" (Freud's *mischperson*; cf. *Traumdeutung* 324)
- "Club Silencio" in *Mulholland Drive* (2001)
- The room above the purple sea in *Twin Peaks* (2017; "Part 3")

Dimension 4: Conceptualizations of dream experience

- *Mulholland Drive* (2001)
  - "and now I'm in this dream place"—Diane's psychological-American dream
  - The interconnection of dream and film ("dream in film," "film as dream," and "dream as film")
- *Twin Peaks* (1992; 2017)
  - Monica Bellucci in Cole's dream ("Part 14"): "Who is the dreamer?"
  - "The dream of time and space"/"We live inside a dream"—Oneiric disruption of space-time ("Part 17" and "Part 18"; *Twin Peaks: Fire Walk with Me* [1992])

Dreams and the oneiric have never been placed at the center of a monographic exploration of Lynch's films. Further, the Lynchian oneiric has never been studied under a phenomenological lens—a surprising fact, especially because the dream seems to provide a blueprint for what Lynch considers a particularly intense and unique *film experience* (cf. Rodley 15 and section "The Lynchian Oneiric and Phenomenology" in Chapter 2).[11] When the oneiricity of his cinema is investigated in existing literature, the conception of dream underlying the analyses tends to be exclusively mimetic. The (implied) question is in what regard his cinema as a whole *imitates* the night dream, and to what extent his films can be called "dreamlike" based on that (e.g., Lahde 98). In a book chapter on "The Dream Logic of *Twin Peaks*," Bulkeley, for example, concludes that "[e]very dream-related phenomenon in the *Twin Peaks* series has some grounding in current dream research" and that "[i]n that sense, David Lynch has presented a 'realistic' vision of dreaming" ("*Twin Peaks*" 72–3). The approach in this study, on the other hand, is *constructivist* to begin with. Rather than asking how "accurate" a given film or scene imitates the nocturnal dream-experience, it asks for the ways in which the impression of oneiricity is constructed *by the film*, departing from the experiences occurring in marked dreams. That is, in a first step, it is the film that indicates what is dream, what is not, and it is the film that hints at what is dreamlike, that is, which elements of the experience as it occurs in marked dreams also occur in unmarked sequences. This requires a thorough description of the former and latter category in terms of their experiential characteristics. It is only in a second step, then, that I ask for potential similarities between the experience of a given sequence and the experience of the nocturnal nonmedial dream. This approach aims at the *creative* aspect of the Lynchian oneiric or, more generally, at the expressive potential of the filmic medium in evoking the oneiric—a potential that, unlike in Bulkeley's conception, is not necessarily rooted in the "realistic" depiction of dreaming.

Concerning the writings of Todd McGowan on Lynch, it is striking that, despite their heavy reliance on psychoanalysis, the dream is not recognized as special among the imaginative abilities of the characters. Rather than being considered in its own right, the dream serves as the formal frame for the experience of *fantasy*. Following Jacques Lacan, McGowan distinguishes between the world of *desire*, defined by "the absence of the object" of enjoyment, and the world of *fantasy*, defined by the excessive enjoyment of the satisfying object (*Impossible* 19). If fantasy rests on the excess of the satisfying object, and dreams and fantasy are essentially the same, then how is it possible to account for those of Lynch's dream depictions that can hardly be called satisfactory for the dreamer—for example, the girl's dream in *The Alphabet* (1968), Fred's dream in *Lost Highway* (1997), and Cole's dream in Part 14 of *Twin Peaks* (2017)? These dreams are less about the desire for or the excess of a satisfying object than about existential fear. Further, McGowan's central argument is that "[t]he great achievement of his [Lynch's] films lies in their ability to break down the distance between spectator and screen" (*Impossible* 2). It is McGowan's basic assumption that "cinema is predicated on distance," that "proximity is imaginary" (1–2). It is crucial to note here that, from a phenomenological perspective, the distance between spectator and screen can only be grasped in retrospect. It is only from the perspective of reflection that the viewer recognizes the imaginary status of proximity. In the immediate pre-reflective experience of film, the viewer is directly involved by the scenario unfolding on the screen. Rather than "break down the distance between spectator and screen" (2), thus, Lynch exploits a potential that film already possesses to begin with, that is, that of pre-reflective sensory address. But it is not just a general neglect of the pre-reflective dimension of the film experience that informs McGowan's approach to Lynch. What McGowan overlooks, further, is the *dream's* significance as a sensory experience. As the dream shows, it is not only the elimination of distance, that is, the viewer's immersion into the film world, that matters—the fascination of Lynchian viewer involvement consists in its ambivalence, as it provokes both immersion and disruption, a play between stabilizing the viewer's material relationship to the film world and de-automatizing his perception of it.

A common question underlies all analysis chapters—they all explore the nature and function of the oneiric on the spectrum of pre-reflective sensory address, on the one hand, and reflective medialization, on the other. How are characters and viewers involved sensorially by the oneiric experiences in Lynch's films? And what is the psychological and media-aesthetic potential of the dream? Does the dream play a role in the film's self-conception? At the same time, this study will do justice to the *specificity* of each film in evoking the oneiric instead of rigidly enforcing a single thematic focus that would risk ignoring the different characteristics of the oneiric in the diverse filmography of Lynch. It will become clear that despite—or rather *through*—its unified methodological approach, this study allows for the films' individuality. If there is one big advantage of phenomenology over other methods of analysis, it is its inherent fascination with what immediately appears to consciousness. That is, it starts with a description of the sensory phenomenon instead of imposing theoretical assumptions upon it from the very beginning. In this "bottom-up" approach, phenomenology proceeds in a way that shows a basic similarity with film itself. As Kracauer observes, films do "not move from a preconceived idea down to the material world in order to implement that idea; conversely, they set out to explore physical data and, taking their cue from them, work their way up to some problem or belief. The cinema is materialistically minded; it proceeds from 'below' to 'above'" (Kracauer 309). Both phenomenology and film are more "bottom-up" than "top-down" in nature, moving from the sensory toward the abstract, from the material toward the conceptual. If film is a "performance of the perceptive and expressive structure of the lived-body experience" (Sobchak, *Address* 299) and phenomenology is the reflection upon that same structure, then film and phenomenology are two different "media" that revolve around a similar core, that is, the particularity of a given experience such as dreaming. The phenomenology-inclined analysis of cinematic oneiricity conducted in this study is firmly rooted in the experiences evoked by specific scenes. Thus, this approach thrives on the variety of scenarios that Lynch's oneiric sequences present.

Part I of this book will show why and how phenomenology acts as the "methodological backbone" of this study. More specifically, it will discuss to what extent this work is informed by the film-phenomenological theory and method (Chapter 1), whether phenomenology *could* and *should* be applied to the study of oneiric film (sections "Framing the Object of Investigation" and "The Implicit Phenomenological Basis . . . " in Chapter 2), how it *has been* applied to do such (section "Explicitly Phenomenological Studies . . . " in Chapter 2), what the potential of phenomenology for the Lynchian oneiric consists in and how *this study* is going to use it (sections "The Lynchian Oneiric and Phenomenology" and "Systematic Approach" in Chapter 2), and what role Freudian psychoanalysis plays in a phenomenological approach to cinematic dreams (section "Dream Phenomenology and Freudian Psychoanalysis" in Chapter 2).

Analyzing seven of Lynch's audiovisual productions, Part II presents the main part of this study. It moves chronologically through Lynch's body of work, starting with *Absurd Encounter with Fear*, a short film from 1967, and ends with an analysis of *Mulholland Drive* from 2001 (the third season of *Twin Peaks* [2017], which came out *after Mulholland Drive*, is included in the preceding chapter on the earlier *Twin Peaks* productions [1990–1; 1992] for the sake of thematic and narrative continuity). In addition to *Absurd Encounter with Fear*, Chapter 3 discusses two more short films, *The Alphabet* (1968) and *The Grandmother* (1970). Chapter 3 explores the significance of the material pre-reflective dimension of the film experience when it comes to potential "dreamlike" qualities. It will show how these early short films challenge perceptual automatisms (e.g., figure/ground perception in *The Alphabet* and *Absurd Encounter with Fear*), attack the viewer's senses in creating an oneiric atmosphere (cf. *Absurd Encounter with Fear*), and undermine the hierarchy of sensory modalities in a tendency toward synesthesia (cf. *The Grandmother*). Further, the change from live action to animation imagery in *The Alphabet* manifests the film's reflection on the otherness of visual perception in dreams—thereby inaugurating a kind of "second-order seeing."

David Lynch's first feature film, *Eraserhead* (1977), was promoted as "a dream of dark and troubling things" (cf. Leigh). Focusing less on viewer–film interaction than the analysis of the early short films, Chapter 4 takes a close look at the transitions between waking and dreaming in this film in order to explore the ways in which dream experience differs from waking experience and what filmic means are used to qualify these differences. I will suggest that the film implies a gradual rather than categorical conception of consciousness, and that waking and dreaming provide two opposite ends of the consciousness spectrum. Further, building on the medial aesthetics of the girl's dream in *The Alphabet*, protagonist Henry's dream displays a second medium (i.e., theater) within the first (i.e., film). Thus, I will argue that *Eraserhead* employs the dream as a meta-medium through which the film reflects on its own poetic possibilities of representation—an idea that will be picked up again at various points in the chapters to follow.

Chapter 5 deals with the world of *Twin Peaks*, as created by the first two (ABC-produced) seasons from 1990 to 1991, the feature film *Twin Peaks: Fire Walk with Me* from 1992, and the third (Showtime-produced) season from 2017. Much of the chapter is concerned with the way in which a particular treatment of time and space is evocative of the oneiric quality of *Twin Peaks*. Building on Michael Gamper's and Helmut Hühn's concept of *aesthetic proper time* (23–4), sections "Proper (Spatio-)temporality in Cooper's Dream . . . " and "Proper (Spatio-)temporality" are interested in the extent to which (spatio-)temporality and the oneiric, understood as both sensory and narrative dimensions of the film experience, are mutually dependent in the universe of *Twin Peaks*. Section "'The Dream of Time and Space' . . . " focuses on the development of the dream as a psychological phenomenon in season one toward its ontological function in the end of season three. Section "The Function of Gordon Cole's Dream . . . " discusses the only unambiguously marked dream sequence in season three, that is, Gordon Cole's (David Lynch) dream in "Part 14: We Are Like the Dreamer." This dream provokes the interpretation of the series as a shared dream experience between its creator, actresses, and viewers.

Chapter 6 is concerned with two dimensions of *Lost Highway* (1997), both of which are crucial to understand the way in which the film is informed by the oneiric: the psychological and the (meta-)medial. It will show the inadequacy of psychological interpretations that remain tied to the textual level of the film. That is, the psychological complexity of the film can only be grasped once it is realized that the film performs the phenomena of dissociation and loss of reality on a phenomenological level, translating them into the viewer's immediate experience of the film. In terms of (meta-)mediality, the movie continues the self-reflexive oneiricity of *Eraserhead*, but it radicalizes it, given that the dream sequence introduces a second order of experience that is in fundamental conflict with the first (waking) order. It will become clear that the dream's distinctive potential consists in the depiction of the protagonist's inability to know the truth, an aspect that also underlies the film's deconstructivist conception of itself.

The last film analysis, Chapter 7, revolves around one of Lynch's most beloved movies, *Mulholland Drive* (2001). In the first part of the analysis (section "The Interconnection of Dream and Film"), it suggests three possible ways of framing the complex interrelationship between dream and film evoked by *Mulholland Drive*—"dream in film," "film as dream," and "dream as film." I argue that the dream-as-film dimension, largely unnoticed in the existing literature on the movie, mediates between the dream-in-film and the film-as-dream dimension. Diane's dream is a film-like experience rather than the (entire) film being a dreamlike experience. The second part of the chapter zooms in on the remarkable Club Silencio sequence, arguing that it shows us what is at the heart of the analogy between cinema and dream established by *Mulholland Drive*. Club Silencio displays the mechanism responsible for our continuing acceptance of an—oneiric and filmic—unreality, despite our better knowledge.

In short, both popular and academic discourse frequently identify Lynch's films by their dreamlike qualities. However, in the existing literature on Lynch, these qualities tend to remain underspecified in terms of their experiential dimension. Departing from an interest in the phenomenon of dream experience, this is the first systematic book-length study exploring the nature and function of the oneiric in the director's different phases and audiovisual formats. It will show that, over the course of fifty years, Lynch has developed a cinematic aesthetics of the oneiric—an ensemble of four dimensions that unfolds its full potential in the dynamic interplay between sensory address and reflective medialization.

Part I

Methodology and Concepts

This study presents an attempt to draw closer to what can be termed "the Lynchian oneiric." That is, my research interest in David Lynch's films concerns the experience *represented in* and *presented by* dream(-like) sequences as well as conceptualizations of dream experience. Often postulated but rarely clarified in meaning, the "dreamlike qualities" often said to inform his cinema as a whole call for a thorough exploration of the aesthetics, structure, and function of the depicted dream experiences. Part I lays the theoretical, terminological, and methodological foundation for the subsequent film analyses. It sheds light on what is in the background of the analyses and elaborates on some important concepts that recur throughout the following chapters. In Gestalt-psychological terms, the methodological-theoretical *ground* of the analyses becomes the *figure* here. Given the research goal of this study, it will be shown how phenomenology—in its application to both film and dream—allows me to investigate the characteristics of the Lynchian oneiric. To do so, this part of the study will proceed in five steps: (1) it sketches some of the main features of the film-phenomenological theory and method and shows to what extent this study is informed by film phenomenology (section "Film Phenomenology"); (2) it discusses the potential of phenomenology for the study of oneiric film in general (section "Phenomenology and the Oneiric Film"); (3) it shows why phenomenology is a promising theoretical framework for *Lynch's* dream depictions in particular (section "The Lynchian Oneiric and Phenomenology"); (4) it points to the phenomenological approach to dreaming and discusses the extent to which psychoanalysis is a valuable interlocutor to phenomenology given my research focus on dreams (section "Dream Phenomenology and Freudian Psychoanalysis"); and (5) it sketches a systematic approach in order for the structure of the analysis chapters to become transparent (section "Systematic Approach").

Given Lynch's popularity and the semantic proximity of the terms "Lynchian" and "oneiric" (cf. Introduction), the lack of studies exploring the dreams in Lynch's entire oeuvre is striking. Lynch is among the most studied directors in contemporary cinema—maybe even in film history—as indicated by the sheer amount of monographs, papers, and book chapters on his films.[1] While dreams feature prominently in many of these studies, they are rarely put into a wider range of the director's filmography, treated as separate phenomena, or discussed in the context of dream studies. This goes in particular for his early short films which, if taken into account at all, are often treated as decorative supplements to his later, supposedly more artistically valuable feature films and television productions.[2] While the idea of a study on the Lynchian oneiric per se may not seem surprising in this light, the idea of using phenomenology as a methodological framework to conduct such a study might seem rather far-fetched. Before we get to the question of why phenomenology can (and should) be used to study Lynch's cinema—particularly his dream depictions—it might be helpful to establish some common ground for further elaborations by briefly sketching some aspects of phenomenology's encounter with film in general and with oneiric films in particular, that is, films that in some way or another deal with dreams or dreamlike structures. Rather than attempting to provide a comprehensive history or theory of the phenomenology of oneiric cinema, it is my aim to bring to the fore some important aspects of the theoretical framework that informs the methodological approach of this study.

1

Film Phenomenology

Gerard Granel has described the aim of phenomenology in the vocabulary of film. He considers phenomenology "an attempt to film, in slow motion, that which has been, owing to the manner in which it is seen in natural speed, not absolutely unseen, but missed, subject to oversight. It attempts, slowly and calmly, to draw closer to that original intensity which is not given in appearance, but from which things and processes do, nevertheless, in turn proceed" (Granel qtd. in Michelson 30).[1] Vice versa, essential aspects of the capacity of film can be described in phenomenological terms. Vivian Sobchak, for example, holds that through its ability to communicate the human activities of seeing, hearing, and moving—the ability to "commute perception into expression" (*Address* 40)—"cinema is able to transpose [. . .] modes of being alive and consciously embodied in the world" (*Address* 4). In this light, the central question of this study could be framed as concerning the potential of film to transpose the existential state of dreaming, "existence in that mode of being of the dream" (Foucault 33). In other words, if cinema transposes "modes of being alive," how does a dream(-like) sequence transpose being in that mode of dreaming? Is there anything like a dream-specific act or mode of seeing, hearing, and moving? While these questions open up an interesting field of inquiry, we should bear in mind that in this study, the focus and point of departure is Lynch's cinema. His films are not treated as a "case study" for a more general phenomenology of the dream. Rather, phenomenology is used as an instrument to illuminate the Lynchian dream experience. This study is only a contribution to the specification of "the dreamlike in film" insofar as Lynch's cinema already instantiates that generic category.

A more standard definition of phenomenology characterizes it as "a philosophical movement devoted to the study of consciousness and of the phenomena (objects and appearances) of direct experience," its project being "to describe the experience of things as they present themselves to us" (Kuhn and Westwell 309). In an attempt to get *to the things themselves*, phenomenology aims at a "theory-free description of what is immediately given in consciousness" (cf. Fellmann 28; my translation).[2] Founded as a philosophical discipline by Edmund Husserl at the beginning of the twentieth century, phenomenology's influence on other disciplines in the humanities is hard to underestimate. Its impact on film studies—visible "sometimes in direct, mostly in oblique ways" in the history of film criticism and scholarship (Ferencz-Flatz and Hanich 14)—has surged since the early 1990s and a renewed focus on the body (the "somatic turn"; Ferencz-Flatz and Hanich 38),[3] which has led to an explicit application of phenomenological methods and concepts to the study of film. Christian Ferencz-Flatz and Julian Hanich suggest two definitions of film phenomenology. Broadly speaking, film phenomenology encompasses "all approaches in which film scholarship and phenomenology intersect in one way or another" (Ferencz-Flatz and Hanich 13). More narrowly it can be characterized as "an attempt that describes *invariant structures* of the film viewer's *lived experience* when watching moving images in a cinema or elsewhere. Here the emphasis can either lie on the *film*-as-intentional-object or the *viewer*-as-experiencing-subject" (13–14). Further, according to the authors, a "focus on the analysis of film reception and the experience of the film spectator [...] is indeed almost unanimously considered to be the key issue of film phenomenology" (26). In this context, Thomas Elsaesser's and Malte Hagener's widely read 2010 *Film Theory: An Introduction through the Senses* could be considered phenomenological, as it organizes the history of film theory along the question of the spectator's material relationship to film. In praising a crucial paper by Dudley Andrew, Vivian Sobchak speaks of the phenomenological approach as "a mode of inquiry that might describe the perceptual, sensuous, affective, and aesthetic dimensions of signification and meaning in the film experience" ("Phenomenology" 435).

Given the focus on dream *experience* in this study, it is worth pondering the conceptual underpinnings of the *film experience*, that is, the logical precondition of any higher-order judgment of a sequence as dreamlike or not dreamlike. In other words, if we ask for the specifically oneiric experiential characteristics of a scene, then a certain understanding of *experience* is necessarily implied in the question. How, thus, can we conceive of that upon which we base our judgment of oneiricity?

Without a doubt, it is the work of Vivian Sobchak that provides the most elaborate theoretical account of how the term *film experience* can be understood. The point of departure for Sobchak's philosophical exploration of film is the existential phenomenology of Maurice Merleau-Ponty, particularly his 1945 *Phenomenology of Perception*. With recourse to Merleau-Ponty, Sobchak calls film "an expression of experience by experience" (*Address* 3). The cinematic medium is characterized by the fact that it tells stories in the mode in which we also perceive our (nonmedial) environment. The film perceives, and it expresses this perception as something that can, in turn, be perceived by the viewer. She calls the film experience "a system of communication based on bodily perception as a vehicle of conscious expression" (Sobchak, *Address* 9). If literature uses words to *refer to* direct experience, then film can be distinguished from it, in that it uses "direct experience as its mode of reference" (11). It achieves this by using "*modes of embodied existence* (seeing, hearing, physical, and reflective movement) as the vehicle, the 'stuff,' the substance of its language," the basis of film language being "the *structures of direct experience* (the 'centering' and bodily situating of existence in relation to the world of objects and others)" (4–5). Cinema's ability to signify is thus rooted in "similar modes of being-in-the-world" shared by the filmmaker, the film, and the spectator (5). Sobchak's conception entails a film-specific type of reception behavior for which it might be worth quoting her at length:

> What we look at projected on the screen [. . .] addresses us as the expressed perception of an anonymous, yet present, "other." And, as we watch this expressive projection of an "other's" experience, we, too, express our perceptive experience. Through the address of our own vision, we speak back to the cinematic expression before us, using a visual language that is also tactile, that takes hold of and actively grasps the perceptual expression, the seeing, the direct experience of that anonymously present, sensing and sentient "other." (Sobchak, *Address* 9)[4]

Not only is film able to express (the camera's) perception by projecting it on a screen, the viewer's perception is also expressive in nature. Sobchak's understanding of the film experience is shaped by the belief that both the film and the viewer (as well as the filmmaker) are able to perceive and express and to change the one into the other (i.e., to "commute perception into expression" [40]). Although ontologically distinct, film and viewer share the ability "to commute the 'language of being' into the 'being of language,' and back again" (21). What enables this commutation is the *act of viewing*, understood as "both an intrasubjective and intersubjective performance equally performable by filmmaker, film, and spectator" (21). Therefore, in terms of its performance, film is a viewing subject, not merely a viewed object. In terms of the film experience, thus, seeing is a shared modality, or a doubled structure. "Watching a film, we can see the seeing as well as the seen, hear the hearing as well as the heard, and feel the movement as well as see the moved" (10). In other words, a camera recording—and thus a film—is a performance of our ability to see because, in terms of its structure and function, it is sufficiently similar to the way in which we perceive the world from a first-person perspective.[5] Hence we can speak of film as a viewing subject.

The Role of Subjectivity in Film Analysis

Despite the subjective modality of film (as an act of seeing made visible), film theory has traditionally privileged the film's status as a seen object, reducing vision to an objective phenomenon. In Sobchak's words,

> cinematic vision is looked at by theorists from outside the structure and experience of the human vision that constitutes cinematic vision and includes that vision within its own. Cinematic vision is regarded as if it were only what is visible in experience, rather than also that which is perceptible in vision and visual in experience. Those aspects of vision that are not visible in vision but that are perceptible to each individual viewer as s/he views are discounted in theoretical descriptions of the film experience, even as the theorist must subjectively live through those "invisible" aspects of his or her perceptual experience in order to see the images, imaginings and spectators s/he so objectively and partially describes. (Sobchak, *Address* 296–7)

Given this imbalance, film's status as a viewed object (Sobchak's "viewed-view" 50) must be extended to include its role as a viewing subject (Sobchak's "viewing-view"; *Address* 50). In order to do justice to this second, subjective modality of seeing, it is presupposed that the subjectivity of the researcher/spectator is always included in the process of analysis—the film exists through an act of viewing that never belongs to *it* alone but always to the spectator as well. In order to understand (a) film, we must therefore always understand *how we see it* at the same time. This implies that a phenomenological study can only be conducted to the extent that the researcher relies on his being a viewer. To stress the importance of the subjective modality of filmic vision in the emergence of meaning, the analyses in Chapter 3 will frequently use first-person description. The film experience is not a monologue between a "merely" seeing viewer and a "merely" seen film. Rather, it requires that film and viewer are understood as always being engaged in a dialogue, both occupying the role of *seeing subject* and *seen object*. More radically even, Sobchak's account seems to imply that the subjectivity of the researcher/spectator *cannot but be* included in the analysis (whether he realizes it or not). At least this is how we may understand her request that, "in a full description of vision in the film experience, as elsewhere, the introceptive and invisible aspects of subjective embodiment *cannot* be overlooked—even if they cannot objectively be seen" (298; my italicization). The "cannot" at the end of the sentence may indicate both that "one should not try to" and that "it is impossible to" take oneself out of the description. Subjectivity is always already part of film analysis because the concept of vision only makes sense as an amalgamation of *seeing* and *seen*. Understanding a film *is* understanding how *we* see (it) because the film performs *our* ability to see. The boundary between experience as depicted by the film and the spectator's experience softens. Elsaesser and Hagener understand Sobchak's "phenomenological logic" of film in this sense when they write: "because [. . .] the expression of experience (in the film) can only be expressed in the form of an(other) experience (of the spectator), film experience and spectator experience can neither be kept apart heuristically nor hierarchically" (Elsaesser and Hagener, *Filmtheorie* 150; my translation).[6]

The question then arises whether we choose to thematize our subjectivity in the co-constitution of a film's meaning or to ignore it. Sobchak holds that in the latter case—that is, if we do not address vision as it is lived "subjectively, invisibly, introceptively"—we would have to assume that "the spectator's visibly passive body [is] 'taken over' by an alien visual consciousness, one that has no 'visual body' of its own and is pure visual intentionality, pure 'introceptive image' of an/other's 'myself, my psyche'" (*Address* 297).

However plausible it may seem conceptually, one may still argue that the subjectivity that is part of phenomenology's methodological paradigm violates the scientific claim to objectivity.[7] Against this view, I would like to propose two observations. First, to describe the approach as purely "subjective" does not seem to be accurate. What is of interest to phenomenology arises in the contact of the subjective with the objective, without one component eliminating the other. That is, we do not understand the concepts of objectivity and subjectivity as necessarily mutually exclusive from the start but as existing in a dynamic relationship to each other. The subjective dimension of the film experience is consciously integrated into the process of analysis, but this does not entail that it "substitutes" what can be said about a film objectively. As Daniel Yacavone argues, "[k]nowledge that *can* inform one's experience of a work includes that of the artist's intentions, techniques, attitudes, problems overcome, and so on" (xix).[8]

If we ignore the subjective, "perceiving" component of the film experience, one could say that we leave out half of what there is to be taken into account (this may be called the "weak version"). One could say this because the film experience results from expression and perception. However, this idea would presuppose that we understand perception and expression as two separate "acts." If we follow Merleau-Ponty and his view of experience as a chiasmatic connection between perception and expression, it is a relation of reversibility that makes experience possible in the first place. If we ignore one of the two components, Sobchak would say that we deny a fact of our existence and the experience-based structure that enables cinematic communication ("strong version"). Both the viewer and the film are at once subjectively *embodied* and objectively *enworlded* (cf. Sobchak, *Address* 135–6). Both are seeing and seen subjects and objects. A full description of vision in the film experience requires subjective and objective characterization of cinematic and human vision.

That the perception expressed by a film is potentially illuminated by my perception *of* it is the result of the structural similarity between filmic vision and human vision (and the genetic dependence of the former on the latter). As Sobchak observes, "the cinema exists as a visible performance of the perceptive and expressive structure of the lived-body experience" (*Address* 299). Thomas Morsch speaks of film as an "aesthetic form of perception anchored in the body [. . .] which is itself embodied by the apparative dispositive and by the forms of filmic expression" (8; my translation).[9] Not only human beings are capable of experience (understood as the reversibility relation between perception and expression) but also the film itself expresses perception in a performative way. To that extent, it is possible that a subjective description of "my" experience illuminates the film and the expression of experience that it is—precisely when the analysis succeeds in coupling "my" individual film experience with the existential horizon of experience which is intersubjectively accessible (to the film and the viewers) and makes an individual experience possible in the first place. Rather than being the center of attention, "my" experience (like potentially anybody's) thus represents the starting point for the analysis of structural aspects of the interaction between film and audience. As Klaus Held observes:

> Phenomenology does not address the facts, the empirically observable individual cases of intentional experience and its objectness in individual people. It abstracts from the coincidental, factual processes of consciousness and objects and takes into focus the laws of essence which determine the composition of the acts and the regions of being appearing in them. (Held 26; my translation)[10]

In this sense, it is not so much a matter of (my) personal experience of the films but rather, as far as the analysis of the subjective modality of cinematic seeing on the basis of "my" subjective seeing is concerned, of the aspects of my experience that I share with all seeing people.¹¹ This being said, the use of the first person (plural or singular) does not intend to represent *all* viewing experiences but refers to a *possible* response that is prestructured by the film—a response that, ideally, will resonate with some readers and viewers, opening up a previously unconscious, pre-reflective, sensory intensity of the film experience to conscious reflection.

Second, against the claim that the inclusion of subjectivity into the discourse of film analysis lowers the degree of objectivity, one can argue that it actually *increases* it, in that the situatedness of the researcher's viewpoint on a given phenomenon is thematized rather than ignored. What Donna Haraway calls "feminist objectivity" builds on this conviction:[12] "objectivity turns out to be about particular and specific embodiment and definitely not about the false vision promising transcendence of all limits [. . .] The moral is simple: only partial perspective promises objective vision [. . .] Feminist objectivity is about limited location and situated knowledge, not about transcendence" (Haraway 582–3).[13] In a similar vein, Christian Bermes speaks of the "realization that it is precisely perspective that enables knowledge" (43; my translation).[14] To illustrate this point, we may think of Lauren Greenfield's approach in her documentary *Generation Wealth* (2018). Dealing with capitalism's obsession with greed, money, and fame in the context of the post-1990s United States, the film, at a certain point, turns into a profound personal reflection on how the director herself is part of the phenomenon she previously tried to describe from an allegedly outside, "transcendent" perspective. She asks to what extent she is driven by the same impulses as the people she had been observing until now. "As I went deeper into my subjects' obsessions, I was surprised they reflected my own" (*Generation Wealth* 01:00:09–01:00:17). What money, fame, and beauty are to her "subjects," she comes to realize, is *work* for Greenfield. When she pesters her sons about their experience of the "pressure of legacy" in the family, her husband intervenes to turn the camera on the filmmaker, mirroring her questions. The turn of the camera is not just of aesthetic value; it also grants us insight into the methodological (and literal) *turn* the film is taking.[15] The roles are reversed now, the observer becomes the observed, and the universality of the documentary's perspective is relativized. Filmic reflexivity coincides with psychological reflection, as Greenfield asks for the basis and negative consequences of her being a "workaholic" (as her son describes her). Thus, the director, like the phenomenologist, makes her subjective access to the phenomenon she is describing—and the film she is making—the subject of inquiry. Arguably, the result is a more nuanced picture of what she is trying to explore. Western obsession with success and self-realization is a phenomenon so pervasive, the attempt to "take herself out" and observe others from a disembodied neutral perspective would have been misguided, in that it would have drawn a less complete (and honest) picture. If the film phenomenologist rhetorically asks why he would leave out the dimension that grounds both the film experience and his subsequent analysis thereof, that is, human perception, then Greenfield, in a similar vein, asks why her film would omit the original impulse that brought it into being, that is, her professional ambition. In *Generation Wealth*, as in phenomenological inquiry, thus, the thematization of subjectivity (as the enabling condition of the film or text) might entail a higher degree of objectivity.[16]

In the context of this study, it should be stressed that one of the advantages of a phenomenological approach is its fundamental methodological openness, its inclusiveness to observations of various kinds, rooted in the fact that it attempts to be "theory-free" from the start. A broad definition of phenomenology is thus preferred here due to its inclusiveness, but this does not mean that the viewing experience is ignored—it is just not the *exclusive* focus of this study. When analyzing a particular film instead of the general structure of *the* film experience,[17] although physiological responses do need to be addressed for a full description of the film experience, one must not "get carried away" by them. After all, a film also tells a story in addition to causing sensory impressions. That is, these impressions also function within a larger semantic context. They are "charged with meaning" that is inextricably linked to its perceptible manifestation. An interesting interrelationship to explore, thus, is that between what is "felt" and what is "understood," to put it bluntly. While this study might not be "phenomenological" in a strict sense—not every observation about the films needs to be phenomenological in nature or about film–spectator interaction in order to be included in the analyses—it is certainly driven by a phenomenological impulse in the sense that its main research interest concerns the experience *of* and *in* dreams and dreamlike sequences. More specifically, it uses concepts and methods from phenomenology (rather than from other film-theoretical approaches) in order to draw closer to and make sense of the Lynchian oneiric. (In that regard, it is *film* phenomenological rather than film *phenomenological*, in that phenomenology is used as a means [to illuminate the Lynchian oneiric], not as an end.) Further, it departs from the fundamental assumption that film "does" phenomenology in the sense that it "'make[s] manifest' certain characteristics of human experience" (Ferencz-Flatz and Hanich 15). Analyzing a film, the phenomenological approach spinges us to describe and reflect on the fundamentally perceptual nature of a scene—on the perceptual acts involved (i.e., [re-]presented in and by the film and afforded by the viewer) and on the question of how they evoke meaning, that is, how the filmic image comes to mean what it means on the basis of an expressed (bodily) perception. Thus, I am not interested in the empirical physiological responses of the viewer but in how a higher-order (semantic) understanding of a film is rooted in the pre-reflective, intuitive grasp of the expressed perception presented by the film.

Given that every film-theoretical approach, every film analysis even, implicitly postulates an ideal recipient (*the viewer*; cf. Elsaesser and Hagener, *Filmtheorie* 13–14), it should be pointed out that, while my subjectivity certainly has its place in the descriptions and analyses, the conceptualization of *the viewer* in this study is not purely informed by introspection. As Adriano D'Aloia's neurophenomenological account suggests, "the embodied-simulation hypothesis provides empirical evidence that not only is the spectator a witness to the actions represented on screen but also, moreover s/he internally *acts out* and simulates the intentional actions executed by a film character" (220). Thus, the film-phenomenological conception of the fundamental nature of the film experience—that is, the reversibility of perception and expression—is backed up by the neuroscientific discovery of mirror and canonical neurons. After all, perceiving and executing an action (or perceiving and using a physical object) rely on the same neural mechanisms; hence perception is more active than it might usually be thought of. Watching a film, I can feel the movement of a character on the screen because my brain activity in the film situation is similar to that of the situation in which I move in such a way in the world. This experience is not exclusively subjective because it rests on the shared neural mechanism of mirror neurons, hence the increased objectivity of perception-based introspection. In this study, the description of *the viewer's/my/our* experience of a scene always implicitly builds on a neurophenomenological understanding of the film experience, *the viewer* being endowed with the ability to inhabit the film's world through a mirror-neural, or "visuomotor"-neural (cf. D'Aloia 219),[18] connection.

In this sense, this study agrees with the approach of Evan Thompson's 2017 monograph *Waking, Dreaming, Being*, in which the philosopher makes a strong argument for the methodological unification of "objective," neuroscientific measurements of brain activity, on the one hand, and "subjective," phenomenological reflection, on the other (xix). If the object of investigation is an experiential phenomenon, first-person description is an invaluable source of knowledge because the study of brain activity alone does not illuminate the nature of experience. Therefore, a new—neurophenomenological—approach shall combine neuroscientific research with firsthand experience: "This approach combines the careful study of experience from within (phenomenology) with neuroscience or the scientific investigation of the brain. [. . .] Combining these perspectives would help scientists to relate the mind and the brain in meticulous ways" (E. Thompson xviii-xix).[19] To be very clear, while brain activity is not measured in this study, my approach to the nature of film experience is shaped by neuroscientific findings. In particular, the enabling condition of film's intelligibility, that is, the reversibility of perception and expression, can be explained in light of the discovery of mirror and canonical neurons.

Auditory Perception in the Film Experience

Sobchak mentions hearing as a "mode of embodied existence" next to seeing (*Address* 4). Her phenomenological approach to film can be read as a critique of ocularcentrism (cf. Elsaesser and Hagener, *Filmtheorie* 139-40)—that is, the prioritization of the visual dimension in film theory. Nevertheless, she explores the phenomenological structure of film by means of the visual rather than the auditory in *The Address of the Eye*.[20] Her focus on vision is due to the structural and functional *directionality* of seeing, which, in her account, demonstrates the intentionality of consciousness as a whole (Sobchak, *Address* 86). When Sobchak argues that "[p]erception, like the structure of consciousness, is never empty but always the perception *of* something" (*Address* 71) and that perception "gives intentionality existential form as a concrete activity" (72), the implied modality of perception is *vision* rather than any other.[21] Hearing, unlike seeing, is a spatial rather than directional phenomenon (cf. Elsaesser and Hagener, *Filmtheorie* 164). While any attempt to establish an absolute hierarchy between viewing and hearing in the film experience is ill-advised, it should be stressed that the auditory dimension is essential to film, in that it *situates* the listener in physical space, both off-screen and in relation to the on-screen scenario. Elsaesser and Hagener stress two aspects of the auditory experience of film, that is, subjectivity and spatiality: "the ear allows cinematic experience to probe deeply into the spectator's (and listener's) inner self. Furthermore, a focus on the ear and sound directly emphasizes the spatiality of the cinematic experience: We can hear around corners and through walls, in complete darkness and blinding brightness, even when we cannot see anything" (Elsaesser and Hagener, *Introduction* 148). Concerning the consequence of acknowledging the importance of sound for the material relationship between spectator and film, the authors observe that "[t]he spectator is no longer a passive recipient of images [. . .], but rather a bodily being enmeshed acoustically, spatially, and affectively in the filmic texture" (148). The sense of *proximity* suggested by hearing stands in contrast to the distance implied by vision, which is frequently associated with a rationalist perspective.

Elsaesser's and Hagener's distinction between the spatial and the subjective dimension of film sound recalls Michel Chion's notion of *point of audition*, which, extending the idea of *point of view*, has a spatial sense ("from where do I hear [. . .]?") and a subjective sense ("which character [. . .] is (apparently) hearing what I hear?") as well (Chion, *Audio-Vision* 90). The theory Chion proposes in his 1994 monograph *Audio-Vision: Sound on Screen* is among the most elaborate and frequently cited in the field. According to Chion, the relationship between image and sound (or between their noetic manifestations seeing and hearing) should not be seen as one of rivalry; rather, the two modalities work together, influencing and transforming one another to the extent that "[w]e never see the same thing when we also hear; we don't hear the same thing when we see as well" (Chion, *Audio-Vision* xxvi). In Chion's view, "a phenomenological analysis of cinema" entails that we do not "fall under the hypnotic spell of technology," according to which a film would "be described as the simple sum of 'soundtrack' plus 'image track'" (136). That is, instead of processing the visual and auditory input separately, we *audio-view* a film as a transsensorial whole. In the words of Walter Murch, "we do not *see* and *hear* a film, we *hear/see* it" (cf. Chion, *Audio-Vision* xxi). Similarly, Merleau-Ponty suggests that "the way they [sight and sound] are put together makes another new whole, which cannot be reduced to its component parts" ("The Film" 341).[22]

Chion elaborates: "A film's aural elements are not received as an autonomous unit. They are immediately analyzed and distributed in the spectator's perceptual apparatus according to the relation each bears to what the spectator sees at the time" (Chion, *Voice* 3). Arguably, "analyzed" is not to be understood in terms of a "conscious decision" here. Much of our auditory experience occurs beneath the threshold of awareness, such that it could be said that there exist two modalities of auditory perception: one, manifested by the verb "to listen to," involves a conscious focus of attention on a specific audible object. Phenomenologists might call listening an instance of *act intentionality*, "which is the intentionality of our judgments and of our voluntary decisions" (Merleau-Ponty, *Phenomenology* xxxii). The second modality, often (but not exclusively) implied by the verb "to hear," is marked by a more diffuse and holistic (i.e., less selective) attention that is not as clearly directed toward any specific object. In phenomenological terms, this kind of auditory experience can be seen in the context of *operative intentionality*, "the intentionality that establishes the natural and pre-predicative unity of the world and of our life, [. . .] the one that provides the text that our various forms of knowledge attempt to translate into precise language" (Merleau-Ponty, *Phenomenology* xxxii). Some form of "pre-predicative unity" also exists between the world of a film and the spectator, and this seems particularly significant for establishing an affective relationship on the phenomenological level. Yacavone observes that "affective response is inherently *audiovisual* and a cinematic product of 'presentational form' (in Susanne Langer's sense), far removed from what may be at work in relation to any linguistic (symbolic) mediation. It thus has little genuine counterpart in any form of literature, however poetically imaginatively 'imagistic'" (Yacavone 175–6).[23]

The interplay between a more diffuse and a more focused form of auditory perception is of utmost importance to cinema in general (e.g., the combination of ambient sound and dialogue prompting both *hearing* and *listening*) and particularly to that of Lynch—a director/sound designer whose soundscapes have attracted as much attention among film scholars (Chion, e.g., has devoted an entire monograph to Lynch's films), critics, and fans as is rarely the case. As will be further discussed in Chapter 4, Lynch's keen awareness of the importance of sound can be associated with his practice of meditation. As Evan Thompson observes, "meditation trains both the ability to sustain attention on a single object"—that is, act intentionality—"and the ability to be openly aware of the entire field of experience"—that is, operative intentionality (xxxiii).

2

Phenomenology and the Oneiric Film

Framing the Object of Investigation

If film phenomenology, generally speaking, is concerned with "film's capacity to present the outward appearance of the world" (Kuhn and Westwell 309), then it might be deemed unfit for the study of dream sequences, as they are concerned with the *inner* experience of the dreamer's mind. But since a dream sequence presents this inner experience as an externalized *projection* (in the true sense of the word), phenomenology is able to tackle it, given that it now *appears* as an object in the world. If, in analogy to this, we are inclined to call the night dream a "projection" of inner states in the form of images (cf. Baudry 53),[1] we should acknowledge that the filmed dream is a projection in a very different sense, as it directly appears to whoever decides to watch it, whereas the night dream only appears to the dreamer, merely "projecting" *her* inner sensitivity. A phenomenology of filmic dream depictions could thus be said to be interested in cinema's capacity to present the inward experience of the mind *as an outward appearance*.

This way of putting it speaks to the interpenetration of subject and world, an aspect that has been observed in regard to both film and the night dream. According to Merleau-Ponty, "the movies are peculiarly suited to make manifest the union of mind and body, mind and world, and the expression of one in the other" ("The Film" 344). Much like existential philosophy, film lets us "*see* the bond between subject and world, between subject and others, rather than to *explain* it" (344). Medard Boss observes in regard to the dream:

> Measured against this immediate dream event, how artificial and false appears the usual mental separation of such a relationship into the two parts of an external world and an internal world, into a mere external object of space, a room space on the one hand, and into any psychic experiences, states and behaviours of the human being that are uninvolved in it on the other hand. (Boss 92; my translation)[2]

Thus, the film experience and the dream-experience resemble each other, in that both express the interpenetration of subject and world. "In the dream, everything"—including all the objects of the dream world—"says 'I,'" as Michel Foucault put it (59). The dreaming subject is "in" the perceived objects (they are *projections* of her self-states) as much as the objects are "in" the dreamer (they are *part* of her psyche). Analogously, a film is both a container of a set of objects appearing "in" it and a certain way of presenting these objects. A world is (contained) "in" a film as much as a film is (situated) "in" that world. Like a dream, a film is both an object for vision and a subject of vision; it is a world and the seeing of that world at the same time.

In the context of this medium-specific double status, Sobchak stresses the temporal character of film when she writes: "Perceived not only as an *object for vision* but also as a *subject of vision*, a moving picture is not experienced precisely as a *thing* that, like the photograph, can be easily controlled, contained, or materially possessed" (Sobchak, *Address* 62–3).[3] In this regard, film could be said to resemble the dream—though a dream can to some extent become a controllable "object" (cf. lucid dreaming), we cannot "materially possess" it due to its transience, that is, its temporal nature. More specifically, in Sobchak's view, part of cinema's phenomenological ambivalence rests on its ability to both "present experience as *representation* (the post hoc fixity of already-perceived and now expressed images that stand as equivalent to noun forms)" and to "represent experience through dynamic *presentation* (the always verb-driven and ongoing present tense of sensory perception)" (*Carnal Thoughts* 74). Reducing the dream to its semantic content (as Freudian psychoanalysis tends to do; cf. Foucault 35),[4] we make it a matter of an *already perceived*, rather than an *ongoing*—which ignores the dream's experiential character. A character *lives through* the dream, the viewer experiences the sequence *in time*; in Merleau-Ponty's view, "film is not a sum total of images but a temporal *gestalt*" ("The Film" 339). The dynamic, verb-driven, presentational modality of dream-*ing* and film view-*ing* constitutes the condition of the possibility to build up emotional tension (for the film) and for the viewer's perception of that tension. If a nightmare scene achieves the feeling of being subjected to uncontrollable forces, this feeling exists, in other words, in function of the possibility that the viewer experiences a change in the scenario. Film can thus evoke "the impact of the dream *as it is being dreamed*" (Flitterman-Lewis qtd. in Dickson 19).

If I were to label my object of investigation, I could call it "the phenomenon of the oneiric," that is, that which can "appear" to the viewer in the film experience, with the film making the dream(-like) "accessible." The phenomenon of the oneiric is that which (in the literal sense of the word) "appears" as conveyed through the film and, as such, is able to affect the viewer in a sensual way. It constitutes the ontological and epistemological basis for what is described, and because this work presents a "study of" (*-logy*) this phenomenon, it presents *a phenomenological approach*. As Held suggests, "[t]he objects *in the how of their appearance* in assigned manners of givenness are the 'phenomena,' the 'appearances' with which phenomenology, named thereafter, is concerned" (16; my translation).[5] In this approach, a close connection is postulated between the "oneiric" and "dream experience." "Dream experience" hereby refers to the fictional experience that the film characters make *in* a dream as well as the viewer's experience *of* a dream sequence. ("Dream-experience" refers to the experience of a nonfictional night dream.) An exploration of dream experience paves the way for a deeper understanding of the *oneiric*, that is, a broader, more abstract category comprising experience in marked dreams, unmarked, merely "dreamlike" sequences, as well as conceptualizations of dream experience. Thus, this study explores four dimensions of the oneiric. First, "oneiric" applies to experience as it occurs in marked dreams (*dream experience*). Second, it denotes experiences that can be said to be *like* the dream experience in a specific sense ("dream-*like*" in the literal sense, with "dream" referring to experience in a marked dream). In a third sense of the word, "oneiric" refers to those aspects of specific sequences that aim for an imitation of the nocturnal dream-experience. A fourth sense of "oneiric" builds upon the way the dream is conceptualized in and by the films. Important about this dimension of the Lynchian oneiric is that, in addition to sequences evoking dream(-like) experience, verbalizations *about* the dream come into play. "Oneiric film," further, refers to all films that in some way or another (directly or indirectly) deal with dreams or dreamlike structures.

The Implicit Phenomenological Basis of the Film/Dream Analogy

Even if it is clear now that phenomenology can be used to study the oneiric potential of cinema, why *should* it be used to do such? First of all, there is the historical dimension to the comparison between cinema and dream. According to Noël Carroll, "analogies between cinema and dream have been with us almost as long as film" (11). By the 1950s already, the idea that "the cinema is a dream" has been called the "key word" of film theory (Morin 7). Striking from a phenomenological point of view is that many attempts, whether at the beginning of the twentieth century or during the peak of the psychoanalytic tradition in the 1970s and 1980s, aim at a certain affinity between *film perception and dream* (as the title of Irmela Schneider's paper, "Filmwahrnehmung und Traum," suggests). Although this study does not depart from the assumption that film is dreamlike per se, it is useful to name some of the reasons why this idea has been entertained in order to be able to contextualize Lynch's own approach to cinema (which will be explored in the next section) and to see how a particular dream(-like) sequence might manifest the oneiric potential that has often been ascribed to the filmic medium as such.

In an essay from 1911, Georg Lukács suggests that cinema is dreamlike in its negation of the distinction between possibility and reality. "Because its [i.e. cinema's] technique expresses in every single moment the absolute (if only empirical) reality of this moment, the validity of 'possibility' as a category opposed to 'reality' is rejected" (Lukács qtd. in Schneider [25]; my translation).[6] Like the dreamer, the film viewer makes an experience in which "everything is true and real, everything is equally true and equally real" (25; my translation).[7] As Schneider observes, Lukács compares the way in which a viewer experiences a film with the way in which someone experiences a night dream (25). It is not the *recollection* of a night dream that serves as a point of comparison—here the difference between possibility and reality has been re-established—but the (manifest) experience of the night dream, that is, "the level of the dream which is not accessible to observation in the strict sense" (25–6; my translation).[8]

In 1921, in the midst of the era of silent cinema (which, as Chion argues, would better be called "deaf cinema" [*Voice* 7][9]), Hugo von Hofmannsthal addresses an aspect of dreams that could be of great importance to the Lynchian oneiric, that is, the withdrawal of language. Like in the first marked dream of Lynch's oeuvre in *The Alphabet* (1968), language is conceived of as "the tool of society" (Von Hofmannsthal 142; my translation)[10] embodying the power dynamics of the waking world. According to von Hofmannsthal, people in the early twentieth century went to the movies to escape from their dull everyday lives. They wanted to find a "surrogate for their dreams" (as his essay is titled) of which they have been deprived by the monotony of modern industrialized urban life (141; my translation).[11] Von Hofmannsthal's use of "dream" might sensitize us for the varying degrees of metaphoricity with which the term is used by different proponents of a film/dream analogy: in addition to its reference to the concrete night dream, von Hofmannsthal seems to conceive of dreaming as a mode of experience driven by a certain curiosity for the unknown (143). So when he compares cinema to dream, he is not so much interested in the actual experience of dreaming as in what a dream *represents*, that is, a sense of magic for life. Arguably, he wants to suggest that people's minds have become so "industrialized," even their dreams need to be fueled by external "manufactured" images. With this kind of metaphorical use of "dream," he anticipated the popular conception of Hollywood as a "dream factory," which was put forward by the anthropologist Hortense Powdermaker's 1950 study *Hollywood, the Dream Factory*.[12]

Even more critical of the cultural climate of their time, and even more important for a contextualization of David Lynch's cinema is the surrealists' approach to film, which is inextricably linked to the dream. As Michael Lommel et al. observe, "[t]he spectacles of the dream are among the constitutive features of an aesthetic of the surreal, which finds in the cinematic an adequate place of realization, most suitable to convey those surreal atmospheres and forms of perception" (15; my translation).[13] By employing hyper-associative montage and by breaking with the rules of continuity editing, for example, Luis Buñuel's and Salvador Dalí's infamous *Un Chien Andalou* (1929) aimed at evoking a dreamlike film experience that undermines the conventional dichotomization into "real" and "unreal," arriving at a reality existing "on top of" or "above" (cf. French *sur*) the regular one determined by rationality and the moral values of the bourgeoisie. "The dream state thus became a model that was to enrich, even change, the perception of reality," as Matthias Brütsch observes (32; my translation).[14] Although the cinematic medium might not be dreamlike per se, compared to the other arts, it has a special potential to evoke a dreamlike experience: for some surrealists, "the film camera possessed a unique capacity to capture and convey the sensation of dreaming" (Kuhn and Westwell 415). In Lynch's own words,

> they [the surrealists] discovered that cinema was the perfect medium for them because it allowed the subconscious to speak. If surrealism is the subconscious speaking, then I think I identify with it and I could say that I was somewhat surrealistic. I think that films should have a surface story, but underneath it there should be things happening that are abstract. They are things that resonate in areas

that words can't help you find out about. These are subconscious areas. ("David Lynch Presents the History of Surrealist Film [1987];" 00:05:20–00:06:00)

From a film-phenomenological perspective, it seems important to stress that, as Laura Rascaroli observes, the writings of André Breton and René Clair provided the basis for "the comparison between spectator and dreamer [which] became the most widely quoted and important similarity between film and dream" (2). That is, the proximity of film and dream was explained by the similarity between the film viewing and the dreaming *subject*. Rather than the phenomena themselves, the conditions of their *reception* lead many to suggest their similarity. Maybe critic Sandy Flitterman-Lewis is most clear about this when she writes about the aim of Antonin Artaud's films being "to create the impact of the dream instead of simply reproducing its irrationality. For him, then, the representation of a 'dream state,' in which the spectator's involvement was one of active participation, was the primary aim of his scenario" (Flitterman-Lewis qtd. in Dickson 19).

Writing in the early 1950s, the film/dream comparison in Susanne Langer's philosophical theory of art, *Feeling and Form*, like the surrealists' approach to film, builds on a more concrete conception of dream compared to that of von Hofmannsthal. S. Langer writes, "cinema is 'like' dream in the mode of its presentation: it creates a virtual present, an order of direct apparition. That is the mode of the dream" (S. Langer 412). What cinema "abstracts" from dreaming is the "immediacy of experience," the "givenness" resulting from the impression of being "at the center" of the situation (S. Langer 413). Like the dreamer in a dream, the camera is "equidistant from all events" (413). Seeing "with" the camera, the viewer's "standpoint moves with it, his mind is pervasively present [. . .] *He takes the place of the dreamer*, but in a perfectly objectified dream—that is, he is not in the story. The work is the appearance of a dream, a unified, continuously passing, significant *apparition*" (413). Further, the similarity of film experience and dream experience relies on a shared tendency toward synesthesia (414),[15] with space existing by virtue of spatial *experience* (i.e., dream and film "are not oriented in any total space"; 415), and an "affective or associative logic" underlying both film editing and dream imagery (N. Carroll 13). Concerning S. Langer's observation as to the film viewer "taking the place of the dreamer" without being physically present in the scenario, most dream researchers would probably speak of a *hypnagogic* rather than an oneiric facet of experience. This is because the dream ego's body only materializes in the dream state as opposed to the hypnagogic phase, that is, the state of consciousness between waking and dreaming. In the words of Evan Thompson, "[t]he experience of being a self in the world, which marks the waking state but diminishes in the hypnagogic state, reappears in dreams" (127).

The significance of Christian Metz's contribution to film theory builds on the combination of semiotics and Freudian psychoanalysis. Interestingly, however, when it comes to the question of the oneiric potential of cinema, Metz writes extensively on the relationship between the spectator and the film. He departs from the observation that the principal difference between the film and the dream situation is constituted by the fact that "the dreamer does not know that he is dreaming" whereas "the film spectator knows that he is at the cinema" (Metz 101). In both cases, however, the degree of awareness is subject to change, as the dreamer may gain insight into her state of dreaming and the spectator may forget that she is at the movies. Although he does not name it as such, Metz evokes the idea of lucid dreaming when he writes about the "open[ing of] a gap in the hermetic sealing-off that ordinarily defines dreaming" (104). As a consequence of this twofold dynamic, "it is in their gaps rather than in their more normal functioning that the filmic state and the dream state tend to converge" (104). That is, by becoming *more* conscious when dreaming and *less* conscious when watching a film, the two states approximate each other. More specifically, the film viewer's state, which is marked by "a general tendency to lower wakefulness," may move the viewer in the direction of dreaming through its "encouragement of narcissistic withdrawal," "indulgence of phantasy," "withdrawal of the libido within the ego," and the "suspension of concern for the exterior world" (107). Metz speaks of film as "a machine for grinding up affectivity and inhibiting action" (107), a point that the phenomenology-inclined scholars Vlada Petrić and Rainer Schönhammer elaborate on (see the next section). It seems important to stress here that the reduction of wakefulness in the cinema entails the "impression of reality" that can move toward—but never reach—the genuine illusion of dreaming (Metz 107). This has to do with the difference between perception and imagination "in terms of a phenomenology of consciousness" (109). Filmic perception requires a stimulus, whereas dreaming does not. The film experience involves a "progressive path" of "psychical excitation," with exterior objects causing the perception (114). Dreaming, on the other hand, is characterized by a "regressive path," that is, from the internal toward the external (114). Strictly Freudian in his approach, Metz argues that the "illusion of perception" in a dream is caused by the combination of an unconscious wish and a recent preconscious memory triggering it (114). Although the filmic situation shows a tendency toward regression by partially blocking the viewer's motor outlet, the regression is never complete when watching a film because filmic perception is "doubly reinforced," that is, encouraged "simultaneously from without and within," that is, shaped by both the progressive and the regressive path (117–18).

Far from being comprehensive, what this brief digression into the film-theoretical discourse around oneiric cinema hopefully showed is the implicit phenomenological basis of many of the influential writings on the relationship between film and dream. Even if it was not named as such, phenomenological reasoning was already a part of the film/dream analogy. Given that these analogies traditionally tended to rely upon the relationship between viewer and film, phenomenology *should* be used as a methodological framework to study the potential oneiricity of film because this relationship is a phenomenological issue par excellence. In addition, opening up the discourse around film and dream provides a theoretical background for the third season of *Twin Peaks* (2017; cf. section "'The Dream of Time and Space' . . . " in Chapter 5) and *Mulholland Drive* (2001), two works which literalize the "film-as-dream" metaphor in evocative ways.

Explicitly Phenomenological Studies on Oneiric Film

The lack of explicitly phenomenological studies on oneiric film is particularly striking in light of phenomenology's tendency to question binary thinking (cf. Bermes 15), on the one hand, and, on the other hand, in light of the filmic dream's inherent challenge to the binary *inside–outside*—the dream sequence presents inward experience as outward appearance. But while it is true that there is no book-length study of oneiric film from a phenomenological perspective, it would be wrong to assume that phenomenological thought has not been applied to oneiric film at all. Simon Dickson's recent important paper, "The Oneiric Film: Refocusing the Film-Dream Analogy from an Existential Phenomenological Perspective," for example, highlights the importance of extending Sobchak's understanding of the concept of *carnal knowledge*. In reference to Sobchak telling us that "we see and comprehend and feel films with our entire bodily being, informed by the full history and carnal knowledge of our acculturated sensorium" (*Carnal Thoughts* 63), Dickson stresses the need to expand our idea of this knowledge to comprise dream-experience. He writes that "one might begin to acknowledge [. . .] that our 'acculturated sensorium' would thus factor in what we experience and sense in dreams. In short, as well as 'carnal,' one might begin to recognise an *oneiric* knowledge embedded in the film spectator" (Dickson 9–10). Whenever we say that a film or a scene has a dreamlike effect on the viewer (in the sense of what I label as the third dimension of the oneiric), we presuppose the existence of what Dickson calls "oneiric knowledge," that is, knowledge as to what it is like for someone to be dreaming—how else would we be able to perceive their similarity? In this sense, when we talk about particular scenes in the film analysis chapter, it is their potential to remind the waking viewer of what it is like to be dreaming—that is, the potential to address the viewer's *oneiric knowledge*—that needs to be judged. In case a scene is reminiscent of dreaming, what aspects of dreaming are evoked? Dickson assumes that oneiric knowledge is rooted in an "affective connection to the dream" rather than a rational one (15).

What might be seen as problematic in regard to an approach that purely builds on the idea of *oneiric knowledge* is the implicitly mimetic conception of film's oneiricity—that is, something is dreamlike only if it, in some way or another, *reflects* the night dream-experience. Only that which activates our knowledge of what it is like to be dreaming can be called "oneiric" in such an approach. On the one hand, this may cause the discourse on oneiric cinema to transcend the limited discussion of marked dreams, given that the ability to cause a dreamlike effect on the viewer is now independent of whether or not a sequence is marked as a dream. However, such an approach might at the same time make it more difficult to speak to some of the creative aspects of those dream sequences which can only be recognized as such due to their markedness. That is, those experiential aspects of a dream sequence which, rather than *imitating* the night dream, aesthetically *construct* an effect that may be termed "dreamlike" simply due to its occurrence in a dream are not part of the discussion at all. Further, excluding the marked dream due to its divergence from the phenomenology of the night dream would not seem fair: it would ignore the *retroactive mode* (cf. Eberwein 160–91) in which we become aware of a scene's dream status only *after* we have already seen it.

In this structure, the retroactive mode corresponds to the passage from dreaming to waking up. But even a sequence with an opening dream marker can achieve an oneiric effect because the viewer engages with the film on a pre-reflective level (where an experience is not yet differentiated into *real* and *unreal*), a dimension that the night dream, too, exploits to create intense moments of sensory co-involvement or disruption.

In order for a sequence to be discussed in this study, thus, we neither restrict it to having to be reminiscent of the night dream nor to having to be unambiguously marked as a dream. Yet we should consider both cases as possibilities in order to obtain the most nuanced picture of the category of the *oneiric*. The implication of this approach is twofold: if a film does not involve any marked dreams, this does not mean that it cannot possess any dreamlike qualities; if a film marks its dream depictions, then this does not mean that it cannot remind us of the night dream-experience.

Neurophysiological Accounts

Vlada Petrić's 1980 paper, "Film and Dreams: A Theoretical-Historical Survey," may be read as a specification of the conditions under which the film viewer's oneiric knowledge is activated, paying particular attention to the pre-reflective, physiological dimension of the film experience. Petrić holds that if cinema uses its medium-specific means properly, it is able to let the viewer "not only [. . .] perceptually follow the dream content on the screen but to experience it sensorially, that is, in a way which approximates the process and impact of dreaming" ("Film and Dreams" 2). Particularly interested in what he calls the "psycho-physiological impact on the viewer" (14), Petrić writes:

> In the process of dreaming, our neural and muscular systems respond differently to various situations in spite of the fact that we accept them as reality. In essence, this unique aspect of dreaming parallels the impact of some cinematic devices on the film viewer. This impact is the subject which must be studied by both film theorists and psycho-neurologists. (Petrić, "Film and Dreams" 14–15)

While dreaming, the dreamer accepts the dream situation as reality and yet, on a (neuro-)physiological level, she reacts *differently* than if she really were in that situation. This dynamic is mirrored in the film situation: "the sensory-motor *responses* (characteristic of film viewing) correspond to muscular *sensations* (experienced by the dreamer)," writes Petrić ("Film and Dreams" 19). While different psychologically, the two responses "*do* stimulate a similar physiological reaction in dreamer and viewer's viscera: each in its own way enhances the dream or film viewer's identification, alienation and comprehension of the dreamed event. The most exciting dream films [. . .] employ the specific cinematic devices to intensify such visceral reactions in the viewer" (19). A creative use of the viewer's psycho-physiological stimulation may intensify the film's metaphorical meaning as well as its oneiric effect and involves the following cinematic techniques: "camera movement through space" causing a "kinesthetic sensation" in the viewer reminiscent of hypnagogia, "paradoxical combinations of objects," "dynamic montage" leading to "vestibular activation" and the enhancement of "anxiety characteristic of the nightmare," "photographic effects" inducing a "hypnotic mood," and "sight-and-sound counterpoint" making for "unusual sound and color combinations" reminiscent of dreams (24). Unlike Dickson, Petrić is interested in both the oneiric potential of the cinematic medium in general and in the way specific (marked) dream sequences may realize this potential. What seems important to stress is that, in contrast to most of the positions presented in the previous section, Petrić does *not* presume the film experience to be oneiric per se. Rather, his approach seems to imply the view that the potential for oneiricity (in the sense of a sensual-oneiric effect on the viewer[16]) is inherent in the medium in a special way but is only exploited by certain films and scenes. This potential exists as a function of cinema's ability to address the viewer's sensory-motor centers, which can result in an oneiric effect on the viewer, thus distinguishing oneiric imagery from merely fantastic imagery (which does not involve such physiological, "hypnagogic," or "hypnotic" stimulation; Petrić, "Film and Dreams" 14).

When it comes to the question of which "cinematic devices" are apt to stimulate dreamlike physiological responses in the viewer, Petrić particularly stresses the importance of camera movements:

> While watching dream sequences executed by a tracking camera, viewers simultaneously experience spatial sensation of the [filmic] environment and muscular activity of their body, supporting a hypothesis that the stimulation of the viewers' neural centers is closer to a REM sleep (desynchronized sleep) than to a NREM sleep (synchronized sleep). [. . .] Thus the most evident similarity between REM sleep and film viewing lies in the phenomenon that both dreamers and viewers, while their muscle potential is relatively high, experience sensory motor activity which creates a unique tension that can enhance an anxious mood or hallucinatory imagery.[17] (Petrić, "Film and Dreams" 22)

Camera movements provoke a twofold spatial experience on the viewer's side. Through activating her sensory-motor centers, they provide an experience of the film's virtual space; due to the physiological experience of movement, the images are perceived as "features of the real world" (Petrić, "Film and Dreams" 21). At the same time, the viewer experiences her own motionless body. For D'Aloia, "the film experience is an intensified *sensory* stimulation that does not correspond to any explicit *motor* activation" (219– 20). At this point, psychologist Rainer Schönhammer's account of perception becomes interesting. In Schönhammer's words, "[t]he viewer's motionlessness is, in a sense, the stage on which inner co-movement unfolds in accordance with the physical events on the canvas" ("Traum und Film" 76; my translation).[18] A source of irritation is constituted by the tension between the viewer's experienced movement and her body's stillness. In the nonfilmic/waking world, someone's execution of such movements would necessarily entail changes in her proprioception, particularly in the vestibular system (Schönhammer, "Traum und Film" 77). In film viewing, it does not. In this regard, the physiological state of the film viewer resembles that of the dreamer. The tension between the viewer's sensory-motor activation and stillness corresponds to the tension between the dreamer's extreme brain arousal and her paralyzed body. Particularly in REM phase dreams, our sensory-motor system is activated while the sleeping body remains still. That is, a part of the brain stem prevents the efferent movement impulses (the brain's commands to the muscles) during REM sleep from being acted out. This again affects the dream. Interestingly, as Schönhammer assumes, the dreaming brain interprets the sleeping body's muscular inhibition as *both* an inability to move in the dream world and as an urge to escape a persecutor (*Wahrnehmung* 62). While in the former interpretation, the body's stillness *carries over* into the dream scenario, in the latter, it is *reversed* by the dream.

When it comes to film analysis, it is crucial to bear in mind that each film viewer has implicit knowledge of this physiological dynamic of dreaming (cf. Dickson's idea of *oneiric knowledge* [10]). Particularly in the context of *Twin Peaks* (2017; cf. section "Oneiricity and the Ambivalence of Sensory-Motor Activation" in Chapter 5), *Mulholland Drive* (2001; cf. section "It [Cinema] Is an Illusion . . . " in Chapter 7), and the early short films (cf. Chapter 3), I will explore the ways in which Petrić's and Schönhammer's understanding of the neurophysiological nature of film viewing and dreaming may account for the oneiricity of particular scenes.

A Strong versus Weak Version of the Film/Dream Analogy

On a more film-theoretical note, the present brief discussion indicates the necessity to distinguish between a strong and a weak version of the film/dream analogy. In the strong version of the analogy, *any film is like a dream* because the film experience shares a number of essential characteristics with the dream-experience (the viewer's bodily stillness while he identifies with a virtual scenario, the immateriality of the film/dream world, the passivity of the dreamer/viewer, the malleability of spatiotemporal relationships, etc.). In the weak version, the medium of *film has a special potential to depict dreaming in its sensory intensity*. But is this still part of the film/dream analogy at all? I argue that it is, because it says that *under certain circumstances*, the film experience can be *like* the (way we remember the) dream-experience, or it can at least lead us to rely on the dream-experience to characterize the film experience.

For the purpose of this study, one may ask: even if film (or the film situation) were dreamlike per se, what would it mean to call (the experience of) *a* film dreamlike? What would render one film more or less dreamlike compared to another, if all films are dreamlike? I want to know what it means to say that Lynch's cinema is dreamlike, what the weight of this characterization is. To investigate that question, the strong version of the film/dream analogy does not seem promising, since for the word "dreamlike" to carry any meaning, there have to be films to which it applies and others to which it does not. What we should not ignore in our denial of the strong version, however—as Brütsch (88–9) seems to do—is the natural inclination of cinema toward the dream. In reducing the film/dream analogy to its extreme version, Brütsch appears to ignore that the reversible nature of the film experience marks out the dream, or rather dream-*ing*, as a particularly interesting phenomenon to explore for filmmakers. Because it presents a primarily audiovisual experience aimed at our pre-reflective sensory involvement, film has a special potential to create an experience that reminds the waking viewer of dreaming (possibly a specific *type* of dream)—that is, a typically audiovisual experience frequently provoking intense sensory involvement.[19] This does not mean, however, that *any* film is dreamlike. Rather, the filmic medium is of the right *category* to evoke a particularly intense dreamlike effect. This being said, to explore the potential of film to depict *the dream* (as a sequence) is not independent of the discourse around a general film/dream analogy: it might just be that particular films or scenes or directors instantiate elements that have been (wrongfully) attributed to cinema itself. The crucial part is *how* a film manifests the oneiric potential of cinema in a particular scene and how the experience of oneiricity functions in regard to the film's story.

The Lynchian Oneiric and Phenomenology

Until now, this chapter has discussed whether phenomenology *could* be applied to the study of oneiric films, why it *should* be, and how it *has been* applied to do such. It is now time to come back to the question asked at the beginning of the introduction: why should one study Lynch's cinema from a phenomenological perspective? In this section, I will show why phenomenology provides a promising framework to study Lynch's dream depictions in particular and why it is justified to use this theoretical approach.

As was indicated at the beginning of the introduction, the idea of using phenomenology as a methodological framework to conduct a study on the Lynchian oneiric might seem rather far-fetched. For one, every film asks for its own analysis, requiring an individual methodological approach. Why is film phenomenology a promising framework for *all* the Lynch films in our corpus? Further, even if the choice of the theoretical approach should be independent of what a given director has or has not read,[20] the theoretical nature of phenomenology might be deemed hard to reconcile with Lynch's creative process and its rootedness in intuition and meditation. Significantly, however, Lynch shares the same object of interest with phenomenologists, that is, *experience*. Film phenomenology provides an interesting macro perspective on his cinema because of its systematic study of experience, which is a dimension of utmost importance to *all* of Lynch's films. Contrasting it with the psychoanalytic approach, Sobchak writes that "semiotic phenomenology begins with an individual performance that describes and inscribes a structure whose 'grammar' is always emerging" (Sobchak, *Address* 100). This is why phenomenology presents a promising framework to arrive at that which is specifically Lynchian in filmic dreams (thus different from the *Tarkovskyan* dream experience, for example) and at that which is specifically dreamlike in the films of Lynch. Given the countless descriptions of Lynch's movies as "dreamlike," the word risks losing its meaning—if everything in a Lynch film were dreamlike, then this attribution would not carry any weight. Thus, a phenomenological specification is desirable.

Lynch, on the one hand, and phenomenologists, on the other, use different means to explore experience. Phenomenologists use words to describe it, coming up with concepts to illuminate structural aspects of the nature of subjective experience, for example, when they talk about the characteristics of dreaming. Filmmakers, on the other hand, use experience as "building blocks" to tell a story,[21] almost in the way a writer uses words to construct phrases, sentences, and so on. A phenomenological approach to cinema, then, to some extent, describes the lived-body experience expressed by a film, illuminating its grammar. In Sobchak's view, "the cinema exists as a visible performance of the perceptive and expressive structure of the lived-body experience" (*Address* 299). Thus, what phenomenological description reveals is also, in principle, subjectively accessible. If, further, film itself already expresses the reflection upon lived-body experience, then film, on the one hand, and phenomenological analysis, on the other, could be considered two different "media" that, despite employing distinct vocabulary and formulae, revolve around a similar core, that is, the particularity of a certain kind of experience such as dreaming. In short, film performs what phenomenological reflection and description seeks to reveal: the structure of subjective experience. Ferencz-Flatz and Hanich put it like this: "if film does indeed 'make manifest' certain characteristics of human experience, as Merleau-Ponty and Sobchak maintain, then one may even claim that film itself 'does' phenomenology (and there has been no shortage of phenomenology-inclined scholars who have made manifest in writing what film makes manifest audiovisually)" (Ferencz-Flatz and Hanich 15). What phenomenological reflection deals with is in principle also subjectively accessible, that is, through intuition. The primary object of investigation, treated "theoretically" by phenomenology and "artistically" by filmmakers like Lynch, is immediate pre-reflective experience. Through the written word, phenomenology attempts to tackle the structure of something that is an implicit part of every film.

Phenomenology is a particularly promising theoretical framework to study Lynch, first of all because he, if any filmmaker, can be considered as falling into Sobchak's category of artists who practice a "phenomenology of vision" (*Address* 91). These artists interrogate the conditions and limitations of our ability to see, "the coming into being of figures from the indeterminate and latent ground of the visible" (Sobchak, *Address* 91). Artists, as Sobchak sees them, practice a constant negotiation of sight and our tendency to interpret the world based on what and how we see: "The painter's or the filmmaker's activity of seeing turns back on itself and looks not to *what appears* as visible, but to the visible's *mode of appearance*" (92). As *The Alphabet* (1968) and *The Grandmother* (1970) show, Lynch's filmmaking organically grew out of his activities as a painter. To stress Lynch's artistic *practice* in the exploration of consciousness should not lead us to ignore his *theoretical* study of such themes, though. In his 2006 book *Catching the Big Fish*, Lynch quotes from the Upanishads, which E. Thompson considers the first exploration of the nature of consciousness (1). Particularly in regard to *Eraserhead* (1977), which was being made at a time when Lynch discovered the Vedic traditions through Transcendental Meditation, Eastern conceptualizations of (dream) consciousness thus provide a theoretical backdrop for our discussion (cf. section "The Emergence of Dream Consciousness" in Chapter 4).

On top of that, Lynch implicitly sets himself a phenomenological goal as a filmmaker, as becomes clear through Chris Rodley's interview, *Lynch on Lynch*. When he is asked why a bad dream stops being terrifying when told to a friend the next day, Lynch replies that

> right there is the power of cinema. And even that can't get it, because the dreamer has bought it 1.000 per cent for himself or herself. The dream was played just for them. It's so unique and powerful to that person. But with sounds and situations and time you could get much closer to putting that together for somebody else with a film. (Rodley 15)

Judging from this excerpt, Lynch's approach to film seems to be driven by an attempt to use it at the service of the dream. To provide through the film experience something that approximates dreaming, especially in its emotional intensity, is what he refers to as "the power of cinema." Intensity and uniqueness are conceived of as the main characteristics of dream-experience. To anticipate a potential misunderstanding, Lynch does not imply that *any* film is like a dream in this passage, nor that the way in which the viewer relates to a film is similar to the way in which the dreamer relates to a dream.[22] What many proponents of the strong film/dream analogy ignored is the ontological difference between the two objects of interest. A film has an intersubjective reality—it is reproducible and can be seen by a myriad of people. A dream, on the other hand, can only be experienced by the dreamer. Lynch's remark points to this difference, implying that the gap between the subjectivity of dreaming and the *inter*-subjectivity of film viewing delimits an artist's authenticity claim of representing dream-experience through the film experience. Lynch's remark, further, appears to imply what I have called the weak version of the film/dream analogy: rather than attributing a dreamlike quality to the medium of film per se, his statement can be understood as expressing that, if used in particular way, one of cinema's potentials is to approximate dream-experience, to imitate some of its aspects, even if "the essential ingredient"—that is, what scares the dreamer so much in her nightmare—"is completely unable to be communicated" (Rodley 15).

Lynch is not alone in stressing the importance of the experiential dimension of his movies. His films are "to be experienced rather than explained," as critic Paul Taylor put it in regard to Lynch's first feature film *Eraserhead* (1979; 10). In the *Oxford English Dictionary*'s definition of "Lynchian," the dreamlike is linked to an experiential quality rather than to a narrative technique, for example. Fans and critics frequently describe their experience *of* a Lynch film rather than what happens *in* it.[23] Since an artwork's reception is considered a crucial dimension of its meaning, my analyses will make use of such reviews or YouTube comments. Maybe Kenneth Godwin is most explicit in stressing the link between the dreamlike aspect of Lynch's cinema and the viewer's relationship to the films: "More than any other filmmaker, Luis Buñuel included, Lynch has managed to capture not only the *matter* of dream, but, more importantly, the *manner*, also. His film [. . .] is not only a fantasy related to us and labeled 'dream,' something which we can stand apart from as passive observers. *It is the dream experience itself*" (Godwin qtd. in Lahde 95). Although the implied co-involvement of the viewer gives us a first hint at a phenomenological specification of the Lynchian oneiric, the dreamlike dimension of his cinema is, generally speaking, presupposed rather than explained. As Maurice Lahde points out, rather than *proving* the dreamlike nature of Lynch's cinema, the more important question seems to be "why these films remind the viewer of dream-experiences" (95; my translation).[24] While the potential to remind the viewer of dreaming may arise due to something *inherent in* the film (e.g., a particular way of representing time or space), it is important to keep in mind that it may also result from the way *we relate to* it. In the latter case, we are interested in the ways in which a film outlines a certain type of viewer response (not in the empirical viewer response).

In literary studies, reception theorist Wolfgang Iser speaks of a text's *implied reader*. The implied reader "possesses no real existence; because it embodies the totality of pre-orientations that a fictional text offers to its possible readers as conditions of reception. Therefore the implied reader is not to be located in an empirical substrate, but is based in the structure of the texts themselves" (Iser 60; my translation).[25] The text itself functions as a "reception template," conditioning a certain type of response on the reader's part (Schutte 181; my translation).[26] Just as any literary text has an implied reader, any film can be said to have an *implied viewer*. That is, a film prestructures a certain type of viewer response, for example, by choosing what to show the viewer and what to leave out or by shooting a scene from the bird's-eye perspective rather than low-angle. The question arises: what kind of cognitive or emotional response is provoked by a particular aesthetic choice? What kind of viewer behavior or attitude is implied by a scene? Lynch's dream depictions in particular are expressions of an acute awareness of the significance of film–viewer interactions—as might be most clearly shown by Monica Bellucci breaking the fourth wall in Gordon Cole's (David Lynch) dream in *Twin Peaks*'s (2017) "Part 14: Who Is the Dreamer" (cf. section "The Function of Gordon Cole's Dream . . . " in Chapter 5).

To be sure, the "implied recipient" of literary theory is a very different concept from what film phenomenology aims at, the latter being interested in the material relationship between viewer and film. Further, an aspect of Iser's theory that is not shared here is its functionalist premise: "the reader must construct the text so as to render it internally *consistent* [. . .] [T]he parts must be made to adapt coherently to the whole" (cf. Eagleton 81). To study cinema's ability to prestructure viewer behavior is of utmost importance to a film-phenomenological approach, however, because it frames the film experience as essentially dialogical, grounding the description thereof in the sphere of *originary givenness*, as Husserl would put it. On the one hand, every film is necessarily made with some idea of a potential viewer in mind: reception is a constitutive part of conception and production and thus is essential to the meaning of the work of art. On the other hand, the film itself constrains the theoretically infinite number of possible viewer responses (which is not to say that it or its meaning is fixed—the film itself acts as a necessary but not sufficient condition for the viewer's activity of meaning-making; cf. Schutte 181). In the phenomenological conception, meaning is intentional: it neither exists exclusively in the text as an objective mind-independent entity nor is it exclusively located in the recipient. Rather, it exists as the relationship between intending subject and intended object.[27] "Aesthetics," "structure," "function" (of the oneiric)—all these categories informing the film analyses in Part II characterize a continuous dialogue between the film (as intended object and intending subject) and the viewer (as intending subject and intended object). Naturally, the possibility of these categories' illumination depends on this study's willingness to explore both the objective and subjective dimension of the films, that is, their being things *in themselves* and their being things *for the recipient*, respectively.

Coming back to the study of the Lynchian oneiric, my methodological shift toward a phenomenology-inclined poetics of experience is motivated by Lynch's films themselves. Concerning Lynch's work since *Lost Highway* (1997), it can be observed that the dreams and dream structures play with the evocation and denial of knowledge—think of Fred's epistemological uncertainty when he sees his wife Renée in his dream, "knowing" that it is not her at the same time. If the dreams in *Lost Highway* (1997), *Mulholland Drive* (2001), and *Twin Peaks* (2017) challenge the notion of knowledge, then these films themselves call for an exploration of that dimension, which functions as a condition of the possibility of knowledge, that is, the dimension of experience and perception, which necessarily *precedes* knowledge. The interest in dream *experience* (i.e., experience *in* the dream[-like] sequences and the viewer's experience *of* them) in these cases is the direct result of the problematization of knowledge. The phenomenological dimension thus structures the analyses. However, this is not so much for theoretical reasons or as an end in itself but because a confrontation with the pre-reflective sensory level is demanded by the films themselves—often they refuse a cognitive decoding by being systematically based on (ontological) ambiguity (cf. sections "'The Dream of Time and Space' . . . " in Chapter 5 and "The Dream and the Human Form" in Chapter 6). Particularly the dream provokes this confrontation, not only because its "formal joy of experimentation" (Brütsch 235; my translation) arguably affects the viewer on the sensual level but also because it provides a model for a radical undermining of cognitive comprehension.[28] In Lynch's words, "[m]ost films are designed to be understood by many, many, many, many people. So there's not a lot of room to dream and wonder" (Rodley 228).

Dream Phenomenology and Freudian Psychoanalysis

What the approach in this book shares with the phenomenology of dreaming is an inherent fascination for the dream's direct appearance to the senses. However, since its object of investigation is not the night dream but its filmic depiction,[29] this section does not elaborate on the phenomenological study of the night dream per se.[30] A major reason for this is that a (if not *the*) central methodological difficulty when it comes to the phenomenology of dreaming—the principal nongivenness of the dream-experience from the perspective of waking reflection and description (Ates 93)—does not concern the study of cinematic dreams. Unlike for the dream phenomenologist, the object of inquiry has an objective existence for the film-dream analyst. Further, while this section does not attempt to summarize the complex interrelationship of phenomenology and psychoanalysis, a certain degree of compatibility is presupposed.[31] In addition to discussing the potential of combining a phenomenological method with psychoanalytic concepts for dream analysis, this section introduces a specific phenomenological distinction that recurs at various points in the following main part of the study.

Based on the thought of Edmund Husserl, Jagna Brudzinska speaks of a fundamentally "bi-valent structure of experience" characterizing all subjective life (59; my translation).[32] That is, she distinguishes between two "order[s] of experience and effectiveness" (54) as forming the elements of a "relation of equal rank and constitutive equilibrium" (59; my translation).[33] She calls the first one the "impressional-apperceptive" order (63; my translation).[34] It characterizes our subjective experience of the real, aiming for the "constitution of the object identities" (over time) and for "control of what can be experienced" (65; my translation).[35] It is attributed "uniformity and relative [. . .] unambiguousness" (65; my translation).[36] The second order is called "phantasmatic-imaginary" (54). It is responsible for the constitution of the possible and prototypically manifested by the dream (65). The phantasmatic-imaginary is characterized by "free transformations" that are not bound to the principle of object identities (65; my translation).[37] What replaces identity formation is the wish fulfillment organizing the "order of transformation" in the imaginary (65; my translation).[38]

What makes Brudzinska's distinction appealing to film studies is that her criterion for distinguishing the two orders of experience is essentially the malleability of matter—a dimension that cinema is particularly prone to, given its "materialistically minded" nature (Kracauer 309).[39] Further, the appeal of Brudzinska's account for the study of cinematic dreams emerges through her characterization of the phantasmatic. First of all, the phantasmatic hinges upon the "primary ability to let go of the bodily self of sensation and to let appear an *other*" (Brudzinska 60; my translation and italicization).[40] Crucially, then, she speaks of the "medial character [. . .] of the phantasmatic" (Brudzinska 60; my translation), in that it "primarily has the function to stand for something else" (Husserl qtd. in Brudzinska 60; my translation).[41] In this conception, thus, the night dream displays mediality by nature. What could be argued to make it film-like in particular is that both "media" operate in a similar mode—they address the same senses, communicating primarily through moving images and sounds. Film and dream display a similarity by nature because of their shared medial character, it seems. In the context of this study, I am not interested in the potentially dreamlike dimension of *the* film experience per se, however, but in what happens when the first medium of film attempts to incorporate the second medium of the dream, that is, when film *intends* the dream. Given that film, in Sobchak's conception, is both an *object of* and a *subject for* vision, there are two (nonexclusive) ways in which it can intend the oneiric. First, on a *noematic* level, it can treat "the dream" (in its noun form) as an object, a fixed "unit of experience" inside the story it is telling. On a second, *noetic* level, it can treat "dream-*ing*" (in its verb form) as a particular manifestation of the subjective modality of experience.[42] In the latter, the film is a subject of consciousness functioning in the modality of dreaming, while in the former it treats the dream as an object of consciousness.

Inherent in Brudzinska's conception of the phantasmatic are thus both ends of the spectrum that organizes my phenomenological interest in the dream (the dream being a noetic manifestation of the phantasmatic). On the one hand, dreaming has a special relationship to corporeality: dreams are able to create intense bodily sensations (think of dreams of flying or of being trapped), and matter becomes malleable without losing its palpable quality for the dreamer. At the same time, in order for a dream to occur, one needs to "let go of the bodily self of sensation" (Brudzinska 60). It seems that the body is both a prerequisite and an obstacle for the dream-experience. This raises the question whether this material dynamic of the night dream—which is based on a fundamental ambivalence—is exploited by films that try to communicate the subjective state of dreaming. The dream experiences depicted in Lynch's films are thus explored on the spectrum of pre-reflective sensory affectivity, on the one hand, and reflective medialization, on the other. In the former respect, their sensory potential is discussed both on the character level—that is, how does the characters' sensory experience of dreaming relate to their waking experience?—and on the level of film-viewer interaction. Phenomenology and the psychology of perception, by describing the experiential particularities of the night dream (as it differs from waking), might provide a model for how (the experience of) a dream differs from (the experience of) a waking sequence here. In the latter respect, I ask for the psychological and media-aesthetic potential of the dream. What role does the dream play in the film's conception of itself as a film? What does it *say* about the characters? Finally, as what kind of an experience is the dream conceptualized in Lynch's oeuvre?

One of the reasons why psychoanalysis becomes of interest here is the significatory potential it ascribes to the dream. It seems like this potential is inherently linked to its medial conception of the dream. Sigmund Freud famously described the interpretation of dreams as the "*via regia* to the knowledge of the unconscious in psychic life" (*Traumdeutung* 595; my translation and italicization),[43] with the dream providing a *means* to know some deeper truth about the dreamer. *Standing for something else*, the dream is conceived of as a "medium" disguising a latent content (the revelation of which constitutes the aim of dream interpretation). Methodologically, thus, one of the crucial questions raised by the opposition between the existential-phenomenological and the psychoanalytic approach to the dream is whether the dream is an existential state purely existing in its own right (that should not be considered in relation to the dreamer's waking experience)[44] or whether it is a form of experience that essentially stands for something else (and that this *something else* is what we should extract from it). The approach of this study tries to combine the best of both the existentialist and the Freudian framework: it explores the particular experiential qualities of the dream(-like) sequences but at the same time remains open to the possibility that the experience signifies something beyond its material surface. The attempt to get "to the dreams themselves" should not exclude the significatory potential of the dream concerning the dreamer's psyche or the story. Importantly, as Cornelius Castoriadis suggests, the question as to *what* the dream signifies is independent of the "validity" of the claim *that* it has a deeper meaning: "The groundbreaking novelty about Freud was his insight [...] that slips of the tongue have meaning, that dreams, deliriums, delusional states, and hallucinations have meaning [...] The validity of this decision is independent of the kind of meaning which he believes to have discovered or the accuracy of the method which he applied to determine it" (Castoriadis qtd. in Ates 128; my translation).[45] That is, we do not necessarily have to agree about what the dream means according to Freud's conception to see his pioneering contribution *that* it expresses a deeper truth about the dreamer.

If one asks for the extent to which Freudian psychoanalysis is a valuable interlocutor of phenomenology in this study, then one could answer on a general thematic level: given that my object of interest is the cinematic phenomenon of dream experience, psychoanalysis obviously is a welcome source of input in its ability to illuminate the nature of the dream phenomenon. In this, I do not ask for the extent to which Lynch's dreams (dis-)confirm psychoanalytic dream theories. Rather, I ask for the ways in which, vice versa, psychoanalytic concepts and observations add to our understanding of the dream phenomenon in the films of David Lynch. Thinking of Lynch's filmic dreams in methodological terms as the locus of conversation between psychoanalysis and phenomenology, it bears emphasis that the aim of this conversation is the illumination of dream experience as depicted by the films: we do not "use" the films to talk about the theories—an aspect that Martha Nochimson criticizes in regard to the Lacanian interpretations of Lynch, particularly that of Todd McGowan (Nochimson xiii).

If phenomenology is the "philosophy of conscious experience" (Sobchak, *Address* 27), then psychoanalysis could be called the "philosophy of *un*-conscious experience." A strictly phenomenological approach might fall short in addressing the particular unconscious dynamic that the dreams put on display (on the character level), the organizational makeup of dreams, as well as the relationship of dream content to the waking world and the psychological implications thereof—aspects that Freudian psychoanalysis has devoted a lot of attention to through concepts and mechanisms such as *condensation, displacement, wish fulfillment, primary* and *secondary process, repression,* and so on. Instead of rejecting these concepts from the start, we will explore the extent to which they do justice to the nature of dream experience as depicted by the films. Where are they illuminating, and where are they reductive?

A dialogue between psychoanalysis and phenomenology promises to be fruitful when it comes to the (filmic) dream because, vice versa, phenomenology addresses what Freudian dream theory tends to underspecify, if not ignore, that is, it engages with the "thickness" of the phenomenon of the dream-experience itself, what Freud calls the *manifest dream* (e.g., E. Thompson 148), the particular imaginative dimension of the dream (Foucault 34–5) that is so important in its filmic depiction. Instead of being seen as mutually exclusive, psychoanalysis and phenomenology are conceived of as complementary approaches that may join each other in illuminating the dream. There also appears to be a historical dimension to the reliance of phenomenology on psychoanalysis when it comes to the dream. Murat Ates, for example, speaks of "every post-Freudian investigation of the dream" (including phenomenology) as a "beneficiary" of Freud's attempt "to rehabilitate the dream-experience" (128-9; my translation).⁴⁶ This is apparent in twentieth-century phenomenologists' writings: although highly critical of his thought, Merleau-Ponty, Boss, Foucault, Jean-Paul Sartre, and others tend to refer back to Freud (either explicitly or implicitly) when it comes to the dream. To some extent, thus, psychoanalysis already *is* the interlocutor of phenomenology if the topic of conversation is the dream because twentieth-century dream phenomenology is a reaction to Freud's dream conception.

Besides the general and the historical dimension of the collaboration between psychoanalysis and phenomenology, there is also a third—arguably most important—reason for the unorthodox methodological combination in this study, and that is Lynch's cinema itself. In the previous section, we have already established why phenomenology is a promising theoretical framework for studying the films of David Lynch. Now it is time to elaborate on why, in addition, the analysis of his cinema calls for psychoanalysis. Again, we could answer this question on a broad level. In general, the extent of the reception of Freud's thought on popular culture is difficult to measure. According to screenwriter Paul Schrader, Freud's influence on (Hollywood) filmmaking cannot be underestimated, particularly when it comes to the emergence of heroes with "flawed character" and complex inner lives in post-Second World War cinema (Cousins 00:25:06–00:27:53).

More specifically, some of the surrealist filmmakers (Man Ray, Réné Clair, Jean Cocteau, and Salvador Dalí) who influenced Lynch—as shown by a documentary the director made for the BBC ("David Lynch Presents the History of Surrealist Film [1987]")—directly engaged with Freud's theories, particularly his dream conception (cf. Brütsch 32). So even if Lynch never read any writings of Freud, he indirectly received Freud "through" the films that he watched. What is particularly striking, further, is the amount of Freudian scholarship on the cinema of Lynch. Lynch's cinema has already been studied extensively under a psychoanalytic lens by psychoanalysis-inclined film scholars and psychoanalysts alike. Just to name some examples, Todd McGowan's *The Impossible David Lynch*, Allister Mactaggart's *The Film Paintings of David Lynch*, Michel Chion's monograph *David Lynch*, and, most prominently, Slavoj Žižek's take on Lynch, emerging throughout *The Pervert's Guide to Cinema* and his essay *The Art of the Ridiculous Sublime—On David Lynch's Lost Highway*—all of these studies are rooted in or engage with psychoanalytic theory. A recent monograph, to give another example, is titled *Freud/Lynch: Behind the Curtain*. It assembles analyses from a variety of scholars, psychoanalysts, as well as film scholars and studies Lynch's films through a psychoanalytic lens.

Taking these studies into account raises the question as to what extent the psychoanalytic approach to Lynch's cinema engages with the dream phenomenon itself, that is, as it is depicted in the films. Do they run the risk of exposing themselves to the same criticism that Freud's dream theory has been confronted with, that is, a neglect of the manifest dream experience in favor of a disguised latent content? If not, how do they evade this problem? In Robert Sinnerbrink's view, there are two opposing types of scholarship on Lynch: one "maintain[s] that Lynch's films defy rational interpretation, which suggests that we should sensuously intuit rather than conceptually analyse" his work ("Everything" 128). The other, represented by Žižek, "insist[s] that we can discern intelligible narrative structures and coherent themes in Lynch's films, provided we assume the appropriate (Lacanian) perspective" (Sinnerbrink, "Everything" 128). Rather than decide for one approach from the start, this study—despite its phenomenological outset—engages with both, looking for the ways in which they inform and benefit from each other. The present analysis attempts not to fall victim to the ideological split between two schools of thinking, which would impoverish our discussion. Interestingly, further, the opposition that Sinnerbrink describes maps perfectly onto the opposition between existential dream phenomenology (focused on the dream's particular experiential qualities) on the one hand and Freudian dream interpretation (focused on the dream's latent meaning) on the other. What was remarked earlier can only be repeated here: the opposition between those who stress the sensory-aesthetic dimension (and therein deny any rationality) of Lynch's films and those who focus on their intelligibility serves as a fertile ground for a deeper exploration of the Lynchian oneiric, which transcends a binary conceptualization of his cinema.

Stressing the significance of psychoanalysis for this study, it is also important to bear in mind which role psychoanalysis does *not* play in the methodology. While psychoanalytic concepts are discussed in relation to the dreams, psychoanalytic *film* theory is not part of this study's methodology. On the one hand, this has to do with some of the ideological presuppositions of psychoanalytic film theory, which are not shared here—particularly when it comes to the conceptualization of the film–viewer relationship. The film experience is not a priori deceptive, and the spectator is not by nature a Jeffrey Beaumont-like voyeur who, driven by a *lack* that defines his identity, is looking for the satisfaction of his perverse desire to see. In particular, Metz's generalization concerning the dreamlike nature of the filmic state (based on its regressiveness) hinders a more differentiated approach to the filmic dream. On the other hand, the neglect of psychoanalytic film theory in favor of phenomenology is motivated by Lynch's own approach to film, given that he aims for a particularly immersive—and in this sense *dreamlike*[47] experience to the viewer. Even in the context of dreams, thus, Freudian psychoanalysis, in its focus on their symbolic character, might not lead us to a deeper understanding of the Lynchian oneiric in its experiential dimension. As Petrić elaborates:

> The interpretation of dream symbols in cinema is [...] less significant for the oneiric impact of a film than the way they are presented on the screen. If Freud stated that "the interpretation of dreams is the royal road to a knowledge of the unconscious activities of the mind," then the cinematic presentation of dream symbols is "the royal road" to their sensory-motor experience in the course of watching a film. The greater the intensity of this experience, the deeper the metaphorical and poetical meaning of a dream film. (Petrić, "Film and Dreams" 16)

Systematic Approach

Before the steps of the analytic process are concretized, a few remarks on the film selection of the present corpus shall be made. Obviously, a characterization of the

Lynchian oneiric is all the more significant the greater the number of films on which it is based, not least because the dreams across Lynch's filmography speak to each other. But it is not just the *number* of films discussed, it is also the treatment of different formats that has its benefits (feature films, short films [animated and live action], TV series); the term *film* is used in a broad sense here, comprising all of these formats. A characterization of the Lynchian oneiric that builds on examples spanning across different audiovisual media surely is more significant than if the analyses were exclusively focused on the short film *or* on the features *or* on Lynch's TV work. Each format has its own regulations that play into the way the oneiric is treated, and if this approach to the Lynchian oneiric transcends these, it stands as a more valuable contribution to the academic discourse around Lynch's art.

But still, why are *these* films chosen and not others? *Absurd Encounter with Fear* (1967), *The Alphabet* (1968), *The Grandmother* (1970), *Eraserhead* (1977), *Twin Peaks* (1990–1; 1992; 2017), *Lost Highway* (1997), and *Mulholland Drive* (2001)—the IMDb lists 100 directing credits for Lynch,[48] why this particular selection of seven of his works? First of all, given my interest in the interrelationship between marked dreams and unmarked, merely dreamlike sequences, what motivates the selection is the question whether there are marked dreams in a film. There are no marked dreams, for example, in *Wild at Heart* (1990), *The Straight Story* (1999), or *Inland Empire* (2006). What stands out in *Blue Velvet* (1986) is the metaphorical dimension of dreaming—a symbolic passage into and out of the protagonist's ear coincides with an exploration of the dark side of the American Dream. While the concept of the American Dream does not constitute a primary research interest of this study due to the "dream's" metaphoricity, it will play into the discussion of *Mulholland Drive* (2001), as this movie *literalizes* the metaphorical dimension of the American Dream by letting it unfold as a psychological dream of the main character Diane. An exception to the orientation toward marked dreams is constituted by our discussion of *Absurd Encounter with Fear* (1967), Lynch's mostly ignored very first film which, in phenomenological terms, anticipates a fundamental aspect of the Lynchian oneiric, that is, an ambivalent relationship between the viewer and the on-screen scenario. Concerning *Dune* (1984), although there are marked dreams in the film, Lynch had no final cut for it, which entailed a significant compromise to his creative expression. It is impossible to tell in this case whether the dreams as they appear in the film are the way the auteur intended them to be.

In addition to engaging with different formats, the selection also reflects different phases of Lynch's creative work: student filmmaker (*Absurd Encounter with Fear* [1967], *The Alphabet* [1968], and *The Grandmother* [1970]), idiosyncratic cult-film eccentric (*Eraserhead* [1977]), mainstream TV-director (*Twin Peaks* [1990–1]), renowned postmodernist arthouse director (*Lost Highway* [1997] and *Mulholland Drive* [2001]), and TV auteur (*Twin Peaks* [2017]). Finally, in addition to addressing different formats and phases of Lynch's creative work, the corpus should also reflect the films he is most known for—that is, those which, most likely, provide the basis for the attribution "dreamlike" (which might not be the perfume commercial *Lady Blue Shanghai* that Lynch directed in 2010, for example).

How can the methodological-conceptual framework outlined so far be translated into a concrete systematic approach that informs the succeeding analysis chapters in Part II? While much of what will be described may have already been suspected, I would like to sketch the systematic approach for the underlying structure of Part II to become fully transparent. To begin with, the structure of Part II reflects the chronology of Lynch's filmography. The chronological makeup facilitates the recognition of developmental changes and tendencies in the filmography of Lynch, thus constituting the possibility for a kind of generalization that would not be given with a nonchronological structure. At the same time, each of the films is discussed in a separate chapter to let it stand on its own. After all, the primary referential framework of a particular film is the film itself—that is, the film as *a single experiential unit*. The overall structure, thus, attempts to both grasp the particularity of each film *and* relate the films to each other.

Leaning on Chion's concept of *audio-vision*, what is seen and heard in the respective film is described at the beginning of each chapter (except for Chapter 5 on *Twin Peaks*—in this case, this kind of description would fill an entire book, given that there are forty-eight episodes and a feature film; here, the discussed scenes will be contextualized in the narrative and described before they are analyzed). This is partly because of phenomenology's call for a "thick" description of what appears in (film) consciousness and partly to provide orientation for the reader. A new paragraph usually coincides with a new sequence in this section. This section, which mostly takes the form of a section titled "Audio-Viewing . . . ," appears particularly useful for Lynch's films due to the often complex and confusing narratives (even after multiple viewings), as can be seen in frequent misrepresentations of events of the films in analyses (in Žižek's recollection of *Lost Highway* [1997], for example, Pete imagines Renée to have sex with Mr. Eddy at the Lost Highway Hotel [*Ridiculous* 17], but this is not what happens in the film—Pete already transformed back into Fred at this point; a similar misrepresentation can be found in Daniele Dottorini [64]; Andrea Minuz writes that Mr. Eddy has sex with Alice in this scene, but it is clearly Renée [95]). As for dream sequences, a particularly thorough audiovisual description of what presents itself is conducted, without interpreting what they "mean" or how they function in the film at this point. Given that the focus at this stage is on *what* appears in consciousness, the *how* of the objects' appearance (i.e., their *manners of givenness*, in phenomenological terms) and the *why* will be discussed later.

One of the major problems concerning the attribution "dreamlike" or "oneiric" is the arbitrariness it implies initially; what is dreamlike in a scene to one person may not be dreamlike at all to another. In this context, this study follows two different approaches to the oneiric, depending on the dream-marking status of a given scene. Both approaches attempt to minimize the arbitrariness in judging a scene to be dreamlike. First of all, dreams and potentially dreamlike sequences are identified. Preferably, I start by taking a closer look at marked dreams. The guiding question here is *how experience as it occurs in a marked dream can be characterized*. Instead of asking what *is* dreamlike about these scenes, I ask what is *suggested* as dreamlike.[49] That is, rather than asking how the night dream works, we ask how the night dream is *reflected* in the film. What this approach naturally implies is the question of how dream experience is different from experience outside of marked dreams. A postulate of this study is that the experience as it occurs in a marked dream provides the paradigmatic manifestation of what "oneiric" refers to.

For unmarked and not unambiguously marked sequences whose oneiricity is merely suspected at first, the procedure is different: given that the meaning of "'oneiric' cannot be determined on the basis of dream markers here, the guiding question now becomes *in what sense a scene can still be called oneiric.*" While in the case of a marked scene, the oneiricity of experience is predetermined, the oneiricity of an unmarked scene is always a subject up for debate. First of all, YouTube comments on the scene in question or reviews of the films can be taken into consideration. If a particular aspect of a scene of the film is called "dreamlike," then we can ask for the reasons for this perception. A first option is the consideration of academic literature on the dream. That is, when is the possibility of considering a scene dreamlike—as referring to the night dream—"backed up" by studies on the dream or on cinema (see my discussion of *Absurd Encounter with Fear* in Chapter 3 and section "Proper (Spatio-)temporality" in Chapter 5)?[50] How can this comparison be critically evaluated? What aspects of dream-experience does a particular scene engage with? There might be structural similarities between dream experience as represented in and evoked by the film and the way the night dream-experience is conceived of in studies and academic literature. Second, we may explore the ways in which a potentially dreamlike sequence relates to experience in marked dreams. That is, when and in what regard is experience that is not marked as a dream similar to dream experience, that is, experience *of* and *in* a marked dream? For example, the third episode of *Twin Peaks* (1990–1) characterizes dreaming through a manipulated time flow (cf. section "Proper (Spatio-)temporality in Cooper's Dream..." in Chapter 5), an aesthetic choice that can hardly be motivated by the attempt to imitate the nocturnal dream-experience. Manipulations of time also exist in the third season of *Twin Peaks* (2017), but they do not occur in marked dreams. However, the manipulated time flow may still be called "oneiric," as season three uses the dream as a metaphor for a disturbance of the impression of reality—ultimately, *Twin Peaks* deconstructs its own diegesis using a dream metaphor—and a manipulated time flow is able to express this disturbance. At the same time, the manipulated time flow is dream-*like* (in the literal sense), as it echoes and expands on an essential element of the dream from season one.

While some of the methodological steps demanded by marked and unmarked sequences are different, others are the same. That is, whether a scene is oneiric from the start or merely potentially oneiric, I will describe and reflect upon the experience *of* and *in* the scene, distill its structural features, explore the function of this experience in the context of the entire film, and compare them to the structure and function of the oneiric in other Lynch films. This involves a constant reflection on the relationship between the *how* and the *what* of the dream(-like) sequence, that is, between the subjective manner of givenness (performed by the film as a "seeing subject") and the objects appearing through it.

Part II

The Oneiric in the Films of David Lynch

A Phenomenological Approach

3

Three Early Short Films (1967–70)

Absurd Encounter with Fear (1967)

Most monographs on the work of David Lynch start with a discussion of *Six Men Getting Sick* (1966)[1] or *The Alphabet* (1968), ignoring his two-minute short film *Absurd Encounter with Fear* (1967).[2] Since his previous *Six Men Getting Sick* was an installation combining elements of painting, sculpture, and film (Kaul and Palmier 24), *Absurd Encounter with Fear* is, strictly speaking, Lynch's first *film*. What I would like to argue is that, while it does not contain any marked dream, *Absurd Encounter* provides an example of how the film experience can imitate certain aspects of the nocturnal dream-experience. The "dreamlike quality" of the short film[3] may be rooted in the pre-reflective and sensual interaction between the film and the viewer rather than being inherent in the film understood as a system of relations between objects.

An audiovisual description of *Absurd Encounter* should note how Lynch's first film, significantly, starts on the auditory level. The crescendoing drum roll of Krzysztof Penderecki's *Capriccio for Violin and Orchestra* (1967) guides the fade-in of the image[4]—a wide shot of a corn field. In the distance, there is a blue-faced man (Lynch's fellow student, friend, and longtime collaborator Jack Fisk), slowly approaching the camera. He passes the camera to approach a crouched girl (Lynch's first wife Peggy Lynch) who does not seem to notice him, as she does not look up. The girl's face is painted white, the same color as her clothes, and she wears red lipstick. She appears to be frightened. When the man stands right behind her, he unzips his pants and, in a grotesque gesture, pulls out flowers and blades of grass. After frantically turning around to catch sight of the camera zooming in on him, he drops to the ground, losing consciousness. The girl remains motionless, as if nothing had happened.

Oneiric Atmosphere

Immediately striking about the film is its underlying sense of threat, whose source can be localized in the soundtrack's *Capriccio*. The orchestra's sheer tempo stands in contrast to the slow movements executed by the man and the girl's complete stillness.[5] In combination with the dissonances, it seems to affect the film material, as becomes visible through the specks hectically buzzing around and the damage the celluloid is taking. It appears to be the same tension, not just underlying but *driving* both the visible and the audible: the specks and strings share a similar sensual quality, consisting in very short and quick movements that, not only according to the postulate of the functioning of mirror neurons (cf. section "The Role of Subjectivity in Film Analysis" in Chapter 1), move me, as a viewer, at the same time.[6] My breathing rhythm accelerates, with a tension building up in the chest. One might say that the specks "do" to the celluloid (and therefore to both the film's and my vision) what the strings and brasses "do" to the soundtrack (hence to the film's and my hearing); but that only speaks to the reflexive ability to direct one's attention toward separate sensory modalities in succession, the visible followed by the audible, to then compare what presents itself in either one of them. At the pre-reflective stage of my viewing experience, however, I do not yet differentiate between the two modalities such that the arousal I feel becomes the diffuse *ground* against which individual elements of perception, that is, *figures*, stand out. This shows how the film evokes an atmosphere of threat. For Rainer Schönhammer, the perception of *atmosphere* is the result of a reduction of an environment's stimuli to diffuse impressions (*Wahrnehmung* 293).[7] Not being able to "pick out" an individual element we can direct our attention to, we perceive a situation holistically. *Absurd Encounter* achieves its atmospheric quality by denying us to single out an element in the music we can cling to. Given its inherent phenomenal qualities, the music creates a sense of overpowering. *Capriccio for Violin and Orchestra* belongs to the musical tradition of sonorism, which is characterized by an orientation toward noise in an attempt to overcome traditional compositional principles focused on tonality and consonance (Granat). The *Capriccio* does not allow for the identification of a rhythm, melody, or musical pattern in general but is focused on sensible qualities produced by the instruments. The effect in Lynch's short film is that, like in a dream, we are completely *absorbed* into the scenario without being able to understand it. The title-giving "fear" evoked by this lack of perceptual discriminability may not only be related to the experience of *atmosphere* in general but also to the atmosphere created by dreaming in particular, as a comment by Lynch suggests. In his view, we do "not see [. . .] the whole thing" when we are afraid, as "[w]e're not experiencing the ultimate reality" (Rodley 243–4). In other words, fear might be a determining factor for a mode of consciousness in which we do not experience "ultimate"—waking—"reality," that is, the dream mode.

Concerning the dream state, this atmospheric absorption is often linked to our rational faculties functioning differently. Sigmund Freud, for example, spoke of the predominance of "primary processes" which are "directly animated by the drives, serve the pleasure principle and work to actualize a free flow of psychic energy" ("Primary Process/Secondary Process"). Secondary processes, which allow for self-reflection while awake, are of less importance in the night dream. Distinguishing between primary *consciousness* (as the "subjective awareness of perception and emotion") and secondary consciousness (as primary consciousness plus thinking and meta-awareness; Hobson 803), neuroscience explains this phenomenon through a decreased activity in the prefrontal cortex, which is associated with cognitive control and metacognition, combined with an increase of activity in the amygdala and the hippocampus, that is, areas of the limbic system processing emotions (Mutz and Javadi 5).

Allan Hobson suggests that dream consciousness "is predominantly primary in the sense that it emphasizes perception and emotion at the expense of reason" (808).[8] Since we are necessarily awake when watching a film, the subjective experience resulting from this dynamic of dreaming cannot be recreated in the film experience. What film can do, however, and this short film proves it, is to present a totally unmotivated, alogical chain of events as causally necessary,[9] resulting in a peculiar logic that belongs entirely to *this film*. Our primary sensual involvement, mainly created through the music, is narratively reinforced by a total lack of logic and psychological motivation. Not only does the film not *give* us a context that would explain why this is happening, but it appears *impossible* to imagine a circumstance that would render the scenario comprehensible. And yet the film contains the sense of necessity, that is, that what we see could not happen in any other way. This feeling is due to the threat inherent in the music. Due to the lack of harmonic and rhythmic orientation it provides, it is constantly and consistently unsettling. As a result, we are susceptible to, that is, we accept to a greater extent, anything presenting itself not only auditorily but also on the screen. In this way, the film provokes a form of reception behavior conditioned by the expectation that the events and our reactions to them need to occur in the way they do, even though nothing makes any sense.

A second aspect that should not go unnoticed concerns the viewer's "fusion" with the film. As mentioned before, the fleetingness of what the orchestra is playing is paralleled visually by the specks on the celluloid. It appears that, in our pre-reflective experience of the film, we cannot be sure of whether this "whizzing" of specks and sounds causes our arousal or whether it is our arousal causing the whizzing. We feel the objects' hectic movement *as* our own bodily tension and this tension *as* the hectic movement. Film and viewer merge in a dynamic interplay in which both occupy the role of active participant and passive recipient. As the active participant, the perceived (external) object becomes the expression of my subjectively felt tension and as the passive observer, my tension becomes the expression of the object. In the former case, it feels as though I *produce* the tension (with the film reflecting it), whereas in the latter, I merely *receive* it (the film being the source of it).

Ambiguity in the Viewer–Film Relationship

The ending shows that the film provokes the viewer's direct confrontation with her double status as participant/observer both on a phenomenological and on a narrative level.[10] After all, the blue-faced man dies because he realizes that he is being "observed by us"; his shock upon being caught coincides with us zooming in on him. The zoom in does not only give expression to his shock but also functions to make us viewers aware of our viewing situation: he is looking at us looking at him. In the title-giving "encounter," it is not only the man being caught in his weirdly perverse act, it is also the viewer being caught in her perverse desire to see "what she is not supposed to see."[11] If our expectation was to witness a rape scene, then this expectation is doubly broken here. First, because instead of his penis, the man pulls flowers out of his zipper—a quirky declaration of love? And second, because the unwritten law that I am merely *witnessing* the film scenario is broken. The effect is particularly strong not only because the zoom coincides with the orchestra's strings playing a sharp and dissonant chord that jolts us but also because the man "walking through" the camera earlier implied our disembodied, fixed, safe, passively observing position.[12] The man's staring suddenly gives me a body, placing me in that world, or better: it makes me feel my material presence both off-screen and in the on-screen scenario, exposing his embarrassment and my voyeurism as two sides of a single (literally understood) act of looking, which is pre-reflectively not yet differentiated into *his* and *mine*.

In a fiction film, a character's look into the camera may fulfill various functions. By nature though, it entails a shift in the communicative situation for the viewer. When a character looks and sometimes speaks into the camera, the viewer appears to be directly addressed. He becomes aware of being the recipient of the filmic discourse while the film puts its constructedness on display. Woody Allen breaks the fourth wall, for example, when he unexpectedly turns to the camera as Alvy in his classic *Annie Hall* (1977; 00:12:04). Annoyed by a "pontificating" intellectual queuing behind him at a movie theater, Alvy seemingly addresses us viewers, asking, "What do you do when you get stuck in a movie line with a guy like this behind you?" (00:12:03–00:12:07). In what follows, he asks us to "team-up" with him (and Marshall McLuhan) against the man, inviting us to laugh at his pretentiousness. As Matthias Brütsch observes with regard to dream depictions in film history, a sudden glance into the camera has become a common means to mark the end of a dream (136). The post-dream glance at the camera "stresses the inner-diegetic boundary between dream and reality by touching or trespassing the boundary between fiction and the real world, between diegesis and off-screen space" (Brütsch 136; my translation).[13] While the former boundary is not present in *Absurd Encounter*—there is no framing dream marker in the film—the observation concerning the latter boundary still holds true. The scene establishes a moment of contact between the viewer in front of the screen and the actor in front of the camera. A certain eeriness lies in the fact that the man's eyes are not revealed but remain dark. As a viewer, I sense that he is looking at me, but I cannot be completely sure. There is something elusive about his gaze and, thus, by extension, about his intentionality. Furthermore, what makes the moment dreamlike, thus distinguishing it from a mere shift concerning the fictional status of the events (as in Allen's case), is the extent and the sort of my involvement in the scenario.

The way in which we ambiguously relate to the film as passive observers *and* actively engaging participants, on a pre-reflective level, shares with the phenomenology of dreaming the double status of dreamer-as-observer (third-person perspective) and dreamer-as-agent (first-person perspective). Back and forth changes from a neutral, observing perspective to an active, participating perspective are a well-documented phenomenon of dreams (cf. E. Thompson 129).[14] According to Julian Mutz and Amir-Homayoun Javadi, this might be due to decreased activity in the right inferior parietal cortex during sleep (5). In waking, such changes would be considered pathological, characterizing states of depersonalization and derealization. As Samuel Lowy puts it, "[i]n the real world 'I' and 'you' are more clearly defined and distinct to our subjective perception than it is the case in dreams where *spectator and actor are one with the* action" (qtd. in Petrić 22). With regard to watching Lynch's short film, the observing and participating modality of my spectatorship merge in the *act of looking*—not just because it is mirrored by the blue-faced man but, more importantly, because through it, I appear to be causally involved—that is, I fall under the illusion of causing the man's breakdown. In Allen's case, though I become aware of my recipient status, I am not under the impression of causing any of the events on the screen to occur; I just *join in on* the tendentious joke attacking the academic. In Lynch, at the pre-reflective stage, my act of looking ceases to be merely perceiving and, as Merleau-Ponty would say, becomes expressive, as I appear to *affect* the events on the screen. It allows me to "talk back" to the film through the primary sensory modality through which I have access to it. If the words I speak while watching a film cannot be "heard" in its world, film can create the illusion that my glance can be "felt," giving the viewer the feeling of *interacting with*, rather than merely *observing*, the film. What this example makes clear, then, is how oneiricity may consist in a particular kind of viewer–film interaction constituted by the film experience, one that is easily overlooked if film is considered a mere object of vision and the viewer a merely passive observer. Oneiricity in this case is a direct result and constitutes an essential dimension of our sensual engagement with the film.

The Alphabet (1968)

Lynch's interest in film naturally evolved from his being a painter. Recalling his transition from painting to film in the mid-1960s, he says, "I'm looking at this figure in the painting, and I hear a little wind, and see a little movement. And I had a wish that the painting would really be able to move" (Rodley 37). Curiously, his motivation does not concern cinema's ability to capture real movement as it occurs in the physical world but departs from the wish to *write movement* (from Greek "kínēma" and "gráphein") into his *painting*, almost as if he could "add it as an ingredient." His four-minute short film *The Alphabet* (1968) bespeaks this transition, displaying a cinematographic interest in painting and a painterly interest in film as two sides of a single creative impulse.

The film deals with a girl's (Peggy Lynch) fear of learning the letters of the alphabet. Inspired by a nightmare of Peggy's niece (Rodley 40), the film fictionalizes this dream report, visualizing it as a sequence of live action and animation scenes. We see the girl falling asleep (or sleeping; see Figure 3.1), followed by the title card's image of her wearing sunglasses (see Figure 3.2).

Animation as the Otherness of Dream Vision

Dimming her sensory input from the outside world, the sunglasses announce a turn toward her inner reality. Besides functioning as a dream marker (the first one in Lynch's oeuvre), the image stands out because it is neither an objective shot of her (she was not wearing the sunglasses in the opening shot) nor is it part of her subjective images (it is unlikely that she sees herself while falling asleep). It occupies a space "in between,"

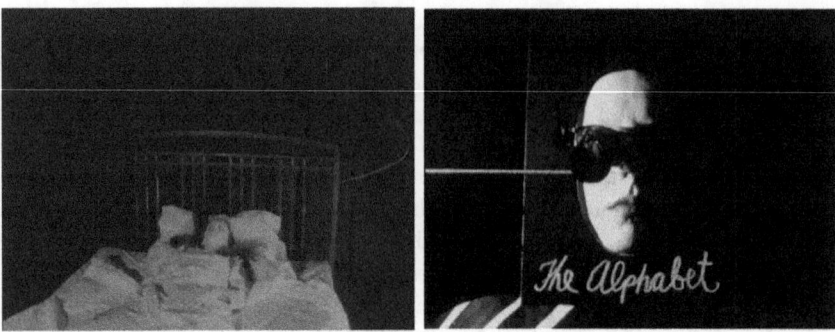

Figures 3.1–3.2 *The Alphabet* (1968), opening with the first dream marker in Lynch's oeuvre (00:01:23; 00:01:30).

not outside anymore and not yet inside, neither in the physical reality where the girl is falling asleep nor in her dream world.[15] Undoubtedly, however, it leads *from* the former *to* the latter. In what follows, the dream status is clearly distinguished through its animation technique (00:01:34–00:03:57) that stands in contrast to the waking world's live action. Animation does not claim the ontological authenticity often ascribed to photographic images and thus lends itself to represent the *otherness* of the dream.

A similarity between filmic vision and dream vision may be worth considering here: inherent in dreaming is a reflexive movement, thus a reflective momentum. By its nature, the dream mode necessarily thematizes waking vision. It draws on the functioning of waking vision and uses memorized images as its raw material, changing them in any number of ways. Thereby, the dream challenges, reflects, or more generally "deals with" our regular, waking ways of seeing the world. Thus, dream vision brings to the fore an aspect that is also implicitly contained within filmic vision. As an externalization of our ability to see—Sobchak speaks of the structural and functional similarity of filmic and human vision (*Address* 4)—film always implicitly reflects on our (and its own) act of viewing. Hence, oneiric and filmic vision involve "second-order seeing." *The Alphabet* thematizes this second-order seeing—belonging to both the film and the dream—through animation. That is, animation manifests the reflective potential of film as the awareness of dream vision's *otherness*.

Introducing the dream is a sequence (00:01:34–00:02:17) that presents a sort of "natural evolution" of the alphabet. The image is divided horizontally, with the sun dominating the upper half and a flat surface representing the surface of the earth on the bottom (see Figure 3.3).[16] As we are watching, the sky is "drawing itself" in small dots forming color fields while the "earth" is being populated by the alphabet's letters popping up in chronological order in the form of squares, circles, and what appear to be speech bubbles. Dreaming is associated with the process of painting. The implication seems to be that visual perception works differently in a dream, and that painted as opposed to photographed imagery is more apt to qualify this difference. Through the constantly evolving drawings, we can watch the girl's creative act unfold such that the malleability of the shapes corresponds to the malleability of the dream

Figure 3.3 The prologue: A natural evolution of the alphabet (00:02:15).

itself. If it is the "fluidity of the dream-world which can be considered its most basic quality" (Engel, "Poetics" 22), stop-motion animation gave Lynch the opportunity of imitating this quality of dreaming at a point in film history long before the advent of digital postproduction, CGI, and so on. Crucially, the constantly changing shapes are the filmic expression of the way in which the dream presents itself to the girl *while dreaming*. As such, the film seems to imply that her act of viewing *is creating* the objects of her vision *through* her vision (i.e., functioning in the modality of imagination), as opposed to a passive viewing that would merely "take up" what is already there to be perceived. Rather than receiving sensory information, thus, her dreaming mind constitutes the perceived object.

The De-Automatization of Perception

That the dream state embodies a strongly modified form of perception becomes clear after the humanized "birth" of a lowercase "a" from its uppercase equivalent (see Figures 3.4 and 3.5). By now, we have entered the darker part of the dream, as announced by the extreme close-up of a teeth-licking red mouth, accompanied by a distorted voice. Its vulgarity stands in contrast to the harmonic atmosphere established by the religious singing's linear up-and-down movement and the sky's soft color palette at the beginning of the dream. It soon becomes clear that the first sequence of her dream (00:01:34–00:02:17) functioned as a sort of prologue, presenting an idealized way of "learning the alphabet as it's supposed to be." As the rest of her dream shows,

 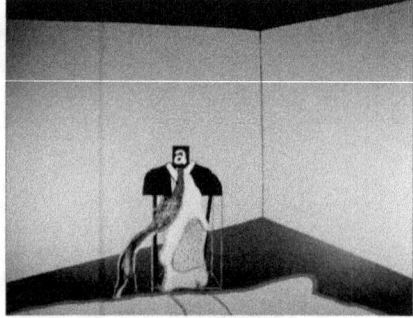

Figures 3.4–3.5 The birth of the (*objet petit*) "a" (00:02:51; 00:02:53).

the girl's actual experience in learning the alphabet is directly opposed to this version. After "a" is born, we hear a baby crying and the muffled sound of a female voice. It is impossible to pick out phonemes, let alone words, so our acoustic impression is limited to prosodic features of the mother's speech. It seems as if the girl were remembering the way she perceived language when she had not acquired it yet. Unable to function semantically, her perception merely extracts the emotional essence of her surroundings, and the dream expresses her memory thereof. Interestingly, the dream points back to a prelinguistic past not by "naming" it or "referring to" it but by entering a deprived mode of speech perception. It seems as if Lynch imagined a way in which a newborn perceives language and recreates that experience in a highly stylized way through the film experience.

In a Lacanian reading, the lowercase "a" not only refers to the first letter of the alphabet but also to the *objet petit a* ("a" standing for *autre*), Lacan's concept of the unattainable "object-cause of desire," which is given with birth.[17] His take on developmental psychology is that the newborn is defined by its separation from the mother and as a consequence by its *lack* of being one with her. That is, from the very moment of birth on, the newborn has a desire that is, per definition, not satisfiable. With the baby's crying and the voice of the mother right after the abstracted birth, the small "a" on the head of the human figure seems like a perfect illustration of Lacan's concept (see Figure 3.5). Further, the *lack* that defines the desire for the other connects the moment of birth to the girl's present situation, which is determined by her lack of command of the alphabet. In a Lacanian reading, the dream circles around the trauma that defines the real. It visualizes the unnamable, impossible truth at the basis of the girl's trauma, her existential fear of the letters, which, due to being unspeakable in the symbolic order, becomes subject to the imaginary.

The movement from the idealization toward the horror of learning the letters coincides with a change from the abstract realm of the prologue, where the human being was only represented by a voice, to an exploration of the human body. Body parts (a breast, head, shoulders, a penis-like shape, faces, etc.) are decomposed and recomposed as painted fragments and geometrical forms. Not only are the forms manipulated, but also the space within which they appear is frequently reduced to two dimensions, which amplifies the impression of the film constituting a moving painting. What *The Alphabet* has in common with abstract painting, further, is an interest in the organizing principles of vision: lines, color, form, the construction of spatial depth (or a lack thereof), perspective. In films and paintings that aim at realism, structuring preconditions that enable visual perception usually remain invisible themselves, but they are employed here to expose the fragility of visual perception. Through a continuous overlaying of salient geometrical forms and painted fragments of the body, Lynch stylizes visual perception in its nascent state—recreating a sort of "seeing for the first time" (cf. Marks 178). It is a kind of seeing that cannot cognitively grasp its object but is rather trying to find out what it is in the process. Merleau-Ponty speaks of the potential of painting to "blow [. . .] up the 'skin of things' . . . to show how things become things and world becomes world" (qtd. in Zechner 74; my translation).[18] In *The Alphabet*, out of an undefined area of white, a human face appears, disappears, and reappears (see Figure 3.6). The initial act of perception thus renders the indeterminate determinate and is followed by what might hint at a first step toward learning to recognize a human face. In Merleau-Ponty's view, "perception orients itself toward the truth, placing its faith in the [. . .] progressive determination of what was previously indeterminate" (Toadvine). It is that revelatory potential of perception in its truth-giving function that is called into question by the constantly changing shapes and bizarre appearances in *The Alphabet*. Normally, perception tends "to forget itself in favor of the perceived that it discloses" (Toadvine). As this function is undermined in Lynch's short, the reliability of perception is put into doubt and perceptual experience

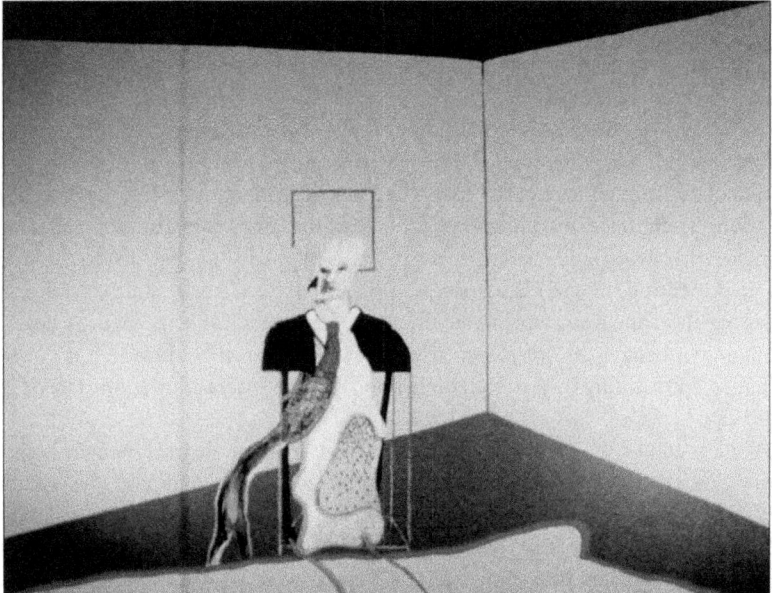

Figure 3.6 Perception in its nascent state (00:03:03).

itself becomes the center of attention. Hence, the dream provides a space within which a fundamental "automatism of perception" is challenged (Šklovskij 15; my translation).[19]

The fragility does not only reflect back on the *act* (or mode) of perception (phenomenologists speak of the *noetic* level) but is also in the perceived *object* (the *noematic* level in phenomenological terms), hence the human figure. Francis Bacon, the only artist whom Lynch quotes as a direct influence on his own paintings (Rodley 16–17), once said that "[t]he greatest art always returns you to the vulnerability of the human situation" (McKenna 15). The human figure in Bacon's painting does not appear as a whole but tends to be deformed, alienated, and frequently distorted beyond recognition. Similarly, Lynch's paintings from the late 1960s, which frequently reference Bacon's famous "cage" (as does *The Alphabet*, see Figures 3.5 and 3.6), are to a large extent fragmentations and transmutations of the human body. *Woman with Tree Branch* (1968), for example, shows a creature with what appear to be five breasts. Her legs resemble the surface of a tree more than human skin. *Sick Man with Elephantine Arm* (1968) shows a human face distorted with pain, as it appears to be dissolving. The human figure, in its physical appearance, becomes transmutable due to the suffering it has to endure. Meanwhile the canvas, in its ability to depict these transmutations, becomes a kind of "proscenium stage for curious occurrences" (McKenna 15). Shifting from painting to film, Lynch transfers this conception of the canvas, applying it to *The Alphabet*, where the dream, in this regard, becomes a justificatory framework for "strange" occurrences and aesthetics and his own experimentation with the new medium. While movement can only be suggested by a static image, film renders it explicit. The type of movement inherent within Bacon's depictions of faces becomes visible in time in *The Alphabet*, as a face is drawing, erasing, and redrawing itself.

Materiality and Symbolism

From 00:03:23 on, the baby's unnaturally stretched-out crying appears dehumanizing and assumes an alarming quality similar to a siren. As such, besides referencing the siren audible throughout Lynch's first video installation *Six Men Getting Sick* (1966), the crying prefigures the quintessential theme of the nightmare: the violence inflicted upon the girl through education. A red rectangle appears, its distance to the human face (representing the girl) being stressed by an enlarged horizontal "tracking shot." Providing the spot from which the letters are catapulted into the figure's head, the rectangle symbolizes the *other*, something that is not herself. Crucially, it is *outside of* the figure, constituting the external force imposing the letters upon the girl (see Figure 3.7).

While much of the film treats its subject matter in an abstract, heavily symbolic manner, one of its crucial moments leading the girl to wake up employs a natural, gestural signifier whose meaning is grasped in a way similar to that of a pointing finger; it is instinctively "read off" of its visible (in this case audible) surface without having to be translated into something else. The danger expressed by the sudden and audible inhale is inherent in the gesture (00:03:44–00:03:45). It provokes an "inner co-movement" (German "innere *Mit*-bewegung," cf. Schönhammer, *Wahrnehmung*

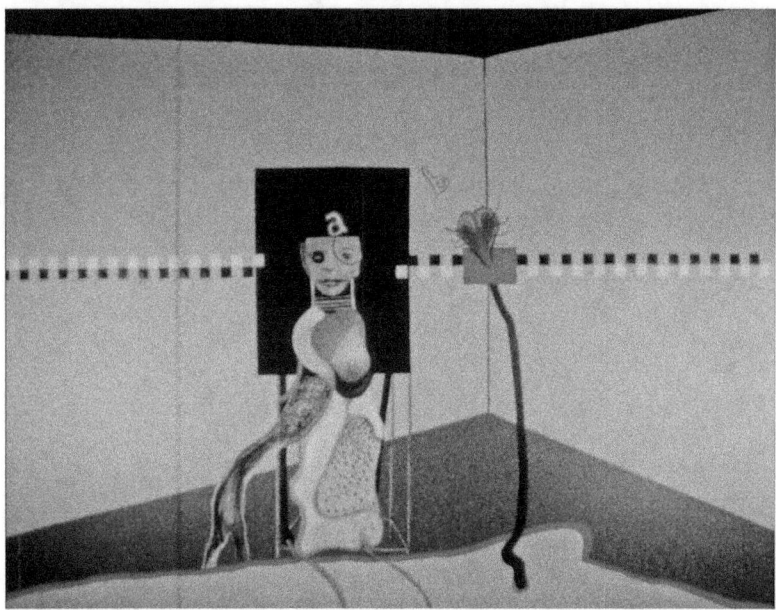

Figure 3.7 The violence of education (00:03:40).

168; my translation and italicization) on the viewer's side, leading his heartbeat to speed up, an effect that is mirrored on the film's visual level as the blanket of the awaking girl is moving up and down faster and faster. Describing the effect of a character looking into the camera upon awakening, Brütsch observes that "the viewer's irritation finds an equivalent in the temporary confusion of the dreamer who has to re-orient himself in the waking world" (136; my translation).[20] This type of viewer–character empathy, in Lynch's case, is thus extended to the interoceptive (i.e., referring to the internal state of the body) dimension. That is, seeing the girl's fast pulse "in" the blanket's movement—another instance of nonarbitrary signification—I sympathize with her, since it is also my own movement. Mutually complementary, my movement seems to be an extension of her movement (an internalized gesture of her expression) just as hers is an extension of my own (an externalized, visible gesture of my interoception), hence the identification. Through the bodily dimension, thus, the scene is able to trigger memories of sudden awakenings from bad dreams.

The audible inhale signifies the dream's imminent collapse. Much like in Lynch's previous *Absurd Encounter with Fear* (1967), the protagonist's collapse is visually prefigured by an act of looking that the camera zooms in on (see Figure 3.8). In *The Alphabet*, though, the girl's look in the mirror—a live action image—symbolizes self-identification with her dream ego. She suddenly realizes that the figure bombarded by the letters is herself, as acoustically reinforced by the doubling of the inhale. In the context of an apparently oppressive educational system, the dream gives her the opportunity to *learn* something about herself: it contains that which she is most afraid

Figure 3.8 *Seeing oneself* in a dream (00:03:45).

of and directly confronts her with it. In other words, the (end of the) dream enables her to (literally) *see herself*. As perceiving subject, act of perception and perceived object fall into one, her identity emerges as determined by fear. Merleau-Ponty would say that the girl's fear *is* the disintegration of the dream ego's body (cf. *Phenomenology* 171–2). It is the way in which the girl experiences her panic in the existential mode of dreaming. In this conception, there is no need for the Freudian separation into a manifest level of dream content and a latent level of dream thoughts that needs to be uncovered in dream interpretation. At the same time, the dream assumes a sociopolitical dimension, laying bare the point of conflict between her individual creativity and the educational indoctrination she has to endure. If the dream is driven by a creative impulse—one that is suppressed by the educational system that imposes the alphabet on the girl—then, if reflected upon, it contains the seed for rebellious action.

The figure crumbles down in bloodshed and the dream is collapsing—the screen being taken over by a dark red with whirling small dots that resemble the seed-like indents on a strawberry's surface (00:03:48). This red screen functions as a transition image, given that its seed-like dots are first transformed into white dots on a black background (see Figure 3.9) and are then carried over into the waking world to reappear on the girl's blanket (see Figure 3.10). The objective shot of the girl waking up is thus informed by her subjectivity, with dream elements swapping into the waking world in the form of hallucinations. (Similarly, when toward the end of the film [00:04:03–00:04:19] the letters "magically appear" in her room, objective space is populated by her visual hallucinations.) Since the dots only comprise the transition

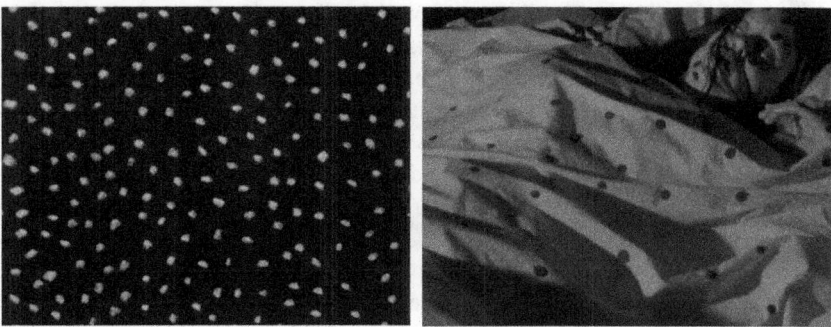

Figures 3.9–3.10 The transition from dreaming to waking (00:03:56; 00:04:00).

from dreaming to waking, they may be seen as purely signifying this change between two states of consciousness. They are neither "in" the dream nor "in" the waking world, but they are there to give a visual representation to the subjective progression from dreaming to waking. In that gradually evolving process, it can be difficult to tell when one is dreaming as opposed to waking, since sensory input from the sleeper's physical surroundings is subjectively integrated and imaginary elements are projected outward onto the physical surroundings. Thus, the progression has a phenomenological basis, but in the way it is rendered in *The Alphabet*, it is purely cinematographic, that is, a moving visual abstraction of a particular kind of everyday experience.

Concerning the transitions between waking and dreaming, the auditory dimension is of utmost importance. The alphabet song leads us into the dream (00:01:22–00:01:30) and back out of it (00:03:54–00:04:02), functioning as an acoustic marker framing the dream. In its second manifestation, it sounds higher and louder, which lets it appear more vivid. More importantly, its connotation has changed, as it is marked by the horror the girl associates with it. The contrast between serenity and horror—the inherence of the latter within the former that the nightmare has established—also underlies the effect of the girl's own chanting of the alphabet song (00:04:03–00:04:27) and constitutes its uncanniness.

A further, more general, aspect of the film's auditory dimension bears emphasis. Audible in dynamically varying degrees throughout, *The Alphabet* features the first occurrence of what has become a distinctive element of Lynch's cinema: an extended roaring sound which has received much attention in Lynch's later films. Michel Chion calls it a "wind" constituting a "cosmic force of divine nature" that "works and moves" the whole; it is "that current between worlds" (*David Lynch* 197–8).[21] For Slavoj Žižek, it expresses the "lost echoes of the big bang bringing forth the universe itself" (qtd. in Heiland 154; my translation).[22] Konrad Heiland speaks of "the unidentifiable sound object, a noise or sound, without reference, without place" (Heiland 149; my translation).[23] It thus qualifies as a primary example of what has been referred to as *acousmatic sound*, which characteristically conceals its origin (Chion, *Audio-Vision* 71). As such, in the context of *The Alphabet*, the roaring sound serves a double function: (1) it expresses how the girl is overwhelmed by a fear she does not understand, a fear whose source is nonlocalizable. The film does not seem to be interested in saying anything about *why* she is afraid of learning the alphabet. Rather, it qualifies the girl's nightmare experience, bringing to light her existence as determined by fear. The roaring sound suffuses the things that appear on the screen, seemingly giving them an agency, hence its mystic quality. Through it, the film creates the girl's sense of being overpowered in the viewer's experience of the film. (2) Like an invisible motor of subjectivity, it drives the changes both in the mental dream world (where it appears related to the creative process, i.e., the dream world "drawing itself") and in the physical waking world (its crescendo appears to be causing the girl to spit out the blood). On the one hand, the roar's effect on the viewer is related to the atmospheric strings in *Absurd Encounter with Fear*—in the roar, too, one cannot pick out individual elements or establish units of perception such that it appears as a whole. On the other hand, the roaring sound is different from the music of its predecessor in how it establishes a connection with the protagonist's inner sphere. Although it encompasses both scenes set in the waking and dream world—and thus does not function as a dream marker—it mutes realistic sounds of the environment, which indicates its proneness to subjectivity. The viewer is "closer to" the protagonist because noises from the outside world are muted.

The Dream as the Human Form

Framed by the red screen—thus gravitating toward the dream end of the spectrum, if we want to read the background color switch (red to black) as pointing toward its waking end—is a particularly perplexing image of a human face turned upside down, with a fake nose attached to the chin (see Figure 3.11). The image is out of focus and framed to the lower part of the face, which tells us: "Please remember, you are dealing with the human form" (00:03:49–00:03:54). Cognitive psychology has observed that object recognition depends upon the correspondence between stimulus and mental representation (McCloskey 101) so that a reversed object is not immediately categorized *as that object*. Constituting an obstacle for the categorization of its optical information, the shot disrupts the viewer's act of perception, causing an initial confusion. Thus, the alienation is not so much in the perceived object itself but in the viewer's way of relating *to* it. The effect of this kind of "seeing without immediate recognition"[24] (Zechner 76; my translation) is particularly strong, because, out of all possible objects, we are shown a human face. We are so familiar with faces that, according to many psychologists, our visual cortex, even if it might not be equipped with an isolated face module, is particularly well adapted for processing and analyzing their visual appearance (Riddoch and Humphreys 66). In this shot, the familiar object becomes unfamiliar through a change in its spatial orientation. In this simple way, it is suggested that the unfamiliar is inherent within the familiar. Thereby, *The Alphabet* evokes on a purely visual plane a notion that Lynch will deal with in great depth throughout his career on the level of storytelling.[25] It is a shot whose oneiric implications are rooted in the fact that "the poetics of dream narration"—or in this case the poetics of dream *experience*—"is based on the dialectical interplay between techniques of familiarization and defamiliarization" (Engel, "Poetics" 22).

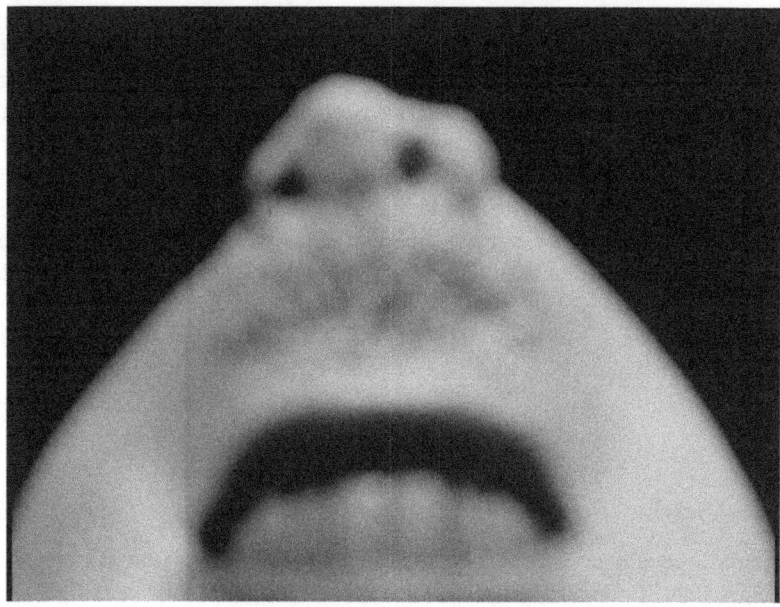

Figure 3.11 The unfamiliar as inherent within the familiar: *The human form* (00:03:52).

But what does this say about *the human form*? "The (literal) human form," that is, the face, appears as familiar and unfamiliar at the same time; we know it and we do not. In the human form, contradictory elements coexist, which is shown by the fact that in our perception, it both is recognized as a face and it is not (although not contemporarily—rather, like in the perception of a figure/ground reversal, we experience this change in succession such that at one point in time, it either is or is not perceived as a human face). "The human form," in the context of the film, also refers to the alphabet; especially the birth of the letter "a" is shown as both horrific and *necessary*. With the human figure (the dream ego) being born *as* the first letter of the alphabet, the film seems to suggest a natural tendency of humans to use symbols and strive for abstraction—a tendency, however, that leads to the girl's suffering. We can see this paradox in the way the girl is both *haunted by* and *longing for* the letters appearing in her room. In a similar vein, Chion speaks of an ambiguity in her relationship to the letters. Although the letters are forced upon the girl from outside, Chion asks whether they originate in her (*David Lynch* 13).

In a double movement, further, the abstract is materialized and the material is abstracted. Both the letters and the body function as (quasi-)living organisms and linguistic signs at the same time (Dottorini 83). Not least through its reference to *the human form*, the film shows the tension between the capacity for abstraction and the need for materialization, whose products, it is suggested, are both the alphabet and the dream. Besides referring to the inverted face and the alphabet, thus, "the human form" also addresses the *experiential form* that dominates the film, that is, the state of dreaming—not only because of the phrase's occurrence on the edge of the dream that is about to dissolve and "look back on itself." But the dream gives form to and is in itself a contradictory and fundamentally *human* experience. It is both the product of an internalization of input from the external world (in *The Alphabet*, the "real" letters hatch, i.e., appear in the girl's very idiosyncratic and imaginative way) and that of an externalization, a projection of an inner sensitivity in the form of moving images (her experienced horror translates into the bloody crumbling down of her dream ego). The dream would accordingly be that form of experience that, although it strongly distorts physical reality (live action becoming animation in the film's passage from waking to dreaming), brings the girl closer to herself, as it contains the "condensate of who she is at the moment."

The Grandmother (1970)

Audio-Viewing *The Grandmother*

The thirty-four-minute short film *The Grandmother* (1970) starts with a prologue that combines a murmuring organ sound with a mix of animation and live action. Drawn representations of father (Robert Chadwick), mother (Virginia Maitland), and son (Richard White) come into being in liquid of a cave belonging to an underground "birthing netherworld" (cf. Olson 74) before their physical bodies "hatch" on a lawn covered in leaves. Catching sight of the boy, the father attacks him. Mother and father act like they were animals in the way they move and in terms of the sounds they make.

In the second scene, the boy, who wears a suit throughout the film, is in his room and finds a vase with flowers next to his bed. One morning, he wakes up and finds that he has wet the bed. The father discovers the orange stain on the bed sheet and rubs his son's face in it. The mother physically abuses him as well: she tries to kiss him and when he refuses, she shakes him heavily while at the same time starting to scratch her own face. The boy escapes.

Sitting on his bed, he hears a whistling sound from the upper floor. He climbs up the dark staircase and finds a room with a bag of seeds and a bed. He plants the whistling seed on the bed, using soil and water. Time after time, the seed grows into an organic structure resembling a tree trunk. The trunk—Lynch calls it "the pod" (Rodley 47)—gives birth to a woman—the title-giving "grandmother" (Dorothy McGinnis)—whom the boy gives his flowers.

At the dinner table, his parents mistreat the boy because he does not want to eat. The boy escapes to the Grandmother who is sleeping on the upper floor. He gives her a kiss, sits down, and eats some fruit.

In the next scene, the Grandmother whistles, waking up the boy in order to meet her. His parents catch him on the way up, however, and an animated sequence is interspersed. In this sequence, the boy executes his parents, chopping his father's head off and crushing his mother with a large ball. The urine on the boy's bed spills over, filling up the room. Then the urine fills up the underground cave from the prologue and the boy drops inside. Mother and father are inflated through pipes and are then shattered into pieces. Back in live action, the boy arrives on the upper floor, falling asleep on the Grandmother's bed.

Grandmother and the boy make each other laugh by grimacing and poking each other playfully. Then they kiss. Snowflakes are falling in front of a black background—a wide-angle close-up on the boy's sweaty face. Then another animation sequence in which a plant is grown, possibly as a result of the presence of two figures representing the Grandmother and the boy. A tree is stung by what looks like a large insect and sprays a white substance. Meanwhile, in live action, Grandmother's arms and head are shaking while she is asleep. Although much weaker than before, her whistling wakes up the boy again. Now the whistling becomes involuntary, however, signaling that she is in pain. The boy tries to help her but does not know how. He runs to his parents for help, but they only laugh at him. The Grandmother "buzzes around" whistling uncontrollably, and as the boy gets back to her, there is a thud. The boy closes his eyes in slow motion and has a vision set on a cemetery.

In the vision, the Grandmother sits on a chair in front of some tombstones. The boy approaches, his head toward the ground. Grandmother looks at him intensely, but then her head tilts up, her mouth opening. As she dies, the boy falls to the ground screaming.

Back in his room, the boy, in low spirits, lies down on his bed, closes his eyes, and, subject to a kind of "pull," is rolled over to the other side of the bed. A still image of the boy's body on the bed and a painted background, combined with a menacing low-frequency sound, concludes the film.

The Dream between Metaphoricity and Literalness

It has been suggested that the film's central physically impossible event, that is, the growing of a person out of a seed, is not marked as a dream. Susanne Kaul and Jean-Pierre Palmier, for example, assume the Grandmother to exist in the diegetic reality (36). There are two elements, however, that challenge this assumption, suggesting that Grandmother's birth might happen inside the boy's dream. The first one concerns the director's association of black and dreaming. Recurring to the paintings of Francis Bacon, Lynch states that

> [b]lack has depth. It's like a little egress; you can go into it, and because it keeps on continuing to be dark, the mind kicks in, and a lot of things that are going on in there become manifest. And you start seeing what you're afraid of. You start seeing what you love, and it becomes like a dream. (Rodley 20)

Two elements of the quote seem important with regard to *The Grandmother*: the boy walks through the pitch-black corridor before reaching the room where he finds the seeds, and he eventually "starts seeing what he loves" (cf. Rodley 20). That is, he grows a caring Grandmother to compensate for the lack of love he experiences from

Figure 3.12 "Like a dream": The boy's (Richard White) symbolic passage through black in *The Grandmother* (1970; 00:12:31).

his parents' side. Walking through the dark corridor can be read as symbolizing the boy's transition from waking to dreaming. In that process, the distinction between *outside* and *inside* becomes blurry, as represented visually by his body merging with the surroundings (see Figure 3.12).

As "cinema does not have a closed list of enunciative signs, but uses any sign [...] in an enunciative manner" (Jost 32), Lynch's way of suggesting the transition from waking to dreaming might appear as purely idiosyncratic. In nineteenth- and twentieth-century art, however, black and the obscure have frequently been associated with subjectivity, creativity, and dreaming. In Odilon Redon's *Limbes* from *Dans le rêve* (1879), for example, black is not a color like any other but assumes an existential dimension. It represents the unknown of the dream, working toward the larger objective of art to put the spectator in the "world of the undetermined"; "to *name* an object would be to destroy the poetic imagination" (Thomas). The underlying reason seems to be that we conceive of vision as related to understanding—the expression "I *see* what you mean" suggests just that. A lack of vision, such as when closing the eyes to fall asleep, coincides with a lack of understanding. Hence, a clear, stable, reliable vision finds its equivalent in a certain ease of understanding on the viewer's side. In a film, the viewer is able to grasp diegetic space to a greater extent if a long shot showing a well-illuminated scenery allows for orientation and the identification of objects. Dark parts of the frame, if used in the way of *The Grandmother*, make it difficult for the viewer to form a mental representation of diegetic space—an effect that is reinforced by the high frequency of close-up shots. The black background is the same whether we are in the kitchen, the boy's bedroom, the room on the upper floor where Grandmother is born, or in one of the corridors that supposedly connect them. The lack of realism in the physical surrounding thus already by itself carries the potential for oneiric defamiliarization—in many dreams, too, we are prone to disorientation, with spaces being blended and transformed constantly. The only scene, however, that exploits this potential for spatial ambiguity to suggest the *possible dream status* of an event is the one in which the boy leaves his room to follow the seed's whistling (00:12:10). He leaves his room and we cut to an image that is almost entirely black (00:12:18). Out of the black, the boy's head and shirt appear and, judging by his movement, he must be walking up the stairs (see Figure 3.12). Since only the white parts stand out against the homogeneously black background, the exact contours of his body remain undetermined. This visual underspecification culminates in his complete absorption by the blackness at the beginning (00:12:18) and end (00:12:50) of the two shots. Considering the artistic tradition that Lynch's work has been associated with (i.e., Rodin; cf. McKenna, "Painting" 14) or directly grew out of (in the case of Bacon), the boy is not only absorbed by blackness but also by the world of the undetermined, hence the world of the dream.

Formally, the sequence showing the boy planting the seed is not marked as a dream at either end, nor is it marked "immanently."[26] In fact, the room where the boy is about to grow the Grandmother is introduced (00:12:59–00:13:07) in the same way his bedroom is (00:07:54–00:08:00): with the camera panning across the room from left to right at the same speed, accompanied by the same extradiegetic murmuring organ. This may lead to the assumption that the events take place on the same ontological level, the rooms occupying a similar ontological space; and the initial effect certainly is such that we do not conceive of the space where Grandmother is born as an imaginary one. As a result, we will not be inclined to judge the scene as "merely hallucinatory" while watching it, as would be the case with a *clear* initial demarcation of its dream status. Hence, at this stage, we are confronted with a purely *symbolic* transition to the dream. This tendency toward ontological ambiguity may be seen as related to a phenomenological aspect of the nocturnal dream, which, too, does not "mark itself" while we experience it—except in the case of a lucid dream. A dream's events only seem impossible from a waking perspective, probably due to a higher potential for self-reflection and critical thinking, what is sometimes called "metacognition" (cf. E. Thompson 136; Hobson 803). While dreaming, our inclination to distinguish between ontological states could be lessened compared to when we are awake (irrespective of whether these distinctions while awake are justified or not). In the words of Hobson, "dreaming is deficient in its failure to recognize its own true condition, its incoherence (or bizarreness), its severe limitation of thought and its impoverishment of memory" (803).

Thus, because we are less likely to question the ontological status of our surroundings in a (nonlucid) dream, we are unaware of dreaming while experiencing a dream. The dream state suspends our disbelief. Following this way of characterizing the dream as a state of nondistinction, we can see how a film may be able to give expression to this facet of dreaming. A film that makes an ontological distinction between rationally explicable phenomena and nonexplicable ones would not be *dreamlike* in that particular sense, as the distinction expresses an underlying intentionality that is governed by rational thinking linked to waking (implying a self-reflexive questioning of the reality status); a film that contains explicable and inexplicable events but does not unequivocally distinguish between them ontologically is *dreamlike* according to this criterion because it gives expression to a phenomenological quality of nonlucid dreaming. *Suggestion* as opposed to determination is thus particularly interesting when it comes to a sequence's ontological status in how it raises the possibility of dreaming without making such a reading inevitable. Further, through the lack of a marker that is linked to the boy's consciousness, the fluid transition into the dream and back out of it indicates that *the boy* does not distinguish between waking and dreaming. This nondistinction also becomes clear in their similar degree of immersion. In Nicola Zippel's Husserl interpretation, the degree of perceived conflict with the immediate present is what distinguishes dreaming from imagining (182). The dreamer's intention does not compete with the present, whereas the intention of the person engaging in imagination does (Zippel 182). To the dreamer, an "object is directly present as it appears, without any mediation" (Zippel 182). In imagination, something not present imposes itself and "wants to be present" (Husserl qtd. in Zippel 182). The film parallels this view: the boy is so immersed in his dream that he is not aware of its unrealistic elements—hence the lack of elements marking his awareness of the "unreal" nature of his surroundings. I will come back to this idea when discussing the boy's cemetery vision at the end of the film.

A second element challenging the Grandmother's existence in diegetic reality is provided by the film's ending. The last scene requires particular attention when it comes to the issue of dreaming. After the Grandmother has died on the cemetery, the boy is lying on his bed, disillusioned. Slowly, his eyes become heavier and heavier. As he rolls over to the side, he closes them (see Figure 3.13). Suddenly, he is "magically" pulled to the other side of the bed. In the film's final still shot (see Figure 3.14), his torso remains on the bed, while his head is not visible. In place of his head, there is a drawing

 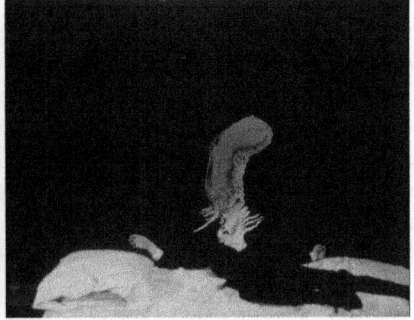

Figures 3.13–3.14 The brain-like "pod" as a self-reflexive symbol of the dream state (00:37:57; 00:38:01).

that resembles the organic matter (from earlier in the film)—the "pod"—that grew out of the seed and then gave birth to the Grandmother.[27]

First of all, the animated pod's vertical orientation recalls that of the material pod seen earlier in the film (e.g., 00:17:15), the hole on the bottom left echoing the opening through which Grandmother crawled out. Interestingly, the opening in the painting points toward the boy's head (or where we would expect it to be), which may indicate that his mind (sitting "in" the head)—not the pod per se—is to be identified as Grandmother's "fabricator." Supportive of this interpretation, the drawing, as a whole, bears some similarities to the human brain: two hemispheres are hinted at, with a brain stem and nerve cords (these white tubes also recall the tree branches from the earlier material pod) attached to it. Considering this, the pod symbolizes the dream, materializing "that towards which the boy is (literally) moving" after falling asleep. Dreaming as a state of consciousness is thus self-reflexively marked by the organ that produces it. To put it another way, when he is "pulled" toward the other side of the bed, he is "pulled" toward the dream. Not coincidentally, the drawn pod only appears once he closes his eyes. The film could thus be argued to use the pod as an *enunciative sign* representing the boy's sensual dream experience. A rare case of Lynch giving his own interpretation of the events in his films, he says in regard to the scene: "[h]e's just back in ... trying to dream" (Rodley 47). In accordance to this reading, the quote shows how the ending points back to the earlier scenes involving the Grandmother, retroactively suggesting the possibility of their dream status (i.e., providing a form of what Robert Eberwein calls the *retroactive mode* [160–91]).[28] In this regard, it seems important to reconsider the pod's location. Crucially, it is growing on the top of a *bed*, that is, a major topos for sleeping and dreaming. In addition, it hints at the boy's bed specifically, due to the soil replacing the urine spot at its precise position. What this shows is how the boy's frustration in waking—the father forcing him into the urine earlier—sparks his wish to grow a caring Grandmother (see Figures 3.15 and 3.16). The visual analogy thus indicates how the realm of dreaming allows the boy to reinterpret the lack of control over his sleeping body into control of his emotional needs while at the same time compensating for the physical abuse through his father.

 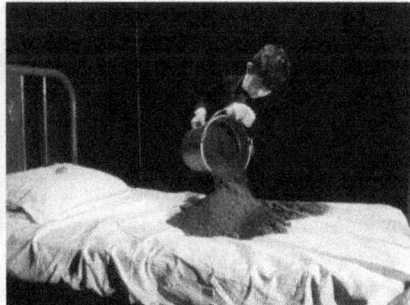

Figures 3.15–3.16 "Real" degradation (left; 00:10:24) and "oneiric" empowerment (right; 00:14:22).

In light of these observations, one might be inclined to assume as a hermeneutic framework that only the scenes in the attic (involving the coming into being and interaction with the Grandmother), but none of the others, occur within the boy's dream. Such an interpretation would enable a "realistic" reading of the film, given that its central, physically impossible event is now rationally explicable. What impedes such a realistic reading, however, is the way the film is edited. That is, the supposed dream scenes in the attic are interrupted several times by other scenes taking place at either the boy's room or in the kitchen. The assumption of a continuous dream, starting each time the boy gets to the upper floor and stopping each time he leaves, is implausible. The retroactive dream marker may speak to the Grandmother's dream *status*, but it challenges the authenticity of the boy's *experience*. How could he go back and forth between the dream and the waking world *without* going to sleep and waking up in between? The assumption of Grandmother's existence in the boy's dream is implausible only if the film is expected to be zero-focalized (cf. Kuhn 123–4), that is, if the narrator's perspective on the action *exceeds* the characters'. What should be considered as a possibility, however, is that the boy's perception determines the narrative perspective (what is often called "internal focalization"; e.g., Kuhn 123–4; my translation).[29] To him, she is real, and the experience they share is not imaginary, as suggested through the lack of an initial dream marker. Like a psychotic, the boy does not distinguish between reality and fantasy, at least initially. It is only after his realization that Grandmother only existed in his mind that her dream status is hinted at by the retroactive marker. Continuing the story of maturation that started in *The Alphabet* (1968), *The Grandmother*, in this sense, is about a boy who painfully learns how to distinguish between reality and fantasy.

Materiality and Oneiricity

While the film's ending itself could suggest the birth scene's (re-)interpretation as a dream, a phenomenological distinction may lead to the same conclusion. A phenomenological approach, in this case, entails a shift of focus. One is now concerned with the question as to what constitutes the oneiricity of the dream sequence "from within," independently of how (or whether) it is marked at either end. As was mentioned before, Jagna Brudzinska characterizes the dream as being dominated by an "order of transformation," which is in turn organized by a "teleology of [. . .] wish fulfillment" (65; my translation; cf. section "Dream Phenomenology and Freudian Psychoanalysis" in Chapter 2).[30] The sequences leading to the Grandmother's birth literally *materialize* this order of transformation: matter is not static but dynamically changes according to the boy's wish. The seed changes its material properties (eventually leading to Grandmother's emergence) *because* the boy longs for a companion. In other words, this process externalizes the transformative capacity of the mind *as* the transformation of matter, the Grandmother becoming a metaphor for the human ability to construct a mental alternative to a harsh reality. While many scenes are internally ocularized and auricularized (cf. Kuhn 122–3)—such that what we see and hear is shaped by the boy's perception[31]—there is no other scene in the film in which matter is subject to the boy's willful manipulation.

Materiality, in its visible malleability, thus assumes a crucial function in regard to the film's oneiricity, but is also essential for the film's aesthetics as a whole. Roy Menarini, for example, calls *The Grandmother* "extremely 'material'" (91; my translation).[32] At this point, it seems important to note that materiality does not only belong to the film and the objects it depicts but also to us viewers. As Shaviro holds, "[t]here is no structuring lack, no primordial division, but a continuity between the physiological and affective responses of my own body [. . .] and the bodies and images on screen" (255). Before addressing the viewer's intellect, films "physically arouse us to meaning" (Sobchak, *Carnal Thoughts* 57). *The Grandmother* is a primary example of film's capacity to "directly stimulate the material layers of the human being" through "the material elements that present themselves" in the film (Kracauer qtd. in Sobchak, *Carnal Thoughts* 55). When I see the parents' distorted faces on the screen in the opening sequence, it is not as a result of reflection that I want to take a step back from the screen. Rather, I am physiologically affected by the father's extreme proximity to the camera (see Figure 3.17). Assuming its point of view in the physical scenario, I intuitively grasp the danger expressed by his corporeality and my body instinctively wants to move away from its source. This mode of perception thus exploits one of our fundamental biological predispositions. Further, his darkened eyes conceal the intentionality of his gaze such that the threat I experience is related to my inability to know what his intentions are. The low-frequency barking indicates a big resonance body and thus directly implies his threat to the boy and to me. The muffled character of diegetic sounds suggests an inability to cognitively grasp them, which is why I

Figure 3.17 An attack on the viewer's sense of safety (00:07:24).

perceive them as threatful. The film does not only *observe* biologically rudimentary behavior from a neutral (documentary-style) perspective—that would be comparable to describing it in a sentence like "the father moves on all fours, thumping on the ground and barking"—but it "throws us in there." Not just *re*-presenting nature and biology psychologically (cf. Menarini 92), the opening sequence *presents* us with impoverished sensory input to create a lived perspective on the scenario in our viewing experience.

There are many more examples for the importance of materiality in the film, but none of them are as radical as the sequences leading to the Grandmother's birth. The degree to which *knowledge* is denied to the viewer is at its peak when the seed is slowly growing into something unidentifiable. Unlike in the examples before, we do not know what the object is (for lack of a better word, I will follow Lynch and speak of a "pod"). As a direct consequence, we are "thrown back" to what presents itself sensorially. Laura Marks uses this term *haptic visuality* when we are "gradually discovering what is in the image rather than coming to the image already knowing what it is" (178). The term seems to apply here because the images invite the viewer to explore what is in the frame "by visual palpation." Based on Schönhammer's conception of *canonical neurons* (*Wahrnehmung* 144),[33] the specific course of my saccadic movements is influenced by what I imagine the pod to feel like, were I to touch it. The film performatively anticipates this reception behavior when it shows the boy in his room, looking at the furniture as if seeing it for the first time. Importantly, the inability to *know* coincides with the inability to *visually recognize* the object *as* something. The mastery of vision over the other senses is undermined and implies a movement away from a knowing attitude toward a sensual experience of the scene. Sobchak writes: "we do not experience any movie only through our eyes. We see and comprehend and feel films with our entire bodily being, informed by the full history and carnal knowledge of our acculturated sensorium" (Sobchak, *Carnal Thoughts* 63). In other words, "our vision is always [. . .] even at the movies [. . .] informed and given meaning by our other modes of sensory access to the world" (60).

What applies to the film-viewing situation in general has particular relevance for the Grandmother's birth sequence, which forces us (whether consciously or unconsciously) to rely on our "carnal knowledge" (cf. the title of Sobchak's 2004 book) in experiencing it. It leaves us no choice but to speculate on the nature of the object that changes its shape in peculiar ways. Leaving the influence of narrative context aside for a moment, this speculation is informed by the way in which our senses are affected by what we see and hear. The pod's growth, for example, is first marked acoustically—with a sound indicating the expansion of a substance that lets us expect the seed to grow (00:15:41–00:15:54), which is confirmed by the next shot showing a small organic structure. In a Sobchakian view, I already "knew" the seed was growing "*before* I refigured my carnal comprehension into the conscious thought" (63) such that seeing the pod emerge from the soil in the following shot comes as no surprise.

Speaking of *knowledge* here is quite different from saying that "I know that two multiplied by two equals four" or that "I know that Nixon was the American president in 1970." In these cases, philosophers speak of *propositional knowledge* or "knowledge-that," which has truth value. In cases of nonpropositional knowledge, it is impossible to name the conditions that make the knowledge claim true or false. I "knew" that the seed was growing in a similar way I "know" how and when to change gears while driving a car. Whether we call it "procedural," "phenomenal," or "knowledge by acquaintance" does not seem to be of importance at this point. It is a type of knowledge that a person has due to her haptic and tactile experience with the world, because she knows "what it is like" to be a touching subject and a touched object. The sound that is audible after the boy planted the seed managed to communicate *something* about the process of organic growth. What Lynch remarks in regard to the importance of intuition in his artistic process—"[y]ou feel-think your way through" (Lynch, *Fish* 83)—may ring true for the viewer's reception behavior as well. I have an intuitive understanding of this signification, and that is because of my own corporeality and my ability to interact with the world directly through the senses. According to Merleau-Ponty, "[i]n the jerk of the twig from which a bird has just flown, we read its flexibility or elasticity" (*Phenomenology* 229). Similarly, while watching *The Grandmother*, we "read" the seed's growth into the acoustic signal indicating the "stretching out of matter." This is only possible because the different sensory modalities collaborate to some extent. Although each one of them modulates the perceived object in a particular way, "they all communicate through their significant core" (Merleau-Ponty, *Phenomenology* 230), the significant core being the lived body. Sobchak defines the latter as "that field of conscious and sensible material being on which experience is gathered, synopsized, and diffused in a form of prelogical meaning" (*Carnal Thoughts* 71). Because the lived body acts as a unifying element, tying together the input from the sense modalities on a "common ground," it is possible for the different forms of sensory input to become transposable to some extent—such that we know what someone means in describing a tone as "soft," for example.

In describing the "mood" of Alfred Hitchcock's *Rear Window* (1954), Lynch implies the intermodality of the senses when he says, "even though I know what's going to happen I love being in that room and feeling that time. It's like I can smell it" (Rodley 57). Aware of the audiovisual medium's limits, he introduces olfaction to testify to the intensity of atmosphere evoked by the film. His hyperbole concerns not only the impossibility of an *actual* olfactory impression through film but also the impossibility of smelling something as abstract as time. *Rear Window*, to Lynch, establishes an atmosphere with which he is so in tune, in addition to the audiovisual dimension, it almost appears to have an olfactory one. In more concrete terms, this could mean: because it creates an atmospheric impression in which the perceived object and the perceiver's attitude toward it are aligned (cf. Schönhammer, *Wahrnehmung* 293), the film viewer ascribes the actual olfactory impressions she has while watching the film *to* the world presented by the film. The evocation of an olfactory dimension is seen as the maximal—if ultimately unattainable—expression of the on-screen world's authenticity. To characterize the film's *mood* by attributing to it a (quasi-)*smell* is interesting in the light of neuroscientific research showing the mutual influence of olfactory impressions and emotional content, that is, a smell may trigger (the memory of) an emotion and vice versa. Further, it is telling that Lynch contrasts narration ("even though I know what's going to happen") with sensation here, favoring the latter over the former. This inclination also informs *The Grandmother*'s birth sequence, whose narration follows a "sensual logic," building up tension as a result of creating increasingly intense affective responses.

The fact that the object giving birth to the Grandmother is never really identified keeps our reception behavior focused on sensual involvement and has interesting consequences for the way in which the film's oneiricity is constructed. In Sobchak's view, when watching the opening scene of Jane Campion's *The Piano* (1993), her own fingers already "knew" that what the camera was looking through were fingers before she was consciously aware of it. In vision alone, the image showed something unrecognizable, a blurred arrangement of long, thin objects. And yet her fingers, "[feeling] themselves as a potentiality of the subjective and fleshy situation figured onscreen [...] comprehended that image" (Sobchak, *Carnal Thoughts* 63). Unlike in most of narrative cinema, where "vision's overarching mastery and comprehension of its objects and its hierarchical sway over our other senses tend to exclude our awareness of our body's other ways of taking up and making meaning of the world," *The Piano*'s opening shot provides an example where "the cultural hegemony of vision is overthrown" (63). This is the case only for a moment though, since the objective reverse shot reveals the presupposition to be true: what we were "looking through" in the previous shot were indeed fingers. As we now "know" what we are looking at, seeing the fingers from a distance and in a sharp image, it is not that our sensual engagement with the image has suddenly become obsolete—our vision is *always* embodied—but once the word "fingers" is retrieved from the mental lexicon, using it will be the more economical alternative to relying on our sensory impressions. Thus, the reverse shot in *The Piano* facilitates a "linguistic reception," so to speak, and in this mirrors a well-established cinematic convention. In the first encounter with a dinosaur in Steven Spielberg's *Jurassic Park* (1993),[34] for example, the director fuels our desire to *see* by stressing the two characters' act of looking, both of them first taking off their sunglasses, then looking at the dinosaur in awe before it is revealed what they are looking at. The scene's tension is structured around a dynamic of *seeing–not seeing*. Appealing to the viewer's senses, it builds up our urge for visual satisfaction, which, like in *The Piano*, we are granted by the reverse shot. Ambiguous sensation serves unequivocal narrative resolution.

In *The Grandmother*, however, vision does not grant us this type of resolution. Sensual comprehension continues to be the primary mode of interaction with the film, as the tension between *seeing* and *recognizing* is not resolved: the question as to the object's identity remains, even after multiple viewings. Even if I pre-reflectively knew *that* the seed was growing, I did not (and still do not) know *what* it was growing into. In this way, Lynch makes sure that the viewer continues to engage with the imagery on the pre-reflective, prelinguistic, and sensual level. As the pod is growing, the boy playfully interacts with it (see Figure 3.18),[35] and our eyes join his hands in exploring the pod's surface haptically. Gestalt psychologists would speak of the "demand characteristics" of the pod's visual appearance (cf. Gibson 138):[36] the combination of the "spikes" and smoothness, the close-ups of water dribbling down its shiny surface, the prominent hole on the bottom with soil coming out—all of these elements provoke the viewer's

Figure 3.18 Exploring the pod's surface by (visual) palpation (00:16:07).

motor involvement, activating the same neural structures that would be active if she really were to touch the object (cf. Schönhammer, *Wahrnehmung* 144). The fact that we still do not know what the object is after the Grandmother was born—the pod has apparently gone into a kind of auto-destruction mode—suggests that the object does not count for what it is but for what it brings about, both on the level of sensual experience (the boy's and the viewer's) and narration. The pod's narrative importance is reducible to its function of giving birth to the Grandmother such that Hitchcock might have called it a *MacGuffin*.

At this point, it may be tempting to see an analogy again. In film viewing—as in dreaming—we are involved on a sensory-motor level, with the brain sending impulses to respective body parts (*efferences*) while the commands are not (or rarely) executed. In both situations, our bodies remain still (no actual movement following) such that *afferences* (impulses sent from the body parts to the brain) are inhibited. From a phenomenological point of view, however, a big difference lies in the fact that for the dreamer, unlike for the film viewer, the dynamic of afferent and efferent nerve pathways does not seem to be functioning differently than in waking. His dream ego's body appears to be interacting with physical objects in a way that is similar to waking experience. If it were not for afferences and their continuing coordination with efferences (determining the "felt position" of the body parts), he would not be able to experience movement and touch in a dream. We are not aware of not actually executing the motor commands while dreaming. When watching film, however, the viewer *is* aware of not executing the film-induced motor commands. Beside this qualitative difference concerning the subjective experience while dreaming versus watching a film, speaking of the body's "stillness" has different groundings in the two cases. While dreaming, the human body is in a state of sleep paralysis in which the execution of motor commands is blocked. The film viewer's stillness, on the other hand, is not biologically determined but results from a culture-specific style of film reception. In regard to Western-centric aspects of film reception, which psychoanalytic film theory has focused on (particularly on similarities between the film viewing and the dreaming or sleeping "situation"), it seems worth adding that the idea of *the* film-viewing situation has not only been challenged by non-Western "ways of seeing" but also by the multiplicity of viewing situations (e.g., film streaming on portable devices) in the digital era.

Interpreting the scenes in the attic as the boy's *dream* allows for an understanding of what "oneiric" means in the context of *The Grandmother* by establishing a connection to the film's merely dream-*like* moments. If the mastery of vision over the other senses is *questioned* by several scenes in the film (such as when the mother's face is blackened while shouting at her son, her aggression being reduced to gestural and acoustic signifiers (see Figure 3.19)), then this tendency, in the logic of the film, is oneiric because it finds its most radical expression in the *denial* of the pod's visual identification, which happens inside a dream. Hence, a more encompassing oneiricity consists in the movement away from "rational vision," which implies the visual recognition of an object *as something*. Typically, rational vision acquires profilmic space from a distance in order to control it and to contextualize the presented objects. What *The Grandmother* moves toward at various points is a kind of vision that is "sunken into"

Figure 3.19 Oneiric aesthetics: Undermining the mastery of vision (00:23:51).

the objects and events it presents, only granting a minimum of depth to the profilmic space (subjugating it to the representation of salient objects) such that the viewer's gaze becomes increasingly haptic and she is sensually involved in the scenario. Thus, *The Grandmother* constructs an oneiricity through the combination of two elements, both of which having to do with materiality. First of all, by representing the pod in its malleability, it echoes Brudzinska's characterization of the phantasmatic-imaginary experiential order; and second, by undermining the authority of visual perception over the other senses. In regard to the second aspect, and much like in *Absurd Encounter with Fear*, oneiricity is the result of a particular kind of film–viewer interaction (even if, in his earlier short film, the viewer's sensual involvement is of a different kind and not marked as a dream at all). Unlike in his earlier film, though, there is no empirical evidence for the disempowerment of visual perception in the nocturnal dream. In fact, the predominance of visual impressions in dream reports may be seen as suggesting the opposite (Kreuzer 40). Even if the hypothesized *mimicry* of dream-experience in *Absurd Encounter with Fear* is echoed by Brudzinska's characterization of dreaming in *The Grandmother*, the latter film complements this mimetic strategy with the nonmimetic undermining of seeing.

Animation, Pixilation, and Trauma

Not only due to its use in the previous *The Alphabet* but also because animation generally has a lessened reality effect compared to live action, one may be inclined to view animation scenes as dream scenes. The film's opening sequence shows, however, that animation is not indicative of dreaming in *The Grandmother* but that it, together with pixilation, relates to the dream's psychological basis. First of all, it becomes clear in the opening sequence how Lynch's use of animation has become more complex in the two years between *The Alphabet* and *The Grandmother*. Animation and live action are now interwoven. The abstract and the concrete,[37] instead of indicating discrete ontological planes or even opposites, are now mutually dependent and stand in a causal relationship: upward-moving figures (animation) give way to the parents creeping out beneath the leaves covering the holes on a lawn (live action); the boy's physical appearance is prefigured by an animated representation of him coming into existence. Causality also works the other way: woman and man kiss, leading to an abstracted act of procreation represented by two drops of liquid mingling to form an organism.[38] Similarly, the first act of violence against the boy is represented through animation. As the father approaches his son to attack him (see Figure 3.20), we cut to two drawn figures, one bending over and hitting the other, the latter spitting fire (see Figure 3.21). While animation may be seen as censoring sex and violence here, it also serves to attribute a higher degree of generality to the scenes. The boy emerges as the "natural" product of the parents' sexual instinct. Through the animation and pixilation technique, the sexual act is both generalized and alienated. Alienated because their staccato movement, a result of pixilation, contradicts the "flow" of sexual encounters, letting the two appear as merely executing their biological determination to procreate. Similarly, in the second case, we understand that the father's attack on his son is not

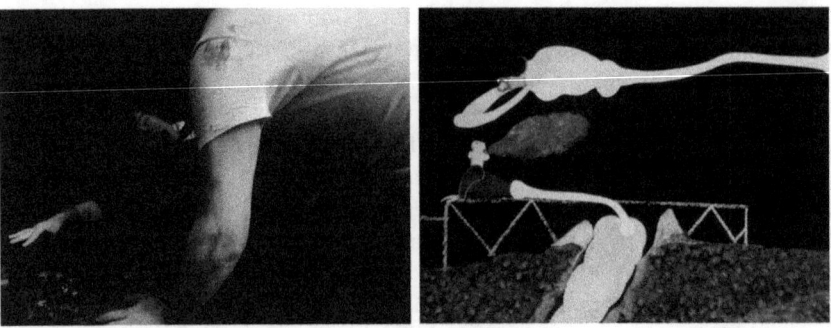

Figures 3.20–3.21 The non-narratability of child abuse (00:07:39; 00:07:44).

a singular event but represents a general truth of the boy's abusive upbringing. To be clear, the change from live action to animation does not let the father's attack appear less real. Animation does not stress the "otherness" of what it presents here. It opens up a wider horizon of meaning because it evokes the *idea* of domestic violence, which transcends the specific scenario of the film. Rather than undermining the reality status of the events, the technical manipulations render the scenes more expressive by suggesting the universality of reluctant parenthood and child abuse. Further, the father's physical attacks on his son (recurring throughout the film) show how pixilation and animation question the possibility of depicting (or narrating) the events. Pierluigi Basso Fossali speaks of "blind spots" related to how "the focalization on the interstices is associated with the presence of unperceived temporal intervals" (48; my translation).[39] The nature of the traumatizing event is such that it causes a phenomenal void in the representation of movement (pixilation)—bits of the movement are "cut out" such that the images appear to be jumping rather than flowing naturally—and a shift to the immaterial world of animation, because the violence cannot be represented in its material dimension. Both of the techniques imply the ultimate non-narratability of trauma.

According to such an interpretation, the reason for the abovementioned censorship is thus a psychological one, that is, the boy's trauma, which prevents him from an accurate recollection of the violent encounters with his parents. In this reading, trauma and dreaming stand in an interesting interrelationship. The traumatic experience forms the basis for the dream, sparking the wish to be loved, which is fulfilled by the dream. At the same time, the dream is what makes him aware of what it is he is missing and has a crucial role in providing what Todd McGowan calls an "experience of loss" ("Lynch on the Run" 50). He writes: "Because it creates the satisfying object that ultimately disappears, the fantasy of the Grandmother enables the boy to have an experience of loss" (50). One may think that it is not so much the fantasy in itself but the transition from fantasy (in which Grandmother exists) to reality (in which she does not) that is responsible for this experience of loss. But as McGowan observes in regard to the boy's cemetery vision, he is rejected by the Grandmother even in fantasy. In McGowan's Lacanian view, reality is *desire*-driven by nature and involves the lack of a satisfying object. Fantasy, on the other hand, provides *excess* of a satisfying object. Crucially, the excess in the realm of the fantastic leads back to the trauma itself—the boy kissing the Grandmother, the maximum of mutual affection, is what announces her disappearance. Instead of allowing for an escape from a grim reality, fantasy, thus, *perpetuates* trauma, showing that it is inherent even in our satisfaction (McGowan, "Lynch on the Run" 45). This would explain why the Grandmother leaves the boy in his cemetery vision.

To see *how* the boy becomes aware of the loving Grandmother being the object of his desire in the first place, it is worth coming back to the moment of her birth. If the film were just about fantasy, then the boy would not necessarily have to be *sleeping* in the last scene. Since Lynch flirts with the idea of bringing the Grandmother into being in the boy's *dream*, though, the dream receives a special status among the mind's imaginative abilities. It involves a surplus of self-knowledge because it appears to "know" what the boy is most longing for and is able to conjure it up. In this, it instantiates a capacity that the waking mind does not seem to possess, distinguishing it from the "fantasies," "visions," or "hallucinations" as they occur while awake. The waking fantasy or vision of the boy in the cemetery only *accesses* what has been revealed and produced by the dream. The vision is secondary to the dream. Freud argues that the dream has this revelatory power, its interpretation providing the royal road to the unconscious (*Traumdeutung* 595). The dream, in his view, arises through the combination of a preconscious and an unconscious wish. The boy's current abuse (triggering the preconscious wish to be loved) triggers the unconscious wish for parental love (hence the prologue's reference to a point very early on in the boy's life, which he might not consciously remember), forming the basis for the dream content. Whether or not one agrees on the psychological reasons behind the emergence of the dream, it seems clear that the film suggests the dream to be special in providing an *experience* of a deeper (because previously unknown) knowledge of the self. It *is* the experiential order that lets his trauma materially appear to his senses. He is first drawn to the attic because he *hears* the whistling seed. He *looks* at the pod, being fascinated by the way it changes its shape. He takes pleasure in *touching* the pod's branches and soil as it is growing. He sees, hears, and touches the object whose lack defines his trauma. This means that the boy already has an "experience of loss" (although he may not be aware of it) *before* the Grandmother dies in the cemetery, and that this experience is sensual. Dreaming may be understood as the experience of *absence through presence*. Since the Lacanian view suggests that the absence-presence dynamic is structured around desire, even the mere presence of the Grandmother carries the indication of a satisfying object's lack in reality. The dream presentifies the desired object, or better, it presentifies desire by translating it into a material object. The way in which physical interaction (poking, kissing, intense gazes, no talking, etc.) with the Grandmother is stressed in the dream appears logical in light of the dream's nature to materialize an object that is actually not there for immediate sensual exploration. Although materiality is of great importance to the film's aesthetics as a whole, the dream stands apart in the quality of the boy's sensual involvement. The only time he is shown as *actively* exploring something sensually is the dream sequence in the attic, showing his physical interaction with the pod and the Grandmother.

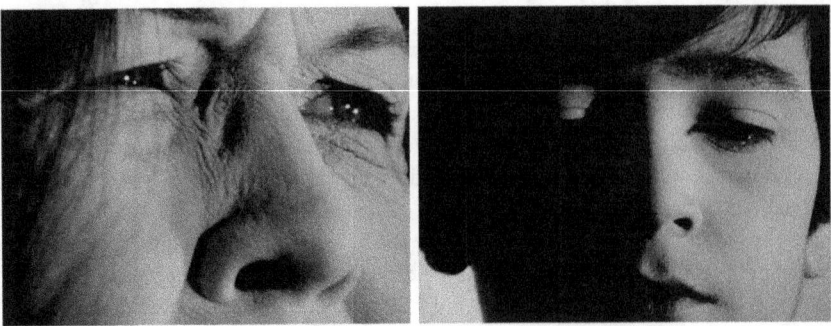

Figures 3.22–3.23 The gaze signaling distance in the cemetery vision (00:36:59; 00:37:00).

In the cemetery vision, their interaction could not be more different. A beautiful extreme close-up on the protagonists' eyes, while recalling the final duel scene from Sergio Leone's *Once Upon a Time in the West* (1968), stresses the importance of the gaze (see Figure 3.22). While the Grandmother's determined look at the boy expects him to return it, the boy avoids eye contact, looking down to the ground (see Figure 3.23). According to McGowan, the scene expresses that she leaves him in isolation ("Lynch on the Run" 49–50). What this reading ignores, however, is that the boy does not ask for her company here. He does not want to see her anymore, which might be due to the realization that he cannot take her with him into his ordinary life. By now, he has come to realize that Grandmother is only a figment of his imagination. Her dying, accordingly, is the expression of this realization. The vision, unlike the previous dream sequence, thus carries traces of his awareness of the experience's fictitious status; in the dream, he was completely immersed. His perceived conflict with waking reality is what distinguishes the cemetery vision from the dream imagery and finds expression in a contrasting physical setting, differences in lighting, and a strongly diverging interaction style between the boy and the Grandmother. Concerning the latter, there is neither eye contact nor physical contact between them. Their physical proximity from the dream is contrasted by a noticeable distance, as stressed by the camera panning across high grass; his hands, which were haptically exploring the pod earlier, are now folded behind his back. The sensual exploration testified to the high degree to which he was "sunken into" the dream. Its lack in the cemetery vision signals a lower degree of sensual immersion in order to anticipate that reality does not possess the material "object" of the Grandmother. In terms of the physical setting and lighting, the cemetery is further away from both the dream and the waking setting (the latter two being very similar). We are outside now: the natural surrounding (the grass, the trees, the sky, etc.) replaces the homogeneously black background from the scenes shot inside the house and facilitates spatial orientation. The natural lighting contrasts with the low-key lighting of the previous sequences. It thereby suggests a higher degree of realism that contrasts with the expressionistic flair of the indoor sequences but is ironized by the fact that what we see is marked as a fantasy—the boy closes his eyes before the cemetery is introduced. In line with Husserl's view mentioned earlier, the clear marker of the cemetery vision's "unreality" coincides with the boy's higher degree of perceived conflict with waking reality (most clearly visible in the contrast in the setting) and a lower degree of immersion (absence of sensual interaction with the Grandmother).

4

Eraserhead (1977)

Audio-Viewing *Eraserhead*

Eraserhead opens with six minutes of abstract imagery whose reference to conception and birth only gradually emerges as the film's theme solidifies. Henry Spencer (Jack Nance) is floating in outer space. A sperm-like creature emerges from his mouth and is cast into an extraterrestrial pool of liquid. The camera enters the liquid and then approaches a circular area of white, which dissolves into a close-up of Henry, who might have been (day-)dreaming.

On his way home, Henry walks through a dystopian (post-)industrial cityscape that does not seem to be inhabited by any living creature. Upon arriving in his apartment, his neighbor, credited as "Beautiful Girl Across the Hall" (Judith Anna Roberts), tells him that his girlfriend Mary X (Charlotte Stewart) invited him to dinner at her parents' house. Inside his apartment, Henry takes off one of his socks and puts it on the radiator, which catches his attention for the first time. His glance inspects it thoroughly.

He then leaves to meet Mary at her parents' home. Judging by the form of greeting, Henry and Mary had not been seeing each other for a while. When Mrs. X (Jeanne Bates) asks him what he does, Henry says that he is on vacation. "What *did* you do?," she continues, with Henry replying, "I work in the Lapelle's factory. I am a printer" (00:20:36–00:20:52). Mary adds, "Henry is very clever at printing," followed by her mother's sarcastic "Yes, he sounds very clever" (00:20:53–00:21:01). The sequence's awkwardness, to a large extent, is the result of deviations from social norms, as becomes clear, for example, when the father (Allen Joseph) introduces himself: "I thought I heard a stranger. We've got chicken tonight. Strangest damn things, they're man-made. Little damn things, smaller than my fist. But they're new. I'm Bill" (00:21:12–00:21:27). As Henry cuts up the chicken, a dark and thick liquid is oozing out and the legs start moving. This appears to cause a moment of ecstatic lusting for Mrs. X, which soon turns into nausea, however. She leaves the room and they never start eating. Coming back, she asks Henry to talk to her in the living room for a moment. "Did you and Mary have sexual intercourse?" (00:28:47–00:28:51)—Henry is "too nervous" to answer (00:29:52). Almost in a single gesture, Mary's mother molests Henry and, announcing the story's central element, tells him that "there is a baby. It's at the hospital" (00:29:54–00:29:57).

The young family moves back into Henry's apartment. The spermatozoon-like "baby"—the doctors were not sure if it really is one—resembles a premature lamb fetus rather than a human newborn. Its entire body is wrapped in a bandage, and it can only be seen lying on a desk. In the mail, Henry finds a tiny box with what appears to be a worm inside. In the apartment, he puts it inside a cupboard. He lies down on the bed to examine the radiator, inside of which a small theater stage lights up. As the stage light goes out again, the baby's crying can be heard. It refuses to eat, crying throughout day and night. In bed, Henry's longing for body contact is harshly rejected by an agitated Mary. She is unable to tolerate her sleep deprivation and escapes to her parents, leaving Henry and the baby alone. Henry has good intentions in regard to the baby: he takes its temperature and, finding it to be sick, sets up an inhaler and sits by its side. The "worm" in the cupboard has not moved, and Henry tries to leave the apartment to check if there is more mail in his box, but the baby prevents him from doing so, starting to cry each time he opens the door.

In what follows, dream sequences play an increasingly important role. Henry lies in bed, looking at the radiator (00:50:08). This time, he is completely absorbed by the stage inside of it. Organ music starts playing and a young woman, the "Lady in the Radiator" (Laurel Near), dances to it, stepping sideways. She is folding her hands in front of her chest. Her cheeks are unproportionally big, and she wears an old-fashioned evening gown. Sperm-like creatures start falling on the stage, and she crushes them with her feet, smiling bashfully. Back in the apartment, Henry is sleeping. A moment later, he wakes up because Mary, who reappears in this scene, is occupying too much of the bed's space. Something else catches Henry's attention: under the blanket, he finds the sperm-like creatures that fell on the stage in the preceding scene. Terrified, he pulls them out to smash them against the wall. The cupboard's doors open and the worm, now brought to life, starts moving. It is crawling about on what resembles the surface of the planet in the film's opening sequence, but apparently "not knowing where to go," it opens up at one end and the camera penetrates it.

Henry is sitting on the bed, wearing his pajamas. His neighbor knocks at his door, telling him that she locked herself out of her apartment. She spends the night with him and they have sex in a bed filled with white liquid, sinking deeper and deeper into the liquid. A sequence of shot/reverse shot shows the neighbor followed by the planet. Then, the Lady in the Radiator appears again on the stage, singing a song about how "in heaven everything is fine" (01:03:44–01:03:52). When the song is finished, Henry walks on stage and approaches the Lady. She opens her hands toward him, but as he reaches out to touch her, the screen goes all white. She disappears and is substituted by the Man in the Planet, who then also disappears again. The model of a pile of earth with a tree on top, which seems like a magnified version of the pile on Henry's nightstand, comes rolling onto the stage. Henry is intimidated by this and by the industrial hissing sounds, pulling back to stand behind a dock as if he were on trial. Suddenly, his head is popped off his body by a penis-like shape shooting upward through his neck. The head falls on the stage. While the baby's head is growing out of Henry's neck, dark liquid oozes out of the heap of earth and engulfs Henry's head, which is then abruptly "swallowed" by it. The head lands on a piece of industrial ground. A boy picks it up and takes it to a pencil factory, where it is drilled and found suitable for the production of pencil erasers, hence the film's title.

Henry wakes up in bed (01:13:42). Neither Mary nor his neighbor is with him. The bed is not a pool of white liquid; the cupboard's doors, which previously opened "magically," are now closed. From his window, he observes how a man beats up another man by a pool in the yard. He knocks at his neighbor's door, but nobody opens up. The baby laughs at him. Lying down on his bed to contemplate, he starts hearing the organ music that the Lady in the Radiator was dancing to. The baby continues laughing. Henry closes his eyes (01:18:00). We see the cupboard, a lamp, the backyard pool, and a close-up of the radiator. The lights do not go on. He opens his eyes again. Determined, he gets up, puts on his jacket, and opens the apartment door. Seeing his neighbor with another man, she being in his embrace as they are about to enter her apartment, comes as a shock to Henry, whose head is temporarily replaced by the baby's head in a reverse shot. Driven to despair by her rejection, he brutally murders the baby with a pair of scissors, first cutting open the bandage that covers its body and then stabbing its organs. Electricity goes out of control as great amounts of organic matter spill out of the body. The neck elongates to resemble the sperms appearing throughout the film. A magnified version of its head appears at various spots in the room coinciding with the lamp's switching on. In the sequence that ends the film, the planet's surface cracks open, the Man "in" it pulls levers under the emission of sparks, and the Lady in the Radiator, bathed in light, warmly embraces Henry.

Dream Experience in *Eraserhead*

To get a sense of the relationship between the dreaming and waking, a relationship that is crucial for an understanding of both the film's structure as a whole and the question of what "oneiric" might refer to in the context of *Eraserhead*, it may be worth considering the following schematic representation:

Prologue and Epilogue

Like Lynch's previous short film, *Eraserhead* opens with a prologue that symbolically anticipates the most fundamental narrative event (00:00:55–00:06:55). And like in his previous short film, the opening shot implies a certain degree of awareness of its own mediality. While *The Grandmother*'s (1970) opening represented the boy's flight from his monstrous parents, a desire that would be (temporarily) fulfilled by his dream, *Eraserhead*'s opening sequence, in light of the film's theme, can be understood as an abstraction of reproduction. The degree of abstraction is much greater in his first feature film, despite having moved from animation to live action in the meantime. The film opens with a shot in outer space, showing a round, planet-like object in the middle. Superimposed on the lower part of the frame,

Eraserhead *(1977)*

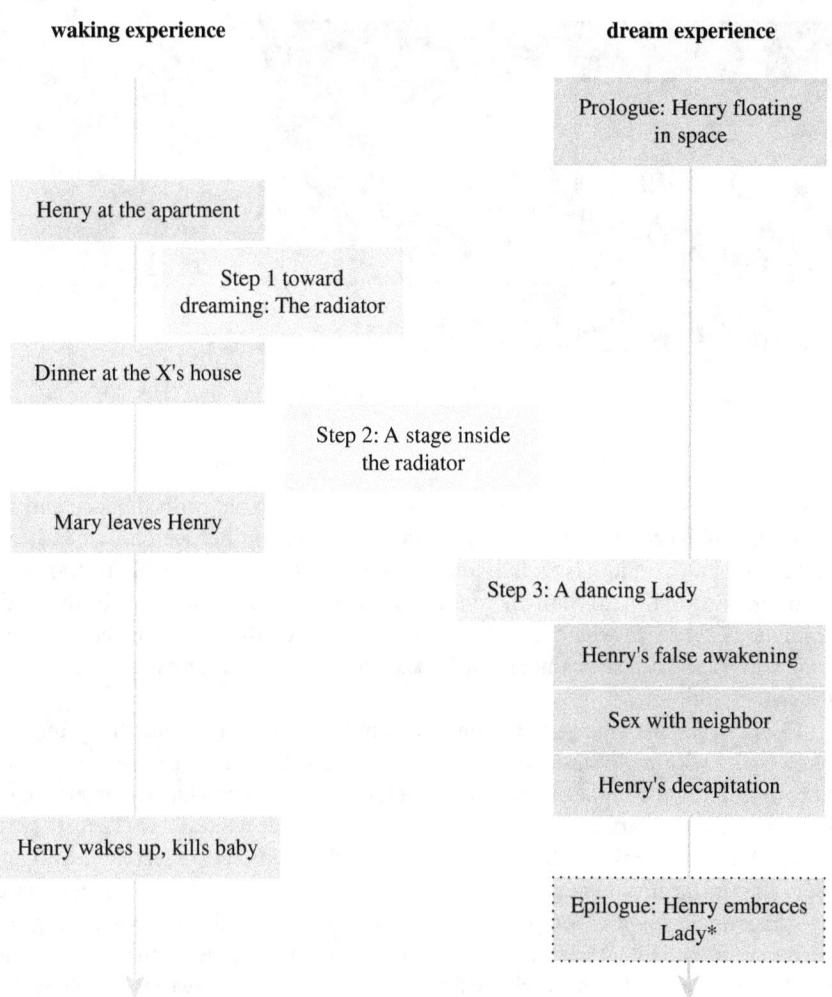

(* the epilogue is the only dream scene in the film that is unmarked)

Figure 4.1 Dreaming and waking in *Eraserhead*.

Henry Spencer's face comes floating in on the vertical axis (see Figure 4.2). As Basso Fossali observes, the protagonist is introduced as a perceiving subject before he becomes an acting subject (63). The apparent lack of gravity ties in with the setting in outer space, but the difference between the planet's horizontal orientation and the face's vertical one, as well as the latter's transparency, indicates that the two objects are not inhabiting the same space. There is a relationship between them,

Figures 4.2–4.3 Henry (Jack Nance) in *Eraserhead*'s opening shot (left; 00:01:39) and Redon's *Germination* (right).

however, as visually suggested by the planet's partial overlap with the face and its vague resemblance of a brain. The associative connection between a human head and a planet also underlies Odilon Redon's *Germination* (1879; see Figure 4.3), and, in the opening of Lynch's film, the connection is linguistically reinforced by the title's ambiguous *-head*. In what follows, the planet might be thought of as representing Henry himself, with the camera slowly tracking in on it marking the beginning of his self-exploration.

Henry's eyes are wide open but do not seem to be focusing on anything. Instead of engaging with a physical environment, they indicate that Henry is caught up in his own mind, possibly seeing the planet before his inner eye while daydreaming or hallucinating: the stars find their visual analogy in the little white dots in Henry's eyes, amplifying the impression that it is Henry *seeing* them, *his* eyes reflecting *their* light. Henry's translucency reflects the permeability of the real-world image experienced by someone having a vision; the person's gaze upon the real world loses its "grip" such that she can direct her attention to her mental image. Thus, Henry could be the focalizing instance, that is, the character through whose perspective we perceive what is about to occur. The prologue's inclination toward Henry's subjectivity as opposed to his objective appearance may be seen in how the planet's image appears as solid and fixed, while Henry's face is translucent and, not bound by gravity, floating about on the screen, in and out of the frame. While suiting the setting—the apparently similar position of the light source adds to this congruence effect—the face's floating is at the same time opposed to the fixity of the image showing outer space. This ambiguous relationship between Henry's face and the background could be seen as the film's way of suggesting that Henry both "is and is not" in outer space, that is, he is imagining it.

Adding to Lynch's anti-realist approach is the fact that a continuous noise is audible on the soundtrack. Since sound waves are unable to travel in space,[1] what we hear cannot be produced by the visually represented physical situation such that the prologue's sound is extradiegetic—at least if we understand the sequence as objective. The impression of a "unified perception," however, suggests the mental nature of the prologue. This kind of perception is rooted in the congruence of image and sound:[2] as the camera approaches the planet, the noise begins to crescendo—both sensory modalities suggesting a movement that supports the perception of the respective other.[3] The intermodality of the viewer's senses, that is, the way in which what she sees and what she hears work together, amplifying each other, is determined by everyday perception: the closer one gets to a sound's source, the louder it will be to her and vice versa. By the measure of natural perception that the scene performatively embodies, the planet is thus implied as the sound's source. But if it is the planet emitting the sound, then we cannot be in an objective space here; we are in Henry's dream space. Now if the planet symbolizes Henry's head, and it is the planet emitting the sound, then the sound is, by way of this symbolization, connected to Henry himself. In the analogy, it is *his head* producing the sound. This seems to be a crucial indication for the way the narration sets up its acoustic perspective—the continuous murmur is audible throughout most of the film. Claudia Gorbman calls film sound "meta-diegetic" if it is neither diegetic nor extradiegetic, expressing a character's subjective experience instead (22–3).

To include the dreaming (or sleeping) figure in the image, dividing up the single pictorial space into two ontological spaces, reflects a well-established tradition in the history of art (Kreuzer 213). It is only in the nineteenth century that dream events can be represented without being framed pictorially; among the earliest examples are Grandville's *Premier rêve.—Crime et expiation* (1847) and *Second rêve.—Une promenade dans le ciel* (1847; Engel, "Traum und Malerei"). Before that, the vast majority of depicted dreams included the dream's originator in the picture. A painting's binary division into a space dedicated to the sleeper and another space representing the dream event, in the medium of film, is usually temporalized. A sequence of images shows a person falling asleep *followed* by the depiction of her dream world. In Percy Stow's and Cecil Hepworth's (first film-)adaptation of *Alice in Wonderland* (1903), viewers were helped in understanding this by the intertitles telling them that Alice *dreams* of the White Rabbit (00:00:46). Like many other examples from the silent era, the film shows how the filmic dream, unlike the painted one, does not necessarily introduce a *new space* but lets Alice's dream ego "wake up" in the same spot where she has fallen asleep, forming a spatial continuity with the waking world.[4] In terms of its composition, *Eraserhead*'s opening shot orients itself toward the pictorial tradition, even if it is met by a uniquely *filmic* technique: a doubly exposed image showing a relatively small planet that overlaps with a much bigger head. Despite this aesthetic difference, the implication stays the same: the planet (dreamed object) is incorporated within Henry's mind (dreaming subject). Now the association between the planet and the brain becomes more tangible. Given the implied connection between the planet and Henry's head, Lynch, collaborating with cinematographers Herbert Cardwell and Frederick Elmes, tells us that Henry's mind is not only the subject of perception but also the object of perception, which the film is about to explore, as shown by the camera slowly tracking in on the planet.

As the next shot shows, "explore" also refers to the planet's material surface. The camera vertically tracks over what appears to be a canyon, whose tactility is evoked by the flat lighting. By highlighting the tips while leaving their counterparts in a deep contrasting black, the lighting stresses the rough texture of the planet's surface. Its roughness is mirrored by the skin surface of the Man in the Planet (Jack Fisk), whose stare out of a broken window has been read as signaling that *he* is dreaming up Henry (Haubner 515). If it is staring that marks the dream, however, then Steffen Haubner ignores that Henry's stare precedes the Man's so that Henry should be the dreamer. Further, Haubner's interpretation bespeaks an ambiguity concerning the dreamer's participatory status in relation to the dream, an aspect that was crucial in my discussion of *Absurd Encounter with Fear* (1967; cf. Chapter 3). What may lead us to assume the Man in the Planet to be the dreamer is his active role in the scenario. The cause–effect relation between the two men is such that, after the Man in the Planet's arm twitches, Henry's mouth opens mechanically and a spermatozoon-like creature emerges from it (00:04:30). Twitching again, then pulling a lever (00:05:15), the sperm floats out of frame to then, after a third and fourth lever, be cast into what appears as a mixture of a lake on a foreign planet and, in the context of the issue of fertilization evoked by the sperm, an ovum; Greg Olson speaks of "an underground amniotic gestation pool that recalls *The Grandmother*'s birthing netherworld" (74). What may underlie Haubner's interpretation is the view that the dream ego cannot occupy a passive role in regard to the scenario. This ignores the ambiguity of how we relate to dream-experiences, as exemplified by the coexistence of two formulations for "dreaming" in German: *ich habe geträumt* (subject actively brings about the dream) and *mir hat geträumt* (subject receives the dream; this mode of expression is now considered antiquated but was used until the nineteenth century[5]). Thus, the dreamer is making the dream happen as much as it may be *happening to* him. Although he creates the conditions for it to occur, while experiencing a dream, he may not perceive himself to be the one pulling the strings, or in Henry's case: the levers. In fact, in *Eraserhead*, Henry's passivity occupies a central role in regard to the symbolic fertilization we are about to witness, as it points toward the dream's psychological cause: Henry is not ready to be a father, so his dream creates a "mental way out," that is, a scenario in which someone else, that is, the Man in the Planet, assumes the responsibility for impregnating his girlfriend Mary X. Henry's unconscious is looking for a way to "outsource" his parental responsibility.

But that is not the only function Jack Fisk's character fulfills. Remarkably, Lynch oscillates between encouraging such a psychological interpretation on the one hand and a metaphysical one on the other, as becomes clear through a spatial ambiguity: the Man is *in* the planet, that is, *in* Henry's head, but he is also *in* outer space. The Man in the Planet assumes a psychological role in Henry's unconscious, but he also personifies the biological instinct to procreate, giving a supernatural face to what guarantees the continuation of the human species. He is often understood as "the one in charge" of the baby's birth (Schmidt 55). Kaul and Palmier refer to him as the "game master" in a self-reflexive sense (41; my translation):[6] he not only personifies Henry's reproductive instinct but also sets the whole story of the film in motion when pulling the levers. When in the epilogue, he fails in "trying to stop the spark-emitting (story) machine with all his power," Kaul and Palmier read this as a sign of Henry's emancipation (41; my translation).[7] He now gained his autonomy and is no longer controlled by the Man in the Planet. But whether he really is to be viewed as the "puppet master"—the film becoming a kind of metaphysical drama instead of a psychosocial one—is, while being raised, put into question through his initial appearance at the same time. Curiously, he pulls the levers due to an impulse that expresses itself as a mechanical muscle twitch in his arm, which does *not* appear as a volitional act. This questions whether he really is the one in control. Though the image demonstrates his power over Henry, it also points to its limits. He might only be executing the cosmic principle that drives procreation. Hence, while he represents that force, he also already instantiates it. The Man in the Planet becomes one out of a myriad of theoretically possible signifiers of an underlying cosmic force, but the signified itself remains elusive, in that it cannot be represented on the screen. The muscle twitch humanizes him in the sense that it makes him more credible as a product of Henry's dreaming mind rather than a God-like figure that would predetermine the fertilization.

Assuming that what we see is the "objective omniscient perspective on the way things are" (Olson 74), it would not be Henry but the Man in the Planet who really *is* responsible for the fertilization. Such a reading would fail to acknowledge that *Eraserhead* is about *human* responsibility and the *human* drama of existence. It portrays a man's path to an extreme choice in the face of an unbearable responsibility and experienced lack of freedom. In that sense, it is not so much *about* the Man in the Planet or the Lady in the Radiator as it is about Henry's longing for what they represent to him. Although the metaphysical and the psychological complement each other, the ambiguity between them yielding a variety of creative interpretations, the film is inclined toward the psychological end of the spectrum in the way it sets up its story. Obviously, this does not entail that psychological interpretations are necessarily able to "explain" everything happening in the film. But the film's psychologization of the story seems to call for psychological interpretations.

Before the viewer might be able to grasp the symbolic meaning of the scene, what announces the prologue's crucial moment is signaled as much on the acoustic level as it is on the visual one. The broad spectrum of noises we heard continually until now is narrowed down to mid-frequency (00:05:52–00:05:55) and high-frequency (from 00:05:55 onwards) noise—a movement that is extended by the inclusion of a more clearly identifiable, high-frequency pipe, coinciding with the sperm hitting the liquid's surface (00:05:58). The acoustic culmination of the prologue is constituted by a deep resonating gong (from 00:05:59 on) that combines beautifully with an extreme close-up of splashing liquid, shot in a slight slow motion. In this way, the traumatic nature of this moment is implied, even if the spectator, upon a first viewing experience, is unable to grasp the implications at this point. Revisiting the scene, however, one can see how *fertilization* constitutes Henry's trauma. After the close-up, the camera plunges into the liquid. The mingling of two substances has formed a third one (in analogy to the animated fertilization in *The Grandmother's* [1970] prologue), whose perspective the viewer adopts as the camera approaches the white light. Tracking in on the white "opening" can be read as a symbolic foreshadowing of birth, as shown by the "pubic hair" on the border between the black and the white area (cf. Seesslen 25; Olson 74). Given that what the prologue represents in a symbolically encrypted way is really going to happen to Henry, it constitutes a prophetic dream vision. The vision's end is marked by an entirely white screen that dissolves into a shot of Henry. The transition builds upon Lynch's association of black and dreaming (cf. section "The Dream between Metaphoricity and Literalness" in Chapter 3), extending it to the optical opposite: "going from black into white" is the visual representation of "going from a dream (vision) into waking life." A close shot shows him chest upward, roughly the same part of his body as before (see Figure 4.4). He is looking back, just past the camera. His eyebrows are furrowed, as if he saw what we just saw and were somewhat confused by it. There is no indication of Henry sleeping, but the prologue can be seen as tied to his interior, given elements that could be interpreted as sequence immanent, and end markers. What the shot in Figure 4.4 may allude to is that, in film history, a glance into the camera has come to suggest the mental nature of what preceded, especially when following otherworldly imagery (cf. Brütsch 134–7). As he seems to have been immersed in the scenario, not perceiving a conflict with his actual surroundings (cf. Husserl 150; and section "The Dream between Metaphoricity and Literalness" in Chapter 3), the prologue could be considered a daydream rather than a hallucination.

By interpreting the prologue as a daydream, one "naturalizes" it to some extent, in that something open, ambiguous, and perplexing is "tamed" by calling it a figment of a character's imagination. But, as I have suggested, there is something specific to the experience of dreaming in the sequence: the aspect of "being and not being" in

Figure 4.4 Henry's glance past the camera—what did he just see? (00:06:56).

the dream world at the same time; and that of being the (active) originator and the (passive) recipient of the dream scenario. Although the second criterion does not apply exclusively to dreaming—in waking, we can be active participants or passive observers, too—the dream provokes a polarization of active (lucid dreaming) versus passive (nightmare) involvement in a scenario. Rather than presenting a categorical distinction, thus, the difference between waking and dreaming is a matter of degree in that respect. Henry's levitation, further, may be understood as an allusion to the phenomenal absence of one's sleeping body in the nocturnal dream-experience. That is, the dream translates the absence of gravity for the dream body (as opposed to the sleeping body) *as* levitation (cf. Andrei Tarkovsky's dream sequence in *The Mirror* [1975], where the dreamer is depicted as hovering over her bed).

Unlike the prologue, *Eraserhead*'s epilogue is not marked by any *formal* element that would indicate an ontological shift—and yet it can also be read as a dream vision. This is because, over the course of the film, a clear division has been established between Henry's dream world in which the Lady in the Radiator and the Man in the Planet exist and Henry's waking world in which Mary and the baby exist (see Figure 4.1). Since, by now, we have learned to distinguish Henry's dream from his waking experience on the basis of *what* appears in a given scene, it seems safe to say that when the Lady and the Man are part of a scene, it takes place in Henry's dream, even if that scene is not marked as such on a formal level.

The Emergence of (Dream) Consciousness

In the three scenes involving the radiator (00:13:59–00:15:07; 00:35:51–00:36:38; 00:49:58–00:53:07), Henry's gradual progression from the waking state into the dream state presents a movement that is inversely proportional to the degree of his sensory-motor activity. Henry is clearly awake when he gets home, plays a record on his gramophone, and sits down on the bed to take off one of his shoes. After he puts his sock on the radiator, the physical interaction with his environment stops as his attention becomes more and more focused on the radiator (see Figures 4.5–4.7): his eyes explore its surface and the dirt below it in close-ups; the crescendo of a hissing sound, indicating Henry's hyper-perception of the radiator valve, is driving away the diegetic organ music. The breadth of visual and acoustic input is narrowed down to a few salient elements. The audiovisual aesthetics of the scene expresses the peculiar way in which the radiator appears *to Henry* or rather the way in which Henry's mind *apprehends* it, examining it meticulously while selectively heightening some of its aspects. In this regard, the radiator symbolizes his turn inward, a transition zone—that moment in experience when the external, physical world meets that point *from which* experience is gathered and both coexist. It is both the external physical object that catches his attention *and* the object that just happens to be "there" while inner experience is beginning to emerge. If waking is "that state in which consciousness apprehends the outer world through sense perception and conceptualization" (E. Thompson 15), then it seems that Henry is not fully awake in that his perspective on his surroundings partly overrides the actual external sensory input, as in the disappearing organ music.

Figures 4.5–4.7 A first step toward dreaming: Henry explores the radiator by "visual palpation" (00:14:10; 00:14:20; 00:14:34).

Concerning Henry's mental and physical state, it may be worth considering Evan Thompson's characterization of insight meditative states: "an overall state of relaxation; the high arousal needed to maintain an upright sitting posture; a complex interplay among attention (focused and diffuse), absorption, and meta-awareness [...] the ideal being a state that's both stable (neither restless nor sluggish) and vivid or clear (not dull)" (E. Thompson 121). Henry's body posture indicates a mixed state, combining signs of relaxation with signs of alertness. First of all, he is *sitting* on the bed, a posture that is more relaxed than standing but not as relaxed as lying down. Further, the fact that he is wearing just one shoe—he stepped into a puddle in the previous sequence[8]—symbolizes his state *between* relaxation and alertness. (Also, the sock, something he wore *on* his body, is put *on* the radiator now, which establishes a relationship between the radiator and Henry's body. After all, the stage will appear not only "inside" the radiator but "inside" Henry as well.) His attention is both focused (object-directed) and diffuse (his eyes are wandering in a way that is similar to the boy's haptic perception of his bedroom in *The Grandmother*), and he is absorbed by the radiator's presence. In regard to meta-awareness, we do not know if Henry is aware of the symbolism involved in his looking at a brick wall right outside his window—a wink to René Magritte's *La saignée* (1939)—which alludes to the inaccessibility of his unconscious at this point. His feeling—he may know that there is something "going on" inside of him, but he does not know yet what it is—is mirrored by the viewers', as they do not know yet what the film will be about.

Even though Henry is not meditating here, he is in a meditation-like state, since the scene depicts a first step toward inner experience as it also occurs in meditation. Henry's subjectivity announces itself, but only on the level of film language (e.g., in the crescendo of the hissing sound). The presence of his subjectivity is marked aesthetically, stressing the peculiar way in which he perceives the radiator. This changes in the second scene (00:35:56–00:36:38), when Henry's subjectivity materializes as a visible object in the film's diegesis: a theater stage lights up inside the radiator (see Figures 4.8–4.10). According to E. Thompson, "[i]n the yogic traditions, meditation trains both the ability to sustain attention on a single object and the ability to be openly aware of the entire field of experience *without selecting or suppressing anything that arises*" (xxxiii; my italicization). In a further analogy to a meditative state, the light's switch on could thus be seen as the externalization of the emergence of inward-directed consciousness. Consciousness directs itself inward *as* the light turns on. But this phrase is ambiguous: is it that consciousness is directed inward *such that* the light becomes visible—the switch on as the product of consciousness having turned inward? Or does the switch on *itself* symbolize that consciousness is directed inward now—the switch on *as* the process of consciousness turning inward? It appears that a third interpretation is possible in light of the director's activities during the making of his film.

In the summer of 1973, in the midst of shooting *Eraserhead*, Lynch started practicing Transcendental Meditation, a meditation technique founded in 1957 by Maharishi Mahesh Yogi.[9] The relevance of his practice for the film is such that Lynch himself establishes a close connection between the start of his meditation and the radiator scenes in particular: "Shortly after I started meditating, I would always do these little drawings in the food room. And one day I started drawing this little woman [. . .] and this woman came to life in my mind. And I realized that this woman lived in *Eraserhead* and that this woman lived inside the radiator" (Lynch and McKenna, ch. 47, 00:02:25–00:03:02). Before meditation, the Lady in the

Figures 4.8–4.10 Step two: A second world emerges "within" the first (00:35:55; 00:36:20; 00:36:28).

Radiator was not part of the script. Hence, inner experience was not only important to Lynch's creative process in the making of the film but also became an essential plot element in it, as becomes clear through Henry's dream sequences in which the Lady appears.

A form of silent mantra meditation, the meditation technique Lynch practices, is rooted in the Vedic traditions as we know them through the Upanishads. In the Brhadānyaka Upanishad, "the oldest of the Upanishads, dating from about 800 BC" (also known as the "Great Forest Teaching"; Shearer and Russell 44),

> the self (*ātman*) is the inner light that is the person (*purusa*). This light [. . .] consists of knowledge [. . .] [T]he "light" Yājñavalkya is talking about is what we would call "consciousness." Consciousness is like a light; it illuminates or reveals things so they can be known. In the waking state, consciousness illuminates the outer world; in dreams, it illuminates the dream world.[10] (E. Thompson 3)

Self thus refers not so much to "personality" here as it does to the "unbounded underlying substratum of consciousness in which all thinking and experience, including that of an individual self or ego, takes place" (Shearer and Russell[11] 14). Hence, *ātman* is also known as "pure consciousness"; "pure consciousness is not the contents of the mind, just as a beam of light is not the object it illuminates" (Shearer and Russell 14).

In an Upanishad-inspired reading, thus, when the light switches on inside the radiator, it is not just another one of Henry's contents of awareness making itself visible, it is *consciousness itself* that emerges, as symbolized through the very process of the light switching on. The dream mode, which announces itself here, hence asks for the genesis of experience per se, for which consciousness acts as a precondition. How does *anything* arise out of nothing?—*Eraserhead*'s image for this process, that is, the emergence of consciousness, could be seen as the illumination of a theater stage. The stage would not become visible if it were not for the light shining on it. It is not only the content of a (daydreaming) mind that becomes visible; it is consciousness itself that surfaces, as symbolized by the very process of the light switching on (no matter what it illuminates). If waking life is illuminated by natural light, then the dream world, which is likened to a theater stage here, is illuminated by artificial light. One might interpret the scene as follows: consciousness has a different quality in the dream, *just like* electrical light has a different quality from natural light. The stage lighting up stands as the metaphorical emergence of consciousness. The light illuminating the dream has characteristics that are different from the light illuminating the waking world: it is directed, forming a perfect circle on the stage's floor. It is created by human beings, just like the light in a dream is the pure product of the dreamer's creation. It appears that the scene stresses the artificiality of the dream world. But: if it is the light itself (*ātman*) becoming visible here (not just the "dream light") and the light has an artificial or constructed quality, then this constructedness is ascribed to consciousness itself, not just to dream consciousness.

The ontological implications would be radical. In a strong interpretation of the light symbolism, reality becomes a matter of subjective construction, as it is mediated through "artificial" consciousness. At the same time, the dream becomes a privileged state not only because it thematizes the emergence of consciousness but also because it obtains epistemological value, in that it lays bare the ultimate constructedness of reality as we perceive it.

An interpretation of this sort might seem radical, but it seems to resonate with interpretations of the film that suggest the complete indistinguishability of waking and dream sequences. If all experience is artificial, then everything might be a dream, one might argue. The present analysis, however, suggests that reality and dream *are* distinguishable in *Eraserhead*. Even though some scenes set in the "waking" world stress their constructed character—for example, when the (cooked) chicken's legs start moving as Henry cuts them up (00:25:36–00:26:29)—they do not serve to undermine the story's sense of a diegetic reality; *Lost Highway* and the finale of *Twin Peaks* do just that to the point of becoming aporetic. The "impossible" movements of the dead chicken in *Eraserhead* can be seen as an externalized expression of Henry's hyperperception, a hyperbole of his anxiety about having dinner with his parents-in-law and the overboiling sexual tension that is unfolding. In scenes like this one, "Lynch breaks down the traditional narrative separation between his characters' inner psychic states and their physical surroundings" (Olson 65). The blending of *outside–inside* is not structured around a dynamic of *waking–dreaming*, however, but is rather a stylistic feature of the film per se. The dream mode, as I will show, has more specific characteristics in *Eraserhead*.

Further, a strong interpretation according to the Indian yogic traditions comes back to the question of the emergence of consciousness in a more literal sense. In parallel to Henry's gradual immersion into the dream, the film gives us an *in nuce* model of an incremental evolution of consciousness. E. Thompson distinguishes between three aspects of consciousness: the first aspect is "awareness, which is often likened to a light that reveals whatever it shines upon" (E. Thompson xxxii). The second aspect refers to the illuminated object, that is, the "content of awareness," while the third characteristic of consciousness is how some of these contents of awareness are experienced *as* "I" or "Me" or "Mine" (xxxii). When looking at the radiator for the first time, awareness is not "there" yet—there is no light going on. Looking at it the second time, "awareness lights up," a setting appears, and the light turns off again—a glimpse of an evolving consciousness. There is no dream *experience*, just a place. The third time, it lights up and new contents of awareness start appearing; Henry is presumably witnessing from a disembodied (or rather not-yet-corporeal) perspective (coinciding with the camera's perspective) from within the dream space (see Figures 4.11–4.13).

The fourth time, his dream ego's body materializes in the dream space and he identifies with it (see Figure 4.14). Henry experiences some of the contents of awareness, that is, the dream ego's body (rather than the setting), as his dream self. In E. Thompson's words, "the dream ego [. . .] centers our experience of the dream world and presents itself as the locus of our awareness" (xxxi).

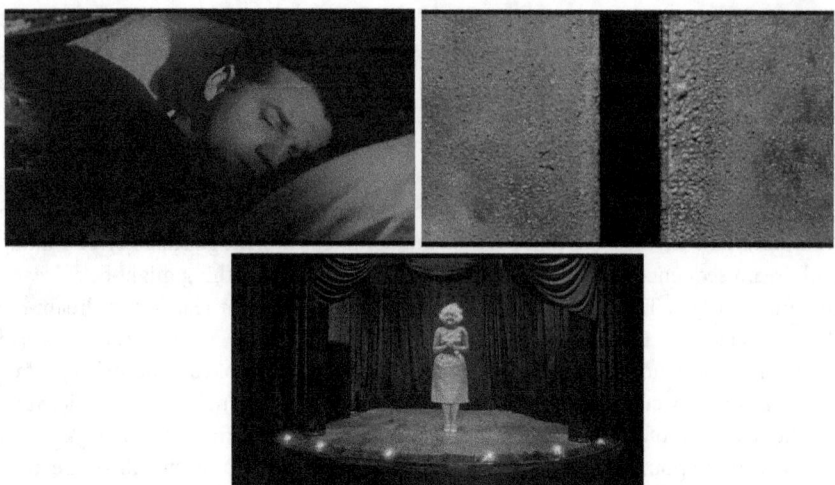

Figures 4.11–4.13 Step three: Witnessing the dream from a disembodied perspective (00:50:17; 00:50:36; 00:51:12).

Figure 4.14 Step four: The dream ego's body materializes in the dream world (01:05:24).

On a different note, the Upanishads provide a simple answer for why a barely noticeable noise of a radiator, an object that does not seem very interesting, leads Henry into the dream world. In the yogic traditions, consciousness is not conceived of in binary terms (*conscious/unconscious*) but rather as a continuum of levels of (phenomenal) awareness that vary in their degree of coarseness. Waking, for example, is a relatively coarse state of consciousness in which awareness is directed outward to apprehend objects in one's physical surroundings (E. Thompson 7). "Dreaming is subtler because you withdraw from the outside world and create what you see and feel on the basis of memory and imagination" (E. Thompson 7). Deep sleep is still subtler featuring "subliminal awareness"—"consciousness without mental images" (E. Thompson 7). Arguably, a conception of this kind is reflected by the film. As Henry directs his attention to something that is only marginally perceptible in waking, his state of consciousness becomes more subtle, that is, more *dreamlike* in the sense that he sees the space that will provide the setting for his dream. The fact that the radiator's noise increases as Henry turns his attention toward it reflects that his subtle state of consciousness renders it more tangible. The stage's illumination, in this context, is an extension of this movement. Crucial to the film's implications concerning the difference between waking and dreaming, Henry is not sleeping when the stage appears. This may suggest that the difference between waking and dreaming is not so much about sleep as it is about qualitative aspects of consciousness, such as the degree of outward- versus inward-directed awareness. Strictly speaking, sleep loses its discriminatory function concerning the difference between reality and dream, at least on an ontological level: the dream *world* is accessible, in principle, in the waking state. Ontology follows phenomenology here: what is "there" (in the film's diegesis) depends on the inclinations of Henry's subjective state and on what he experiences. The dream world is "in" the waking world *because* awareness is able to linger in an in-between state, directing itself outward and inward at the same time. This being said, sleep is not denied as a necessary condition for the dream *experience* to unfold. Crucially, Henry wakes up after seeing the Lady in the Radiator, first at 00:53:08. Most likely, this is a false awakening, though, given the following elements: Mary is now present—she should not be part of the waking reality in which she left—and then disappears again; the sperms, previously falling on stage, appear in the bed now; the cupboard's doors magically open; the dead worm moves; and Henry and his neighbor have sex in a bed filled with white liquid. He wakes up again at 1:13:27; since all the elements that were impossible in the previous sequence have now disappeared, there is no reason to assume that he is still dreaming.

Dreaming and/as Unconscious Experience

As I have just shown, *Eraserhead* implies a nonbinary conception of consciousness—possibly as a result of Lynch's commencing meditation practice during its making. If we speak of "the unconscious" in regard to the film, thus, it does not refer to the absence of consciousness—Henry does not visit a place that is completely inaccessible to him when he is awake; quite the opposite: in principle, it is already predefined in the waking state, it is just a matter of directing the (literal) "spot" (cf. Figure 4.10) of awareness. But in what sense can we still speak of an "unconscious" then? This section asks to what extent *Eraserhead* stands as a cinematic exploration of the interrelationship between the unconscious, experience, and dreaming. It will show how the film raises the ambiguity of the unconscious as *location* and as *experience*—the dream constituting its prototypical manifestation.

The (Im-)possibility of a Freudian Unconscious

In an interview from 1979, when the film was still gaining popularity, Lynch stated that many people have described *Eraserhead* to him as a "subconscious experience," and he does not seem unhappy with this reaction ("David Lynch interview from 1979" 00:08:44–00:09:20). To Lynch, this description expresses that the film "unearths things that are inside of people" and he links this aspect to the "dream theme," which was mentioned earlier by the interviewer. (The latter described the whole film as a dream at the beginning of the interview.) Further, Lynch hints at the importance of his own subconscious in making the film. In light of his biography, the implication seems to be that through meditation, Lynch "unearthed things inside of himself"—most likely, "things" associated with the birth of his own daughter Jennifer in 1968 found their way into the film—and the film unearths things inside of the viewers. So Lynch postulates the transfer of an "unearthing" process here: *Eraserhead* stands as the expression of Lynch's subconscious that speaks to the viewer's subconscious.[12] It might be obvious that this process is not without reference to the film's plot, that is, to Henry Spencer's own self-exploration and the discovery of his subconscious.

Concerning the terminology, it may be worth considering the vagueness of the term "subconscious" and its lack of conceptual distinguishability from the *unconscious*. Freud commented on this problem:

> If someone talks of subconsciousness, I cannot tell whether he means the term topographically—to indicate something lying in the mind beneath consciousness—or qualitatively—to indicate another consciousness, a subterranean one, as it were. He is probably not clear about any of it. The only trustworthy antithesis is between conscious and unconscious. (Freud, "Lay Analysis" 198)

Following Freud, whenever someone uses the term "subconscious," it could be the case that what they really intend to refer to is the unconscious. Although it is questionable whether the term "unconscious" avoids said ambiguity between a qualitative and a topographical meaning, it is preferred here, given its dominant use in systematic approaches to the topic.

But what does speaking of *Eraserhead* as a "sub- or unconscious experience" entail on a theoretical level? How can this notion be rendered plausible in relation to the film? And what does it build upon on the practical level of the film experience? Is it an apt description of experience as it is represented in and/or embodied by the film? Before turning to the possibility of "phenomenologizing" the unconscious and its consequences for filmic representation (cf. section "Phenomenologizing the Unconscious"), it seems necessary to discuss the relevance of Freud, both in regard to the conception of the unconscious and the composition of the dream—not because Lynch studied Freud's thought—he claims not to have read any of his work (Rodley xi)—but because it is Freud who shaped the concept of the *unconscious* like no other. What is most important to keep in mind at this point here is that my goal is not to decide whether *Eraserhead* (dis-)confirms the Freudian conception of the unconscious. Rather, I am interested in the extent to which Freud's theory illuminates the implications of calling the film a "sub-/unconscious experience," that is, an experience *of* the unconscious as conceived of by Freud.

In Freud's conception, it is impossible to have a direct experience of the unconscious. It rather presents itself indirectly in slips of the tongue, spontaneous "free associations," and in the dream-experience. In these instances, the unconscious, that is, a characteristically obscure intentionality, can be inferred based on someone's immediate experience. This is particularly true for the dream, whose analysis led him to speak of "unconscious psychic activity" in the first place (Freud, *Anwendungen* 36; my translation).[13] Dream analysis revolves around the uncovering of "latent dream thoughts" within the "manifest dream content" (Freud, *Traumdeutung* 284; my translation).[14] The former are "stored" in the unconscious and find their expression in the language of the dream, which articulates the dream thoughts in a way that bypasses censorship.

It is debatable whether the theater stage can be interpreted as the unconscious in the Freudian sense. It seems that this interpretation has three components: (1) the intentional structure and focalization/ocularization status, (2) the exact meaning of "as," as well as (3) the meaning of "unconscious" in this expression.

Concerning (1), his unconscious cannot directly appear to Henry, otherwise it would become an object of his awareness; but it cannot appear to the camera either, because it has no visible form per definition. The unconscious cannot be known directly, otherwise it would become conscious. Thus, speaking strictly, any attempt to visualize it is paradoxical in itself, in that it would visualize something which, by nature, has no appearance or any other immediate experiential form. The paradox only refers to an internal ocularization, though, that is, if we assume to be seeing what Henry is seeing. The camera's act of looking, however, does not necessarily coincide with Henry's perspective. Kuhn's model of film narratology speaks of "zero-ocularization, if what the visual narrative instance shows is not bound to any of the characters, like in the so-called *nobody's shot*" (128; my translation).[15] Hence it could be the case that what the camera reveals is unperceived and unknown to Henry, which is why we might use the term "unconscious" from the perspective of Henry's limited point of view; the camera grants us viewers—but not him—insight into the depths of his psyche such that we see more than he does. (Even here, images on the screen could only be an approximation to Henry's unconscious [not a visualization of the unconscious itself]; just like in a dream, the unconscious does not present itself directly to the dreamer but has to be inferred based on the impressions she is having.) But zero ocularization seems unlikely here due to the gradual progression described before (cf. section "The Emergence of (Dream) Consciousness"). The gradual progression toward the dream is clearly tied to Henry's perception, as becomes clear by the subjective camera introducing the theater stage inside the radiator. Kuhn observes the conventional ABA structure of point-of-view shots (141), which *Eraserhead* instantiates in all three scenes involving the radiator (00:13:59–00:15:07; 00:35:51–00:36:38; 00:49:58–00:53:07). A first shot shows

Henry from the outside, looking at something that is not in the frame (A), which is followed by what Henry sees from his subjective perspective (B), and closes with a second shot from the outside (A). In this way, the stage is unambiguously introduced as an imaginary object appearing to Henry. When Henry goes to sleep, then, Lynch would not have needed to cut to a point-of-view shot again to make clear that the stage is a product of Henry's imagination. But he does, and by doing so, he makes sure that the viewer understands this. In Kuhn's terminology, the three radiator scenes are thus an example of internal focalization combined with internal ocularization. That is, what the visual narrative instance shows us corresponds to "what a character knows *and* perceives" (Kuhn 140; my translation).[16] The stage is thus neither "unconscious" to the camera (we see an image of it) nor to Henry (he sees it, too). In terms of intentionality, that is, in the sense of someone's "*consciousness of* x," we therefore cannot speak of an unconscious. (In the section "Phenomenologizing the Unconscious," however, Jagna Brudzinska's phenomenological account of *unconscious experience* will show that the unconscious does not have to be defined in terms of a total lack of "conscious" qualities but can be conceived of as a "quasi-present phantasmatic *re-presentation-consciousness*" [Brudzinska 63; my translation].[17])

(2) The question of the meaning of "as" in the expression "the theater stage *as* the unconscious" addresses the film's mode of depicting the unconscious. Is the stage a "representation" of the unconscious? A "visualization" of it? Given that, by definition, it cannot directly appear to the senses, the image on the screen is a *symbolic* rendition of Henry's unconscious, not the unconscious itself.

(3) In regard to the meaning of "unconscious," what leads us to see the connection to psychoanalysis is that a new *place* appears, one that is connected to Henry's interiority (as shown in the section "The Emergence of (Dream) Consciousness"). According to Freud, "[o]ur psychic topology [. . .] refers to regions of the psychic apparatus, wherever they may be located in the body" (*Psychologie des Unbewußten* 133; my translation).[18] The unconscious is conceived of topographically and dynamically, its "core [. . .] consist[ing] of drive-representatives that try to discharge their cathexis, i.e. of wish-excitations" (*Psychologie des Unbewußten* 145; my translation).[19] Given its intimate connection to the unconscious, the dream makes these processes visible through symbolization (not in their actuality). In addition to considering the topical aspect alluded to by the stage, one may thus be inclined to interpret the objects on the stage as symbolic representations of Henry's repressed wishes, fears, and drives. In this reading, the unconscious is what "shines through" the dream figures.

The Lady in the Radiator crushes the sperms falling on the stage with her feet (see Figures 4.15 and 4.16), so it does not seem far-fetched to see this as the manifestation of Henry's drive to "erase" the fertilization. Her 1950s-style evening gown, bashful smile, and hairdo indicate chastity and innocence, but she cannot prevent the sperms from falling on the stage. She is an imperfect fantasy object. To "hide the sin," to undo what cannot be undone, she destroys them; the deformed, swollen cheeks may hint at the immorality of this act. She has a crucial function in representing Henry's self-interest and its assertion at any cost. The first dream sequence, in that light, presents the film's plot in a nutshell. Henry's world is "invaded" by an unwanted baby, as represented

 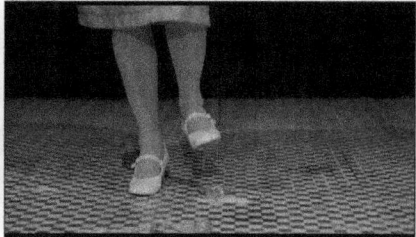

Figures 4.15–4.16 Henry's repressed wish for freedom? The Lady in the Radiator (Laurel Near; 00:52:40; 00:52:38).

through the sperms falling on stage. Crushing the sperms, the Lady provides him with a way out of his hopeless situation.

What is really at stake for Henry becomes clear when the Lady appears for the second time. In her song, she promises Henry how "in heaven, everything is fine" (01:03:44–01:03:52). The second verse goes, "you've got your good things, and *I*'ve got mine" (01:04:06–01:04:15); but in its repetition, it becomes, "you've got your good things, and *you*'ve got mine" (01:04:40–01:04:49). The changing pronoun implies that the song's addressee has obtained the narrator's "good things," without any further specification of who assumes these roles or what these things may be. What this change may hint at, however, is Henry's loss of freedom and independence due to his parental responsibility. It is the baby who took away Henry's good things, that is, his freedom. Alternatively, the change of pronouns may also imply Henry's wish for self-dissolution. With "I" becoming "you," "I" ceases to exist. In this interpretation, the Lady is not only the harbinger of murder but also the harbinger of self-destruction. The film's last scene, while also readable as Henry's vision, could imply that Henry has committed suicide, the pure white light of heaven redeeming him from the darkness of his earthly existence. Whether he "only" killed the baby or also himself, Henry has violated the human instinct for self-preservation, as represented by the Man in the Planet losing control over the levers—in the prologue, he used them to set fertilization in motion.

Another dream moment that deserves attention from a Freudian perspective occurs when Henry's head pops off and is replaced by the baby (see Figures 4.17 and 4.18). According to the *Cambridge Dictionary*, someone losing their head does "not have control of their emotions" and does "not act in a calm way" ("Lose Your Head"). Idiomatic expressions such as this one, in Freud's conception, are stored at the level of latent dream thought and are not directly accessible in their linguistic form in the unconscious. The unconscious only contains "object representations" (*Sachvorstellungen*), no "word representations" (*Wortvorstellungen*; cf. Freud, *Psychologie des Unbewußten* 160; my translation). This is what distinguishes it from the (pre-)conscious, which contains both.[20] Through the primary process (condensation and displacement), the idiom is translated into the dream image of Henry actually losing his head. Translating the image back into the idiom, dream interpretation

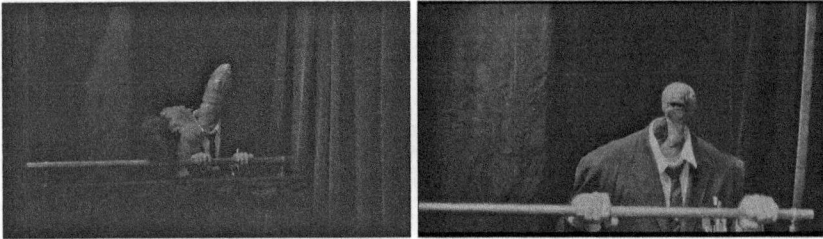

Figures 4.17–4.18 Henry loses his head (01:07:36; 01:08:26).

reveals that Henry panics at being a father.[21] He is afraid of literally "losing his head" over his parental responsibility—after all, his head is replaced by the baby whose recent birth tackled Henry's (supposed) wish for freedom. Before Henry's head pops off, the Lady is replaced by the Man. In a causal interpretation of the montage, this expresses a conditional: if Henry follows the Man, who represents procreation, he will lose his head because of the baby, thus eliminating his own existence. What he then does in waking life can be understood as a reaction to the second half of the dream (01:05:30–01:13:27). He chooses the Lady's way out: not wanting to lose control over his own life that is now ruled by the baby—in order to "keep his head"—he kills it. But this would imply that Henry "understands" the dream's message in the sense that he now sees filicide as a possibility. This presents a clear contrast to Freudian psychoanalysis where the dreamer is in need of the psychotherapist to arrive at the dream's meaning.

A more fundamental concern imposes itself. In Freud's logic of the dream's origin, the baby acts as a threat to Henry's initial (positively charged) wish for freedom. Through an act of repression (*Verdrängung*), this wish for freedom is translated into fear of his own death in the unconscious. The dream makes this fear visible because it does not maintain the suppression (*Unterdrückung*) of the unconscious through the (pre-)conscious. Importantly, though, the repression is not in the film, and neither is the unconscious wish that would be necessary for the composition of a Freudian dream.[22] So the hypothesis that Henry formed a wish for freedom (in his early childhood) is not motivated by what the film shows us and would be the result of adhering to a "causal determinism" implied by psychoanalysis—which the film gives us no reason to accept. Unlike in psychoanalysis, where the unconscious becomes the metaphysical entity filling in the gaps in a causal chain of (conscious) experiences (Heidegger 260),[23] the unconscious does not assume an explanatory function in the film.[24] It is precisely *not* the case that it resolves the mystery posed by the film; it rather perpetuates it. Questions as to why the world that Henry inhabits is so strange, why his "baby" looks the way it does, and so on, are not answered by the unconscious as it appears in the dream. In regard to understanding Lynch's cinema in general, Martin Heidegger's observation begs the question if speaking of an unconscious should be seen as an oversimplifying attempt to make sense of complex works of art. The ambiguities and causal discontinuities are frequently seen as the products of an obscure unconscious, which fills in the gaps of explainability. In other words, the assumption of an unconscious runs the risk of creating causality where there is none.

Further, what we see in the dream sequences does not make any claim as to the specificity of psychoanalytic mechanisms concerning the dream's unconscious origin. Judging from *Eraserhead*, Freud and Lynch might agree *that* there is symbolism involved in the dream. It should be stressed, however, that the symbolic value of (dream-) experience has nothing to do with psychoanalysis per se. Further, in clear contrast to Freud, *what* is symbolically expressed in *Eraserhead*'s dreams is not some repressed element from Henry's early childhood but his current emotional state. In this regard, Lynch seems closer to Binswanger's existential dream conception, which considers the dream a "consistent expression of the dreamer's living situation" (Gehring, *Traum und Wirklichkeit* 200; my translation).[25] The Lady in the Radiator and the Man in the Planet perform his recent inner turmoil, the dream being a stage play putting it on display.

If we continue speaking of "symbolization," then the term has assumed a connotation that is different from the way in which it is used in Freud's writings. In his *Interpretation of Dreams*, elements of the manifest dream are mainly discussed in terms of their symbolic function, which falls short of addressing the *way* in which wishes are represented. To a great extent, however, the dream matters for what it presents (at what Freud calls the *manifest* level), not for what it *re*-presents. A Freudian reading does not speak to those elements of the dream (e.g., the dream characters' peculiar appearance) that are not explainable in light of Henry's past, that is, to the genuinely *creative* momentum of dreaming. Since we are not given any information as to Henry's distant past, this aspect of dreaming is of great importance in the film. Further, the Lady in the Radiator and the Man in the Planet do not only *signify* abstract principles, but they *are* also material agents Henry interacts with. Taking into account the materiality and active nature of meaning-making, Umberto Eco speaks of "sign-vehicles" rather than "signifiers," which seems appropriate in this case (52–4). The Man's and Lady's bodies are "charged with" meaning; they are the "stuff" that carries meaning. This meaning is not solely abstract—it cannot be, since it is "bound to" their individual bodies. An essential part of the characters' "meaning," one that would be ignored by a strictly Freudian approach, is constituted by the way they appear to Henry's and to the viewer's senses at the manifest level. The material character of meaning guarantees the individuality of that expressive act and roots it in Henry's subjectivity. Exclusively focusing on the symbolic character of the dream is to ignore its particularity, because "what the symbol means is not some individual trait of our lived-through experience, not some recurring quality, not some property, as Husserl puts it, 'of reappearing identically to itself,' for we are in the presence of an ideal content presenting itself through the symbol as a unity of meaning" (Foucault 40). In other words, symbolization does not exhaust the particularity of *that* experience. What makes the Lady the product of a nongeneric, but individual act of imagination, for example, is her imperfection. Her body is not a mere shell for an "ideal content" communicated through it, but her grotesquely disproportional cheeks make her unique. This idiosyncrasy problematizes the exclusivity of her symbolic function.

An existentialist approach to the decapitation scene shows that the psychoanalytic interpretation is by no means mandatory. It seems that its meaning is directly "read off" the visible surface by any competent English speaker, without presupposing the existence of psychoanalytic mechanisms. Merleau-Ponty understands dreaming as the "experience of a latent content through a manifest content" (*Vorlesungen* 80; my translation).[26] In an erotic dream, the dreamer does not "begin by perceiving clearly the stimulations of a genital origin as genital to *then* translate this text into a figurative language" (Merleau-Ponty, *Perception* 171). Rather, "such a sexual drive is immediately this image of a wall being scaled or a cliff being climbed that is found in the manifest content. [. . .] The dreamer's penis *becomes* this serpent represented in the manifest content" (171–2). Analogously, we are not bound to conceive of Henry's head loss as the mere result of a symbolization process of the dreamwork, but it can be understood as the expression the dream is choosing in light of the panic he feels at being a father. Merleau-Ponty would say that the panic *is* the decapitation; it is the way in which Henry experiences his panic in the existential mode of dreaming. He experiences his own existence as determined by panic and he experiences panic *as* the disintegration of his body. The body experience unveiled by the dream is what underlies the idiomatic expression ("to lose one's head"), hence the dream engages with the (imaginary) structure at the basis of everyday language and is not just the result of it.

But even if the mechanisms underlying the dream's composition were specifically psychoanalytic in nature, these observations have already hinted at the fact that psychoanalysis falls short in addressing the particularity of Henry's experience on the phenomenal level of dreaming. What is true for the nocturnal dream, in this case, is also true for its filmic representation. Concerning Freud's dream conception, Foucault wrote, "the image is somewhat more than the immediate fulfillment of meaning" and that "the peculiarly imaginative dimension of the meaningful expression is completely omitted" (35). Freud, as is often the case, cannot be unaware of this problem when he writes, "[i]n our view, the perceived phenomena must be subordinate to the merely assumed aspirations" ("Fehlleistungen" 62).[27] Freudian dream analysis does not speak to the dimensions that are so important for an artist like Lynch in representing the dream: the peculiarity of its expressive act, the pictoriality of its language, the creation of a unique "mood" that the viewer is immersed in and that is specific to the dreams.[28] To approach the experiential structure of dreaming (as opposed to waking) as depicted in *Eraserhead*, phenomenology will prove to be useful.

Dreaming as Phantasmatic-Imaginary Experience

Phenomenology provides a means to describe the *otherness* of Henry's subjective dream experience, addressing the question in what sense the dream "speaks another language." First of all, an interpretation according to Brudzinska would agree with an Upanishad-inspired reading that, as Henry makes the acquaintance with his dream world, it is not just the transition from one *kind* of experience to another. As mentioned in the section "Dream Phenomenology and Freudian Psychoanalysis" in Chapter 2, Brudzinska distinguishes between "two *orders* of experience," that is, the "impressional-apperceptive" and the "phantasmatic-imaginary" order (58–9; my translation and italicization).²⁹ Arguably, the radiator in *Eraserhead* acts as the nexus between waking reality and dream reality (ontologically), between the conscious and the unconscious (psychologically), and, on a phenomenological level, between the impressional-apperceptive order of experience—in which the identity of people and objects is stable—and the phantasmatic-imaginary order of experience, in which that is not the case. The radiator is not only the gate to another world and marks the threshold of two layers of consciousness, but it also introduces a different experiential order which is structured by material instability and frequent transformations and a general lack of spatiotemporal continuity. This order reflects the structure of the phantasmatic-imaginary. In his second (night) dream, after Henry reaches for her, the Lady disappears for no apparent reason (1:06:22); then, the Man materializes in her spot before he vanishes in the same way; Henry transforms into the baby; the liquid oozing out of the pile of earth becomes a "portal" through which his head falls on an industrial site (see Figures 4.19–4.21); Henry's head is drilled, its brain matter being extracted and mechanically processed into an eraser (see Figures 4.22 and 4.23); to test its quality, a man uses it to remove a pencil stroke; he sweeps away the eraser's remaining particles (see Figure 4.24); the image of the eraser's swirling particles, functionally and aesthetically similar to the hypnopompic transition image in *The Alphabet* (1968; compare Figures 4.25 and 4.26 to Figures 3.9 and 3.10), brings us back into waking reality, where Henry's hands are folded behind the back of his head, as if he tried to hold on to it after just losing it in his dream.³⁰

What stands at the end of this long chain of transformations is Henry's complete material dissolution. To Seesslen, freedom can only consist in an attack against oneself (218). The dream shows Henry the possibility of deciding against his instinct for self-preservation, that is, to choose death. However, it does not show death to him as a possibility but as something that happens to him. The dream creates a material scenario for it to occur and "throws Henry in there." An extraordinary facet of this experience is that he assumes an impossible perspective that transcends the biological limits of his existence. He sees his own death, but, unlike what happens in Christopher Nolan's *Inception* (2010), he does not wake up in that moment. Instead, he continues witnessing what happens to his head after his death from a (literally)

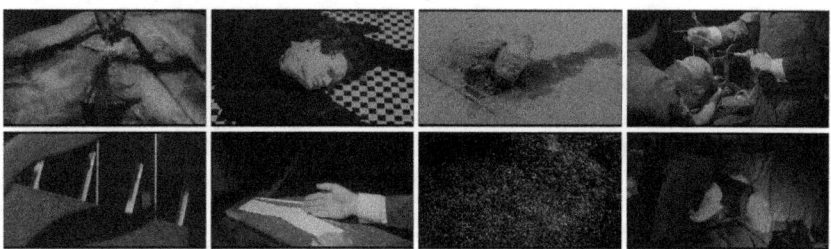

Figures 4.19–4.26 Material transformation as the dream's syntax and theme (01:07:52; 01:08:04; 01:08:50; 01:11:27; 01:12:19; 01:13:15; 01:13:22; 01:13:28).

disembodied perspective. Ironically, the head is not just eliminated, but turned into an eraser, which is used to eliminate "traces of existence." "Eraser-head" thus becomes the metaphor for Henry's ultimate self-annihilation. As each step in the chain of transformations gets Henry a little bit closer to the vaporization of his self (the head being the material representation of his personal identity), self-annihilation can be identified as the principle driving the transformations. If self-annihilation is called the "wish" underlying the dream, then there is nothing necessarily Freudian about that. First, because speaking of a wish does not entail the psychoanalytic implications concerning any "latent content"; waking Henry does not necessarily have a "death wish"[31] if he dies in his dream. Further, Freud was not the first or only person to observe the importance of the wish for dreaming and imagination. Rather than to psychoanalysis, the dream speaks to the existential dimension of the crisis Henry is going through at the moment. The prologue-daydream transcended the initial boundary of conscious life, while the decapitation-dream transcends its final boundary. The latter thus continues the evolution of consciousness from its emergence (i.e., "birth," cf. section "The Emergence of (Dream) Consciousness") over its experience (i.e., "life") to the dissolution of consciousness (i.e., "death"). Should the decapitation sequence's transformational structure be seen in function of the existential nature of its content? It seems that permanent material transformation,[32] while characterizing the dream's peculiar syntax, also serves its thematic destination of death and annihilation.

Further, Henry's head loss stands an image that fits the change from the impressional-apperceptive to the phantasmatic-imaginary order, in that this change involves a loss of control of what can be experienced (cf. Brudzinska 65). Losing his head, Henry loses control over what is happening to him. The head, as his "control instance," pops off. In E. Thompson's conception, this would involve a change from "self-as-dreamer" (i.e., an acting dream ego) to "self-as-dreamed" (i.e., a dream ego that is acted upon; 134). Since the head is also a topos for knowledge, Binswanger's conclusion in regard to dreaming, "[t]o dream means: I don't know what is happening to me" (102), resonates with Henry's experience of this dream moment.[33]

Phenomenologizing the Unconscious

Following the intuition that *unconscious* refers to "amputated, unperceived consciousness" (Bernet 330), a film cannot depict it because it always implies an act of perception. In order for something (an image) to be seen, something (a camera) must see first.[34] Because cinema speaks in images that, through their prior act of perception, have become conscious, it seems impossible to depict not only the unconscious in the Freudian sense but also more generally the elements of the mind that have not arisen to consciousness. In Bernet's view, however, the unconscious is conceived of as the appearance of another form of "(self-)consciousness" (330) that is not defined "in terms of this appearance being itself devoid of a certain 'conscious' quality or accompanying representation" (Kozyreva 203). Instead, its definition depends on "what appears (the absent, the alien) and how it appears in consciousness (reproductively as opposed to impressionally)" (Kozyreva 203).

In a similar vein, Brudzinska holds that we encounter the unconscious (not "just" the realm of fantasy) beyond the boundary of the impressional-apperceptive:

> The unconscious can be grasped [. . .] as that which, although it goes beyond the scope of impressional-apperceptive givenness, immediately realizes itself at the same time as a quasi-present phantasmatic *re-presentation-consciousness*: in the dream-experience, in the symptom, in the slip [. . .] But the unconscious as a phantasmatic-imaginary is also constantly interlocked with the impressional-apperceptive, namely as a polyphonic *intervention* into perception, as a phantasmatic *inscription* during protentional impulses.[35] (Brudzinska 63–4; my translation)

Through her specification of the "experiential-theoretical sense" of the unconscious (Brudzinska 55; my translation)[36]—the unconscious as "a phantasmatic-imaginary structure of intentionality" (Kozyreva 203)—the unconscious cannot only be brought to fruition by phenomenology but also by film. In her understanding, the unconscious is the "manifestation of *another presence*" (63; my translation)[37] such that it ceases to be a pure "anti-phenomenon" (63; my translation),[38] the negative value of what can be experienced, an "absence, gap or rupture of the conscious flow," a "derailment or lack of experience" (62; my translation).[39] Brudzinska's "phenomenologization" of the unconscious provides the theoretical basis for the possibility of a filmic "performance" of unconscious experience. Since filmic representation is able to give the unconscious an experiential form, film is able to engage in a dialogue with phenomenology concerning the question of what *unconscious experience* is supposed to be, which brings us back to the question of calling *Eraserhead* a "sub-/unconscious experience."

In *Eraserhead*, the "interlocking" Brudzinska talks about is graspable through the image of the radiator. In the way it is depicted in the film, the radiator presents the "scope of impressional-apperceptive givenness" (Brudzinska 63; my translation).[40] As an object with a stable identity throughout the film, it is part of what Henry experiences as real. At the same time, it provides the material ground for that which goes *beyond* impressional-apperceptive givenness, that is, the theater stage. As I have argued earlier, the appearance of the theater stage is dependent upon Henry's state of consciousness and thus the stage does not qualify as a "real" (or mind-independent) object. To the contrary: when Brudzinska speaks of human beings' "originary ability to let go of the bodily self of sensation and to let appear an *other*" (60; my translation and italicization)[41]—a process we can see in Henry's gradual progression toward dreaming—she characterizes the *phantasmatic*. Henry's dreaming thus provides the experiential form to the phantasmatic as understood by Brudzinska. Brudzinska speaks of the "medial character of the phantasmatic-imaginary" (60; my translation),[42] in that it "primarily has the function to stand for something else" (Husserl qtd. in

Brudzinska 60).⁴³ In this context, it is interesting that, out of all possible objects, it is a *stage* that appears in the radiator. Like the phantasmatic itself, a theater stage, generally speaking, functions to stand for something *else*, letting appear an *other*. Theater puts human interaction on display and thus always implies a reference to something that transcends the immediate spatiotemporal scope of the play. As two sides of a coin, the theater stage represents the medial character of the phantasmatic, and the phantasmatic represents the medial character of the theater stage. An analogy between the mediality of the phantasmatic and the Upanishad's light symbolism becomes apparent: an illuminated object always contains a reference to the process and source of its illumination, pointing to something "beyond itself." Similarly self-reflexive, a stage performance also implicitly points to its own stagedness. In both cases, the necessary ontological precondition is concealed, while at the same time being inscribed into what can be immediately experienced.

The mediality of the phantasmatic is not only evoked visually, though, but also acoustically. If Lynch's "sound cuts [. . .] achieve an inscription into time, amounting to a creation of time by a director" (Chion, *Lynch* 42), then dream time (as presented in the first dream sequence) stands apart in this regard because its diegetic electronic organ determines rhythm and tempo, unlike the nonmusical sound textures evoked by the "constant rush of boiler sounds, whirlpools, electronic organ chords" (Chion, *Lynch* 36). Thus, the dream structuralizes time rhythmically, or better: it transforms time into a rhythmic structure. As we enter the dream, the realm of art is not only evoked visually, through the change of the physical setting to a theater stage, but also acoustically: through the transformation of a nonmusical soundscape into music. There is music in the "impressional" waking world as well, but here it is produced by the gramophone. In the dream, there is no visible source of the music that would explain where it comes from. The scene leaves it open whether the music's source is located in the off-screen space or whether the music is "produced" by the dream space itself.⁴⁴ In the latter case, we could speak of *phantasmatic ambient sound*, drawing on Brudzinska's understanding of the phantasmatic and Chion's conception of ambient sound—"sound that envelops a scene and inhabits its space, without raising the question of the identification or visual embodiment of its source" (*Audio-Vision* 75). (Considering the organ music as "internal sound"—"although situated in the present, [it] corresponds to the physical and mental interior of a character" [Chion, *Audio-Vision* 76]—would ignore that, from within the dream's perspective, the organ music is part of the material surrounding. Neither Henry nor the viewer tends to question the source of the organ music consciously, so it appears as ambient sound, although, upon reflection, it cannot be.) It is clear, however, that it does not constitute nondiegetic underscoring: the Lady in the Radiator dances to it, so it must be audible in her space. In regard to the music, the boundary between waking and dreaming is the boundary between on-screen and off-screen (or acousmatic) sound or between on-screen and phantasmatic ambient sound. In any case, the second reason for why the music draws attention to its mediality is the concealment of its source: like the illuminated object and the theater stage, the music points to something beyond itself.

The acoustic dimension, however, does not only mark the *difference* between the (nonmusical) impressional-apperceptive and the (musical) phantasmatic-imaginary, it also *interlocks* the two orders of experience. A roaring sound is present throughout the film. At various transitions between the impressional-apperceptive and the phantasmatic-imaginary, it crescendoes but maintains a "smouldering presence" throughout both dream and waking sequences. This constant but dynamically variable sound may thus imply the interlocking of impressional-apperceptive and phantasmatic-imaginary experience. We are never, one might argue, in just one world: the external world is always structured, to some extent, by our imaginary perception of it, just like our imagination builds upon sensory impressions from the external world. In other words, the imaginary transcends the impressionally given and is itself transcended by (because materially bound to) it. The perceiving or imagining subject, as an embodied consciousness, can never be completely absorbed in either one of them; there can be no total exteriority or interiority, we are always in an in-between state, feeding on input from both realms. Lynch speaks of "room tone" as "what we hear when it's silent, in between words or sentences" (Rodley 73). Room tone is able to create "a certain image of a bigger world" (Rodley 73).[45] Given the way in which the room tone swells into roaring or hissing sounds at the ontological transitions in *Eraserhead*, "bigger world" refers to the respective other fictional level (to that of waking reality from the dream's perspective and to the dream reality from the waking perspective). To think backward for a moment, Lynch's claim as to the shortcoming of the phenomenally given, whether this refers to the external physical world or to the internal mental one, is "translated" into an immediately perceptible in the film experience. On an acoustic level, we are thus constantly reminded of the respective other mode of experience, of the *other* within the *present*. In Chion's theory of film sound, what Lynch refers to as "room tone" is called "ambient sound" (*Audio-Vision* 75). Interestingly, his model locates ambient sound at the boundary between diegetic and nondiegetic sound.

While watching a film, its ambient sound can be hard to distinguish from the sounds emitted by the film viewer's physical surroundings. The film's ambient sound, like the phantasmatic-imaginary, acts as a (literally) "*polyphonic* intervention" (Brudzinska 64; my translation and italicization) into the viewer's natural auditory perception of her nonmedial environment.[46] General film sound perception reflects what *Eraserhead* uses the phenomenon for: the intermeshing of ontological levels (dream–waking and film–reality). Ambient sound's natural disposition for undermining the boundary between fictitious film scenario and nonfictitious external world, in Lynch's film, is exploited for the interlocking of the dream and the waking world. *Eraserhead* expresses the interlocking of fictional levels (dream–reality) as the merging between the film's ambient sound and the viewer's respective sound environment.

In light of the director's biography, this interlocking is possibly rooted in the Upanishads' fluid model of consciousness, because practitioners of Transcendental Meditation enter more subliminal states of awareness *based on a sound mantra*, similar to how the viewer enters Henry's dream world through the increasingly noticeable roaring sound.

The interlocking between the two orders of experience also underlies the second dream (00:53:08–01:03:42), but it acquires a different sense here: the particular mode of experience carries over into Henry's allegedly "real" environment. Dream experience and dream location are now differentiated. Previously, the dream took "place" in an environment that was distinct from Henry's waking world, that is, the theater stage (and later the "eraserhead" factory). Now, Henry's bedroom becomes the dream's setting. The effect on the viewer is such that we initially believe that Henry is back in the waking world now. Inherent in the subsequent realization that Henry is still dreaming is the observation that dreaming is no longer bound to any particular place. Thus, Henry's dream experience has emancipated from a dream location. The interlocking, then, consists in how the alleged impressional-apperceptive environment is "filled with" a phantasmatic-imaginary experience. The principal accessibility of the dream world in the waking state (cf. section "The Emergence of (Dream) Consciousness")[47] now finds its inversion: the waking world is also accessible from within the dream. While it was a particular quality of awareness allowing for the dream world to emerge in waking, it is now memory providing the basis for the waking environment's appearance in the dream state. The waking world is "in" the dream world *because* the dreaming mind is able to recollect elements from the dreamer's past and integrate them into the dream. The continuity occurs on a textual and aesthetic level. The sperms that fell on the theater stage before now magically appear in Henry's bed (00:54:40–00:55:34); the spot illuminating the stage before now encircles the worm that is about to start moving in Henry's small cupboard. An aesthetic element from the original dream world, one that stresses its mediality, has thus carried over into his alleged waking space.

The Dream as the Meta-Medium of Lynch's Films?

The high value that the dream sequences attribute to mediality is striking in light of Brudzinska's elaborations on the intentional structure of dreaming and the phantasmatic. Her interpretation of Husserl[48] can account for the mediality of the dream. The dream, she proposes, has a medial character because the phantasmatic-imaginary (which it instantiates) is conceived of as a reproductive inner consciousness. Through dreaming, Henry has an experience that transcends his impressional surroundings, letting appear a reproductive, medial, and phantasmatic other. This being said, it is not the case that the waking sequences are devoid of medial character. Schmidt, for example, comments on the scene in which Mary "welcomes" Henry at her parents' house, saying that the "action *in* the scene [is] to be subordinated to the absurd image *of* the scene" (45; my translation).[49] Similarly, while calling Lynch's films "unreadable," Seesslen says that "their places and their times [emerge] from pure filmic language" (32; my translation).[50] (There is no "veritable place" or "veritable time" that would guarantee their "readability" [Seesslen 32; my translation].[51]) Hence the display of mediality might be a more fundamental feature of Lynch's cinema in general and not specific to his dream depictions. When Bill is ranting about the world, his rage is symbolically accompanied by the sound of a thunder, which, as soon as he is interrupted, disappears again. *Eraserhead* also displays a tendency toward synesthetic perception when Henry dreams of his neighbor coming over to his apartment. In what might be the film's most beautiful scene, the acoustic and the visual impression are aligned, expressing a type of "unified perception." The dimmed light mirrors the extremely reduced soundscape. The neighbor and Henry speak very softly, but this does not reduce the dialogue's crispness.[52] It might be here that we learn what "subtle state of consciousness" (cf. section "The Emergence of (Dream) Consciousness") means to Lynch.

Even if mediality is not exclusive to the dream sequences, it is striking that only dream scenes display a second medium (i.e., theater) within the first one (i.e., film)—unlike *The Alphabet* (1968), which *switches* from live action to animation in its passage from waking to dream imagery (cf. section "Animation as the Otherness of Dream Vision" in Chapter 3), Lynch's first feature film *incorporates* the "dream theater" within the waking world of the film. In this, it is reserved to the dream scenes to depict mediality *as* a visible object in the diegesis. But why is the dream particularly prone to an exploration of mediality? It cannot be a mimetic motivation underlying the connection because we do not dream in that way, at least not on a textual level: the nocturnal dream is unlikely to display its own mediality on a content level. Rather than mimetic dream representations, Henry's "staged" dreams, in this regard, stand as cinematic reflections on the structure of dream-experience.[53] They revolve around how a dream appears in principle, not in its experiential actuality during sleep. As such, they constitute an abstraction of what "experiencing a dream" means. The same goes for the transition into the dream, that is, the opening of metal doors (see Figure 4.12). It is not about an imitation of the process of falling asleep, but it is a cinematic reflection, an abstraction of the "what it is like" to mentally visit another environment and be immersed in it. In these cases, Lynch finds images that attempt to tackle the "universal" phenomenal structure of going into a dream. Creating a dream analogon, they symbolize this process, aiming for the *universal* in it, rather than attempting to portray a *particular* instantiation of that structure in a "realistic" way, that is, in such a way as it appears to somebody experiencing that transition.

At the same time, since light is a necessary precondition for film, *Eraserhead* becomes self-reflexive when it depicts the illumination of the theater stage as the dream begins. Given my previous analysis of *The Alphabet* and this chapter, it stands as a hypothesis that through the dream, Lynch's cinema reflects on its own poetic possibilities of representation in making mediality a phenomenological characteristic of dream experience. As the dream provides a space for reflection for human beings, it is obvious that it will also do so for the characters in a story. As this chapter has shown, Henry's dream is, to a great extent, a reflection on his diurnal experience and provides him with a possibility for action. Since the dream constitutes an experience of reflection for human beings, that is, a reflection on experience *through* experience (i.e., in the mode of experience),[54] experience necessarily reflects on itself in the dream. Phenomenologically, this expresses itself as an inclination toward a certain "reproduction character" (as opposed to an "impressionality character") in the nocturnal dream-experience. This means that its own "producedness" is, to some extent, inscribed in the experience as it occurs in a dream (even if the nonlucid dreamer is usually unaware of this). If the dream becomes the medium of an experience of reflection on real events, then for film (which already is a medium), the dream becomes a "meta-medium." In the dream, film reflects on its own functioning and the conditions of its coming into being. Based on Brudzinska, we could say that the nocturnal dream reflects on nonmedial, "real-life" events, staging them in a *medial* way. The filmic dream, further, reflects on medial, fictitious events, staging them in a *meta-medial* way.

5

Twin Peaks (1990–1; 1992; 2017)

Proper (Spatio-)temporality in Cooper's Dream (Season One of *Twin Peaks*)

The main plot of the first seventeen episodes of *Twin Peaks* (1990–1) revolves around the investigation of high school student Laura Palmer's (Sheryl Lee) murder. Special agent Dale Cooper (Kyle MacLachlan) is assigned to the case in the pilot. In the third episode, he uses a "deductive technique" that requires him to throw rocks at a glass bottle after the names of a list of suspects have been read out by the Sheriff ("Episode 2: Zen, or the Skill to Catch a Killer"[1] 00:18:37–00:27:40). Cooper repeats each name before throwing a rock, so the closer he gets to breaking the bottle, the more suspicious the person is whose name has just been called out. This peculiar investigative method is based on "intuitive knowledge" that Cooper gained in a Tibet-related dream. In the same episode, Cooper has a dream that supposedly hints at Laura's murderer ("Episode 2" 00:40:05–00:46:50).[2] The dream's aesthetics, including the peculiar flow of time in this sequence, quickly became symbolic of the series as a whole. *Twin Peaks* managed to stand out in the early 1990s media landscape not least through its willingness for experimentation.[3] This quality is already visible in its curious blend of genres, which was all the more unconventional in the conservative medium of television: soap opera, crime/mystery, coming-of-age story, and psychological horror (cf. Frank and Schleich 6). In the Red Room, that is, the dream's setting, the dream is characterized by a manipulated time flow. Vice versa, to Lynch, the dream provides the opportunity to experiment with time as the medium of inner consciousness. As such, much like in *The Alphabet*, where it "justifies" the use of animated painting, the dream offers the framework for the experimentation to be taken to the formal-aesthetic level of an individual scene. In the setting of the dream, "time" becomes visible in its technical manipulability. One could also say that time and dream become each other's fields of experimentation.

If film's verisimilitude depends on the indistinguishability of filmic movement from real movement, then the manipulation of movement provides a possibility to mark an *un*-reality. Shooting the scene, Sheryl Lee and Michael J. Anderson (whose character is known as "Man from Another Place" or "the Arm") pronounced the phrases and executed the body movements backward. On the language level, the technique is called "phonetic reversal." For example, "I've got good news," instead of the regular [aɪv gɑːt gʊd n(j)uːz], becomes [zuː(j)n dʊg tɑːg vɪa] in Anderson's speech production. The scene as the viewer sees it on the screen is the reversal of that recording (both in image and sound), resulting in the impression of a "paradoxical movement": the (speech) movements, while appearing to be directed "forward," carry the traces of time flowing in the opposite direction. Plosive sounds appear as ingressives (i.e., with air streaming inward instead of outward), wrong syllables are stressed, prosody becomes completely unnatural, pauses are misplaced, and so on. In the Arm's speech, the word "style," for example, does not sound as the standard [staɪl] but as [staˈiːl]. When recording the word backward, Anderson must have produced the long high front vowel [iː] ([ˈliːats]) instead of a centralized [ɪ] ([lɪats]), which would have entailed a more natural impression of the word.[4] It is obvious, however, that the distortion of natural speech is exactly what this technique aims for. The viewer may also notice the strange way in which Laura and the Man from Another Place blink—a slow closing of the eyelids is followed by an abrupt opening (e.g., "Episode 2" 00:44:23)—or the way Laura's hair abruptly "jumps" right after she kisses Cooper (00:46:23–00:46:26).

The resulting defamiliarization effect prevents the viewer from grasping oneiric time as either "flowing forward" or "flowing backward" and, through this, characterizes the otherness of the dream. In other words, when time "flows through" Laura and the Man from Another Place, it is manipulated in such a way as to make the identification of *direction* impossible. In Sobchak's view,

> the cinema is able to demonstrate the heterogeneity of time: on the one hand, in its objective mode, the film gives us to see time as a linear, irreversible progression while, in its subjective mode, and through such technical and narrative devices as flashbacks and altered motion, it presents time as discontinuous and differently paced depending on the desiring investment of the experiencing agent. (Morrey 15)

This seems related to a more fundamental phenomenological particularity of film, that is, its ambivalent representation of experience. Cinema "presents experience as *representation* (the post hoc fixity of already-perceived and now expressed images that stand as equivalent to noun forms)" while at the same time "represent[ing] experience through dynamic *presentation* (the always verb-driven and ongoing present tense of sensory perception [. . .])" (Sobchak, *Carnal Thoughts* 74). Through the predominance of the latter dynamic, presentational modality, the scene in *Twin Peaks* anchors the viewer sensorially in the *here and now* of the dream, stressing the subjective experiencing (*Erleben*) of time,[5] both the viewer's and also (by implication) that of Cooper. As the waking sequences in seasons one and two are more likely to evoke the idea of an "already-perceived" rather than visualizing "perception in the making," time is marked as something that belongs entirely to the dreaming Cooper in this sequence.

If, then, time marks a particularity of this individual dream experience, the dream constitutes the setting for the emergence of a *proper time*, that is, an autonomous, idiosyncratic, and, in this case, uniquely filmic temporality. Michael Gamper and Helmut Hühn understand "aesthetic proper times as exposed and perceptible forms of the complex design, modeling, and reflection of time," that is, as entities that "form past, present, and future differently from the way in which they appear in linear time" (23–4; my translation).[6] The particular appeal of filmic temporalities is evoked when Gamper and Hühn suggest that "'[t]ime' emerges aesthetically in non-semantical qualities, if it generates presence-effects rather than meaning-effects, for example as rhythm, measure, mood, tempo, duration, rhyme, breath, body-performance and moving picture" (17–18; my translation).[7] Cornelius Castoriadis speaks of the "proper temporality" of the dream: "A dream unfurls in a dream time; and it creates, it makes be a dream time. There is a proper temporality of the dream, as, more generally, a proper temporality of the Unconscious. This is not 'our' temporality of socialized adults, and noon can be switched to before 9AM; that matters little, there is a before/after" (Castoriadis 376).

One might be inclined to reduce the proper temporality of Cooper's dream to the peculiar, technologically manipulated time flow already mentioned. And much of its idiosyncrasy does rest on the otherness evoked by the time flow in which, radicalizing Castoriadis's observation, there precisely is *no* "before/after." Time in Cooper's dream is not only different from conventional cinematic representations of time but arguably from the way in which time moves in the real world as well, that is, in one direction. The alienating effect in the viewing experience—which can be called "oneiric" in the context of the dream setting—is thus achieved through the phenomenological divergence from learned patterns of cinematic representations of time *and* the divergence from our minds' "regular" waking perception.

But reducing the dream's proper temporality to its subjective modality of time would ignore Cooper himself. Even though he is affected by temporal manipulation as well—his wrinkles let him appear much older than he is—time flow is not distorted in his case: the sound of his voice is normal, his movements do not seem unnatural. This distinguishes him from the strange dream occurrences, making him an observer of the strange events; and it solidifies his status as the character with whom the viewer identifies, even within the dream. One might say that time is displayed as an objective, irreversible flow here, just like we know it from the waking sequences (and from everyday life, e.g., when we say that "an hour has passed"). This speaks to Sobchak's objective modality of filmic representation of time.

In regard to the time flow, thus, the dream's proper temporality does not consist in the subjective modality replacing the objective modality of time but in their juxtaposition, which shows the heterogeneity of time. In terms of the dream events' point in time, the sequence weaves past (Laura died before Cooper has this dream) and future (in the form of Cooper's older self) into an indeterminable present. The elusiveness of a present moment is verbally expressed by Mike's/Phillip Gerard's[8] (Al Strobel) poem at the beginning of Cooper's dream: he speaks of "the darkness of future past" ("Episode 2" 00:41:00–00:41:03). Combined with the indeterminability of the flow direction of dream time, the sequence could be understood as a figuration of "atemporality"—being outside of time, the detachment from a linear temporal sequencing of events.[9] That is, on a *rational* level, the attempt to grasp the *now* of the dream will fail; on the level of *sensation*, however, the viewer is firmly anchored in the dream's present. A present moment, in the sense of a "presence-effect" (Gamper and Hühn 17–18), is solely perceptible, not determinable.

Hermetic Space and Music

Essential to the sequence's presence effect, that is, the viewers' immersion in the *now* of the dream, is their immersion in the *here* of the dream, that is, the dream's space (see Figure 5.1). It could be argued that the mise-en-scène achieves this by creating a distinct spatial interiority: the red heavy curtains "encapsulating" the viewer; the lack of objects that would be found in a regular room; the dim lighting that almost lets the Arm disappear in front of the curtain; the impossible shadows that do not need physical objects creating them. All of these elements create the impression of a space that is unlikely to be "anywhere in the world," a denaturalized, hermetic space that belongs to Cooper's interior. The evocation of a body's "interior" could be understood quite literally here, given the reduction of the color spectrum to shades of red, that is, the color of blood. If this leads to the viewers' sensation of warmth, it may be worth considering the way in which Lynch spontaneously conceived of the scene on the basis of a physical sensation: "I was leaning against a car—the front of

Figure 5.1 Hermetic dream space in *Twin Peaks*' (1990–1) "Episode 2: Zen, or the Skill to Catch a Killer" (00:43:47).

me was leaning against this very warm car. My hands were on the roof and the metal was very hot. The Red Room scene leapt into my mind. 'Little Mike' was there, and he was speaking backwards. . . . For the rest of the night I thought only about the Red Room" (Rodley 165).[10]

What ensures the dream being set in a "space of its own," further, is not just the result of the mise-en-scène but also seems to hinge upon the music. Basic physics tells us that sound is a spatial phenomenon, in that sound waves need air to be able to travel in space. That is why the Arm is, scientifically speaking, right when he talks about music always being "*in* the air" ("Episode 2" 00:45:12–00:45:17). Composer Angelo Badalamenti's *Dance of the Dream Man* acquires a bodily dimension in how the combination of a grounding bass (on the first and third beats) and upbeat snapping (on the second and fourth beats) suggests an up-and-down movement (00:45:27–00:45:42). Due to the firing of mirror neurons, the arousal of the viewer's body rhythm is reinforced visually while seeing the Arm dancing. The first two bass notes define the tonal boundaries of the bass line, one octave, that is, the "space" within which the bass melody is moving. Then the bass starts playing on every beat (from 00:45:43 onwards). Its melody is suspenseful in how it chromatically wanders down an octave and back up again, as if "it" were taking small steps in one direction and then turning around to go back, not really knowing where it is going. The expression "*walking* bass" seems to support such an anthropomorphic perception of music. This impression is again matched visually by the way in which the Man from Another Place moves about in the Red Room.

Further, a more fundamental semiotic-phenomenological property of music is crucial to the effect of being "anchored" in the *here* of the dream space. Elements in a (minimally figurative) painting or text refer to real-world objects; one cannot but think of a real arm when seeing an arm in a painting, just like the written word "tree" will evoke the mental image which the reader has formed of a real-world tree (even if the painted arm is an indexical sign, whereas the word "tree" is a symbolic sign). Music is different in that regard because a tone is, in principle, self-contained. Tones relate to each other, but they signify nothing outside of the song, at least not in a direct way. A melody might trigger the idea of movement (as it does in *Dance of the Dream Man*) and an instrument's timbre may be associated with a real-world object or emotion (the saxophone is often said to create a feeling of warmth, for example), but the relationship between signifier and signified tends to be less stable with musical objects. *Dance of the Dream Man* exploits this semiotic property of music, "sealing off" the listener/viewer from what is "outside of" the music and the space with which it is identified such that she is "tied" to the Red Room. Her immersion in the music may also be seen as qualifying Cooper's immersion in the dream. The connection of music and space is all the more intimate here because its source is not visible in the frame and thus it seems to be a product of the space itself. Hence, like the organ music inside Henry's radiator in *Eraserhead*, this is another instance of *acousmatic sound* that is not "de-acousmatized" (cf. Chion, *Audio-Vision* 72; and section "Phenomenologizing the Unconscious" in Chapter 4).[11] It is not

Figure 5.2 "Open" waking space in Episode 2 (00:27:45).

only diegetic, that is, audible to the three characters in the scene, but it appears to originate from the diegetic space itself. Since this is impossible, the Red Room characterizes itself as a dream space.

Cooper's dream presents time and space in their manipulability. Not corresponding to either the laws of physics or to conventional cinematic representations of time and space, the dream scene articulates time and space according to its own logic. The dream's "proper spatiotemporality,"[12] if you will, is rooted in the divergence from natural(ized) modes of waking perception. *Twin Peaks*' first two seasons establish a relatively stable waking world: characters have continuous storylines, space is "open" and continuous (see Figure 5.2), time is linear, and characters' movements are indistinguishable from real movement. The spatiotemporal stability of the waking diegesis acts as a reference point for the phenomenological divergence of dream time and dream space. In Cooper's dream, space is not presented as continuous and open but as hermetic and interiorized; time, while usually going unnoticed, is put on display here by being "un-directionalized."

Oneiric Temporality as the Experiential Otherness of Dreaming

The proper time of Cooper's dream is embedded in a context of time moving linearly. The whole story kicks off as an "*after* Laura's death." Arguably, Cooper's dream is the most fundamental narrative element of the first seventeen episodes. John Thorne, for example, divides season one into two phases based on the dream: the pilot together with Episodes 1 and 2 comprise the "establishing phase," while Episodes 3–7 constitute the "post-dream phase [. . .] translating the perplexing elements of Cooper's dream into a legible story" (Thorne 11). Elements from the dream serve as symbolic hints to the investigation of Laura's murder. Considering its conception and pivotal importance for the narrative of the first seventeen episodes, the dream could be considered an autopoietic element, providing the material that the investigation plot will revolve around. Cooper is well aware of the significance of his dream when he tells Sheriff Truman, "our job is simple: break the code, solve the crime" ("Episode 3: Rest in Peace" 00:05:46–00:05:50).

When the Man from Another Place tells Cooper's dream ego that the woman next to him is his cousin, for example, Episode 3 "translates" this into the series' waking narrative: Laura's cousin Maddy Ferguson (Sheryl Lee) arrives in the town of Twin Peaks (00:12:02–00:12:15). In Cooper's dream, the Arm asked him if she does not "look almost exactly like Laura Palmer" ("Episode 2" 00:44:28–00:44:38), which is then alluded to by the fact that Maddy is played by the same actress as Laura. In his dream, Cooper does not understand: "But it *is* Laura Palmer. Are you Laura Palmer?" The woman's answer, "I feel like I know her, but sometimes, my arms bend back" (00:44:38–00:44:58), does not make any sense at this point. The autopsy results, however, indicate that Laura's arms were bent back before she was killed ("Episode 3" 00:19:08–00:19:12). Similarly, the red curtains in Cooper's dream reference the curtains of a cabin in the woods where Laura was taken before she was killed ("Episode 5: Cooper's Dreams" 00:33:22). The Arm's mentioning of birds alludes to a speaking bird named Waldo that was present in the cabin ("Episode 5" 00:33:45–00:33:50). Waldo is of such importance to the investigation that, after it has been taken to the Sheriff's department, Leo Johnson (Eric Da Re), a local mobster involved in events leading to Laura's death, shoots it through the window to prevent it from giving the police any clues ("Episode 6: Realization Time" 00:31:01–00:31:27). The music that the Arm talks about refers to the music played in the cabin, at least in Cooper's view. When Cooper and his colleagues Truman (Michael Ontkean) and Hawk (Michael Horse) get to the cabin in Episode 5 and Julee Cruise's *Into the Night* is playing on a record player, Cooper repeats the phrase, "and there's always music in the air" (00:33:42–00:33:45), that the Arm first uttered in his dream ("Episode 2" 00:45:19–00:45:23). Leland's compulsive dancing after Laura's death mirrors the Arm's dancing in the Red Room ("Episode 5" 00:39:46–00:41:11). Similarly, in season two, messages that Cooper receives from The Giant (Carel Struycken) in a comatose state anticipate important plot elements ("Episode 8: May the Giant Be with You" 00:08:18–00:10:50). Finally, it is the repetition of a particularly perplexing utterance from his dream that allows Cooper to find the killer in "Episode 16: Arbitrary Law." When an elderly waiter (Hank Worden) offers a gum to Cooper, Leland recognizes it as his favorite brand from when he was a child. The waiter tells Leland, "that gum you like is going to come back in style" (00:30:15–00:30:20), a signal phrase from Cooper's dream ("Episode 2" 00:44:02–00:44:14) that causes him to revisualize a part of his dream. This time, when Sheryl Lee's character whispers into old Cooper's ear, we can hear her saying, "my father killed me" ("Episode 16" 00:30:36–00:30:42).

Hence, the dream's elements stand in a relationship of *anticipation* to the course of the (waking) narrative. Cooper's dream is prophetic, in that its events are progressively realized in the linear time of narration. (It is not the case, however, that Laura's killer is found by Cooper analyzing his dream; rather, the real occurrence of elements from his dream assures him that he is on the right track in the investigation.) While the post-dream phase *translates* the dream elements into a "legible story" (cf. Thorne 11), vice versa, the waking narrative could be said to *rationalize* the dream events by actualizing them to some extent. By providing a context in which they function in relation to the criminal investigation, the waking narrative attributes meaning to elements of Cooper's dream that would have remained meaningless otherwise (even if the manner in which dream elements end up in the waking narrative appears random at times [e.g., the music playing in the cabin or the waiter offering Cooper the gum] and thus ironizes what has become a formula in the tradition of films like Alfred Hitchcock's *Spellbound* (1945) in which dreams are used as riddles to solve a crime). The dream *means something* in regard to the rational undertaking of a criminal investigation. Interestingly, however, the dream's proper temporality is not "covered" by this rationalization; its "proper spatiality" can be accounted for, at least to the extent that the red curtains are in the dream *because* similar curtains cover the windows of the cabin where Laura was tortured. There is no such logic underlying the detemporalization of time, though. It serves no narrative purpose. Why is it there then?

Vlada Petrić writes that "ninety-nine percent of commercial films use dreams only as the narrative material or as a contribution to a literary interpretation of the film plot" ("Film and Dreams" 5). Arguably an overstatement, this perception does testify to what has frequently been observed as a narrative schema concerning the function of dreams in commercial film and television. Petrić continues, saying that "such films are no more than verbal dream reports to be resolved by the symbolic reading of the narrative, behavior of the characters, dramatic situations, and scenery" (5). While it does use the dream as "narrative material" for the plot, it is crucial to note that the first season of *Twin Peaks* also displays a keen interest in the experiential otherness of dreaming, as most visible in its treatment of time in Cooper's dream. To be clear, through the manipulation of a fundamental dimension of everyday life, that is, the directionality of our experience of time, Cooper's dream constitutes a performance of *otherness*. Unlike in *Absurd Encounter with Fear* (1967), for example, what constitutes the reference point for the depicted dream is not the nocturnal dream as experienced by a human being but its otherness from waking experience: the dream scene differs from the waking scenes in a way that is *similar to* how nocturnal dream-experience differs from diurnal waking experience. In this logic, otherness becomes a measure of oneiricity—x is oneiric because x differs from y—just like oneiricity becomes a measure of otherness—x differs from y because x is oneiric.

Oneiricity and Temporality in Season Three of *Twin Peaks*

Proper (Spatio-)temporality

The Red Room's proper time from Episode 2 still exists in the same way in the third season, that is, the 2017 continuation of *Twin Peaks*. Based on the previous analysis, it could be argued that proper temporality is expanded in the new *Twin Peaks*. Till Schröder traces the various compressions and extensions of image and sound back to Cooper's dream in season one (82). Michael Ewins observes that "time moves differently through, and makes distinct impressions in each space" depending on the character and the mood (34); "in Audrey Horne's (Sherilyn Fenn) 'house,' time stretches interminably across the same limited sequence of shot/reverse-shot" (Ewins 34; "Part 12: Let's Rock" 00:36:40–00:47:22). Similarly, "Part 13: What Story Is That, Charlie?" shows Sarah Palmer (Grace Zabriskie) watching a boxing match on a loop, apparently unaware of its repetitiveness (00:49:00–00:50:07). In these cases, the stretching and looping of time hints at the distorted perception of the characters, a possible result of their traumatization in the past. (Audrey was raped by Cooper's doppelgänger and Sarah's emotional disturbance by her husband's raping and killing their daughter Laura possibly continues to this day.) Another temporal stretch seems completely unmotivated. In "Part 7: There's a Body All Right," almost two and a half minutes of screen time are devoted to a bartender sweeping the floor while the Booker T. & the M.G.'s song *Green Onions* is playing (00:49:26–00:51:46). The camera's static observation of this everyday scene acts as a modification of the establishing shot: the selection of a particular part of the frame is massively delayed. During that time, no material is condensed in order to create conflict or narration. Scenes like this one might be seen as a counterpoint to the temporal economy of contemporary mainstream television and film, insofar as those constitute a facet of the fast pace of modern life in general. For critic Matt Zoller Seitz, "Lynch and Frost are forcing everybody to take a slow train without Wi-Fi." Dominique Chateau relates the rhythm of the series' narration to dreaming because "fantasizing requires slowing down, insofar as it involves a process of interplay between attraction and repulsion" (127). This observation might be too generic to be meaningful in regard to *Twin Peaks* (2017) because, according to Chateau's criterion, any slow film may qualify as "oneiric." There seem to be more specific aspects concerning the interrelationship between temporality and oneiricity as depicted by the series.

To begin with, it could be argued that the series' oneiricity is related to its high degree of narrative fragmentation. Even if Lynch already experimented with fragmented storytelling in his previous films *Lost Highway* (1997), *Mulholland Drive* (2001), and *Inland Empire* (2006), this strategy acquires new meaning in *Twin Peaks* (2017), which embraces the fragment as a poetic form.[13] When the first part (Diane's dream) of *Mulholland Drive*, for example, opens up a number of narrative threads (e.g., the cowboy, Adam Kesher, the hitman) whose relevance for the main plot of Betty seems negligible at first, a sense of closure is achieved through the second part (Diane's reality) in which these elements are retroactively marked as unconscious displacements inside Diane's dream.[14] In *Twin Peaks* (2017), there is a variety of sequences and narrative threads that are completely irrelevant to the two main plot lines, that is, (1) Cooper's odyssey back to Twin Peaks and (2) the FBI's investigation of a series of mysterious murders throughout the United States. Scholar Antonio Sanna, for example, speaks of "events that are inconsequential and untied to one another" (11). One might think of "Dr. Amp's Great American Radio Show" ("Part 10: Laura Is The One" 0:18:36–0:20:42), which could be a YouTube channel in its own right, or Jerry Horne's (David Patrick Kelly) aimless wandering in nature (e.g., "Part 9: This Is The Chair" 0:32:50–0:34:42), as well as some conversations in the Roadhouse about otherwise unknown characters talking about unknown and seemingly insignificant events in Twin Peaks ("Part 9" 0:52:20–0:55:07). While the bizarreness is inherent in some of the scenes (e.g., Jerry Horne talking to his foot), it is amplified by their lack of relevance to the narrative. Rather than narrating, these fragments characterize the diegesis, creating moods that are specific to a situation, character, or place. The most obvious example for this aspect is the Roadhouse with its musical performances occurring in or at the end of fifteen out of eighteen episodes. It is not coincidental that fans came to believe that everything happening inside the Roadhouse is actually a dream.[15] Like dreams, the fragments present "pocketed" (counter-)realities that, in the way they are presented, seem to exist in isolation from what is outside of them. Further, the dream comparison may be seen as alluding to the way in which the nocturnal dream is available to the waking mind solely through a necessarily fragmented recollection. The dream itself remains unknown to us in its entirety. Lynch once said that "fragments of things are pretty interesting. You can dream the rest. Then you're a participant" (Rodley 26). The fragment would be both a dreamlike element of the text and, by virtue of that, an expression of the invitation to us spectators to fill in the story's gaps in our imagination. It is as if, by giving us only fragments of the whole story, Lynch and Frost make sure that *Twin Peaks* continues to exist in our minds' imaginative faculties. Audrey Horne, for example, finds herself in an entirely white, utopic space after the abrupt ending of her solitary dance at the Roadhouse ("Part 16: No Knock, No Doorbell" 00:54:00–00:55:54). Her fate is only hinted at by *not* telling us what happened to her in the twenty-five years between the end of season two and season three.[16]

In these cases, fragmentation implies an absence of temporal units that would produce a coherent story. In this context, the lack of time (i.e., time as negatively specified) may be seen as responsible for the series' oneiric character. As the next sections of the chapter, "The Room Above the Purple Sea" and "The Convenience Store," will show, however, temporal oneiricity may also be positively characterized.

Out of the third season's many instances of proper temporality, the scenes involving the Convenience Store ("Part 8: Gotta Light?" 00:21:27–00:24:10) and the building on the purple sea might be the most striking ("Part 3: Call for Help" 00:04:20–00:09:04). Unlike the previously mentioned examples from the new *Twin Peaks*, both of these scenes embody a mechanical intervention in the flow of time. Both of the scenes display Gilles Deleuze's key feature of what he calls the *time-image*. Unlike in the precedent (pre-Second World War) *movement-image*, time is no longer subordinate to movement, because the image's commitment to providing a "sensory-motor link" between the viewer and the depicted situation is no longer required (Deleuze 173). "This is no longer a sensory-motor situation, but a purely optical and sound situation, where the seer [*voyant*] has replaced the agent [*actant*]: a 'description' [. . .] Now, if it is true that the sensory-motor situation governed the indirect representation of time as consequence [*sic*] of the movement-image, the purely optical and sound situation opens onto a direct time-image" (Deleuze 272). In light of what Deleuze says, we may note how Cooper seems unable to "act" in the scene above the purple sea ("Part 3" 00:05:00–00:09:04). His distorted movements, rather than making him an "agent," "describe" the space he finds himself in by characterizing the deviating laws of space-time.[17] A sensory-motor identification between the viewer and what is depicted seems impeded given the way in which the characters' body movements are denaturalized. In this context, Ewins draws our attention to the importance of Maya Deren (34), possibly an influence on Lynch's cinema: "For an action to take place in time is not at all the same as for an action to be created by the exercise of time" (Deren qtd. in Nichols, *Maya Deren* 45). Rather than being determined by the characters, action emerges as a result of an "exercise of time" at the Convenience Store and at the place on the purple sea. In both cases, a heavily manipulated time flow drives the movement.

The Room Above the Purple Sea

Oneiric Implications of the Narrative Context

Concerning the narrative context of the scene at the mauve building, it is necessary to recall what happened at the end of season two. Villain Windom Earle (Kenneth Welsh) kidnapped Cooper's partner Annie Blackburn (Heather Graham), taking her to the Black Lodge, an extradimensional place of evil ("Episode 29: Beyond Life and Death" 00:06:21–00:09:00), part of which is constituted by the Red Room that Cooper had seen in his dream in Episode 2. Cooper followed them and saved Annie, at the cost of being "split" into two beings: Good Cooper (Kyle MacLachlan) remains trapped in the Lodge, while Bad Cooper (also Kyle MacLachlan), possessed by the evil spirit Bob (Frank Silva) gets back into the diegetic reality in the last moments of season two ("Episode 29" 00:43:05–00:49:49). Season three continues this storyline. Good Cooper, now twenty-five years older, is still in the Lodge ("Part 2: The Stars Turn and a Time Presents Itself" 00:15:25). His return to Twin Peaks turns out to be complicated and has to take a detour as his evil doppelgänger manages to circumvent his fatefully predestined return to the Black Lodge. Originally, he was supposed to return to the lodge to redeem the good Cooper; the latter would then have been dismissed in that case. But the story takes a different path, as Bad Cooper created a tulpa, that is, a kind of "manufactured duplicate" of Cooper by the name of Dougie Jones (Kyle Maclachlan playing a third character). Dougie is an insurance broker who lives in Las Vegas. He is sucked back into the Lodge instead of Bad Cooper ("Part 3" 00:21:54). Thus, Dougie was Bad Cooper's trick to not have to return to the Black Lodge himself. In the Lodge, Good Cooper meets Phillip Gerard who, alluding to the poem he recited in Cooper's dream in the first season's third episode ("Episode 2" 00:41:00–00:41:21), asks: "Is it future or is it past?" ("Part 2" 00:15:25–00:15:50).

Good Cooper breaks through the floor of the Black Lodge while the "Evolution of the Arm,"[18] a tree with human flesh on it that sparks electricity, cries out "nonexistent" ("Part 2" 00:45:00–00:45:27). After appearing briefly in a mysterious glass box in New York ("Part 2" 00:45:45–00:47:26), Good Cooper is falling through space at the beginning of Part 3 (00:01:46–00:02:30), then landing on the balcony of a building above a purple sea. He enters through a window and finds Naido (Nae Yuuki) sitting by a fireplace. Her eyes are sewn shut and she is unable to speak. Cooper becomes interested in the room's large power socket on the wall, but Naido stops him from getting too close. They climb up a ladder and find themselves on the roof of a box floating in outer space. Naido pulls a lever on a mechanism and receives an electrical shock that throws her into space. The face of Major Briggs (Don S. Davis) sails past in the distance saying "blue rose" and Cooper climbs back down again. The light in the room has changed, and there is now a blue rose on a table. Another woman, credited as "American girl" (Phoebe Augustine), sits on the sofa. As her watch strikes 2:53:00, a humming sound is emitted by the wall socket and she tells him to hurry. With the sound impression of her voice mirroring that of the Red Room, she says that "when you get there, you will already be there" ("Part 3" 00:15:32–00:15:46). Good Cooper is then "sucked in" by the power socket (00:16:40) and, after exiting through a regular socket in a Las Vegas apartment, replaces tulpa and insurance broker Dougie Jones (who has just been transported into the Black Lodge; 00:26:01–00:26:31).

In terms of the narrative, thus, the building on the purple sea functions as an interstation for Cooper's journey from the Black Lodge "back to earth."[19] Although Cooper does not access the "Mauve Zone" (cf. Djurdjevic 99) in a state of sleep, the scene is indirectly connected to dreaming, given the way the series deconstructs its own diegetic reality through a dream metaphor as it approaches the end. After Bad Cooper is defeated in "Part 17: The Past Dictates the Future," Cooper talks to Diane (Laura Dern). What establishes a connection to the scene at the mauve building is that it was previously Naido who just transformed into her. Then the clock freezes at 2:52:59—unlike at the mauve building, 2:53:00, whose checksum 10 represents the "number of completion" ("Part 17" 00:06:04–00:06:08), cannot be reached. Cooper's face is superimposed on the screen. In a distorted and reverberating voice, it says, "we live inside a dream" (00:34:45–00:34:51), which initiates a series of transformations of place and time that appear to dissolve what has been conceived of as the diegetic reality of the series until now. The standstill of time allows for the realization that "we live inside a dream" and forces Cooper to act.

Oneiricity and the Ambivalence of Sensory-Motor Activation

In the scene set inside the mauve building, fragments of time are skipped, stretched, accelerated, reversed, and replayed over the course of almost five minutes of screen time ("Part 3" 00:04:20–00:09:04). The scene gravitates toward certain moments either through acceleration or repetition, such as when a menacing pounding is heard from a dark corner of the room. Over the course of one minute, Cooper's gesture of turning toward this sound-emitting spot can be seen around ten times (not counting the camera's close-up point-of-view shots of the spot), which creates an attentional focal point around this moment (00:06:17–00:07:20). Similar to the first encounter with the dinosaur in Steven Spielberg's *Jurassic Park* (1993), an emphasis on the act of looking (even if very different aesthetically) is responsible for the viewer's urge to see what is being looked at (see also section "Materiality and Oneiricity" in Chapter 3). Unlike Spielberg, Lynch intersperses the act of looking with the seen object, only to stress the shortcoming of the former. We see what Cooper is looking at, but it is not revealing: a black surface with two flickering white holes on it (see Figures 5.3 and 5.4). The acoustic impression of a metal door being knocked at is neither confirmed nor denied by what is in the image. The scene creates a profound sense of dread by not revealing the source of the apparent danger. It is a play between visibility and invisibility, disclosing *some* information but not enough to make the viewer understand what is happening. And even the visible appears unreliable. The editing, in its combination of repetition and a stuttering rhythm, creates different versions of *that* moment, neither of them claiming objectivity, as if the film itself were unable to properly process the information it is receiving. In its inability to grasp the scenario, the film questions its own act of looking such that the "actual" scene remains elusive.

The play with the dynamic of *visible–invisible* is not only expressed as a temporal manipulation concerning the *act* of looking but also underlies the representation of a seen *object*. Eyeless Naido might be thought of as the "opposite" of a camera: she is not a seeing subject, merely a seen "object-body"; she is unable to see and can only *be* seen. The camera, on the contrary, is a purely seeing subject and has no body at all. Although filmic vision depends on the existence of a camera, and although one might agree with Sobchak that "watching a film, we can see the seeing as well as the seen" (*Address* 10), we do not "see the seeing" in the same way as we see an object in the world. That is, we see the *activity* of seeing but not its material precondition. Naido's inability to see, combined with her inability to speak, forces her to communicate through gestures. Although she initially seems to reject Cooper, she reaches out for his hands and then touches his arms, torso, and face (00:05:14–00:06:17). The importance of the tactile dimension is also evoked by the editing, as particularly plastic sounds precisely coincide with every temporal jump. Thus, tactility—as a function of invisibility—is thematized both on the formal and on the content level of the scene.

When Cooper asks, "Where is this? Where are we?" he does not get an answer, or rather, Naido's response is not verbal but consists in a sound effect (00:05:41–00:06:17). While in Cooper's dream in season one, spatial indeterminacy was implied by describing the space self-referentially as the "Red Room," the impossibility of localizing Naido's room is now rendered explicit by Cooper's question not being answered. Further, the shift from a predominantly verbal and visual to a tactile-acoustic form of communication is reminiscent of what was observed in regard to the encounter between the boy and Grandmother in *The Grandmother* (1970; see section "Materiality and Oneiricity" in Chapter 3). Here, too, not understanding coincides with sensory intensity, and, more specifically, the dominance of vision over the other senses is subverted.

Many YouTube comments ascribe a dreamlike quality to the scene in the room above the purple sea. For example, user Mildly Amusing Channel writes that "this scene was like stepping into a dream, truly." Based on what was observed so far, the dreamlike feel may result from the nonrational perspective opened up by the scene. The insignificance of words (on the film level) and our incapacity to grasp the source of fear in the scene (on the film and on the viewer level) may be related to the fact that in nonlucid dreaming, activity in the prefrontal cortex—associated with cognitive control and metacognition—decreases considerably (Mutz and Javadi 5). At the same time, areas processing emotion, that is, the amygdala and the hippocampus, fire up, possibly providing the neural basis for a dream's emotional intensity (Mutz and Javadi 5). The dreamlike atmosphere may also be linked to the alienating effect that the scene generates. Although there is no reason to assume that dream time in the nocturnal dream-experience literally moves in the way depicted by the scene, Lynch's temporal manipulation achieves *that* type of alienating effect that reminds viewers of "what it is like" to be dreaming. Film, in that logic, uses filmic means to mirror what the nocturnal dream achieves in a different way, that is, the creation of a feeling of subjection and alienation.

Further, the scene's heightened sense of emotionality, as a function of oneiricity, is connected to the described dynamic of *visibility–invisibility*. According to André Bazin, "the analogy between dreams and cinema should be extended even further. It lies no less in what we deeply desire to see on the screen than in what could never be shown there" (171). Although the issue of censorship is on Bazin's mind here, stressing cinema's potential to create dreamlike effects as a function of invisibility seems highly relevant to the purple scene in *Twin Peaks*. That is, due to withholding crucial information as to the source of threat, the scene embodies an overbearing, "oneiric" emotionality. In other words, due to the lack of information provided, reflective distancing is impossible and the viewer is forced to process the input emotionally. The lack of information in the viewing experience, thus, corresponds to the dreamer's inability to judge and reflect on what she experiences.

Petrić suggests that the viewer's emotional processing of a film scene depicting movement has another, physiological component, in that it is directly related to his degree of sensory-motor activation: "the greater the stimulation of the film viewer's sensory-motor centers, the greater the abatement of his critical judgement" (Petrić, "Film and Dreams" 10). But, as Chapter 2 pointed out, cinema's potential to provoke a physiological response characteristic of the dream state is even more specific in his account. He particularly stresses the depiction of movement as a possibility to create an oneiric impact. As mentioned previously, Schönhammer's hypothesis is that the sleeping body's muscular inhibition is interpreted by the dreaming brain as *both* an inability to move in the dream world and as an urge to escape a persecutor (*Wahrnehmung* 62; cf. section "Explicitly Phenomenological Studies on Oneiric Film" in Chapter 2). While in the former interpretation, the body's stillness *carries over* into the dream scenario, in the latter, it is *reversed* by the dream.

But what does this entail for the dreamlike effect of *Twin Peaks*' purple scene? If a film depicts movement as inhibited—the purple scene provides a rather extreme example thereof—then the viewer experience may echo those interpretations of efferent REM sleep movement impulses which stress their nonexecution. The filmic depiction of akinesia, in a neurophysiological conception, alludes to the dreamer's sleep paralysis as well as to the film viewer's stillness (obviously, while the former is biologically determined, the latter results from a volitional act). In this understanding, thus, watching the purple scene could be associated with those sleep phases in which the stillness of the sleeper's body causes the inhibition of movement in the dream. If it is one of the dream state's physiological characteristics for the dreamer to be "in" his sleeping body and "in" the dream world at the same time, then this double perspective can be evoked through the representation of movement *and* nonmovement. While the representation of inhibited movement (nonfluidity, repetition, backward flow, stretching) refers back to the dreamer's body affected by sleep paralysis, Cooper's movement (which succeeds despite of the manipulations) alludes to the dreamer's identification with the agile virtual body of his dream ego, which is free to move about in the dream world. The recurring threatful knock heightens the tension between those two poles: biologically hardwired to escape potential danger, the viewer's impulse to *move away* is denied on several levels. First, Cooper, with whom we identify, does not escape—we are not granted the satisfaction of car chase sequences here. Second, the viewer cannot escape in Cooper's place. Hence, our stillness while watching the scene is perceived as contributing to the relative stillness depicted on screen. And most importantly, the recurrence of the knocking, combined with the inhibited movement suggested by the editing, significantly increases this feeling of having to move away while being unable to do so. Following Schönhammer, one could say that we know this feeling because we know what it is like to be temporarily paralyzed during sleep, with our brains interpreting the paralysis *as* a dream scenario that revolves around movement.

A further aspect that intensifies the viewer's feeling of being trapped is constituted by the scene's set design and the image's visual appearance. Similar to the Red Room in season one, production designer Ruth De Jong creates the impression of an *inside*, with thick stone walls and no doors or windows (except for the one through which Cooper gets in). The artificiality, a result of an unusual combination of objects as well as a geometrically shaped floor in the Red Room, is now evoked through a distorted color palette, with the light sources (e.g., an open fire) plunging the room into different shades of purple. Also, the bright surfaces have a shininess to them, which further reduces naturalness (see Figure 5.3). Interestingly, as soon as space opens up—Cooper and Naido climb up a ladder and reach the top of a small-sized "box" floating in outer space—the manipulation of movement stops. Time changes as a function of space here: the characters' movements are naturalized as they are no longer part of the interior's claustrophobic atmosphere. When Cooper climbs back down by himself after a while, colors are natural and there are no temporal manipulations in the flow of images.

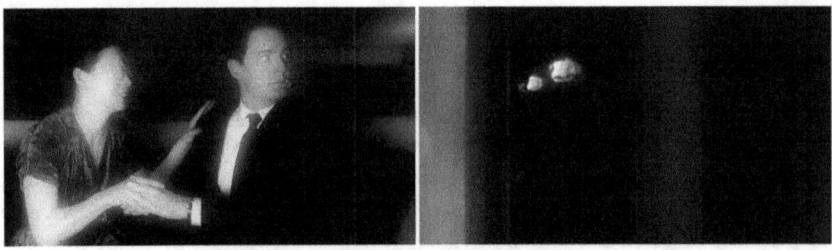

Figures 5.3–5.4 A play between visibility and invisibility in *Twin Peaks*' (2017) "Part 3: Call for Help" (00:06:33–00:06:40).

Instead, the speech of the American Girl matches the Red Room's proper temporality. The manipulations, thus, seem to have been the result of the copresence of Cooper and Naido *in* that room.

I would like to come back to Deleuze's suggestion concerning the absence of a sensory-motor scheme in the time-image. In regard to the scene at the mauve building, it might be worth specifying that a sensory-motor identification is not simply "impossible," but the scene problematizes it by provoking the viewer's inner co-motion while denying it at the same time. An analogy between the way in which the scene deals with the dynamics of *movement–nonmovement* and *visibility–invisibility* now becomes apparent. In regard to the latter, the aesthetics reflects Naido's access to the world in a disturbing way: seeing does not reveal but provides us with a glimpse of the elusive. The scene urges the viewer to *see* and *move with* what happens in the on-screen scenario, yet it points to the shortcoming of these acts, problematizing their functioning. What the acts aim at—*seeing* leading to recognition, (self-)movement leading to a change of position—is obstructed by the manipulations.

The Convenience Store
Oneiric Implications of the Narrative and Formal-Aesthetic Context

The scene at the Convenience Store ("Part 8" 00:21:27–00:24:10) is not explicitly marked as a dream. There are, however, elements connecting it to the dream theme, which runs through the whole series. The Convenience Store is first mentioned in Cooper's dream in season one ("Episode 2"). In the hypnagogic phase, Phillip Gerard says that when he and Bob were killing together, they lived *above a Convenience Store* ("Episode 2" 00:41:19–00:41:30). In the most perplexing sequence of the film prequel *Twin Peaks: Fire Walk with Me* (1992), FBI agent Phillip Jeffries (David Bowie) participates in a meeting taking place above the Convenience Store, where spiritual creatures like Bob and the Arm feed on "garmonbozia," which, in the series' mythology, symbolizes human pain and sorrow. Recalling the meeting at the FBI headquarters in Philadelphia, Jeffries screams that "it was a dream . . . we live inside a dream" before he disappears mysteriously (*Twin Peaks: Fire Walk with Me* 00:29:40–00:29:47). This sequence (00:27:05–00:31:24) deserves a closer look because it stands out not only in the film but is also essential to the ontology of the *Twin Peaks* universe as a whole.

At the Philadelphia office, Cooper tells FBI chief Gordon Cole (David Lynch) the exact date and time, adding that he was "worried about today because of the dream I told you about" (00:27:20–00:27:24). Cooper then tests the functioning of a surveillance camera in the hallway. He stands in front of it and then checks its image on a screen. Showing an empty hallway after Cooper left, it seems to work just fine. The second time he repeats this, Phillip Jeffries passes through the hallway just after Cooper left for the monitoring room. Curiously, in the image on the monitor that Cooper looks at, that same Cooper is still standing in front of the camera as Jeffries passes by. Then, everybody meets in Cole's office. Cole wants to introduce Cooper to Jeffries, who has been missing for almost two years. Jeffries, however, is visibly upset, points at Cooper, and asks Cole, "who do you think this is there?" (*Twin Peaks: Fire Walk with Me* 00:28:58–00:29:01). With static superimposed on the screen, an enigmatic long-nosed figure appears and brings us to a meeting between some of *Twin Peaks*' supernatural spirits. Attended by Jeffries, the meeting took place "above a Convenience Store" (00:30:06–00:30:09). Most likely, we see what Jeffries tells Cole, Albert (Miguel Ferrer), and Cooper, with snippets of his monologue interspersed throughout the scene. He calls out, "it was a dream ... we live inside a dream" (00:29:33–00:29:40). Moments later, he vanishes, and the front desk insists that "he was never here" (00:30:52–00:30:54), although he does appear on the surveillance camera footage. The scene set above the store feels like an extension of the Red Room from Cooper's dream in season one. But its ontological implications are far more radical, given that they tackle questions of the diegetic reality as a function of questioning the camera's (both the surveillance camera's and the film camera's) act of looking.

"A kaleidoscopic montage of images and sounds," Thorne calls the sequence "so bizarre that it seems impossible to reconcile it with any waking 'reality'" (310). Moreover, it is edited "as if the dreaming mind of Dale Cooper is receiving this information and his mind is struggling to process it" (Thorne 312). One of the questions such an interpretation leaves open, however, is why the scene would use the same blue static as in the film's opening if that were the case. If we were inside Cooper's dreaming mind, the meaning of the static would be unclear, the reference to the film's beginning confusing. Thorne's interpretation ignores the self-reflexivity by which, on the one hand, the dream meeting above the Convenience Store is introduced, and, on the other hand, the film questions the reliability of its own act of viewing.[20] As the sequence is externally focalized, the static assumes a crucial role in how it marks the ontological struggle of *Twin Peaks*' reality planes, as well as hinting at the instability of its diegetic reality. That is, it introduces us to the dreamt "supernatural" meeting above the Convenience Store. However, particularly through the way in which more intense short intervals of static frame the images of Jeffries at the FBI office, his presence— and the film's objectivity in making him visible—is radically put into question. He appears on the surveillance camera footage; we can see him walking into the office— yet "he was never here" (*Twin Peaks: Fire Walk with Me* 00:30:52–00:30:54). The scene is paradoxical until we understand it as questioning the reliability of its own act of viewing. He "was there" only in the sense that he was present to someone's (or in the case of the camera some-*thing*'s) act of seeing him.[21] In that logic, he "was not there" to the front desk *because* they did not see him. Curiously, the viewer never gets to see the front desk, so its judgment is ironically undermined by its absence to the camera lens. Through the potential discrepancy between what *is* and what *seems*, the visual perception of human beings, on the one hand, and that of films, on the other, are thus equated in their susceptibility to illusion and are, in this sense, prone to dreaming ("we live inside a dream"; 00:29:35–00:29:40).

Showing how the (surveillance) camera performs what the characters and viewers do—that is, *seeing*—the sequence illustrates one of Sobchak's crucial observations in regard to the film experience in general. In her words: "The camera its perceptive organ, the projector its expressive organ, the screen its discrete and material occupation of worldly space, the cinema exists as a visible performance of the perceptive and expressive structure of the lived-body experience" (Sobchak, *Address* 299). In the scene of Lynch's film, there are two categories of vision involved: (1) the human experience of vision, for example, when Cooper looks into the camera or the coworker watches the surveillance screen (human vision is explicitly represented on the film's "textual" level); and (2) technologically enabled vision, which again subdivides into two types: (a) the vision of the video surveillance system (also explicitly represented on a "textual" level) and (b) the film camera's vision (implicitly performed on a "formal" level). The surveillance system splits up visual perception into two components, the camera representing the (act of) viewing and the screen representing the "viewed," that is, the content of this perception. The mismatch between these two components constitutes the scene's disruptive momentum, in the context of which the phenomenon of dreaming becomes relevant. The dream fills in the gap opened up by the mismatch. In regard to the whole film, Seesslen speaks of "the attempt to enable a pluralized vision within the same image" (136; my translation),[22] which seems particularly true for the impossible doubling of Cooper at the FBI headquarters. The scene's dream perspective, one could say, allows for the two contradictory perceptions to coexist in a single image, without prioritizing one over the other.[23]

Jeffries's experience in the room above the Convenience Store is directly related to his view that "we live inside a dream." The scene directly translates the incompatibility of this assumption with that of an objectively existing world in a cinematic way by calling into question the camera's capacity to represent the world objectively. Although this remains without a consequence for the rest of *Twin Peaks: Fire Walk with Me* (in the main part of the film, the existence of the diegetic reality is not undermined by the dream sequences, such as Laura's dream), it lays the foundation for the ontology of season three (cf. section "The Dream as a Psychological and Ontological Phenomenon") as well as for the audiovisual presentation of the Convenience Store itself (cf. section "The Oneiric as Audiovisual Disruption").

In Part 8 itself, the scene at the Convenience Store is part of a forty-two-minute flashback sequence that opens with an image of the first detonation of an atomic bomb in July 1945 in New Mexico (see Figure 5.6). Coauthor Frost describes the sequence as "a 'Twin Peaks' origin story, [showing] where this pervasive sense of darkness and evil had come from" (R. Reed). Curiously, the atomic bomb sequence is initiated by cutting back to Bad Cooper after a concert of the Nine Inch Nails at the Roadhouse (00:11:28–00:16:07). At the beginning of the episode, he was shot down by his partner Ray (George Griffith) and then saved from death in a kind of supernatural intervention by the "woodsmen," the sooty men in lumberjack shirts who act as helpers for the dark Black Lodge (00:07:14–00:10:50). Bad Cooper awakes from his comatose state and rushes up (see Figure 5.5). His eyes, only slowly opening after he has been sitting upright for a moment, do not yet seem to fixate anything in his physical environment but suggest that he is still occupied by an "overhang" from sleep. This raises the question whether the following atomic bomb sequence represents what he just saw in his dream. Did Bad Cooper, possessed by the evil spirit Bob, dream up his own "origin story?" The idea imposes itself, because if no connection to Bad Cooper was intended, why would he be seen again immediately before the flashback sequence, waking up from the coma? This being said, a literal interpretation of the sequence as Bad Cooper's dream should be relativized on several grounds.

First of all, there is no end marker to the alleged "dream" or, to be more specific, no end marker that would link the sequence *to Bad Cooper* as the dreamer. At the end of the episode, the woodsmen descend to earth in 1956 New Mexico (where the atomic test took place earlier) to punish humanity for using the atomic bomb. One of them (Robert Broski) captures a radio station, crushes the host's skull, and recites a hypnotic poem that lets the radio listeners lose consciousness upon hearing his words. In the episode's final shot, a young girl (Tikaeni Faircrest) falls victim to the curse. Frost's novel *Twin Peaks: The Final Dossier* identifies her as the

Figures 5.5–5.7 Possible dream markers at the beginning and end of the flashback sequence in Part 8 (00:16:20; 00:17:59; 00:54:40).

young Sarah Novack (later Sarah Palmer; 136)—Laura's mother—but the episode's credits do not give her character's name. Lying in bed, she is listening to the radio until the woodsman's curse causes her to fall asleep while a large insect—Lynch calls it a "frog-moth" (Cruz)—crawls into her mouth (see Figure 5.7). Might the entire flashback sequence be understood as *her* dream instead of Bad Cooper's? Cooper finds out in season two that he and Laura had the same dream involving the dancing Man from Another Place ("Episode 16" 00:08:50–00:09:47), so in the world of *Twin Peaks*, Bad Cooper and the girl could "share" the dream that makes up most of Part 8.

But is it plausible to see the sequence as a literal representation of the characters' dream? The additional information from Frost's book is interesting precisely because it hints at the *actual* origin of Sarah Palmer's trauma (which goes beyond the continuing grief over the loss of her child and husband). If the whole flashback sequence was just the dream of her younger self, then it loses its narrative relevance. Interpreting the sequence as a literal representation of Bad Cooper's dream, it equally loses its attractiveness. The sequence's narrative potential consists in the way it sketches a possible scenario for how Bob actually came into the diegesis of the show. Reducing it to the status of a figment in Bad Cooper's mind would mean to relativize the significance of the atomic bomb for Bob's coming into being and would weaken the reprehension of the bomb's use that is inherent in the episode's conception. By choosing the first detonation of an atomic bomb, that is, a real-life historical event (even the exact date, time, and location are given on the screen; 00:16:46), Lynch and Frost do the exact opposite: they give additional weight to the sequence, as their fictional story is historicized to some extent. Weaving the story of *Twin Peaks* into the moral fabric of *this* world, Bob's existence is put on a par with the use of nuclear weapons. Bob's horrendous acts, the murder and rape we saw in the old *Twin Peaks* seasons and the film, reflect back on the atomic bomb, implying a condemnation of its use. Most importantly, the root of all evil in the world of *Twin Peaks* is not identified as metaphysical but as human; this is what the post-Convenience Store image expresses: as a reaction to the nuclear test, an abstracted human figure (credited as "Experiment") vomits Bob into the world. Humanity, by using the bomb, "called for" something as terrible as Bob, who stands as the ultimate personification of human evil in the series' mythology. Rather than being the sole product of Bad Cooper's subjectivity, the images have a quasi-objective allure. It seems as if, in a liminal state between life and death, Bad Cooper gained a glimpse of Bob's (hence his own) "actual" birth.

The Oneiric as Audiovisual Disruption

Hence, to see Part 8's flashback sequence as a literal representation of the characters' dream does not seem to make much sense, even if the possibility of such an interpretation is opened up by how the sequence is embedded. And yet, the dream figures as the most important hermeneutic concept, putting the scene at the Convenience Store into context. As mentioned before, the dream functions as an act of disruption in the narrative and diegesis of the new *Twin Peaks* (2017). When Cooper realizes that "we live inside a dream" in Part 17, this does not only refer back to his strange encounter with the eyeless woman in the room above the purple sea but is also a quote of Jeffries's Convenience Store-related utterance from the film *Twin Peaks: Fire Walk with Me*. Arguably, the narrative disruption entailed by Cooper's dream realization (cf. "Part 18: What Is Your Name?") is translated into filmic form most purely by the Convenience Store scene in Part 8, given the way in which it is presented to the viewer as a sensory intensity.

The image stutters and jumps like a bumpy time lapse that eludes any law or regularity; the image's own mediality is thematized here by giving the impression that the digital reproduction is disturbed. It could be called "grotesque," following Annie van den Oever's view that "the experience of the grotesque [. . .] is not merely or exclusively a perceptual experience of grotesque (fused, hybrid, monstrous) beings; it is, more fundamentally, an experience of the distorting powers of the new technologies themselves effectively 'working' on the percipients in the perceptual process and destabilizing their notion of images, representations, beings and meanings" (101–2). The flashes of light, the constant defocusing and refocusing, the use of still images, and the resulting corrupted flow of time create discomfort, in that temporal fragments seem to be "skipped over" and cannot be perceived (cf. Basso Fossali 48 and section "Animation, Pixilation, and Trauma" in Chapter 3). The sound level is of enormous importance here: according to Michel Chion, Lynch's "sound cuts [. . .] achieve an inscription into time, amounting to a creation of time by a director" (*Lynch* 42). This general description seems to resonate with Gamper and Hühn's concept of *aesthetic proper time* and appears to be confirmed here. In *Eraserhead*, organ music transformed dream time into a rhythmic structure, distinguishing it from the nonmusical soundscape of the waking sequences (cf. section "Phenomenologizing the Unconscious" in Chapter 4). At the Convenience Store, to the contrary, the acoustic dimension does not provide any structure. The sound cuts, perfectly synchronized with the visual editing, disorient the viewer and are hectic through their arrhythmic succession. One might argue that the sequence constitutes the peak of disruption because the sound level is now unified with the image in their susceptibility to the same underlying source of disturbance. The effect is twofold: on the noematic level, the Convenience Store eludes a natural way of representation and perception and thus shows its *super*-natural character; on the noetic level, the ontological disruption works phenomenologically, in that the scene runs counter to an organic (i.e., a continuous, gliding) perception of movement and thus makes our sensory-motor identification with figures or camera movement impossible. This presents an alienation of our normal perception of time and movement, which results from the technical manipulation possibilities of film (especially digital postproduction). Recalling Šklovskij, van den Oever speaks of grotesque imagery's "profound deautomatisation of perception and a destabilisation of the ontological status of the image" (100).

Unlike in the scene at the mauve building in Part 3 (see previous section), narration comes to a complete halt at the Convenience Store. Whereas the former created the impression of the image always being "on the brink of becoming," the tension created by the latter is entirely phenomenal. It does not have any narrative dimension that would create an urge to know "what happens next." Accordingly, a sensory-motor link between the viewer's body and the bodies represented on the screen seems entirely impossible, which makes for the "purely optical and sound situation" of the time-image (Deleuze 272). Since the viewer is unable to "pick out" a body whose movement would provide orientation within the depicted space, she does not identify with any of the characters. At the mauve building, even if sensory-motor identification was problematized due to the manipulations, the viewer wanted Cooper and Naido to *get somewhere*, that is, to escape the menacing pounding, which implied the identification with the characters' bodies. In this, the shot size and the question of camera movements was also of importance: the scene at the mauve building consisted of many (medium) close-ups and contained camera movements, while the static long shots of the Convenience Store further inhibit the identification of or with a character on screen.

To sum up, the Convenience Store was first mentioned in a dream; it lets Jeffries come to believe that "we live inside a dream" (after which he mysteriously disappears); it is part of a sequence that hints at the possibility of a dreamer at the beginning (Bad Cooper) and end (the girl that could be young Sarah Palmer in 1956); and its direct audiovisual presentation constitutes an act of disruption that is "dreamlike" in the sense that the dream functions as an ontological disruption with respect to the narrative of season three as a whole.

"The Dream of Time and Space"—*Twin Peaks* as Oneiric Disruption of Space-Time

The Dream as a Psychological and Ontological Phenomenon

Now it is time to explore an idea that has been implicitly presupposed in the last two sections, that is, the view that in *Twin Peaks* (2017), the dream functions as an ontological disruption. In the first two seasons of the series, the dream was introduced as a psychological phenomenon, even if it bore some epistemological peculiarities. Sarah Palmer's visions and Cooper's dreams, for example, were connected—they both saw the same Bob (cf. "Episode 1: Traces to Nowhere" 00:32:20–00:32:26 and "Episode 2" 00:42:02–00:42:30). Cooper dreamt the same dream Laura did the night before she died ("Episode 16" 00:08:50–00:09:47). And after all, the Black Lodge, originally thought to be a purely subjective space, is found to have a quasi-objective existence by the end of season two, where Earle, Annie, and Cooper are able to enter it due to the temporary alignment of Jupiter and Saturn ("Episode 29" 00:08:40–00:09:00 and 00:17:51–00:18:19). Even in the first two seasons, the dream, one might argue, is not an entirely inner, psychological phenomenon, because it accesses another plane of objective reality. Cooper's dream, in this sense, presents a metaphysical experience. But even if the Black Lodge exists outside of dreams, the "common" reality of Twin Peaks is not put into question by that. In seasons one and two, the town of Twin Peaks is a place where the intersubjective reality (where Laura was killed and where Cooper investigates her murder) collides with the metaphysical Black Lodge (where the Arm and "Laura"—or her cousin—are and that Cooper first accesses through his dream). The dream world is an *additional*, a coexisting reality to the side of the intersubjective one. When Donna says that "maybe our dreams are real" ("Episode 12: The Orchid's Curse" 00:13:38–00:13:41), this is just a cheesy line of dialogue without any deeper implications for the diegesis. This changes in season three.

In Part 16, Cooper awakens from his trance-like state in which he lived the life of Las Vegas insurance broker Dougie Jones. He travels to the Twin Peaks Sheriff Station. Thanks to Lucy Brennan (Kimmy Robertson) and Freddie Skyes (Jake Wardle), Cooper's evil doppelgänger is defeated ("Part 17"). Cooper puts the ring on the dead doppelgänger's hand, which lets him disappear, while the ring is transported to the Black Lodge. As Cooper's face is subtly superimposed on the screen, Cooper catches sight of Naido, who has been found in the woods after her fall into the void in Part 3. She approaches Cooper and places her hand against his. The flesh of her face is transformed, first revealing the Black Lodge and then changing her into the missing FBI secretary Diane Evans (Laura Dern; 00:32:26–00:33:12; see Figure 5.8). Diane and Cooper kiss, and she tells him that she "remembers everything" ("Part 17" 00:34:10–00:34:18). By now, several of the most important characters of season three have gathered at the Sheriff Station, among them the FBI and police team and the Mitchum brothers. As the minute hand on the clock moves back and forth between 2:53 and 2:52, Cooper's superimposed face says that "we live inside a dream" in a dark and distorted voice ("Part 17" 00:34:38–00:34:42; see fig. 57). Cooper says that he hopes to see everybody again. Gordon and Cooper call out each other's names as the room goes dark, leaving only Cooper's transparent face on the screen.

Figure 5.8 Cooper's realization that "we live inside a dream" in Part 17 (00:34:47).

Next, we see Cooper, Diane, and Cole walking through a pitch-black space that makes it impossible to say where they are. They get to a door which is unlocked by Cooper's old key to his room at the Great Northern Hotel (but the door is definitely not at that hotel). Cooper tells the two of them not to follow him and, hinting at the possibility that everything has been a performance, tells Diane, "see you at the curtain call" (00:37:09–00:37:12). The door falls into the lock in a halting slow motion. Cooper walks through a completely dark space again. He meets Mike/Phillip Gerard, who recites the poem we first heard in Cooper's dream in season one:

Through the darkness of future past
The magician longs to see.
One chants out between two worlds
Fire walk with me. ("Part 17" 00:37:42–00:38:03)

Phillip Gerard and Cooper are passing by two places connected to transgressions of reality witnessed earlier in the series and the 1992 film: the stairs they walk up are connected to the woodsmen, as becomes clear through an interdimensional spiral opening up in the sky in "Part 11: There's Fire Where You Are Going" (00:12:00–00:13:36); the parking lot they cross recalls a similar one in a scene of *Twin Peaks: Fire Walk with Me* in which a young boy with a long-nosed mask (Jonathan J. Leppell) walks and jumps in circles and then just disappears in the frame (01:30:48–01:31:05). Phillip Gerard and Cooper then get to a human-sized tea kettle, which embodies the FBI agent Phillip Jeffries. The tea kettle sends Cooper back to February 23, 1989, the night Laura Palmer died ("Part 17" 00:42:34–00:43:55). The image is in black and white now. Cooper witnesses a scene that was part of Lynch's 1992 film. Laura and her lover James Hurley (James Marshall) are having an argument that ends with Laura escaping into the woods. In *Twin Peaks: Fire Walk with Me*, which presents the "actual" series of events leading to Laura's death, she finds Leo Johnson (Eric Da Re), Jacques Renault (Walter Olkewicz), and Ronette Pulaski (Phoebe Augustine) there (01:58:37). They go to Leo's cabin, from which the girls are abducted by Leland Palmer (Ray Wise). Ronette escapes, but Laura is killed by her father in a train car. In Part 17, however, Cooper intervenes to save Laura (00:48:53–00:51:25). He thus fulfills the mission of Leland Palmer who told him to "find Laura" in Part 2 (00:42:50–00:42:57). Shown in a slightly low-angled shot, Cooper, "the hero," waits for Laura in the woods to prevent her death (see Figures 5.9 and 5.10). Laura realizes that she has seen him before in her dream (cf. "Episode 2" 00:40:05–00:46:50).

It seems as if the series tried to erase itself as it approaches the end: Laura's murder, that is, the central event upon which the whole story of *Twin Peaks* is based, is prevented. Intercut with Laura taking Cooper's hand is footage from the original pilot in which her corpse has been cast ashore. Crucially, however, Laura's corpse is now digitally removed from the shore (see Figures 5.11 and 5.12).

Taking her hand, Cooper tells her that "we're going home," as the image changes from black-and-white to color, indicating that the past has been altered ("Part 17" 00:51:08–00:51:11). This is only the second time in the third season that we hear

Figures 5.9–5.10 Cooper's attempt to save Laura ("Part 17" 00:50:13; 00:50:28).

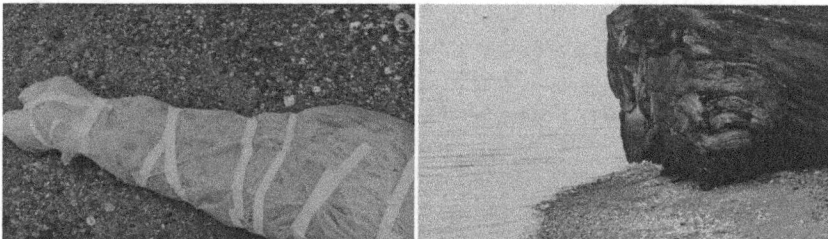

Figures 5.11–5.12 Laura's corpse being removed from the shore ("Part 17" 00:50:35; 00:50:53).

Badalamenti's *Laura Palmer's Theme*, and it serves to increase the emotionality of Laura's changed fate. Her tragic fate, evoked through the music in the early seasons, is now reinterpreted due to the same musical theme being used. The opening images from the original pilot are then recast: Josie Packard (Joan Chen) looks at herself in the mirror, Pete Martell (Jack Nance) goes fishing (00:51:19–00:52:35)—the difference being that now there is nothing for Pete to find and the premise of the narrative has vanished into thin air.

If season three ended at this point, the viewer would get a kind of happy ending, which would even hint at some Hollywood stereotypes. After his evil doppelgänger is defeated, Cooper realizes that "life is a dream" such that, like in lucid dreaming, everything becomes manipulable according to the dreamer's—that is, *his*—will. Our male hero travels back in time to save a desperate girl who would have been the victim of a horrible crime. The satisfied viewer could lean back now, identifying with the seemingly omnipotent protagonist of the series. But the series does not end here. Intercut with the scene of Cooper leading Laura through the woods is a scene set at the Palmer's house, that is, Laura's *home* (hence a possible hint at what Cooper referred to when he just told Laura that they are going "home" 00:52:36–00:54:30) in the present. We are in the living room. Sarah, Laura's mother, can be heard wailing in the distant. Pills, filled ashtrays, bottles of alcohol, and a framed picture of Laura can be seen on the tables. The image is relatively dark. An intensely ominous atmosphere is evoked by the combination of Sarah's wailing and the continuous low, whooshing sound. Over more than one minute, the camera moves only very slightly, which is essential to the creation of emotional tension. Similar to the horrifying scene in which the son is killed in *Funny Games* (1997), an emotional intensity fills up the space due to the reduction of camera movement. In Michael Haneke's film, the camera remains completely static for several minutes, as if *it* was traumatized by what just happened, unable to move due to a state of shock-induced paralysis. Though the camera executes minimal movement, traumatization due to losing one's child also informs the scene in Part 17 of *Twin Peaks* (2017), as becomes clear when Sarah takes Laura's photo, grabs a glass bottle, and smashes the glass on it while continuing to wail. We then cut back to Cooper leading Laura through the woods, holding her hand. At one point, the wide soundscape is narrowed to a soft scratching noise[24] and, as Cooper turns around, Laura is gone (00:55:32)—only her intense scream can be heard. Cooper is not the protagonist of a lucid dream but the subject of a nightmare whose nature he fails to understand.

The scene set in Sarah Palmer's living room thus functions as the turning point in Cooper's attempt to save Laura. It is interesting that an image of Sarah Palmer is chosen as the expression of the impossibility to change the past. In her character, the trauma of Laura's tragic death lives on. Out of all the characters in the series, she continues suffering from her daughter's death most visibly. Her brokenness is palpable in every scene she appears in in *Twin Peaks* (2017). Crucially, her trauma cannot be overcome by smashing Laura's photo; it cannot be reversed, as expressed by the sound loop. In a causal interpretation of the montage, the scene's embeddedness suggests the irreversibility of trauma as the reason why Cooper is unable to save Laura. The reason why "the past dictates the future" (cf. the episode's title), thus, is a psychological one. Interestingly, despite all the play on the reversibility of time, this turning point reflects the causal order of reality. *The past dictates the future*, but not in a deterministic sense, rather in an existential one: actions and events have consequences and are not reversible. Ultimately, the realm of art does not offer an escape from this fundamental aspect of reality but rather echoes it. The causality of "real-world" mental experiences, that is, the irreversibility of trauma, seeps into the fantastical attempt to change the past, which could only be possible in stories—stories that satisfy our tendency for escapism. *Twin Peaks* (2017) does the exact opposite.

Throughout his career, Lynch has shown a keen interest in that moment where "reality" breaks into fantasy. In *The Alphabet* (1968), a nightmare confronts a young girl with her real fear of learning the letters of the alphabet after she fantasizes about an ideal, naturalized evolution of the alphabet. After the boy in *The Grandmother* (1970) creates his ideal fantasy object, that is, the title-giving grandmother who cares about him, he realizes in a daydream that she does not exist. In *Lost Highway* (1997), Fred's dissociative fugue, that is, his escape into a fantasy world where he becomes Pete, cannot hide the fact that he killed his wife in real life. Similarly, in *Mulholland Drive* (2001), the dream stops when Diane's dream ego Betty finds the blue key in her purse; in Diane's waking reality, the key signals that the hitman she commissioned to kill her former lover Camilla finished the job. For all the significance that Lynch's films attribute to dreams, it is important to notice that their escapist tendency is always problematized and never uncritically celebrated by the narrative. In this sense, his art displays a rather *realist* interest in dreaming. Not conceiving of the dream as a pure "realm of possibility," it asks for the compensatory function of the dream, for the things inside the characters that the dream tries to—but eventually cannot—hide.

Whether it is just a *principle* of reality (i.e., the irreversibility of trauma) or "reality itself" breaking into fantasy in the last two episodes of *Twin Peaks* (2017) is a subject up for debate. As the narrative time approaches its end with the end of the seventeenth out of eighteen episodes, one could argue, the diegetic break following Cooper's *we live inside a dream* anticipates the transition from film experience to world experience that fans necessarily go through with the end of the last episode. Accordingly, the series could be said to anticipate within its narrative the fact that it cannot continue beyond its own end. As some features of Part 18 show, it is this border in particular that is to be thematized here, that is, the border between the fictional world of the *Twin Peaks* characters and the "real" world of the audience.

But first, it seems necessary to recall the main plot of Part 18. The importance of the mentioned scene of Cooper losing Laura in the woods at the end of Part 17 is such that Lynch repeats it at the beginning of Part 18 (00:03:19–00:04:37). After losing her, Cooper is transported into the Red Room, where yet another scene is repeated, this time from Part 2 ("Part 18" 00:04:38–00:05:03; "Part 2" 00:15:25–00:15:50). Phillip Gerard asks Cooper, "Is it future or is it past?" The precise repetition of the scene,[25] including the short halt at the beginning, may suggest that what played out between that moment in Part 2 and the corresponding one in Part 18 was a merely *possible* scenario, not what "actually" (must have) happened—Part 2 is called "The Stars Turn and *a* Time Presents itself" (my italicization), not ". . . and *Time* Presents itself"; the indefinite article stresses the contingency of the unfolding events as opposed to their absoluteness. This view may lead to the assumption that whatever comes next will be yet another merely possible course of events.

The rest of the episode could be seen in light of the question posed by the evolution of the Arm: "Is it the story of the little girl who lived down the lane?" (00:06:29–00:06:44; a further intratextual reference to Part 13). One of the interpretative frameworks clearly provoked by this explicit self-reflexivity is the deconstruction of the myth of the male hero. Cooper meets Diane and they cross over into another dimension. They stop at a motel, where they have sex. When Cooper wakes up in the morning, Diane left and he finds a note addressed to "Richard" signed by "Linda."[26] The motel and car are different from when they arrived. In Odessa, Texas, Cooper/Richard has breakfast at a place called "Eat at Judy's" (he chooses this place because the name Judy refers to a powerful, mysterious, dark entity in the *Twin Peaks* universe). He asks the waitress if there is another woman working at Judy's, which she confirms. When the waitress is harassed by three men wearing cowboy hats, Cooper/Richard stops them in an unnecessarily violent manner. "Protecting the woman," he shoots one of the men in the foot and kicks another one in the genitals. Out of fear rather than gratefulness, the waitress gives Cooper/Richard the name and address of her colleague, a woman named Carrie Page (Sheryl Lee) who looks exactly like Laura Palmer. Cooper/Richard is convinced that Carrie is Laura and, wanting to keep his promise and take Laura home—even in another dimension—drives her to Twin Peaks. Once they get to "her parents' house," a woman named Alice Tremond (Mary Reber) opens the door. Sarah Palmer neither lives there nor does Ms. Tremond know her. On their way back to the car, Cooper/Richard and Laura/Carrie stop to turn around and look at the house again. Cooper/Richard is baffled by something and asks: "What year is this?" ("Part 18" 00:54:02–00:54:04). Sarah Palmer's distorted voice can be heard faintly, shouting "Laura!" and Laura's/Carrie's intense scream concludes the series (00:54:23–00:54:56). Instead of saving her, thus, Cooper/Richard takes her back to the place where the violence of *Twin Peaks* originated from, that is, the Palmer's house (Laura was a victim of domestic abuse).[27] In this way, Cooper/Richard reinstalls her trauma instead of relieving her from it. With the credits rolling, we see a subtly superimposed black-and-white image of Laura whispering into Cooper's ear in the Red Room (see Figure 5.13), an image recast from Part 2 (see Figure 5.14), which in itself has already been a self-quotation of Cooper's dream in Episode 2 of the first season (see Figure 5.16). The background image of the closing credits thus raises the possibility that the narration is caught in a time loop.[28]

Coming back to the question of the ontological status of the events occurring after Cooper/Richard wakes up in Part 18, it may be worth considering some elements that could be interpreted as "reality markers" in the episode. First of all, the Odessa sign shown in *Twin Peaks* appears to be a real street sign that could really be found in the city of Odessa, Texas. No such thing can be said of the Twin Peaks sign in the opening credits of the original series (the image is recast in Part 1 of season three), not least because there is no real town called Twin Peaks. A similar observation can be made about the gas station appearing in Part 18. The Valero gas station Cooper/Richard

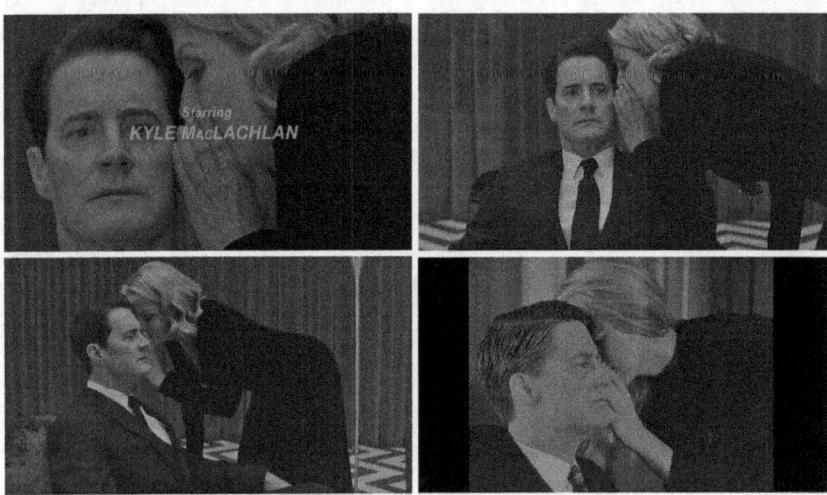

Figures 5.13–5.16 A dream circle of suffering and pain? ("Part 18" 00:55:38; "Part 2" 00:21:12 and 00:21:08; "Episode 2" 00:46:37; top left to bottom right).

Figures 5.17–5.18 The gas station in Part 18 (left; 00:44:24) and Big Ed's Gas Farm (right; "Pilot" 00:44:24).

and Laura/Carrie stop at on the way to Twin Peaks is as close to a real gas station as possible. Again, the verisimilitude stands in contrast to the previously featured "Big Ed's Gas Farm" (see Figures 5.17 and 5.18).

The proximity to the nonfictional "real" world extends to the level of the characters. Alice Tremond is not played by a professional actress but by Mary Reber, who now lives in the house in Everett (Washington) that was used as a shooting location for *Twin Peaks* (1990–1). Further, Cooper/Richard is now deprived of his charm, his eloquence, and his wit. He appears cold and indifferent and no longer has the traits that made him Dale Cooper, the protagonist of *Twin Peaks* (see Figure 5.19). Even coffee, once Cooper's great passion, has no particular fascination to him anymore. His idiosyncrasies and his sense of humor have disappeared. He seems "unformed" in a way, with nothing left that would turn him into a(ny) fictional character. In regard to time, there is the long, quiet, uneventful drive through the night, taking up nine minutes of screen time ("Part 18" 00:38.54–00:47:53). Drama and aesthetics are reduced to a minimum here. Upon a glimpse of action—another car's headlights hint at the possibility that they might be followed (00:41:07–00:42:00)—nothing happens, as the car just leaves the highway. We do *not* hear the *Twin Peaks* theme as Cooper and Carrie arrive in the small town; we do not even see a sign that would confirm that the town of Twin Peaks, as it appears in Part 18, exists on this diegetic level. No material (dialogue or anything else) is condensed or even processed into a conflict. Rather, the narrative time approaches the narrated time—following Sobchak, one might speak of the domination of the objective modality of time due to minimized subjective investment. Recalling the final sequence of Michelangelo Antonioni's *L'Eclisse* (1962), it is as if the already impalpable narrator of the series wanted to dissolve completely here: time, as it appears to someone during a long drive, becomes perceptible in the film experience to some extent. In the context of these observations, it is important to note that all the fantastical elements, around which so much of the third season revolved, have disappeared in the Cooper/Richard–Laura/Carrie section of Part 18. There is no Black or White Lodge, no nonlinear time flow, there are no mythological creatures or spirits, no interdimensional portals, and so on.

Based on these observations, one might argue that it is our nonmedial, external, waking world that is represented here as unfiltered as possible. That the episode does

Figure 5.19 A changed Cooper in Part 18 (00:30:24).

not simply "take place" *in our reality*, however, is made clear by the reference to the name Tremond and Chalfont (these are known from the *Twin Peaks* universe), as well as by Carrie's deeply distressing final scream, in which she resembles Laura and which thus, affectively,[29] contains the entire fictional story of *Twin Peaks*. Her scream produces an ultimate "presence-effect" (cf. Gamper and Hühn 17–18) due to Cooper's previous question, "What year is this?" which, significantly, is *not* answered.[30] Section "Proper (Spatio-)temporality in Cooper's Dream ... " has shown that, from the viewers' perspective, Cooper's dream in Episode 2 combined the rational indeterminacy of the present with their sensual anchoring in *this* moment of the film experience. It is only at the very end of season three, though, that the temporal indeterminacy passes from the aesthetic to the textual level—the question as to the narrative present is raised but not answered. To be clear, we are in a new alternative reality here; the old one, as Cooper suggested in Part 17, had turned out to be a dream. If the present point in time, however, is equally indeterminable here—we know this from Cooper's *dream* but also from the scenes at the purple sea and at the Convenience Store—the question arises whether the end suggests that the oneiricity of the *Twin Peaks* world is insurmountable. The lack of knowledge about the present point in time indicates the existential emergency situation of Cooper/Richard and Laura/Carrie, who are deprived of any certainties concerning their identities (cf. the episode's title, "What Is Your Name?") and the nature of their reality. The apparent dream reality of Cooper and Laura stands in a conflicting relationship with the current reality of Richard and Linda. When Cooper/Richard wakes up in Part 18, seemingly everything has changed: the motel, his car, Diane's and Cooper's identities. But the dissonance between the diegesis of Part 18 and that of (the rest of) *Twin Peaks* is not resolved by identifying the latter as a "dream," at least not in the psychological sense.

In keeping with Lynch's aim to create a dreamlike experience through a film (cf. Rodley 15), however, Ludwig Binswanger's "conclusion" regarding the dream probably applies equally to film characters and viewers—"To dream means: I don't know what is happening to me" (102). This would mean that, even if the end of Part 18 does not involve a marked dream, the existential dread characteristic of the nightmare—Binswanger's "basic ontological element of all dreaming" (102)—lingers with the viewer, constituting the emotional resonance of the ending. Blending different planes of reality, Laura's/Carrie's final scream can be seen as the affective expression of *not knowing* and could hence be called dreamlike in Binswanger's sense. It "extracts" the emotional tension of the nightmare, not least because it is designed to disrupt the viewer's sense of familiarity with Part 18's diegesis. Even if the world of Part 18 in itself presents a strong alienation from the fictional universe created by the preceding forty-six episodes, it creates a new sense of familiarity with a new diegetic level that appears to be classifiable as the real world. In a second alienation, Laura's/Carrie's scream even breaks with this new sense of familiarity, as it picks up a motif that was essential to *Twin Peaks*, that is, *Laura Palmer's* screaming. The alleged waking reality of Richard and Carrie turns out to be neither a part of the *Twin Peaks* universe nor can it be seen as completely independent from it. Its ontological status indeterminable, Cooper/Richard and Laura/Carrie are caught in an "in-between-state"—they appear to be "between" the fictional *Twin Peaks* universe and the viewers' shared world—which recalls the line, "one chants out *between two worlds*" from Phillip Gerard's poem in Episode 2 of the old *Twin Peaks* (00:37:42–00:38:03). If the viewer thought she was able to grasp the ontological nature of what just happened in the Cooper/Richard–Laura/Carrie part of the episode, at the end she is forced to realize that, like a dreamer experiencing a nightmare, she is helplessly exposed to a world whose nature she does not understand.

But the view that the ending of season three is related to the dream is not solely based on hypothesizing about the meaning of Laura's/Carrie's scream, it is also suggested by the image that is gently superimposed as the closing credits roll. As mentioned before, the image constitutes an intratextual reference to both Part 2 (season three) and to Episode 2 (season one; see Figures 5.13–5.17). In the latter, it is part of Cooper's unambiguously marked dream. In the particular moment captured by the image, Laura whispers something into Cooper's ear. In season one, Cooper then wakes up and calls Harry, telling him that he now knows who killed Laura Palmer ("Episode 2" 00:46:51–00:47:21). Episode 2 ends with a big cliffhanger. The next morning, though, he confesses that he forgot who the killer was ("Episode 3: Rest in Pain"). In season two of *Twin Peaks*, Episode 16 picks up that dream moment, revealing that Laura whispered, "My father killed me" (00:30:36–00:30:42). Lynch was neither involved in writing nor in directing that episode,[31] and it is known that he was particularly averse to the idea of revealing Laura Palmer's killer. After all, the viewer's immersion in the world of *Twin Peaks* hinged upon the desire to know who Laura's killer was (Frank and Schleich 9–10; Rodley 180). The television network ABC, which produced the series, however, gave in to the pressure by the television audience, forcing Lynch and Frost to reveal the killer in the middle of season two (Rodley 180).[32] The result was that, in

Lynch's view, "the second season sucked" (Desta). He said that "we were never able to get going creatively" after the killer was revealed (Desta).

In the context of Lynch's frustration with ABC, his film *Twin Peaks: Fire Walk with Me* (1992), released only one year after season two, can be seen as a polemical response to the power of television networks—in the opening image, a TV is brutally smashed with an axe. Twenty-five years later, season three of *Twin Peaks* (2017) stands as a continuation of that impulse, which, in the spirit of auteur cinema, leaves full creative control over the production to Lynch and Frost, allowing them to reinterpret a crucial moment of the original series. To be sure, we could not hear what Laura whispered into Cooper's ear in Episode 2 of season one. Presumably, in the view of its creators, *Twin Peaks* sacrificed part of its artistic integrity by revealing Laura's killer in season two. Not only does Part 2 in season three reaffirm the inaudibility of what Laura whispers into Cooper's ear (00:21:01–00:21:09), but this moment is chosen as the very last image of the series—a symbolic image that reinstates the fundamental mystery of the show. Are we stuck in a time loop, still caught up in Cooper's and Laura's dream? What happened to Laura Palmer and why did she have to suffer? In terms of genre, thus, the series' ending comes full circle with its very beginning. The only certainty that remains consists in Laura's suffering—the mystery, particularly that of "who killed Laura Palmer," prevails.[33]

The Function of Gordon Cole's Dream of Monica Bellucci

As I have observed in regard to the end of season three, temporal and existential indeterminacy are intertwined. While the former is expressed by Cooper's/Richard's question, "What year is this?" the latter is implied by the question, "Who is the dreamer?" that Gordon Cole is asked in a dream—the only marked dream sequence in season three ("Part 14" 00:10:59–00:14:41). In Part 14, FBI director Gordon Cole (David Lynch) tells his two colleagues Albert Rosenfield (Miguel Ferrer) and Tammy Preston (Chrysta Bell) about his dream from the night before in which he met Monica Bellucci (Monica Bellucci) at a Paris café. "When we met at the café, Cooper was there. But I couldn't see his face. Monica was very pleasant. She had brought friends. We all had a coffee" ("Part 14" 00:11:38–00:12:01). As Cole is recalling his dream, the scene he describes is shown in black-and-white imagery, possibly testifying to the lack of affective intensity or immersion compared to the original impression of experiencing the dream. He continues: "And then she said the ancient phrase." Bellucci says, "We're like the dreamer who dreams and then lives inside the dream," with Gordon repeating it in his recollection of the scene (00:12:20–00:12:40). This "ancient phrase" is the direct quotation of a passage from the Upanishads, one which Lynch quotes in his 2006 book *Catching the Big Fish: Meditation, Consciousness, and Creativity*. Opening the chapter on his movie *Inland Empire* (2006) are these lines from Egenes's and Reddy's *Eternal Stories from the Upanishads*: "We are like the spider. We weave our life and then move along in it. We are like the dreamer who dreams and then lives in the dream. This is true for the entire universe" (Lynch, *Fish* 139; Egenes and Reddy 71).[34]

Up to this point, Bellucci's quote of this passage can be seen as her commitment to a constructivist worldview. There is a web (object of perception) and there is a spider (subject of perception), just like there is a dream and a dreamer. Instead of the web's "givenness," the spider's act of creation is responsible for its existence. The spider creates its own habitat. In the sphere of human experience, dreaming serves as the analogon: the dream world does not exist as a given but is created through (or merely consists in) the dreamer's activity of dreaming. Crucially, then, the dream—and the spider web as its symbolic, material manifestation—serves as a model for the description of the constructedness of reality ("This is true for the entire universe"). In a strong interpretation, reality does not exist *outside of* our act of perceiving it: *esse est percipi* ("to be is to be perceived"), as George Berkeley's philosophy suggests (cf. Downing). This view can easily be related to the ontology of film, particularly to vision and hearing, that is, the two primary sensory modalities through which film operates. A film, in Sobchak's view, exists as an "expression of experience by experience. A film is an act of seeing that makes itself seen, an act of hearing that makes itself heard" (Sobchak, *Address* 3); it has no essence, so to speak, outside of its visible (and audible) act of perception.

In a weak interpretation of Bellucci's utterance, the way we *relate to* the world is fundamentally dreamlike. The Log Lady's "watch and listen to the dream of time and space" ("Part 10" 00:45:40–00:45:48) establishes a connection between the act of perception (visual/auditory) and the dreamlike nature of what is perceived such that in a causal interpretation, what makes "the world" dreamlike is the act of perception that grants us access to it. Though the present chapter does not attempt to provide a critical evaluation of this hypothesis, it may be interesting to note that there is neuroscientific literature supporting the claim that perception is fundamentally dreamlike. Robert Llinás, for example, suggests that "wakefulness is nothing other than a dreamlike state constrained by external sensory inputs" (cf. E. Thompson 186). In his neurophysiological account, consciousness is generated through an ongoing dialogue between the thalamus and the cortex (E. Thompson 186). Whether we are awake or dreaming depends on the extent to which sensory input influences this dialogue (186). The participation of external sensory input in this dialogue generates waking perception, while its absence results in dreaming. From the brain's perspective, thus, "wakefulness is a case of dreaming with sensorimotor constraints, and dreaming is a case of perceiving without sensorimotor constraints" (187). In a similar vein, philosopher Thomas Metzinger writes:

> A fruitful way of looking at the brain is as a system which, even in the ordinary waking states, constantly hallucinates at the world, as a system that constantly lets its internal autonomous simulational dynamics collide with the ongoing flow of sensory input, vigorously *dreaming at the world and thereby generating the content of phenomenal experience*. (Metzinger qtd. in E. Thompson 188; my italicization)

Arguably, the Log Lady's imperative provokes a more radical interpretation, though. Due to the ambiguity of "of" in the phrase "the dream of time and space," one could understand it as suggesting that time and space are not the objects of the dream (whose dream we do not know) but the dreaming subjects, with us being merely passive onlookers; x is not dreaming time and space, but time and space are dreaming x. Though such an interpretation is incompatible with the idea of the dreamer as an active (spider-like) creator of the (web-like) dream world—a possible reason why the spider part is left out in the *Twin Peaks* episode—it speaks to the question Bellucci poses at the end of her monologue. Unlike in the Upanishads, what follows the words, "[w]e're like the dreamer who dreams and then lives inside the dream," is not the generalizing claim that "this is true for the entire universe" but the question, "but who is the dreamer?" ("Part 14" 00:12:17–00:12:44). Cole recalls that "a very powerful, uneasy feeling came over me" ("Part 14" 00:12:46–00:13:07). Given that we are in his dream, Bellucci's question obviously relates to his identity. *Who are you*, Monica asks Gordon; then, she "looked past me [Gordon Cole] and indicated to me to look back at something that was happening there" (00:13:07–00:13:15). As the next moments show, *past* and *back* have both a spatial and a temporal meaning here, which exemplifies the bodily basis for expressions of time.[35] Cole turns around. "I saw myself from long ago," continues Cole, as a beautiful 180° cut establishes a uniquely cinematographic moment of contact between a present-day Cole and his much younger self, a black-and-white rendition of footage from the film *Twin Peaks: Fire Walk with Me* ("Part 14" 00:13:15–00:13:30; see Figures 5.20 and 5.21). This part of Cole's dream brings us back to "the day Phillip Jeffries appeared, and didn't appear" ("Part 14" 00:13:51–00:13:57), a sequence that was looked at in the section "Oneiric Implications of the Narrative . . . " in this chapter. Cooper had been worried about that day because of a dream he had had. Cole did not remember Jeffries asking him, "Who do you think that is there?" while pointing at Cooper, and now says that "this is really something interesting to think about" (00:14:10–00:14:28). Albert, who was present on that day, is "beginning to remember that, too" (00:14:28–00:14:35).

Given that the question, "Who is the dreamer?" is not unambiguously answered, it evokes the idea of a dream *without* a dreamer. It could be argued that the dream—as a theme, that is, the sequence is clearly marked as Cole's dream—is decoupled from a dreaming subject, and becomes ontological, taking on a life of its own. Counterintuitive as it may seem, this idea has received some attention in the past, for example, by Johann G. Fichte, who writes:

Figures 5.20–5.21 "I saw myself from long ago."[36] ("Part 14" 00:13:21; 00:13:23).

Images are: they are the only things which exist, and they know of themselves after the fashion of images; images which float past without there being anything past which they float . . . I myself am one of these images; nay, I am not even this, but merely a confused image of the images. All reality is transformed into a strange *dream, without a life which is dreamed of, and without a mind which dreams it.* (Fichte qtd. in Pattison 1; my italicization)[37]

Petra Gehring considers this passage a reformulation of Kantian philosophy. If Kant says that "not things-in-themselves, but only the consistent structures of our subjective epistemological faculties give us the world" (Gehring, *Traum und Wirklichkeit* 114; my translation),[38] then Fichte reformulates this idea in terms of *image* and *dream*, opening up a dream perspective onto the world. "We can only have knowledge in the form of images" (Gehring, *Traum und Wirklichkeit* 114; my translation),[39] which is why the world is actually a dream. There is the possibility that our means of access to the world, that is, our faculties of perception and cognition, do not represent the world accurately to us, just like an image does not depict the actual world, always bespeaking the limitations of what produces the image (e.g., a camera). In other words, *dream* is the concept that Fichte chooses to describe the elusiveness of the thing-in-itself. The idea that the world is a dream without a dreamer is, paradoxical as it may seem, still rooted in the possibility that our perceptual faculties may be failing to represent the world accurately. Hence the decoupling of the dream from a dreamer cannot be rendered plausible without reference to the activity, and by implication to the person, bringing it about. After all, if it is impossible to describe the world in a way that is independent of one's subjective access to it, then this must also be true for the claim that the world is a dream. Interpreting Fichte on the basis of Kant, the claim that "all reality is transformed into a [. . .] dream" does not express a proposition about how the world (as a set of things-in-themselves) is, but, in a paradoxical form, it describes our incapacity to make any factual claim about the world. The activity of dreaming is a necessary precondition to "the dream," that is, its subsequent noun form. In short, "the world is a dream" because "we" are dream-*ing*.

If there is a deeper meaning to Cole's dream, it is that it provides him with the possibility of realizing that the world is a dream. Not coincidentally, the dream brings Cole back to a moment of his life that showed him the essential unreliability of his perceptual apparatus. "Jeffries appeared *and* didn't appear," he recalls ("Part 14" 00:13:51–00:13:57). But it is not just his perception that is unreliable: Albert agrees with Cole's recollection of the scene, and more importantly, the surveillance camera—that is, the technological externalization of human vision—is not of help either in determining what actually happened that day. The "world" in which Jeffries appeared is impossible to reconcile with the "world" in which he did not. Similar to the unresolved discrepancy between the Richard/Carrie and the Cooper/Laura diegetic levels in Part 18, neither of the two worlds is prioritized over the other. Instead, the contradictory worlds coexist within a single image (cf. Seesslen 136), which makes for the scene's dream perspective. In the words of the Log Lady, the dream brings forth "that which is and is not" ("Part 10" 00:45:58–00:46:02). This does not only mean that the dream *is* for the dreamer and *is not* for anyone outside the dream, but it also means that within the dream, contradictory elements coexist. This is why the ending does not overcome the oneiricity of the world. Although it is logically impossible, Kyle MacLachlan's character both "is and is not" Cooper and Richard, just like Sheryl Lee both "is and is not" Carrie and Laura. In this regard, the ending can be said to embody a dream perspective because it conforms to the way the series itself conceptualizes the dream, that is, as a state that embraces contradiction. Due to the persistence of contradictory elements, it becomes clear that the ending does not show us a (or *the*) waking world. The dream, thus, is not part of a *dreaming–waking* dynamic but of a *dreaming–dreaming* dynamic: "we live inside a dream" that we cannot wake up from.

Even if the oneiricity of the Twin Peaks universe is insurmountable in the end, the nocturnal dream, as a microstructure, has special significance in providing the dreamer to grasp that oneiricity. Like in Friedrich Nietzsche's *The Birth of Tragedy from the Spirit of Music*, the dream provides the possibility to see the illusory nature of the world. The "*we live inside a dream*" of Part 17 is anticipated by Cole's dream. The psychological unambiguously marked dream thus implies an ontological truth, which is then widened to the scope of the series. To Cole, Jeffries's questioning of Cooper's "reality status" is "something interesting to think about" ("Part 14" 00:14:10–00:14:28). It lays the foundation for Cole reconsidering the preconditions of what makes something "real," even raising the possibility of the thought that the world is a dream. The dream that Cole has is, in this sense, the experiential mode of reflection, providing him with the opportunity to question his most fundamental beliefs. If life is a dream, then, as Fichte says, thinking is the dream of that dream (66). In *Twin Peaks* (2017), the intertwinement of the dream and reflection is even more visible because reflection takes the form of thinking about who the dreamer is. That is, out of all possible things she could say, Bellucci's question as to the *dreamer* lets Cole's dream enter a mode of reflection. There is no way Lynch and Frost could make it any clearer that the dream carries great reflective potential: in a dream within a dream (Cole's dream as part of the dream world of *Twin Peaks*), the question concerning the identity of the dreamer triggers self-reflection. The radicalness of this reflection becomes visible once we compare Bellucci's words in the episode to the quote from Lynch's version of the Upanishads. In the latter, "we" precedes "dreaming." Who "we" are is a given upon which the activity of dreaming builds. In other words, the subject precedes the activity. This hierarchical relationship, that is, the precedence of identity over activity, is what Bellucci's question puts into doubt. Due to the dream, it is not only that we cannot have an objective sense of the world—we also cannot have a sense of who "we" are. Hence the relationship is reversed: dreaming is implied as that which defines *us*, as that which precedes us and thus enables our identity to emerge. *That we dream* or rather *that there is dreaming* is the only certainty, prior to the certainty of who "we" are as human beings. Focusing on the "who" in the question ("Who is the dreamer?"), dreaming might be what prevents us from knowing who we are. Focusing on the "dreamer," however, the subject is identified by the activity of dreaming such that the dream makes it possible *to be someone* in the first place. Bellucci's question thus implies the existential significance of the dream and could be seen as a reinterpretation of Foucault, who wrote that "the dream is not a modality of the imagination, it is the first condition of its possibility" (67). Analogously, one could understand Bellucci as implying that "the dream self is not a modality of someone's identity, it is the first condition of its possibility." In an existentialist interpretation, it is not just that "existence" precedes essence—crucially, what precedes identity is "existence in that mode of being of the dream" (Foucault 33). While dream-*ing* in *Twin Peaks* is not a modality of existence that can be overcome, *the dream* serves as an opportunity to grasp the dreamlike nature of the diegetic world. The dream marks the extreme point of the characters' way of being in the world and thus points to the ultimate truth about it.

What points to a further interpretive dimension of the scene is the way it was shot and some particular choices that were made in conceiving of and shooting it. So far, the scene has been discussed on a textual level. The *we* in "we're like the dreamer" has been thought to refer to the fictional characters of the series, one of which is FBI chief Gordon Cole. It is striking, however, that the character played by the actress Monica Bellucci is Monica Bellucci. This is the only time in all of *Twin Peaks* that a character plays herself. When she says "we," thus, she does not only speak as a fictional character but also as her "real" self, which gives the scene a metafictional spin. To whom is she speaking? Not coincidentally, she is speaking to Gordon Cole who is played by David Lynch, that is, the series' (co-)creator. Asking, "who is the dreamer?" she alludes to Lynch being the creator of the world of *Twin Peaks*. His double status is hinted at by the term "director," which applies to both the function of his fictional character Cole in regard to the FBI (he is the FBI *director*) and his function as the *director* of *Twin Peaks*. Lynch portrays himself as the spider that created its web and then forgets that it did so and is now just living inside of it.[40] In light of this self-reflexiveness, the black-and-white aesthetics of the scene could be read as a signifier of a specifically *filmic* ontology. Especially to the young Lynch, watching a movie must have been a primarily black-and-white experience. Born in 1946, Lynch even shot his first two feature films *Eraserhead* (1977) and *The Elephant Man* (1980) in black and white. The fact that Lynch chooses black-and-white imagery for the dream in particular shows that he considers dream and cinema, especially the cinema from the past, to be inherently connected.

In support of an author-centered interpretation in this case, after Bellucci's question, her glance turns toward a particular spot behind Cole. As pointed out by YouTuber Twin Perfect, right next to the "certain café" where the scene was shot at Rue Montparnasse in Paris, there is an art gallery that exhibited some of Lynch's lithographs in 2016 ("David Lynch—Plume of Desire"), possibly even during the time of shooting (01:04:02–01:04:14). If there were a dreamer, it should be Lynch-as-Cole, but he fails to realize this. Lynch enacts the role of the author as someone who does not see through the work of art that he created himself, someone who even does not seem to accept that he is its originator. In *Twin Peaks: Fire Walk with Me*, Lynch already dealt with his role as the creator of *Twin Peaks*. Cole meets FBI agents Chester Desmond (Chris Isaak) and Sam Stanley (Kiefer Sutherland) at an airport and presents them with a "surprise," an enigmatic woman named Lil (Kimberly Ann Cole), introduced as Cole's "mother's sister's girl" (*Twin Peaks: Fire Walk with Me* 00:05:26–00:05:30). She wears a red dress and wig and acts peculiarly—grimacing, and with her hand opening and closing continuously, her body spins in circles while its upper part is in a stooped posture. This random combination of elements is followed by agent Desmond's random interpretation ("tailored dresses are a code for drugs") by which Lil is turned into a prophetic figure in regard to an imminent murder investigation (*Twin Peaks: Fire Walk with Me* 00:06:02–00:07:40). Arguably, this scene stands as an ironic reflection upon the viewers' reception process in regard to the preceding first two seasons of *Twin Peaks* (1990–1). Not only does Lynch mock the viewers' often absurd attempts at meaning-making that result in overinterpreting details,[41] but he also seems to oppose an approach to art that tries to reduce it to a question of puzzle solving. In the third season, Lynch takes a different approach, turning the discourse around authorship into an evocative metaphor bespeaking the shared, dreamlike experience of art. Lynch's fictional manifestation Cole is portrayed as someone who does not seem to understand the strange events of the series to any greater extent than the other characters. Due to his hearing impairment, he frequently misinterprets utterances and makes incongruous remarks. We do not really learn what his qualifications for being the chief of the FBI are, and he seems just as perplexed by the strange events of the series as anybody else, including the viewer. The series appears to suggest that Lynch (the film director) and Cole (the FBI director) are only nominally in charge, both of them not entirely in control of the events surrounding them or even their meanings.[42]

And there is a third, arguably most obvious, element indicating the attempted transcendence of the fictional Twin Peaks universe. When Bellucci asks who the dreamer is, the camera takes Cole's position such that she not only addresses him but also the viewer, speaking directly into the camera (see Figure 5.22). In addition to Cole, the viewer is invited to contemplate his own identity. Breaking the fourth wall, she gives additional weight to her question and provokes a self-reflexive, metafictional reading

Figure 5.22 Monica Bellucci as herself, asking (us), "Who is the dreamer?" ("Part 14" 00:12:49).

in which I am asked to think of myself as the dreamer. If each viewer understands the question as being addressed to them, answering it for themselves saying "I am the dreamer," then dreaming is implied as the mode of experience through which the viewer "accesses" the world of *Twin Peaks*. The referentiality of "we" changes: now, Bellucci also speaks on behalf of the TV audience engaging in a collective dream experience. *Twin Peaks* is a collective dream world inhabited by the viewers. The implication that the viewers co-create(d) the world of *Twin Peaks* does not seem exaggerated in light of the massive fan culture inspired by the show. After all, what turned the first season of *Twin Peaks* into a cultural phenomenon was a remarkable fan base around the globe. Rarely has a TV series provoked a comparable degree of public interest, particularly regarding the persistence many fan communities displayed in keeping the series alive. It may not be surprising that the idea of a *collective* dream experience is evoked in a *serial* format, as we viewers keep coming back to the story every week, incrementally becoming a part of it. Unlike a film, television does not involve a single temporally fixed experience, hermetically "sealed-off" and inserted into the continuity of my waking life. It provides a continuous story that I *share* with a myriad of people rather than *possess* individually. Even more than a film, a television series appears to have an independent "world" existing *to the side of* my own, a world which I only get a glimpse of every week during the hour I tune in.

The scene thus evokes the idea of a shared world between actress, creator, and recipient, joining each other in creating a dream world called *Twin Peaks*. While the depicted world presents the object of dreaming, the act of dreaming serves as the metaphor for the shared experience of art. The dream mode is conceived of as that which underlies both the creative process bringing the work of art into being and as the form of reception assumed by the viewers. To liken the film-viewing experience to dreaming is an idea almost as old as the medium of film itself (cf. Schneider 25), but rarely is it reflected *inside* a film. In what could be seen as Lynch's personal film/dream analogy, Bellucci's appearance functions as a nondiegetic insert, pushing Cole to wake up to his real identity as the creator of the world, which he only considers himself to be a part of. From Cole's perspective, she acts as a supernatural, almost angelic entity sent to his world to hint at the illusory nature of his reality. Crucially, though, when Cole turns around to look at the gallery displaying Lynch's art—that is, when Cole is about to meet his "real" self—he does not see it, instead seeing a younger version of himself (see Figures 5.20 and 5.21). Cole is bound to his existence as a fictional character in a fictional universe (although there is the possibility that he at least starts questioning that world). By addressing us, Bellucci anticipates the transcendence toward the viewer's world evoked by Part 18. Like in Part 18, however, this transcendence remains unsuccessful, in that it is incomplete. Its incompleteness could be explained in light of the series' self-reflexivity. That is, because *Twin Peaks* is aware of its ontological status as a fictional story, it portrays the transcendence toward the real world as incomplete. Cole does not see Lynch's art gallery but a younger version of himself, that is, a younger version of Lynch's fictional character in the story of *Twin Peaks*. The incompleteness functions to express the awareness that ontologically, the series remains tied to the edge of the screen, unable to depict *actuality*. Even though the possibility of transcendence—of crossing over into the real world—is hinted at, going beyond the dream is impossible in the end. *Twin Peaks* presents itself as a dream *without a dreamer*, that is, an entity that is unanchored in reality. The series displays an awareness that it can only "have knowledge in the form of images" (cf. Gehring 114) and, due to this, conceptualizes itself as a fictional, ontologically contradictory (it "is and is not")—and in this sense *dreamlike*—entity. Like in Fichte, where viewing is the dream (66), *Twin Peaks* conceptualizes its own act of viewing as oneiric, in that it is willing but ultimately unable to transcend the boundaries of its fictional universe. While characterizing the oneiric, the ontological contradictoriness in *Twin Peaks* (2017) can also be related to the phenomenology of the film experience in general. The Log Lady's *"that which is and is not"* ("Part 10" 00:45:58–00:46:02) arguably describes the experience of film in general. "It is" to the extent that *it is* to the viewer's senses at the pre-reflective stage of the film experience, that is, the viewer is sensorially involved in the material scenario depicted on the screen. I feel addressed by Bellucci's gaze. "It is not" in the sense that the world depicted in a film *is not* real in the same way the nonmedial external world is. Upon reflection, I know that Bellucci does not address me but the camera, which serves as the "opening" (cf. Sobchak, *Address* 64) through which I have access to the film world.

6

Lost Highway (1997)

Audio-Viewing *Lost Highway*

In the title sequence of *Lost Highway* (1997), car headlights are speeding over a highway road through a pitch-black night, as David Bowie's song *I'm Deranged* is playing: "funny how secrets travel" (00:01:32–00:01:36). The medians are at the center of the image and the camera is shaking due to the high speed of the car whose bumper perspective we share. Each of the yellow credits comes rushing toward the screen, holds for a moment as if it was sticking on the windshield like a fly before the airstream blows it off, and continues past our point of view. As the song fades out, a soft thudding sound melts into a menacing low-frequency tone, reverberating as the screen goes black.

The face of protagonist Fred Madison (Bill Pullman) is dimly lit by the glow of the cigarette he is smoking, the camera taking the texture of his skin into focus. The automatic shutter goes up, and there is the sound of someone ringing at the door. After a moment of hesitation, Fred answers. Somebody says, "Dick Laurent is dead" (00:04:30–00:04:39), and when Fred goes to a window to check who is at the door, there is nobody there.

Fred's wife Renée (Patricia Arquette) tells him that she is not coming to his concert tonight; she prefers to stay home and read. "Read . . . read . . . read what?" (00:06:31–00:06:49), Fred asks, as he is approaching her, with Renée evading his attempt to make eye contact. She answers with a chuckle, and Fred finds it "nice to know I can still make you laugh.—[Renée:] I like to laugh, Fred.—[Fred:] That's why I married you" (00:06:55–00:07:11). At the club, Fred performs a saxophone solo of almost violent intensity, which is shot in a flickering white light. After the concert is finished, he, shown in bold red light, calls at his house, but nobody picks up the phone. When he gets home, he finds Renée in bed. She is sound asleep.

The next morning, Renée finds an anonymous videotape outside the front door.[1] It shows amateur footage of Fred's and Renée's house, the camera zooming in on the door toward the end. Renée assumes that it is from a real estate agent. "Maybe," says Fred (00:12:48).

Lying in bed, Fred thinks back to one of his gigs during which Renée left with another man; we will come to know him as Andy (Michael Massee). Then, Renée and Fred have sex. It appears passionless on both parts, and Fred ejaculates prematurely. To Fred's humiliation, Renée responds to this by tapping him on the back, saying that "it's okay" (00:16:25–00:16:26). Then, Fred recalls that he "had a dream last night. . . . You were inside the house. . . . You were calling my name" (00:17:17–00:17:37). The scene shows Fred wandering around in the house. His head tilted, his eyes slightly squinted, he appears filled with suspicion. We hear Renée's reverberating voice calling out Fred's name. Then, an open fire whose exaggerated volume displaces Fred's audible, nervous breathing for a moment. "I couldn't find you," he continues (00:17:58–00:18:00). White smoke emerges from the staircase. Slightly disoriented, he walks through the corridor, facing downward. With the Lynchian roar swelling into an unsettling soundscape of industrial hissing sounds, we get to the bedroom with a point-of-view shot from Fred's perspective: "then there you were, lying in bed. . . . It wasn't you" (00:18:20–00:18:27). The camera slowly pans across the floor to reveal Patricia Arquette's character in bed. "It *looked* like you . . . but it wasn't," he insists (00:18:28–00:18:32)—we rapidly move toward her, approaching her face from above, as she is screaming while trying to protect herself. With an abrupt inhale, Fred wakes up from his dream. Renée sits up to check on him. When he looks at her for the first time, her face remains in the dark. The second time, a pale face of an old man (Robert Blake) with a serious expression is superimposed on Renée's face; the image is accompanied by a slightly delayed, deeply unsettling whooshing sound. After Fred turns on the light, the mysterious face on Renée's has disappeared and she asks if Fred is all right. Still breathing heavily, he touches her face and we fade to black.

In the morning, Renée finds a second videotape on the door steps. The tape includes imagery shot inside the house: the living room, corridor, and the bedroom with Fred and Renée sleeping. Renée calls the police. Two detectives, Al (John Roselius) and Ed (Louis Eppolito), arrive and half-heartedly look for weak spots where someone might have broken in. At some point, one of them asks whether Fred and Renée own a video camera. "No, Fred hates them," says Renée, with Fred explaining that "I like to remember things my own way . . . how I remembered them, not necessarily the way they happened" (00:24:47–00:25:12). The cops leave, promising to keep a watch on the house.

Andy (Michael Massee), the friend of Renée who appeared in Fred's memory earlier, is hosting a party. Andy appears very happy to see Renée and, as she is falling into his arms, she sends Fred for drinks. At the bar, Fred orders two shots for himself. Upon finishing the second one, he catches sight of a pale-faced man—he is credited as "Mystery Man" (Robert Blake)—whose face was superimposed on Renée's when Fred woke up from his dream. Besides the ambient music fading out, the hue shifts to a slightly colder gradation as he is approaching.

Mystery Man:	We've met before, haven't we?
Fred:	Yeah I don't think so. . . . Where was it you think we met?
Mystery Man:	At your house, don't you remember?
Fred:	No, no I don't. Are you sure?
Mystery Man:	Of course. . . . As a matter of fact, I am there right now.
Fred:	What do you mean, you're *where* right now?
Mystery Man:	At your house.
Fred:	That's fucking crazy, man. (00:29:40–00:30:33)

Following the Mystery Man's instruction, Fred dials his own number. What the man suggested proves to be true, as he really does pick up the phone there. Fred is flabbergasted; how did he do that? Fred asks him how he got inside his house. The man responds that "you invited me. It is not my custom to go where I'm not wanted" (00:31:30–00:31:35). Fred asks the host Andy about the mysterious man. He tells him that he does not know his name, but that the man is a friend of Dick Laurent's. This name reminds Fred of the other morning, when some mysterious person told him via intercom about Dick Laurent's death.

The incident is so unsettling to Fred that he and Renée instantly leave the party. On the way home, he asks Renée how she met "that asshole Andy" (00:33:38–00:33:40). Andy and Renée met a long time ago, and he told her about "a job," but she does not remember what job it was. As they get home, the inside of the house lights up for a moment while we hear a disconcerting, dissonant, reverberating glissando. Fred wants Renée to stay in the car while he checks to see if there is anybody inside the house. In a suspenseful moment, a slightly slanted camera "floats" through the corridor. Alluding to the encounter with the Mystery Man at the party, the phone is ringing. With the camera approaching Fred, he looks at something that scares him at first, then he relaxes.

Later on, as Renée is getting ready for bed, Fred passes through the dark corridor and looks at himself in the mirror. Recalling Fred's dream, Renée calls out for Fred, asking where he is. Then, an image of the living room. This time the fire is out; the shadows of two human figures on the wall. Out of the dark corridor, Fred appears and walks by in such a way that his unlit head overtakes the screen, making it all black. An eerie synthetic sound, vaguely resembling whining. Seamlessly, then, the camera pulls back out of the black television screen. We are in the living room now and it is day. Fred enters carrying another envelope with a new videotape inside. On the tape is Fred, bloodstained, kneeling over pieces of Renée's corpse. Fred is in shock upon seeing this and calls out for Renée.

A hard cut: Fred's call for Renée is "answered" by Al, the police officer from earlier, shouting at him, "sit down, killer!" (00:42:21–00:42:23). Fred responds ambiguously: "I didn't kill her. . . . Tell me I didn't kill her" (00:42:28–00:42:35). Through a voice-over, we learn that Fred is found guilty of first-degree murder and is sentenced to death.

In prison, he is tormented by headaches, flashbacks to the murder scene, and insomnia, which is why the doctor gives him sleeping pills. Fred is pale and has a dark spot on his forehead now. In strong pain, he hallucinates a burning cabin in the desert. With the smoke entering the cabin instead of emerging from it, it appears to "burn backwards." The Mystery Man comes out, stands on the porch for a moment to look at Fred, and goes back inside. Then, blue light above Fred's head coupled with an engrossing soundscape. The light bulb goes dark. We can see the dark highway from the opening images, this time there are two solid median strips, though. By the side of the road stands a young man (Balthazar Getty) whom a young woman calls Pete, telling him "not to go." An extreme close-up on Pete's eyes. In the prison cell, bloodstained Fred is rocking from side to side in great pain, holding his head. In the cathartic moment of the montage, under the light flashes and sounds of thunder and the presence of white smoke, the camera penetrates the opening of a bloody piece of flesh.

In the morning, a prison guard checks the cells and is surprised to find a young man named Pete Dayton (Balthazar Getty) in place of Fred Madison. His parents pick up their 24-year-old son Pete, who, as we are told, once stole a car and was arrested, getting one year of probation. Why he was in prison now remains unknown, though. The two detectives Hank (Carl Sundstrom) and Lou (John Solari) are tasked to surveil him. Similar to Fred, Pete has an injury on his forehead—a small wound encircled by a swelling, and a drooping eyelid—and does not remember a number of recent events.

Pete works at a car repair shop where his best client is the terrifying mafia-boss type Mr. Eddy (Robert Loggia). The detectives surveilling Pete refer to him as (Dick) Laurent. Mr. Eddy/Dick Laurent takes Pete on a ride with his car to fix a minor problem about the sound of the engine. When someone tailgates on Mulholland Dr., Mr. Eddy first lets the tailgater pass and then goes after him. He punches him in the face while threatening him with a gun, "teaching him a lesson" about the danger of tailgating.

In the evening, Pete emerges from the dark to examine his face in the mirror (similar to what Fred did earlier). He picks up a young woman named Sheila (Natasha Gregson Wagner) and they have sex in his car. At the car repair shop the next day, the saxophone solo performed by Fred at the beginning of the film is playing on the radio. It gives Pete a headache and he changes the channel. Mr. Eddy comes by, leaving another car that is to be repaired. Over Lou Reed's *This Magic Moment*, Mr. Eddy's wife Alice (a blonde Patricia Arquette) gets out of the car in slow motion, with an awestruck Pete watching. She comes back by herself in the evening, introducing herself as Alice Wakefield. She asks Pete out to dinner and they have sex at a motel, which marks the beginning of an affair.

After a while, Mr. Eddy grows suspicious, so Alice and Pete cannot see each other as often anymore. One night, Pete has a frightening hallucination about Alice. He leaves his room and meets Sheila at a motel, where they sleep with each other. Later on, Pete's parents tell him that "that night" (01:26:03; they are probably referring to the night that is in some way related to his reappearance in Fred Madison's prison cell), there were a man and Sheila with him, but they are not saying anything about what happened to Pete. Recalling "that night," Pete appears to have a brief flashback, seeing the dead body of Renée at Fred's house as well as the penetration of flesh that marked the "morphing" of Fred into Pete.

Pete and Alice plan to "just get some money and go away together" (01:29:51–01:29:56). To do so, they want to (and eventually do) rob Andy (Michael Massee again), a man who "pays girls to party with him" (01:30:05–01:30:08). Before, though, Sheila breaks up with Pete. Then, Mr. Eddy calls Pete to ask "how he is doing." Even more intimidating to Pete is the fact that Mr. Eddy passes the phone on to the Mystery Man, whom he introduces as "a friend" of his (01:39:42). Pete and the Mystery Man "repeat" a piece of the dialogue heard between Fred and the Mystery Man at Andy's party earlier on in the film. In place of Fred, it is now Pete who does not remember meeting the man at his house. Unlike earlier, though, the Mystery Man continues saying that "in the east, the far east, when a person is sentenced to death, they are sent to a place where they can't escape, never knowing when an execution may step up behind them and fire a bullet into the back of their head" (01:40:11–01:40:27).

As Alice and Pete planned, they rob Andy. Pete first knocks him out but then, trying to take revenge on Pete, Andy is killed—by Pete, as Alice insists. Disoriented by the scenario—a porn film starring Alice is screened in Andy's living room all the while—Pete looks at a photo that shows Mr. Eddy, Renée, Alice, and Andy. "Is that you? Are both of them you?" Pete asks (01:46:32–01:46:36), and his nose starts bleeding. Looking for the bathroom, he stumbles through a corridor that is illuminated by flashes of thunder, as Rammstein's *Rammstein* is playing. Pete and Alice drive out to the desert to meet a "fence [. . .] at his cabin" (01:50:53–01:51:01).

Images of the highway in the dark (from the opening) and of the backward-burning cabin in the desert (from when Fred was in prison) reappear. When Pete and Alice get to the cabin, the "fence" is not there yet. Pete asks her why she chose him. She asks him whether he still wants her. In the headlights of the car, they have sex, as This Mortal Coil's *Song to the Siren* is playing. During the act, Fred repeats "I want you" over and over again—until Alice says, "you'll never have me" (01:55:47–01:56:47). She gets up and goes inside the cabin. When Pete gets up, it is no longer him but Fred.

The Mystery Man briefly appears in the car and then on the porch of the cabin. Fred follows him inside the cabin, asking him where Alice is. The man insists that her name is Renée. "And your name, what the fuck is your name?" he asks, as he pulls out a video camera, pointing it at Fred (01:59:04–01:59:09). Fred escapes and gets to the "Lost Highway Hotel" where Renée and Mr. Eddy are having sex. Fred walks through the same corridor that Pete stumbled through at Andy's house. Again *Rammstein*, and again flashes of thunder, as Fred approaches the room of Mr. Eddy; Renée just left. He punches Mr. Eddy in the face and puts him in the trunk of his car, taking him back to the desert. With the help of the Mystery Man, Fred cuts Mr. Eddy's throat. As he is dying, the Mystery Man hands him a portable device with a screen. He watches a scene from a porn movie starring Renée, and we cut to a porn screening at Andy's house attended by Mr. Eddy and Renée. With the sound of two strikes, the portable screen's image changes to depict the Mystery Man and Fred, mirroring what Mr. Eddy has in front of his eyes. The Mystery Man shoots Mr. Eddy in the head and then whispers something into Fred's ear. In the next shot, the man has disappeared and Fred is holding the gun in his hand.

At the crime scene at Andy's house, Andy's corpse is in the same position as before (his skull is cracked by the glass table in his living room). In the photo from earlier, there are Mr. Eddy/Dick Laurent, Renée, and Andy; blonde Alice is missing. Both sets of cops with monosyllabic names, Al and Ed (from the first part of the movie) as well as Hank and Lou (from the second part), are there, looking at the photo. Ed explains that "that's Fred Madison's wife with Dick Laurent" (02:07:31–02:07:34). Lou adds that "we got Pete Dayton's prints all over this place" (02:07:38–02:07:41).

Coming full circle, in the film's last sequence, Fred drives up to his own house, rings the doorbell, and speaks the words "Dick Laurent is dead" into the intercom (02:08:55–02:08:58). Chased by the police, he escapes by car, racing into the night.

Tension is building up, not least due to the high volume of Trent Reznor's *Driver Down* on the soundtrack. In a final climactic moment, Fred starts screaming and shaking heavily. White light flashes, and smoke is emitted as we zoom in on his face, which is deformed by great pain. Another transformation? A moment of silence. The opening images of car headlights speeding over a dark highway return to conclude the film, as does Bowie's *I'm Deranged*.

The Dream between Loss of Reality and Dissociative (Identity) Disorder

Given my phenomenological interest in the aesthetics, structure, and function of the oneiric in Lynch's films, two dimensions of *Lost Highway* are of importance in this discussion: the psychological and the (meta-)medial dimension. Most interpretations of the film are rooted in psychological explanations. A standard interpretation, found in academic as well as popular discourse, suggests that only Fred exists in the diegetic reality, Pete being a figment of his imagination. Patricia Arquette, the actress playing Renée and Alice, came up with an explanation for dividing *Lost Highway* into reality (populated by Fred and Renée) and fantasy (Pete and Alice), which Rodley sums up like this:

> [A] man murders his wife because he thinks she's being unfaithful. He can't deal with the consequences of his actions and has a kind of breakdown. In this breakdown he tries to imagine a better life for himself, but he's so fucked up that even this imaginary life goes wrong. The mistrust and madness in him are so deep that even his fantasies end in a nightmare. (Rodley 231–2)

Lynch, too, is not disinclined to interpreting the film through a concept that implies a clear separation between reality and fantasy: the diagnosis of a *psychogenic fugue* (now called *dissociative fugue* in clinical terms) applies to the main character Fred Madison (cf. Rodley 239).[2] A fugue state is a dissociative disorder involving "sudden, unexpected travel away from home or one's customary place of daily activities, with inability to recall some or all of one's past. This is accompanied by confusion about personal identity or even the assumption of a new identity" (APA, *DSM-4* 525).[3] As a protective mechanism against a horrible reality in which he killed his wife out of jealousy, Fred, awaiting execution, creates an alternative identity in his imagination, Pete, who embodies Fred's idealized version of himself: a young, potent man who seems to understand the "feminine mystery," as Žižek calls it (*Ridiculous* 11). Through Alice, who "personifies the nocturnal side and sexual debauchery of Renee" (Kaul and Palmier 94; my translation),[4] Fred partially justifies his murder because Alice "confirms" the suspicion he held against Renée in reality.[5] What seems to speak for a reading of Pete as Fred's fantasy product are the points of reference in the stories of the two: both have severe headaches or wounds on their foreheads around the time of the transformation; both are romantically involved with a figure embodied by Patricia Arquette and become increasingly jealous; Fred's saxophone solo from the beginning of the film causes Pete's headache when it plays on the radio while he is working on a car; also, the Mystery Man plays an essential role for both Fred and Pete. Arguably, Fred's story increasingly "shines through" Pete's experiences as the film continues. Although co-screenwriter Barry Gifford, like Arquette, interprets Pete as a product of Fred's fantasy,[6] he suggests that this fantasy reading is not without problems: "That's just one possible explanation [. . .] [Y]ou can say, 'Oh yes, it's a guy who goes crazy and has some kind of psychotic episode, and a schizophrenic split,' but there are many things in there that don't fit easily into that category, including the ending [. . .] [o]r endings" (cf. Hughes 215). In this context, the phenomenological approach in this analysis seeks to account for the ending without disregarding the original appeal of the fugue interpretation.

On the psychological level of the movie, Daniela Langer observes two aspects in regard to Fred's pathology: first, schizophrenia ("the feeling of observing oneself—no other, second personality—from the outside" [88; my translation]),[7,8] and second, as a possible basis of a fugue state, dissociative identity disorder (DID),[9] in respect of which she follows Henning Saß's understanding as the "inability [. . .] to integrate different aspects of identity, memory and consciousness" (Saß qtd. in D. Langer 88; my translation).[10,11] Through the dream scene, I will examine two phenomena in more detail, that is, loss of reality and dissociation. To some extent, the former will be discussed in the context of the psychotic dimension (which includes schizophrenia), but in terms of clinical categories, my focus is on the phenomenon of dissociation.[12]

The medial dimension of the film is just as prominent as the psychological dimension, since the ordinary world is disrupted by the videotapes whose origin is a mystery.[13] The central significance of the videos for the plot becomes clear at the latest when the videotapes allow us to witness the event that sends Fred to prison: his murder of his wife Renée. Tanja Michalsky even sees *Lost Highway* as a "filmic contribution to media theory," as her essay is titled (397; my translation).[14] To put it briefly, the dream is located at the interface between the psychological and the medial (or meta-medial) dimension of the film: it suggests that the video images "belong to" Fred, albeit in an initially mysterious way, possibly as a split-off part. The dream thus shows that the medial dimension of the film has merged with the psychological one.

First of all, though, I shall take a closer look at the dream scene and, based on this, consider what interpretation of the film seems plausible. What kind of experience does Fred have in the dream? Through which aesthetic means does the dream address the viewer and what kind of affective response is provoked? What is the role of the dream experience in relation to the whole film? And finally, how can its relationship to the oneiric in other Lynch films be described?

The Dream and the Human Form: Cognitive Ambivalence and Loss of Reality

After Fred and Renée have sex, Fred recalls his dream from the night before. Structurally, it is striking how a change in the narrative perspective seems to take place. First, we find ourselves in the here and now of the moment after sex. From here, the dream scene seems to be retold. Hence, there are two temporal levels. While the scene visually traces Fred's dream experience of the night before, we remain anchored in the present through Fred's voice-over. It is interesting to note how the "linguistic narrative instance" (i.e., the voice-over; cf. Kuhn 124) and the "visual narrative instance" (i.e., the images; cf. Kuhn 123) contradict each other ("it looked like you . . . but it wasn't"; 00:18:28–00:18:32). In the (viewing experience of the) dream, the power of the image is thus contrasted with the power of the word: I *see* Renée, but it is *said* that it is not her. Equally important, the voice-over does not bring us back to the present of the post-sex moment. Instead of seeing Fred finishing his dream recollection, we see Fred startling out of the dream and we thus inevitably join his subjective experience. *Lost Highway* thus provides a counterexample to Brütsch's assertion that "[e]specially with regard to the dream, it is important to keep apart the experience and the narration of this experience" (393; my translation).[15] The consequence of this disappearance of the narrative present for viewer's perception is considerable because we no longer have the impression of a stable waking world within which the dream scene is embedded.[16] This destabilization is intensified particularly by the fact that the eeriness of the dream (Renée is not herself) only manifests itself after waking up, that is, in the supposed moment of safety: the moment of the awakening from the dream, which usually restores the stability of reality, suggests the exact opposite here. Here she *really* is "not herself," because in place of Renée's face, there is the ugly grimace of a mysterious, Mephisto-like figure—the Mystery Man—which is reminiscent of the expressionistic appearance of the figures in *The Alphabet* (1968) and *The Grandmother* (1970; see Figures 6.1 and 6.2).

As in Lynch's early short film *The Alphabet*, it is the manipulated image of a face which demonstrates a potential to shock the viewer on the threshold between dreaming and waking. Addressing the viewer, the face in *The Alphabet* spoke the phrase, "please remember, you are dealing with the human form." It was left open whether this referred to the physiognomy of the human face itself or to the human experience of the dream (or to the alphabet; cf. section "The Dream as the Human Form" in Chapter 3). It seems clear that *Lost Highway* echoes the strategy of the short film to undermine the default perception of the viewer. While in *The Alphabet*, it was an inverted face that we could not immediately recognize as such, in *Lost Highway*, a strange face takes the place of the expected one. The disruptive potential of these images results from our original familiarity with faces, that is, from the attunement of our perceptual apparatus to the visual appearance of faces, due to which we attribute great significance to the most

Figures 6.1–6.2 "It looked like you . . . but it wasn't"—"Renée" in Fred's dream (left; 00:18:39) and after he wakes up (right; 00:18:57).

subtle mimic changes. In other words, the shock effect of the manipulated face is so great because it represents such a blatant break with our default mode perception (in which faces remain the same).

With regard to the story of *Lost Highway*, it is important to note that this image anticipates the dissolution of identity at the end of the film.[17] Here, too, the deconstruction of identity is represented by a deforming face (see Figure 6.3). As mentioned before, Merleau-Ponty speaks of painting as "a blowing up of the 'skin of things' . . . to show how things become things and world becomes world" (qtd. in Zechner 74; my translation). If skin is conceived of "as the symbolic space between self and world" (cf. Elsaesser and Hagener, *Filmtheorie* 140; my translation),[18] then by "blowing up," skin loses its discriminatory function with respect to the categories *outside* and *inside*. The "human form" (that was first brought into play by *The Alphabet*) remains indefinable at the end of *Lost Highway* and it is no longer possible to think of the protagonist as *one* person or to conceptualize the world he lives in. Based on the destabilization of perception, the dream/wake-up scene phenomenologically anticipates the theme of the story told by the film: the story of a man who loses his sense of reality and identity. The dreamlike character of the psychotic state does not have to be presupposed here on the basis of an intrinsic kinship between the two phenomena (Hobson, e.g., speaks of the "psychosis of dreams" [810]) but is created by the dream/wake-up scene, in which Fred cannot distinguish for a moment between reality and fantasy—a characteristic of the third part of *Lost Highway*, in which the realities of Fred and Pete have merged into an ontologically indeterminable world.

Although we seem to be back in Fred's reality in the third part of the film, the murder of Andy (from the second part) really did happen and "Pete Dayton's prints [are] all over this place" (02:07:38–02:07:41). Also, both cop couples (Ed and Al; Hank and Lou) are united here. This challenges the interpretation of the film as the portrayal of a psychogenic fugue because if Pete was just a (fantasized) alter ego of Fred, then it should not be possible for Pete's fingerprints to be present in Fred's reality. By labeling the story as a psychogenic fugue, a clear hierarchy of reality levels seems to take place, which is already expressed when one speaks of Fred (whom we assume to be real

Figure 6.3 The dissolution of identity at the end of *Lost Highway* (02:10:26).

or superior to Pete) experiencing a psychogenic fugue, in the sense of a dissociative episode from which he returns. However, the film does not portray the loss of identity and reality from an objective external perspective. Rather, the depicted pathological state seeps into the very structure of the narrative, so to speak. Seesslen asks: "How could we say that the film 'deals' with a schizophrenic murderer, when it so obviously lets itself be infected by schizophrenia[?]" (Seesslen 172; my translation).[19] Similarly, D. Langer suggests that "Lynch by no means limits himself to the depiction of the insane and their relationship to the (normal) environment. Rather, the rules of insanity also affect the formal design of the films" (D. Langer 69; my translation).[20] Arguably, *Lost Highway* is an insane film rather than a film *about* insanity. Seesslen speaks of the "Dostoevsky level" of *Lost Highway*, in that the film represents "the inner description of a dissolution of person, perspective and perception" (171; my translation).[21] Fred's loss of reality is a model for the psychotic perspective of the narrative, to the extent that in the third part of the film, the viewer no longer succeeds in distinguishing between different diegetic levels. So if *Lost Highway* is seen as a psychological film, it is interesting on this level how the pathological state of the protagonist is "recreated" in the viewing experience: *because* Fred/Pete is not able to distinguish reality from fantasy, the viewer cannot establish a hierarchy of diegetic levels. Ultimately, the tension between internal and external perception is characteristically *not* resolved (D. Langer speaks of an "equation of 'inside' and 'outside'" [89; my translation][22]).[23] In other words, the viewer is not granted a cognitive resolution (instead feeling the ontological paradox of the diegesis) because the psychotic state, that is, the film's subject, is marked by that same paradox. The "world-of" the film eludes cognitive closure because the "world-in" the film does.

In the film experience, thus, the protagonist's psychotic perception manifests itself as the viewer's inability to grasp the ontological status of the narrative. Put this way, watching *Lost Highway* sounds like a purely cognitive endeavor: the viewer generates hypotheses while watching the film. The hypotheses attempt to render the film explicable but ultimately fail to do so, as "irresolvable ambiguities and inconsistencies" (Buckland 55) persist (e.g., the fact that the person who speaks the phrase "Dick Laurent is dead" into Fred's intercom at the beginning of the film is Fred himself; time is not linear but structured as a loop). Warren Buckland observes: "Lynch's films are open to analysis as long as we do not try to reduce these ambiguous moments to a rational logic, but recognize that a *non-rational but meaningful energy* governs them" (Buckland 57). Lynch himself may have something similar in mind when he responds to the question about the difficulty of understanding *Lost Highway*: "[i]t's not to confound, it's to feel the mystery. Mystery is good, confusion is bad" (Rodley 227). Arguably, Lynch wants that feeling of "an explanation being just out of reach" to prevail. The quote shows his inclination toward the emotional over the cognitive or rather his view that the emotional stands out as a result of cognitive ambiguity. Crucially, that same emotion characterizes the dream sequence, where it is accompanied by cognitive ambiguity as well ("You were lying in bed . . . it wasn't you"). The emotional stance of the dream thus becomes the emotional stance of the whole film.

At this point, it may be useful to think of Yacavone's distinction between *local* and *global* expression of cinematic affect. "Local" (or "episodic") expression "pertains to potentially *any* emotions, feelings, and affects that are associated with specific and given images, sounds, and sequences" (Yacavone 170). Local expression can be subdivided into three forms, "the *sensory-affective*, which tends toward the immediate, visceral, and 'natural'"; "the *cognitive-diegetic*," acting as "the bridge that connects the film viewer's capacities for comprehension of the representational contents of the film image with emotional contents and response"; and "the *formal-artistic*, involving responses to features of a film that center on their evincing aesthetic properties of form, design, and artistic intentionality and significance" (170, 179). "Global expression," as opposed to local expression, "pertains to a film work as a temporal whole and as incorporating and integrating some number of local or episodic or affective sources" (170).

Experiencing *Lost Highway*, it is the "cognitive-diegetic" dimension that allows the viewer to connect the "sensory-affective" intensity of the Mystery Man's face in place of Renée's with the global expression embodied by the film's storyworld as a whole. The viewer engagement evoked by Fred's dream provides a "local expression," an affective model for the "global expression," the particular "cine-aesthetic" world-feeling (Yacavone 170) that is specific to *Lost Highway*. The rest of the film could be said to "explicate" or "narrativize" what was essentially already prefigured by the dream. The de-automatization of perception, which, in addition to the dream/wake-up scene of *Lost Highway*, was already observed in *The Alphabet*, is thus extended to the entire narrative, where it results in a "de-automatization of the understanding of the (diegetic) world," for example, with regard to the linearity of the narrated time or concerning the stability of characters' identities. That is, Alice both *is* Renée and she *is not*. It is her, although it cannot be her; it is not her, although it seems like it is. Like in Fred's dream, the logical law of the excluded middle is suspended. The sameness of Renée and Alice is suggested by the two characters being played by the same actress and by the continuity of her (back) story; their difference is stressed by the change of hair colors. Semantically speaking, "re-née" could be understood as the anticipation that her character will be (literally) *reborn* in the second part of the film. In this light, the name *Alice* can be seen as a reference to Lewis Carroll's *Alice's Adventures in Wonderland*; *wake* hints at the possibility of sleeping and dreaming. The viewer is thus asked to think of Renée and Alice as both the same and different. The effect of this cognitive ambiguity between sameness and difference is similar to what we experience in dreams in which dream characters, in addition to being themselves, are somebody else at the same time. Although that dream character looks like x, *I know* that it is (also) y. Freud speaks of a *mischperson* in this context (*Traumdeutung* 324). But what the film itself suggests is more important than this comparison to the night dream-experience. We are to think of Renée as Renée (first part), of Renée as Alice (second part), and of Renée as both Renée *and* Alice (third part).

If *Lost Highway* globally generates the "feeling [. . .] as if the ground were being pulled out from under [the viewer's] feet" (Sellmann 252; my translation),[24] this affective logic of the film is already anticipated "locally" by the dream. The affective dynamics of the third part thus rely on those of the dream. The feeling of being able to trust what one sees and hears, of being able to trust the world, breaks away for Fred and, to some extent, for the viewer. Affectively, we do not return to the waking world, in the sense of a "safe environment." But this does not mean that everything after the dream sequence *is a dream*, it is just that the third part of the film is dream-*like*, in that it is the dream that introduces an experience that undermines the viewer's cognitive grasp and thus makes us feel unsafe.[25] Seesslen speaks of "uninhabitable images [. . .] that are terrified of themselves" (156; my translation).[26] What seems crucial here, besides the anticipation of later elements, is the particular kind of repetition of what has happened before. Namely, the dream "repeats" the scene in which Fred comes home from his concert, looks for Renée, and finds her in bed. In the dream, Fred experiences the same thing as different. The dream represents a different experience of the same, an uncanny repetition of the familiar, if you will. The fact that the dream makes the familiar uncanny is epitomized by the breakdown of personal identity—Renée is not herself in Fred's dream perception, although she looks exactly the same.

The overall structure of the second part of the film could be understood in this way. The same thing happens again under a different guise: the male protagonist is in love with Patricia Arquette's character, who (in his view) neglects him, which entails murder and the protagonist's mental breakdown. The third part offers yet another experience of the same, that is, the known worlds of Fred and Pete are merged into a new, unknown, uncanny world that cannot be conceptualized and in this sense "inhabited." The possibility of what serves as the basis for calling something else "similar" (Pete's world being "similar" to Fred's world) is radically undermined. It is in this sense that the dream introduces the principle that underlies the experience of the whole film. In the context of *Lost Highway*, thus, any momentum that questions or undermines the clear separability of reality and fantasy can be understood as oneiric (or "dream-*like*").

Mediality and/as Dissociation

In *Eraserhead*, the theater stage behind the radiator introduces a second world within the diegetic reality. Chapter 4 has shown that its accessibility is a function of Henry's state of consciousness, for Henry enters the stage only when he is dreaming. In *Lost Highway*, the videotapes sent to Fred and Renée's house appear to constitute a formal resemblance to the stage in *Eraserhead*. They act as the element that transforms the ordinary world of the story, while at the same time being embedded within it. The Lady in the Radiator led Henry to kill his baby; the tapes reveal that Fred killed his wife Renée. While it is clear, though, that Henry's "visit" to the theater stage was introduced as a dream, the tapes, particularly the third one showing Renée's murder, appear to depict reality, thereby questioning the ontological status of the scenes within which the tapes are embedded. (At the very least, they make us question whether the film is really presenting us with the bigger picture or a very distorted—i.e., Fred's—view of things.) Alluding to the mediality of Henry's dream, however, Fred's dream should not be viewed in isolation to the tapes either. Significantly, the camera angle and composition of the tracking shot through the corridor, which may have been inspired by Maya Deren's pioneering avant-garde short film *Meshes of the Afternoon* (1943), is identical to the tape (see Figures 6.4–6.7). When Fred watches the new tape with Renée the next day, he is shocked not only because someone has apparently invaded their home but also because *he* has already seen some of these exact images in his dream.

Andrea Minuz observes that, even before the dream, Fred's perception is associated with the video footage. In Fred's first scene of the film, he looks out of the window to check who spoke the enigmatic words "Dick Laurent is dead" into the intercom. His gaze wanders right (front door) to left (street), and an establishing shot of the house concludes the opening scene (Minuz 96). The video footage from the first tape *opens* with a similar establishing shot and then shows a movement from right to left, literally mirroring Fred's gaze (96). Minuz thus speaks of "an enigmatic relationship of reversibility, a splitting of the same scene into two gazes" (96; my translation).[27,28] Even if the space of the first video is introduced by these shots, however, the relationship between the second video and the dream remains special because the tape *repeats* the exact images from the dream. That is, the second video turns Fred's *lived* point of view from his dream into a point-of-view *shot*.

Concerning the relationship of Fred's dream and the video footage, a question that imposes itself is whether the objectivity of what the tapes depict is put into doubt by the fact that the same imagery appeared in the dream—the dream de-authenticates the videotape; or whether, vice versa, the dream is epistemologically "upgraded" because it anticipated what is *really* about to happen, as testified to by the tapes—the tapes as an authentic representation of reality. Michalsky observes: "The status of images is highly precarious in this film which, on the one hand, declares its protagonist Fred to be the murderer of his wife through video recordings alone, thus even sentencing him to death by electric chair, and, on the other hand, undermines the evidential value of its images by suspending its narrative logic itself" (Michalsky 400; my translation).[29] Thus, the images in this film have an ambiguous status, and the viewer is left uncertain

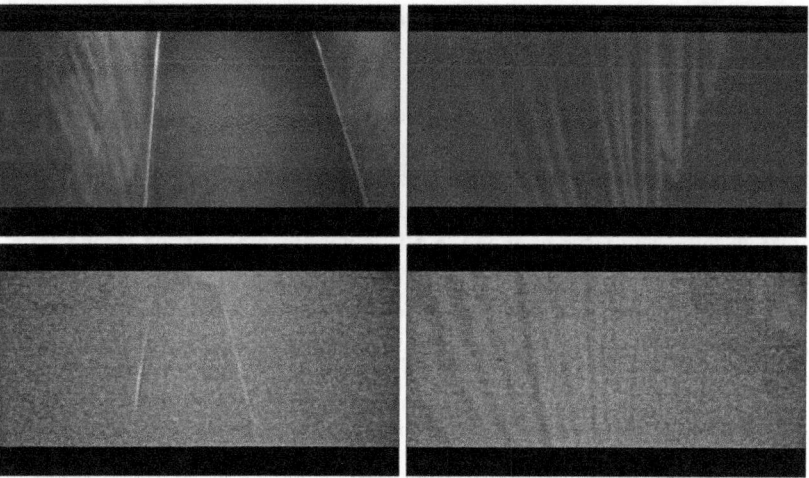

Figures 6.4–6.7 Fred's dream images (top; 00:18:20; 00:18:26) and the video footage (bottom; 00:22:05; 00:22:14).

whether any images are to be trusted. What seems important to note about Michalsky's observation is that it refers to two different kinds of images within the film. On the one hand, it refers to the video footage that is produced *within* the film and plays a specific role there; on the other hand, it is about the images of the film, that is, the images *through which* the film as such comes into being in the first place. Regarding *The Alphabet*, I have argued that the animated dream images present a kind of "second-order seeing," that is, a reflexive seeing which, unlike a "first-order seeing," is conscious of its own seeing (similar to Hobson's distinction between a primary and a secondary consciousness [803]; cf. section "Oneiric Atmosphere" in Chapter 3). In the short film, animation expressed the awareness of the otherness of dream vision (in relation to the live action images of the framing waking scene). In *Lost Highway*, the bifurcation of vision into first-order and second-order seeing, or the separation into film and video images, can be understood as an expression of the protagonist's dissociative identity structure. Elisabeth Howell describes dissociative identity disorder (DID) like this:

> The person with DID essentially lives with various simultaneously active and subjectively autonomous strands of experience that are rigidly and profoundly separated from each other in important ways, such as in memory, characteristic affects, behavior, self-image, body image, and thinking styles. These different segments of experiencing have their own sense of separate identity—their own sense of an "I"—including a sense of personal autobiographical memory; they may have different names. (Howell 3)

In *Lost Highway*, vision splits up into two irreconcilable forms, on the basis of two parts of the protagonist's personality that are equally irreconcilable. "On the basis of," however, does not mean that one form of seeing is simply "assigned" to one part of the personality and the other form to the other part. One could rather say that *because* the nature of dissociative identity disorder is such that fragmented units of self-experience cannot be integrated into a coherent and continuous sense of self, the film does not allow the viewer to integrate the two incompatible parts ("Fred" and "Pete") into a coherent whole. This seems to be true for both plot and aesthetics. On the plot level, an integration of the "Fred" part and the "Pete" part would imply that a reconstruction of temporal chronology is possible (in the sense of "Fred fell asleep at point x, experienced abc as Pete, and woke up again at point x+1"; such a reconstruction is at least possible for *Mulholland Drive*, for example), but it is not. To speak of the second (and/or third) part of *Lost Highway* as Fred's dream is different from calling the first part of *Mulholland Drive* a dream. In *Mulholland Drive*, someone (Diane) goes to sleep at the beginning and wakes up in the course of the story such that there are good reasons to assume that she dreams the first part of the film (cf. section "The Interconnection of Dream and Film" in Chapter 7). To a much greater extent, thus, *Mulholland Drive* suggests the first part to be a dream. *Lost Highway*, on the other hand, makes sure that Fred is *not* going to sleep before he "morphs" into Pete, and neither does he "wake up" again. Unlike *Mulholland Drive*, thus, *Lost Highway* does not juxtapose the first and second part through a dynamic of waking and dreaming.

If *Lost Highway* is called a filmic rendition of dissociative identity disorder, then it should be considered *how* the film translates the logic of this condition, applying it to itself. In a first step, this means: instead of witnessing the story of a dissociative person from a neutral, distanced, external perspective in which we would see Fred behaving *as if* he were Pete, *we see Pete*. Fred's transformation into Pete can be associated with "[t]he phenomenon generally considered most characteristic of DID," that is, "*switching*: Different internal identities can be prone to suddenly taking executive charge, in effect pushing the identity that had previously been in charge, out of charge" (Howell 4). *Lost Highway* grants the viewer an "internal perspective" on switching in how it objectifies Fred's transformation into Pete. For the viewer, Pete is as real as a film character can be, which echoes the subjective realness of "alters" (i.e., subidentities) for dissociative people. The internal perspective on dissociation relies on the inexplicability of Fred's transformation into Pete. What happened "that night?" Since there is no resolution from the subjective point of view, "that night" must remain a blind spot for the plot.

In the literature on the subject, further, two forms of DID are distinguished: in the *serial form*, two or more alters take turns in controlling the body. "When one is active, the other(s) usually is (are) not," writes Andrew Brook (213). In the *coconscious form*, on the other hand, the alters are present at the same time (Brook 213); "The unit in control of speech, for example, will report that another 'person' inside her is talking to her or giving her orders, these orders being experienced not from the standpoint of giving them but from an external standpoint, as coming from another person" (213). While Fred's transformation into Pete corresponds to the serial form of DID, the two also show a degree of coconsciousness, for example, in their shared (albeit fragmented) memory of Renée's murder (00:45:14–00:45:16 and 01:27:12–01:27:15) and in Pete's implied familiarity with Fred's saxophone solo (00:07:27–00:08:14 and 01:12:25–01:12:52), the latter constituting a "polyphonic intervention" into Pete's perception (cf. Brudzinska 64).

Beyond the interior view on the phenomenon, the film treats itself as the subject of this dissociative state, as if *it* were affected by it. The *what* of the narrative shapes the *how* of *Lost Highway*'s self-conception as a film. After all, on an aesthetic level, there is an unbridgeable gap between the technological perception of the video camera, on the one hand, and, on the other, the natural, human perception of the characters, whose perspective is transcended by the former. The video image remains something inaccessible to Fred in the first part. It evokes the sense of a "surplus" of reality, a surreality perhaps,[30] so that a glimpse of a second world within the first is hinted at but never fully revealed to us. Fred "likes to remember things his own way" (cf. 00:24:47–00:24:50), not by means of a video camera that objectively records them "the way they happened" (00:25:07–00:25:12).

Striking about the film is that the radical *otherness* of this medial image, that which is inaccessible to Fred due to his dissociative amnesia, is nonetheless tied to him via its connection to the dream. It is from the dream that Fred already knows the video images showing the hallway and the bedroom. In the dream, *he* took the perspective of the camera. Regarding the video, Seesslen writes: "An observing entity [...] has entered this house, which at the same time has a symbiotic communion with the man. 'It' [or 'Id'] perceives what Fred cannot perceive" (Seesslen 171; my translation).[31] Along with the video camera, the dream also embodies this perceiving agency. The dream perceives that which is not perceptible to Fred, it perceives "in his place," so to speak. It is that "something" in Fred that enables an experience of the nonintegrable, of that which has been split off. In this way, the dream points to the splitting of the protagonist into different parts, which underlies the division of the film into Fred's story and Pete's story.

Dream, on the one hand, and video, on the other, function as two "media" which, technologically speaking, enable perception from a (spatial and temporal) point of view at which the viewer is not situated. Semantically speaking, tele-vision allows her to "see" that which is "far," to see from a spatiotemporal vantage point which is not identical to her own. The viewer sees and hears things that are not in her immediate (nonmedial) environment; the sleeper is immersed in her subjective, virtual dream world and thus also perceives from a vantage point at which she is not physically located. In this sense, the dream can be understood as medial or, conversely, the video as dreamlike. If the medium, by its nature, allows an *other* to appear (cf. Brudzinska 60 and section "Phenomenologizing the Unconscious" in Chapter 4)—and this refers not only to a different spatial or temporal perspective but also to a different quality or order of experience—then both the video and the dream display a medial character. The dream stands as the natural, intrapsychic equivalent of the video, the video as the technological, externalized equivalent of the dream. The criterion of this analogization is difference. For the dream in *Lost Highway*, the medium "video" is a model for representing the other, the inaccessible, that is, for making the other "communicable." It gives aesthetic expression to otherness. According to Fichte, one could say that the dream shows that Fred already knew about the impending murder *in the form of images* (65–6). Vice versa, the dream is the video's possibility to anchor itself inside Fred's psyche despite its difference (from the cinematographic image). On the one hand, the dream is the medium of difference: it shows the absent, the gap in the chain of Fred's conscious experiences. Similar to the nocturnal dream, however, it simultaneously shows this absence *as present* (cf. section "Animation, Pixilation, and Trauma" in Chapter 3) and as an absence bound to Fred precisely by being identified as *his* dream.

The dream thus unites the two poles of the film's spectrum between subjectivity and objectivity. It is a general characteristic of the film to simultaneously encourage subjectivizing and objectivizing interpretations, as can be seen most clearly in the transformation of Fred into Pete: on the one hand, Pete compensates for Fred's negative self-image and is plausibly conceivable as his fantasy product; on the other hand, Pete is introduced as objectively existing in Fred's cell (as a "guarantee" of objectivity, Pete's presence is first conveyed to us through the perception of a guard). While the spatiotemporal continuity suggests the objectivity of Pete's world, the penetration of flesh could also be read as a subjectivization (i.e., Fred wants to wake up as somebody else the next day). The dream encompasses, for one, Fred's subjectively distorted perception of Renée: "it wasn't you [Renée]" (00:18:20–00:18:27) to the extent that he had seen in her only the embodiment of his own fears, his envy—things he wanted to get rid of; it might only have been through this projection that he was able to kill her in the first place. The other side of the spectrum is constituted by what supposedly "really" happened, irrespective of a character's subjective perspective (which includes Fred's amnesia for the murder). Obviously, I am referring to the video images through which Fred is "declared the murderer of his wife," as Michalsky put it (400). Minuz focuses on this objective dimension of the dream when he writes:

> This dream is now entirely objectified in the double regime of the images of the story (Renee searches for Fred, calling him by his name after he seems to have disappeared in the darkness of the corridor [. . .]) and in the images of the video recordings that show us the scene of the homicide, where the dream abruptly stopped [. . .] Therefore, the oneiric regime coincides with the narrative regime here, but, most importantly, the circuit that separated the video images and the film declines, thus canceling that sort of "staged" objectivity implemented by Fred himself. (Minuz 100; my translation)[32]

Regardless of whether or not the video footage in the film is actually reliable, it can be said that it provides a counterpoint to Fred's perception, which seems to have no memory at all of the murder of his wife depicted on the footage (he calls out to her as he watches the video showing her murder). Thus, and Minuz seems to overlook this, the dream introduces a dialectic between internal and external perception, the irresolvability of which is essential for the film's ontology.[33] It is true that the dream creates a strong connection between Fred's inner life and the objective events of the first part of the film. However, this does not mean that the dream is exhausted in its psychological function. It does prophesy the central event of *Lost Highway*'s plot, but it does so only insofar as one conceives of this event as diegetically real in the first place. In other words, how can the dream be "entirely objectified" (Minuz 100), if the world within which it is embedded is increasingly *de-*objectified, as the third part of the film suggests? The dream offers a model of derealization for the entire film rather than acting as an objectified element in a diegetic world with a solid ground. Perhaps, though, the two readings should not be set against each other. In any case, the dream does not provide a clear argument for one *or* the other reading: if the world of the first part is understood as real, the dream functions as a psychological phenomenon that prophesies Renée's murder (local function; only the first part is considered); if the first part is understood as unreal, the dream, in terms of a mise-en-abyme structure, functions as an ontological phenomenon that anticipates the self-undermining of the diegetic world (global function; the focus is on the third part).

Oneiric Self-Reflexivity and Meta-Mediality

A psychological interpretation of *Lost Highway* remains insufficient if it, first of all, insists on the idea of a clear separability of the events into reality and fantasy.[34] Not only the internal perception of psychosis embodied by the third part but also the mode of representation of dissociation (without return) ultimately renders an objectivist interpretation impossible. Lynch shows a radicalized form of identity disorder, which can be understood as psychologically motivated at the outset—Fred creates an idealized version of himself in order to both justify and cover up the murder of his wife. At the same time, however, there are clear hints at the objective existence of Pete (at least in the same sense of Fred's "objective" existence): he has a prehistory instead of beginning to exist when Fred's story "meets" his. He also has some characteristics that let the assumption of Pete as Fred's wish fantasy appear unlikely, for example, the fact that he lives with parents. Concerning the appropriateness of the idea of the film as a psychogenic fugue, Rodley comments:

> More revealing than "psychogenic"—which basically means "having origin in the mind"—is the definition of "fugue." Although it's primarily a musical term, it completely describes the picture: one theme starts and is then taken up by a second theme in answer. But the first continues to supply an accompaniment or counter-theme. Doesn't this perfectly describe the complex relationship between Fred and Pete? (Rodley 239)[35]

Besides the questionable assumption of a fugue state as a wish-fulfilling fantasy, an argument against a purely psychological reading of *Lost Highway* as a representation of a fugue state is suggested by the fact that Fred does not return to a superordinate level of reality. Rather than a temporary dissociative episode, the protagonist experiences a complete, irreversible dissolution of identity and world. Arguably, the role of the Mystery Man is most apt for characterizing the complex relationship between psychology and ontology in the film. While his first appearance on Renée's face could be understood as Fred's hallucination in retrospect, the Mystery Man's status at Andy's party is more ambiguous. Though he could be seen as Fred's hallucination, possibly as a result of having two shots at the bar, other people see the Man as well. Andy tells Fred that the Man is a friend of Dick Laurent (which will be confirmed in the second part of the film, when Dick and the Mystery Man call Pete). The Mystery Man has been understood as a representation of Fred's superego, in that he "is an intruder from an external place into an internal one" (McGowan, "Finding Ourselves" 58). Although it is interesting to observe how the dynamic *inside–outside* informs McGowan's Freudian conception of the superego (and thus the Mystery Man),[36] McGowan presupposes the Mystery Man's purely subjective status—which is not what the film suggests. That is, although he is functionally related to Fred's psyche, he *also* has an objective existence in the diegesis of all three parts of the film. Concerning his status and role in the film, it has been observed how he drives the events, to the point of becoming a manifestation of the director inside the story (cf. Sellmann 241–2). His metafictional status seems particularly appropriate in light of his role in the third part of *Lost Highway*, where, like a filmmaker, he points a camera at Fred (see Figure 6.8). He has been understood as "the author of the videos" that were sent to Fred and Renée earlier in the film (Minuz 95; my translation).[37]

A psychological interpretation also remains inadequate if it remains tied to the textual level of the film; or rather, we only recognize the psychological dimension of the film in its fullness if we take into account what kind of film experience *Lost Highway* is aiming at, that is, what kind of viewer experience is prefigured by the film. When Seesslen speaks of *Lost Highway* also being "about a discourse on the forms of perception" (168; my translation),[38] this should definitely include the self-reflexive level of film perception. That is, the phenomena of dissociation and loss of reality are not only represented on a textual level but also *performed* on a phenomenological level and thus translated into the viewer's immediate experience. The Pete-as-fantasy interpretation of *Lost Highway* ultimately cannot account for its ending because it remains tied to a textual conception of the film. That is, this reading treats the inability to distinguish reality from fantasy as a phenomenon *represented within* the film rather than also being *presented by* it.

The dream evokes the experience underlying the entire film in a condensed form. A phenomenological approach is able to combine the advantages of two existing types of literature on *Lost Highway* by connecting the meta-medial to the psychological dimension of the film. That is, the film radically denies the claim of representing truth (which would imply depicting an inhabitable world without logical contradiction) *because* its protagonist suffers from a highly distorted perception of himself and the world around him. The film loses its sense of reality *like* the dissociative or psychotic person may lose her sense of self and the world. Strictly speaking, the person at the basis of the psychological condition remains elusive. We see the facets of an anonymous, ungraspable person about whom we cannot say anything such that the psychological condition becomes the film's "protagonist," in a way. As the film's end suggests, further, dissociation of identity is only a step toward the total annihilation of self.

Besides implying the prophecy of murder, the distinctive potential of the dream consists in the depiction of the protagonist's inability to know the truth. The basic perceptual mechanism of recognizing a person is undermined by the dream. That is, the dream provides a model both for the protagonist's inability to recognize himself and the world and for the viewer's inability to grasp the world of the film. Thus, the dream points ahead to the meta-medial dimension of the film, namely to the fact that the images of *Lost Highway* are self-referential, that is, they exist only *as images*,

Figure 6.8 The Mystery Man as the expression of the complex relationship between psychology and ontology (01:59:05).

having no coherent "world" as a reference. Thus, when the possibility of illusion is addressed for the first time through the dream sequence ("it looked like you ... but it wasn't"; 00:18:28–00:18:32), the epistemological self-reflexivity of the film is already discernible in this. It is true that the version of Renée in Fred's dream is not the real Renée but only a dream figure. However, the principle of unreliability (of perception) becomes the principle of the film—irrespective of the boundaries between waking and dreaming. Thus, one could say, the dream raises a "world problem" in addition to a problem of personal identity (cf. Gehring, *Traum und Wirklichkeit* 250). That is, we cannot "think it [the dream] into a reality" (cf. Gehring, "Existentielle Psychologie" 00:56:18–00:56:26; my translation),[39] since *Lost Highway* does not let us conceptualize this "reality." The dream, then, manifests the ontology of the film.

In the previous chapter, I argued that the dream represented a state of ontological contradiction in the third season of *Twin Peaks* (2017; it brought forth "that which is and is not"; cf. "Part 10" 00:45:58–00:46:02 and section "The Function of Gordon Cole's Dream ... " in Chapter 5). The scene at FBI headquarters in the film *Twin Peaks: Fire Walk with Me* (1992), which preceded *Lost Highway*, already questioned its own act of seeing by negotiating the ontology of the camera image (cf. section "The Convenience Store" in Chapter 5). Here, too, the reliability of video footage was called into question, as Agent Cooper was simultaneously seen on the live image of the surveillance camera footage and in the room where he was watching that very footage. Seesslen referred to this as "the attempt to enable a pluralized vision within the same image" (136). The dreamlike perspective of the scene was to allow two contradictory perceptions to coexist in a single image, without elevating one over the other, thus raising the question of the "safe ground" of the diegetic world. *Lost Highway* takes up this idea— the title, in this context, can be understood literally as the absence of a material ground. This idea is again associated with the dream (as was shown, the dream anticipates the composition and movement of the video camera footage). *Lost Highway*, however, takes this kind of self-questioning even further by radically subverting the ontology of its own world, which remains intangible and exists only in images and sounds. In *Twin Peaks: Fire Walk with Me*, oneiric self-reflexivity was already implied but ended with the film's prologue. Its narrative potential is only fully exploited by *Lost Highway* through the creation of an ultimately self-referential world. If one wants to see in this a paradigmatic example of postmodern cinema, one should keep in mind what the film is about. The film does not deny a truth claim as an end in itself; it "only" deconstructs itself as a function of its subject. (Lynch's subsequent film *The Straight Story* [1999], for example, lives up to its name and straightforwardly tells a simple story about the relationship between two estranged aging brothers, without creating any doubts about the authenticity of the diegetic world.)

Lost Highway could be called a deconstructivist film. After all, it consistently deconstructs its own world. Like in *Eraserhead*, the dream announces a second world, but unlike in *Eraserhead*, it is not a second world *within* the first (the dancing Lady existed "inside" Henry's radiator); it is a second world *against* the first. This second world is first constituted by the videotapes and then by Pete's plotline. Both elements are related to, but never rendered fully reconcilable with, Fred's reality. Up to this point in Lynch's filmography, the otherness expressed through the dream may have perplexed the viewer; it may have introduced a new (order of) experience to the story that was otherwise inaccessible, but the dream never introduced a second ontological layer that was *fundamentally in conflict with* the first. Structurally, it never introduced a dialectic to the film that dismantled its own ontology. This is the groundbreaking novelty of *Lost Highway*'s dream sequence in Lynch's oeuvre.

Eraserhead displayed its self-consciousness in a mild way through the illumination of the theater stage at the beginning of the dream. *Twin Peaks* (1990–1) continued the theatrical aesthetics of the dream, but it let go of the self-reflexivity of *Eraserhead*'s light symbolism. Instead, Cooper's dream, aware of the dependence of cinematic realism on natural movement, marked its *un*-reality through the manipulation of movement. The *direction* of time flow was impossible to determine, showing a "paradoxical movement." *Lost Highway* not only expands the atemporality of Cooper's dream—the backward-burning cabin in the desert alludes to the backward-speaking occurring in the Red Room in *Twin Peaks* (1990–1; cf. section "Proper (Spatio-)temporality in Cooper's Dream . . . " in Chapter 5)—but it also connects it to the cinematic self-reflexivity that was first discernable in *Eraserhead*. It is not just that in hinting at Renée's murder, the dream shows an event that *has not happened yet*; but the version of reality in which Fred killed his wife, and possibly Dick Laurent, is logically irreconcilable with the version in which he did not, as can be seen by the impossibility of Fred *sending* and *receiving* the message "Dick Laurent is dead" at the same time (00:04:30–00:04:39 and 02:08:55–02:08:58). So the dream introduces a second world whose incompatibility with the first world expresses itself in the atemporality of the film's narrative structure. As it does not elevate one diegetic plane over the other, melting them together instead, the film shows itself to be aporetic. *Lost Highway* reflects on its own possibilities of representation (cf. section "The Dream as the Meta-Medium of Lynch's Films?" in Chapter 4), in that, through the dream, it suggests that it cannot represent truth. In this, *Lost Highway* anticipates the role of the dream in the last episodes of *Twin Peaks* (2017), which deconstructs its own diegesis using a dream metaphor (cf. section "'The Dream of Time and Space' . . . " in Chapter 5). In both cases, an oneiric, in the sense of "dreamlike" (because rooted in a dream sequence), disturbance in time flow expresses the larger ontological disruption.

7

Mulholland Drive (2001)

Audio-Viewing *Mulholland Drive*

In the film's opening images, the blurry silhouettes of two dancers are moving in front of a purple background. As the offbeat drums of composer Angelo Badalamenti's *Jitterbug* kick in, several dancing couples, shot in varying angles and distances, are covering the screen. There are large black silhouettes in the background and multiple versions of the same couple in the foreground. As they continue dancing, a heavily overexposed image of Naomi Watts's character—named Betty Elms in the first 117 minutes of the film and Diane Selwyn in the remaining 26 minutes—is superimposed. She is with an elderly couple (Jeanne Bates and Dan Birnbaum) and wears a bright smile. A cheering crowd could suggest that she won a prize. The music stops and the image fades into an out-of-focus shot of what turns out to be the floor of a bedroom. Somebody's heavy breathing is audible as the camera pans to reveal red bedsheets and a yellow-green blanket, then closing in on the pillow until the screen goes black.

The street sign of Mulholland Dr. (a famous scenic drive in Los Angeles) reflects the headlights of a car, introducing the opening credits sequence. As the credits are rolling, a limousine is driving on a road at night, presumably Mulholland Dr., and we get a panoramic view of Los Angeles at night. Badalamenti's synthesizers establish an atmosphere that has a floating quality and combines dramatic, melancholic, and mysterious elements. In the back of the limousine, there is an elegantly dressed, dark-haired woman (Laura Elena Harring) who complains that "we don't stop here," as the limo comes to a halt at the roadside (00:05:10–00:05:15). The driver points a gun at her, telling her to get out of the car. Two speeding cars are approaching from the opposite direction, one of them crashing into the limousine. The dark-haired woman survives the crash, but she is bleeding from her forehead. She makes her way into the city, passing by Franklin Avenue and Sunset Boulevard (referencing Billy Wilder's film *Sunset Boulevard* [1950] for the second time already; cf. Figures 7.14 and 7.15). Hiding from an approaching couple in the front yard of an apartment building, she lies down and falls asleep. At the site of the crash, two policemen suspect that a woman who was in the limo's back seat had left before they arrived.

The dark-haired woman wakes up in the morning, as another woman—we will come to know her as (Betty's) "aunt Ruth" (Maya Bond)—is leaving her apartment with a number of heavy suitcases. The dark-haired woman sneaks into Ruth's apartment and hides beneath the kitchen sink. Suffering from a head injury inflicted by the crash, she falls asleep again.

The next scene, which may or may not be read as her dream, is set at Winkie's diner where two men named Dan (Patrick Fischler) and Herb (Michael Cooke) talk about a recurring dream of Dan's. He recalls that his dream took place at this particular restaurant, and that he was very scared, as was Herb. Dan connects his fear to a "man in back of this place . . . he's the one who's doing it" (00:13:46–00:13:55). Dan hopes to never see the man's face outside of a dream. Herb understands that Dan "came to see if he's out there" (00:14:26–00:14:30). When they approach the back alley behind Winkie's to make sure that he is not there, the terrifying "Bum" (Bonnie Aarons) does appear and Dan faints.

At Aunt Ruth's apartment, the dark-haired woman is still sleeping under the sink. The following short sequence shows a series of mysterious phone calls revolving around a missing girl.

In the company of the elderly couple from the opening images, Betty—the protagonist of *Mulholland Drive*—arrives at the Los Angeles airport. She seems absolutely euphoric about coming to Los Angeles, or more specifically about becoming an actress, as we learn from the older woman's encouragement: "Remember, I'll be watching for you on the big screen" (00:19:03–00:19:05). Betty gets to her aunt Ruth's apartment in West Hollywood, and the property manager Coco (Ann Miller) gives her the key to it. She is confused to find the dark-haired woman in the shower of the apartment but assumes her to be a friend of her aunt. Unable to remember her real name, the dark-haired woman calls herself Rita after a movie poster of Charles Vidor's noir-classic *Gilda* (1946) starring Rita Hayworth. Betty tells her that her aunt is working on a movie in Canada, which is why she can stay at her apartment while trying to get a job as an actress. Originally she is from Deep River, Ontario, "and now I'm in this dream place" (00:26:33–00:26:37).

Due to her head injury, Rita needs to sleep some more. Like the Winkie's scene, the two next sequences seem unrelated to the main plot. The first sequence is set at an entertainment company in downtown Los Angeles. Director Adam Kesher (Justin Theroux) is in the process of recasting the lead actress of his film, *The Sylvia North Story*. The Castigliane brothers (Angelo Badalamenti and Dan Hedaya), who play a crucial role in the film's production, bring the photo of an actress named Camilla Rhodes (Melissa George) to the meeting. Trying to force Adam to cast her, they repeatedly tell him that "this is the girl" (00:31:03–00:31:05). Adam refuses to accept, saying that "that girl is not in my film," upon which Vincenzo Castigliane threatens that "it's no longer your film" (00:33:10–00:33:20). Mr. Roque (Michael J. Anderson), a mysterious man sitting in a room that is enclosed by heavy curtains, has been listening in on the conversation over the phone. He seems to be in control over the production, as suggested by the way in which a producer of *The Sylvia North Story* tries to find out whether Roque wants to "shut everything down" (00:35:49–00:35:52).

In the next sequence, set at a downtown office, hitman Joe (Mark Pellegrino) talks with Ed (Vincent Castellanos) about a car accident. When Joe catches sight of "Ed's famous black book" containing "the history of the world in phone numbers"

(00:37:42–00:37:53), he kills him as well as two other people working on the same floor.

Back in the apartment, Betty talks to her aunt Ruth over the phone. Ruth does not know Rita and wants her niece to call the police. Rita, who just woke up, is crying and confesses to Betty, "I don't know who I am" (00:43:07–00:43:11). Betty suggests to check Rita's purse for papers. What they find inside, however, is a large amount of cash and a triangular blue key whose origin Rita cannot recall.

Meanwhile, Joe asks a blonde woman (Rena Riffel) who seems to work for him whether there have been "any new girls on the street lately," particularly a "brunette" who might be "a little beat up" (00:45:39–00:45:53), which the blonde woman denies.

The only thing Rita seems to remember until now is that she was going to Mulholland Dr. on the night of the crash. At Winkie's, the waitress's (Missy Crider) name tag, which reads "Diane," triggers a memory in Rita; "Diane Selwyn—maybe that's my name," she says full of hope to rediscover her identity (00:55:41–00:55:45). Back in the apartment, Betty and Rita retrieve Diane Selwyn's number from a phone book and call her, but she does not answer. Listening to her voice on the mailbox, Rita says it is not hers, but it seems familiar. An ominous neighbor named Louise (Lee Grant) knocks at the door, telling Betty that "someone is in trouble" (01:13:12–01:13:15). Louise asks Betty who she is and what she is doing in Ruth's apartment. When she says that her name is Betty, Louise insists, "No, it's not . . . . That's not what she said" (01:13:27–01:13:30). Then Coco comes and resolves the situation.

Meanwhile, Adam is informed that his movie set has been closed, with everyone having been fired. He drives home to his Hollywood villa and, in a comical scene, finds his wife (Lori Heuring) in bed with another man (Billy Ray Cyrus). Adam takes her jewelry and smears pink paint all over it. The lover punches him in the face and throws him out of his own house, so he moves to a cheap downtown motel. The owner (Geno Silva) informs him that he is broke, which Adam finds hard to believe. His assistant confirms this and tells him to go and see "the Cowboy" (Monty Montgomery) who seems connected to the bad things that have been happening to him. Adam drives to "a corrall" at the "top of Beachwood Canyon" (01:01:23–01:01:27) to meet the Cowboy, who tells him to choose the woman whose photo was shown to him earlier on for the lead role of his film.

Coco is growing suspicious of Betty's new friend and tells her to get rid of potential trouble in the apartment. Betty and Rita rehearse a melodramatic scene for an audition that Betty is going to participate in. Betty finds the scene lame and makes fun of its over-the-top emotionality. At the audition, however, she gives a great performance and impresses everyone who is present—so much so that a casting agent (Rita Taggart) immediately takes her to the set of *The Sylvia North Story*, where she locks eyes with the director Adam Kesher. Following the Cowboy's instruction, Adam tells the producers that "this is the girl" when Camilla Rhodes is auditioning for the lead role (01:26:28–01:27:02). Dropping the opportunity to meet Adam, Betty suddenly runs off because she just realized that she had promised Rita to go to Sierra Bonita with her to meet Diane Selwyn.

At Diane Selwyn's apartment, nobody opens the door, so Betty sneaks in through an open window and opens the front door to Rita. There is a bad smell in the apartment. As Diane's neighbor (Johanna Stein) knocks at the front door—she wants to get some of her things back from Diane—Betty and Rita find a decaying corpse in the bedroom, which causes them to escape. Back in Ruth's apartment, possibly as a reaction to seeing the dark-haired corpse at Sierra Bonita, Rita cuts off some of her hair and puts on a blonde wig. Betty offers to share the bed with her, and Rita accepts. Rita thanks Betty for everything and they have sex. Betty says that she is in love with Rita.

In her sleep, Rita repeats the words, "Silencio . . . no hay banda . . . no hay orquesta" over and over again until Betty, awakened by the sound of her voice, wakes her up (01:42:38–01:43:23). Waking up does not seem to calm her down, though. Rita asks Betty to "go with me somewhere" (01:43:37–01:43:39), even though it is 2 a.m. They take a cab and enter a place called Club Silencio.

As Rita and Betty are finding their seats inside Club Silencio, a man on stage (Richard Green)—he is credited as "The Magician"—exclaims, "no hay banda. There is no band. Il n'est pas [sic] de orchestra [sic]" (01:45:25–01:45:36). As he says these words, we can hear (but not see) an ensemble of high and low strings playing. "This is all a tape recording," he continues, "no hay banda, and yet we hear a band. If we want to hear a clarinet, listen" (01:45:38–01:45:55)—and a clarinet can be heard. The same happens with a trombone. The Magician announces "a muted trumpet," and a trumpet player (Conte Candoli) enters the stage (01:46:26). A loud and crisp trumpet is audible, apparently originating from the stage performance, but the player soon moves the trumpet away from his mouth, stretching out his arms (01:46:41). The sound of the trumpet, however, remains audible in the same intensity. "It's all recorded," reaffirms the Magician (01:46:47–01:46:50), with the trumpeter commenting ironically through a perfectly synchronized, shrill sound (01:46:50). Yet again, the Magician insists that there is no band—"it is an illusion" (01:47:16). He then tells the audience to listen and raises up his arms abruptly, conjuring up a thunder. Blue light floods the theater, as intense hissing sounds can be heard (01:47:29–01:47:43). In response to the thunder, Betty's body is shaking heavily and Rita holds her tight. As soon as the Magician takes his arms down, the thunder stops, as does Betty's previously uncontrollable shaking. The Magician then crosses his arms, tilts his head, and disappears in blue smoke, smiling diabolically. The theater, once again, is bathed in blue light. Next, we see a performance by Rebekah Del Rio (playing herself), singing the Spanish version of Roy Orbison's *Crying*. The song deals with the pain of a romantic relationship that has come to an end. As Betty and Rita are watching the performance, they start crying themselves. At some point, Del Rio loses consciousness, dropping to the ground, while her voice remains audible in the same intensity (01:51:46–01:51:52). As she is carried off the stage, Betty opens up her purse, finds a mysterious blue box in it (01:52:38), and they leave Club Silencio.

Betty and Rita take the blue box back to the apartment. Betty puts it on the bed and then disappears, with Rita asking in Spanish where she is. Rita takes the blue key they found earlier on in her purse and opens the blue box. The camera approaches the blackness inside the box and the box drops to the floor. Both Rita and Betty are not in the bedroom anymore. Instead, aunt Ruth briefly appears. She has a look around the room and leaves again.

The second part of the film is introduced through a shift in space-time, which brings us back to the Sierra Bonita apartment. A woman in a black nightdress is lying in bed at the same position as the corpse from earlier on. The Cowboy appears, saying, "Hey little girl, time to wake up" (01:56:37–01:56:41). In the reverse shot, the corpse lies in the bed. After a longer fade to black, it is daytime and Naomi Watts's character is lying in bed, wearing a light-colored nightdress. A persistent knocking at the door wakes her up. The neighbor (Johanna Stein again) wants to get her things back. She calls Naomi Watts's character *Diane* (not Betty). A blue key—this one looking more like a real key compared to the one we saw earlier—can be seen on the table. The neighbor informs her that two detectives have been looking for her. While preparing coffee, Diane fantasizes about Laura Elena Harring's character. In what is most likely Diane's memory—the ashtray that the neighbor just took with her is on her table again, indicating that this scene must have happened within the last "three weeks" (01:58:35–01:58:37)—Diane calls Harring's character *Camilla* (not Rita). Diane and Camilla are topless on the sofa, kissing and caressing each other. Although she seems to be enjoying it at first, Camilla says that "we shouldn't do this anymore" (02:02:46–02:02:49), which upsets Diane. "It's him, isn't it?" she responds (02:03:23–02:03:25), and we cut to a film set, another scene from Diane's memory. Adam instructs an actor on how to shoot a romantic scene with Camilla (Laura Elena Harring[1]) and Diane is watching as Adam and she kiss. The scene is embedded within another scene showing Diane's and Camilla's break-up.

Next, we see Diane desperately crying while trying to masturbate. A ringing phone in the present triggers another memory sequence in which Diane picks up the phone in an elegant dress. Camilla tells her that a car is waiting to take her to Mulholland Drive.

Now, images from the film's beginning are recast: the street sign of Mulholland Dr., the limousine driving through the night. Instead of Rita, though, it is now Diane sitting in the back. Again, the limo stops where it is not supposed to, the reason being, however, that Camilla surprises Diane, picking her up to walk the rest of the way through the Hollywood Hills. They get to a party at Adam's villa, where Diane introduces herself as Diane Selwyn to Adam's mother Coco—like the property manager from earlier on, she is played by Ann Miller. At dinner, Diane tells Coco that winning a Jitterbug contest in the past was what "lead to acting . . . you know . . . *wanting* to act" (02:12:55–02:12:59). Diane used the money her aunt left her to move to Hollywood from Deep River, Ontario. We learn that she met Camilla on the set of *The Sylvia North Story*, for which director Bob Brooker chose Camilla over Diane as the lead actress. Diane then sees several characters that we are familiar with from the first part of the film: the man we came to know as Luigi Castigliane, the actress who was forced upon Adam ("this is the girl") named Camilla Rhodes (Melissa George), and the Cowboy, all of which are guests at the party. Diane then watches as "Camilla"[2] (Melissa George) bends down and kisses Camilla (Laura Elena Harring), which brings her to tears. As Adam and (Harring's) Camilla are about to announce their engagement, we suddenly cut to Winkie's.

At Winkie's diner, Diane is served coffee by a waitress named Betty (still played by Missy Crider). She is with hitman Joe and hands him a photo of Camilla Rhodes (Laura Elena Harring), telling him that "this is the girl" (02:15:53–02:16:56). She shows him a large amount of money, and he shows her a blue key, which she is going to find once the job is done. Diane looks over to the counter and sees Dan, who told Herb about his nightmare at the beginning of the film. Diane asks Joe what the key opens and he starts laughing.

The image then dissolves into a night shot of the back alley behind Winkie's. The Bum is holding the blue box in his hands and puts it in a small paper bag, then drops it to the ground. From inside the bag, a miniature version of the elderly couple from the film's beginning emerges, moving strangely.

A cut brings us back to the blue key on Diane's living room table. Diane is wearing the same bathrobe she wore when she opened the door to her neighbor, which indicates a temporal continuity (everything in between constituting a series of flashbacks). She gazes at the key and, after a while, there is the persistent knocking at the door again. With the sudden onset of a heavy thunder, the old couple, still in miniature, enters the apartment through the slit under the door. A moment later, they are life-sized and approach a screaming Diane. She is pushed back into her bedroom where she shoots herself on the bed as white smoke is emerging. The smoke covers the screen.

In what might be called the film's epilogue, a montage shows us the Bum, a blue curtain, and Hollywood at night with an overexposed superimposition of Betty/Diane and Rita/Camilla. In the film's final moment, a blue-haired woman (Cori Glazer) in Club Silencio says, "Silencio" (02:22:27–02:22:30), as the image fades to black.

The Interconnection of Dream and Film

In order to draw closer to what "oneiric" means with regard to *Mulholland Drive*, it is essential to ponder three possible, but not necessarily mutually exclusive, ways of framing the interrelationship between dream and film in Lynch's movie. The first—"dream-in-film"—speaks to the psychological plausibility of dividing the film into Diane Selwyn's dream and her waking world and allows for a chronological reconstruction of the narrative events (i.e., a translation of the *plot* into the *story* of *Mulholland Drive*; cf. Figure 7.3). The second—"film-as-dream"—exists in two versions. The strong version considers the entire film to be an autonomous dream representation. The weak version addresses the unusual production history of the film and suggests that Diane's dream, making up about four-fifths of the final feature film *Mulholland Drive*, exists as a film-within-the-film. The third way of framing the interrelationship between dream and film—"dream-as-film"—reveals that "the stuff that Diane's dream is made on" is *film*. It draws our attention to the subtly exposed cinematic nature of Diane's dream and mediates between the dream-in-film and the film-as-dream hypotheses, favoring the weak version of the latter. Thus, it shows that Diane's dream is a film-like experience rather than the (entire) film being a dreamlike experience.

"Dream in Film"—The Psychological-American Dream of Diane Selwyn

The dream-in-film hypothesis, feeding one of the dominant interpretations of the film, hinges on what may be interpreted as formal markers of a dream's beginning and end. What we see from the opening credits ("Justin Theroux . . . ") until 01:56:58 is the dream of Diane Selwyn (Naomi Watts). The breathing we hear before the opening credits as someone is sinking into a red pillow is Diane's, which becomes clear through the same color of the bedsheets and blanket at the two points in time. The two images of the bed thus act as the opening and end marker of a long dream sequence making up almost two hours of the film (see Figures 7.1 and 7.2).

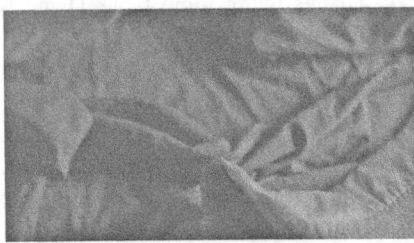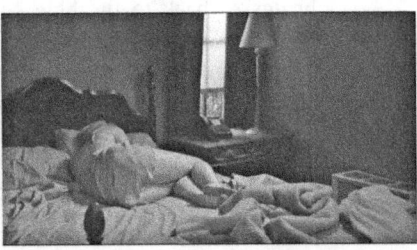

Figures 7.1–7.2 The opening (left) and end marker (right) of Diane's dream (00:02:25; 01:57:03).

Arguably, what makes this interpretation so attractive is the combination of two factors. For one, it seems to stick closely to what the film itself suggests: what, if not a dream, do the bracketing shots of one and the same bed indicate? And whose dream could it be except Diane's? A second reason for the popularity of the dream-in-film interpretation is its explanatory potential. Not only does it allow for the reconstruction of a temporal chronology of the film's story elements (see Figure 7.3), but it also provides an explanation for the modified recurrence of events and characters in the two ontologically distinct parts of the film (see Figure 7.4). That is, the dream-in-film hypothesis fills in the causal gap between the two parts of the film, acting as a nexus. Without it, *Mulholland Drive*, as a whole, would become causally and ontologically incoherent. The events of the first (roughly) two hours of the film would not follow from or be rooted in the world depicted in the last half hour. As I will show, however, rather than in causal or ontological incoherence, the difficulty to understand the movie is grounded in its apparent temporal incoherence—an incoherence that the dream-in-film hypothesis resolves.

To break down the plot into four temporal units, (1) a long dream sequence is followed by (2) Diane's recollection of the recent (waking) past from the perspective of (3) a narrowly defined present (the neighbor comes to get back some things that Diane borrowed; Diane makes coffee and looks at the blue key) and (4) her fantasy of a suicide that might really (have) happen(ed). The timeline of *Mulholland Drive*'s story may thus be represented as follows:

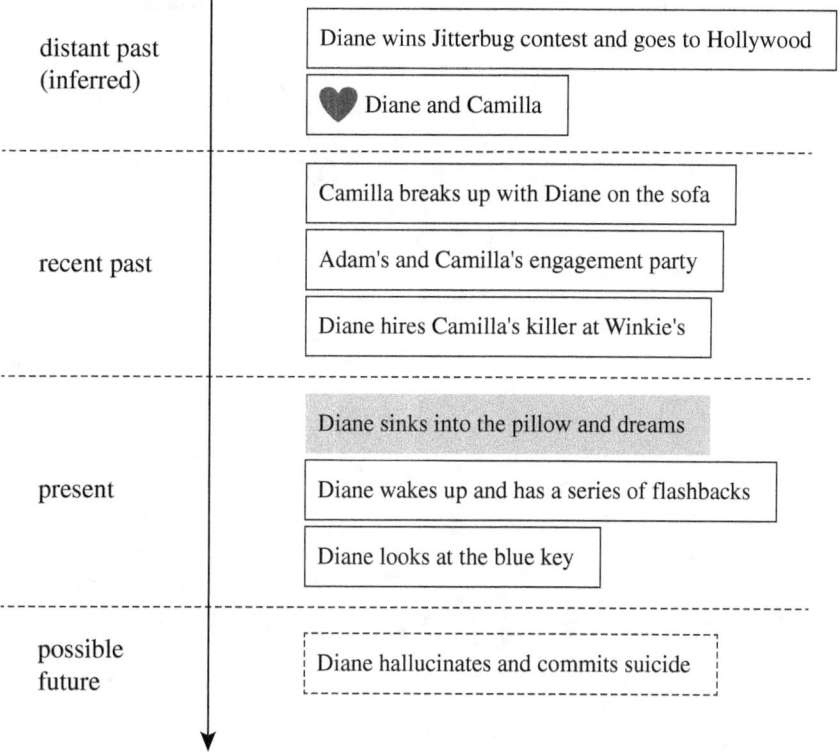

Figure 7.3 A chronological reconstruction of *Mulholland Drive*'s plot elements according to the dream-in-film hypothesis.

Diane came to Hollywood wanting to become an actress, but unlike her dream ego Betty, she was found to have no talent. Bob Brooker (Wayne Grace), the director of *The Sylvia North Story* (a film she auditioned for), "didn't think so much of me" (02:13:57–02:13:59), as she recalls at the engagement party. This explains why, in her dream audition, Brooker's comments are appreciative but also nonsensical. Brooker calls Betty's performance "very good, really [. . .] I mean, it was forced, maybe, but still . . . humanistic" (01:20:15–01:20:25). His response builds on a double motivation on the part of Diane's unconscious, as her dream's mockery of his pseudo-intellectual criticism ("humanistic") signals her aggression against the director who hurt her feelings in reality (and thus discredits his opinion), while also implying Diane's need for the recognition of her talent ("very good").

On the set of *The Sylvia North Story*, Diane fell in love with Camilla Rhodes, and they have had an affair until recently. When Camilla leaves Diane for Adam, Diane hires a hitman to kill Camilla. After Camilla's murder, Diane has a dream that, by and large, compensates for the lack of success in her career and love life. Reprocessing her real-life disappointment, her dream ego Betty essentially experiences what Diane

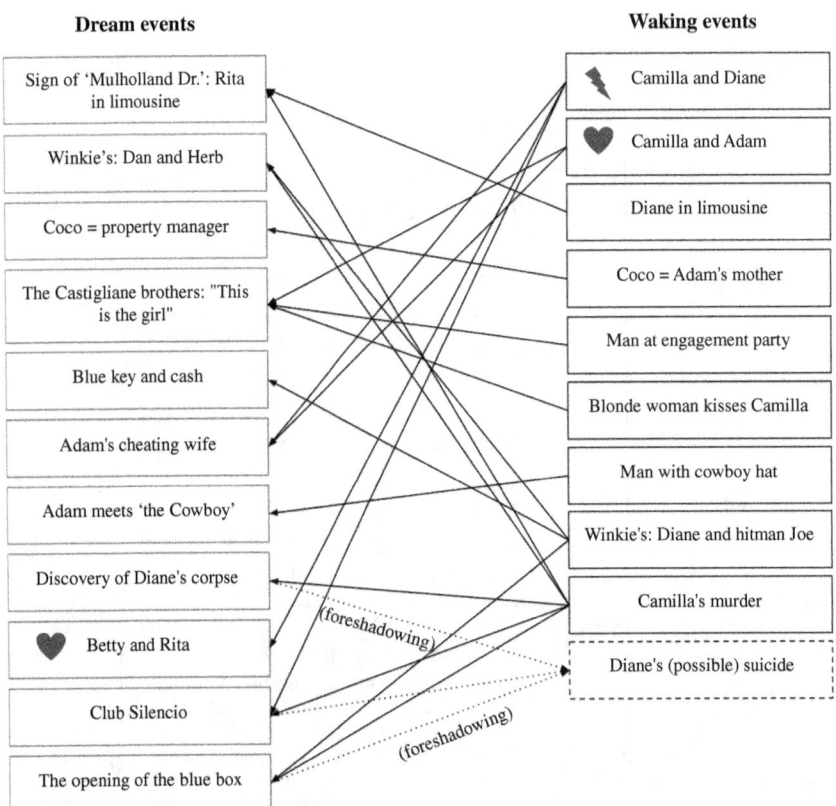

Figure 7.4 The complex relationship between dream events and waking events.

wished for most deeply: to be loved by Camilla and the film industry. Camilla's dream character (who will name herself Rita) loses her memory in a car crash at the beginning of the film/dream, and it seems crucial that she is unable to act autonomously. Diane's dream reimagines Camilla as having lost her identity ("I don't know who I am"; 00:43:07–00:43:11), which makes her completely dependent on Betty. Hence, waking Diane's fear that something bad might happen when the limousine takes her to Camilla's engagement party and suddenly stops turns into control in her dream. Betty is in full control over amnesic Rita. At the same time, the car crash could be seen as a symbol for the status of Diane's career. If Mulholland Dr. represents Hollywood in the film—Camilla can only afford to live there due to her success as an actress—then an accident on this road expresses the failure of Diane's acting career in Hollywood. It is not a coincidence that the accident happens on the road that is the new home of the successful Camilla. Besides allowing Diane to "hurt back" who hurt her in real life, thus, it becomes clear in retrospect that the crash is a symbolic, censored image for Diane's failed career as well as an aggression toward Camilla and the film industry, that is, Diane's two principal desired objects.

After giving an amazing performance at the audition and visiting the set of *The Sylvia North Story*, Betty suddenly leaves to meet with Rita instead of being introduced to Adam—a moment that deserves some attention if we are to grasp the psychological nature of Diane's dream experience. By choosing to leave the soundstage, she sacrifices both a romantic opportunity and a professional one. Betty behaves like a child participating in a competition who, when it becomes clear that the chances of winning are narrowing, pretends to have joined "just for the fun of it." Betty did not *really* want a big role, just like the child did not *really* want to win the competition. In this context, it seems like Diane's dream has conjured up a second reason for her lack of success in the film industry. Given her resemblance to the blonde Camilla Rhodes (Melissa George), the dream seems to imply that Betty's chance at getting the lead role in Adam's movie was barred by Mr. Roque and his disciples who, in a totalitarian fashion, determined that the blonde Camilla gets the part. Had it not been for the dark forces of Hollywood's cartel-like film industry, Betty might have been the "blonde girl" playing the lead role. But it is not only Diane's failure in the movie business that is reinterpreted here, Diane also "blames" Camilla for dating Adam,[3] which led to their break-up. Again, it seems crucial that Betty *chooses* to leave the set. Locking eyes with Adam, she "could have had" him, too, but she chooses Rita instead, just like Diane wanted to be chosen by Camilla over Adam in waking reality. Through Betty's leaving, thus, Diane proves to herself that it would have been possible for Camilla to choose her over Adam. In this way, Diane's dreaming mind expresses the wish that Camilla should have stayed loyal to her, even if it would have meant dropping a big career opportunity.

Further, as both Sinnerbrink and McGowan ("Lost on Mulholland" 78) argue, Diane's unconscious splits Camilla into two people: the "blonde Camilla" (Melissa George) who gets the part in Adam's movie and the amnesic "Rita" (Laura Harring). The real Camilla (Harring) is both the object of Diane's unrequited love and the manifestation of her unsuccessful acting career: in reality, she got the part Diane wanted and she lives on Mulholland Dr.—representing Hollywood—that is, the geographical manifestation of that which inspires the idea of "wanting to act" in many people. Hence, both the personal and the professional dimension feed into the dream's representations of Camilla. For McGowan, the blonde Camilla represents the real Camilla's name, that is, "the undesirable part of Camilla," given that "the name 'Camilla Rhodes' comes to signify corruption and undeserved success" ("Lost on Mulholland" 78). Rita, in his view, represents the real Camilla's body, that is, the "desirable part of Camilla" (78). In other words, Diane's dream turns Camilla Rhodes into an "object" she can handle: her body is wounded and in shock, her memory is not functioning, and her name belongs to somebody else, which makes it bearable that Camilla has the success that Diane wants. Possibly rooted in the blonde woman kissing Camilla at the party (due to the kiss, Camilla's name carries over to the blonde girl in Diane's unconscious), the function of the splitting seems to be twofold: first, Betty's and Rita's relationship is not compromised by the blonde Camilla getting the part (as it would have been if the dark-haired Camilla got it); and second, Camilla's acting is discredited because external forces (the mafia-like structures involving Mr. Roque) rather than skill are shown as responsible for Camilla's success. By making Adam the victim of a

Hollywood mafia, Diane's dream also takes revenge on him. After all, her lover Camilla left her *for him*, so it seems natural that her dream would be fueled by aggression toward him. Most clearly, Diane's revenge on Adam takes the form of his wife cheating on him with another man. Hence the dream does to Adam what he did to Diane in reality, at least in Diane's perception. Instead of Diane, it is now Adam, the object of her jealousy, who is being cheated on.

Concerning the blue key and the money found in Rita's purse, it seems crucial to understand the temporal and causal relationship between the two parts of the film. That is, as Diane is dreaming, Camilla is already dead. Hitman Joe, paid by Diane to kill Camilla, uses the blue key as a signifier of the job's completion. (Although we only see the key after Diane wakes up, its location on the living room table indicates that she has seen it before—i.e., *before* going to sleep.) The key's subsequent appearance in Diane's dream is thus both a *hint at* and a *concealment of* the fact that she ordered her ex-lover's death—a concealment because it has lost the symbolic function of the waking world (in her dream, she is unaware of the key signaling Camilla's death) and because of its modified, now geometrical shape. A similar observation can be made in regard to the initial car crash and "Rita's" subsequent loss of identity. Her physical injury alludes to Camilla's death and, given her amnesia, implies the inability of Diane's dream to see the dark-haired woman for who she is: Camilla.

One of the things that are remarkable about *Mulholland Drive* is that its dream-in-film dimension not only speaks to the psychological dream of Diane but also to the concept of the American Dream. Arguably, the film intertwines the literal psychological dimension of dreaming with its metaphorical cultural dimension: Diane has a dream in the psychological sense while living (her own version of) the American Dream at the same time. The film seems to agree with Leandro Drivet who, paraphrasing Freud, observes that "myths are to humanity what dreams (and deliriums) are to individuals. Both phenomena show unconscious regularities in symbolization that lead to surprising parallels" (Drivet 1683). *Mulholland Drive* makes this link visible, in that the myth of Hollywood fame (as part of the collective American Dream) is intertwined with, or rather *literalized as*, Betty's delusional state (i.e., Diane's dream). Hollywood acts as the both literally and metaphorically dream-inducing entity of the film because it provides the root of Diane's culturally formed wish for fame and its concomitant idea of a happy and successful private and professional life—a wish that also informs her psychological dream. Metaphorically speaking, Hollywood made her "dream" of becoming a famous actress: Betty says that being "discovered and becom[ing] a movie star" is "sort of the reason why I came here" (00:26:10–00:26:23), which conforms to Diane's recollection, "I always wanted to come here.... I won this Jitterbug contest. That sort of lead to acting... you know, *wanting* to act" (02:12:45–02:12:59). But the "dream place" (00:26:31–00:26:37) that Betty perceives Hollywood to be does not only echo the idea of the American Dream (the promise that anybody can make it to success in America) but also denotes the current ontological reality (even if Betty is unaware of this). Hollywood thus makes Diane "dream" both in the metaphorical and in the literal sense. Diane's idealization of Hollywood is so powerful that, even after her real-life professional failure, it still fuels her escapist dream fantasy.

Mulholland Drive—Lynch calls its eponym a "dream road" ("Making-of 'Mulholland Drive'" 00:01:28)—thus psychologizes the American Dream and, in this, points to the individual dimension of the collective metaphorical dream as well as to its psychological basis. (After all, the conceptual metaphor of the *American Dream* is rooted in the concrete psychological experience of dreaming.[4]) At the same time, the film hints at the collective dimension of an individual dream because desires (i.e., potential dream sources) do not emerge in a vacuum but are, to a large extent, generated by a culture.[5] A psychological dream is thus never *just* psychological, in that it is rooted in culturally formed wishes that are to some extent determined from "outside" the individual. I am susceptible to cultural influences such as Western celebrity cult because, as Merleau-Ponty says, "I am immediately outside myself and open to the world" (*Phenomenology* 483).[6]

"Film as Dream"

Some scholars disagree with the interpretation that the film can be divided into a long dream part and a subsequent shorter part depicting waking reality. For Kaul and Palmier, *Mulholland Drive* does not distinguish between a dream and a waking world but combines two incompatible parts into a logically impossible world, the story being contradictory (118). Eva Laass, similarly, speaks of "an equal parallelism of the presented fictional worlds" (277; my translation) that does not allow for the distinction between subjective and objective elements (Kaul and Palmier 148).[7] What their interpretation seems to ignore is the Cowboy's *time to wake up* (01:56:40–01:56:41) prominently introducing the second part of the film, thus at least stimulating the reading of the first part as a dream. Even if one may argue that the dream-in-film interpretation cannot be upheld consistently, it should be acknowledged that the juxtaposition of the film's two parts is accomplished through a dynamic of waking and dreaming.

Stefanie Kreuzer sees the opening and closing images of the film (see Figures 7.5 and 7.6) as indicating an "overall and general dream state" (662; my translation).[8] Granted, the image at the very beginning showing the dancing couples multiplying in a purple nonspace has a dreamlike quality, and it precedes Diane going to sleep, so it is unlikely to be *her* dream. Similarly, the closing images cannot be the product of Diane's mind—she just died—and yet they contain elements of Diane's unconscious such as the terrifying oil-smeared Bum. These observations seem appealing to those who share the feeling that the cliché of *film-as-dream* is not just a metaphor here but is taken literally by *Mulholland Drive*. Is the film to be viewed as an "autonomous dream representation" (Kreuzer 662; my translation)[9] what I call the *strong version* of the film-as-dream interpretation—without a hierarchy between a dream level that is subordinate to a waking level?

If the film intended to deny any waking-dreaming hierarchy between the two parts, then this would raise the question why would it show the same bed (with the same

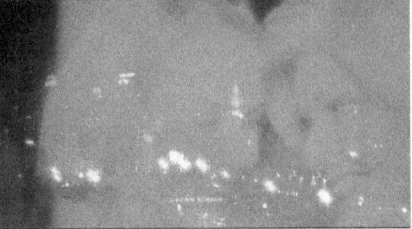

Figures 7.5–7.6 Opening (left) and closing (right) images of *Mulholland Drive* (00:00:43; 02:21:49)—is the entire film an autonomous dream?

colors of the sheets and the blanket) again at the crucial moment that separates the film's two ontologically distinct levels. The recurrence of the bed seems to indicate a spatiotemporal continuity between the shot introducing the opening credits and the shot of Diane waking up, implying the embedded forty sequences[10] to be Diane's internally focalized dream images.[11] The opening shot of the dancing couples, by the way, could also be considered internally focalized, if Diane's point-of-view shot is seen as a brief moment of waking up while falling asleep. What would support such an interpretation of the opening shot as subjective imagery is that it displays some essential characteristics of hypnagogic hallucinations. E. Thompson writes that "in the hypnagogic state, we look at visual patterns and they absorb us" and that "consciousness spontaneously visualizes while holding attention spellbound" (127). Arguably, Diane's consciousness is "absorbed" by the memory-fueled "visual patterns" she "spontaneously imagines" as she is falling asleep. As is typical for the hypnagogic state, Diane's dream ego (Betty) has not materialized yet. It is only in the dream that "the experience of being a self in the world, which marks the waking state but diminishes in the hypnagogic state, reappears" (E. Thompson 127). Curious about the prologue's treatment of hypnagogia is the setting in a monochromatically purple nonspace, through which it stresses the mental nature of what is about to occur. In addition, the deprivation of visual input—as shown by the silhouette-like figures, the lack of depth of the visual field, and the doubling of the dancing couples[12]—hints at the distorted perspective of what follows. Given the shot's position at the very beginning of the film, this distortion can also be related to the film's perspective as a whole, but it cannot be ignored how the Jitterbug dance is both structurally and thematically tied to Diane's character.

To grasp the first part of the film as Diane's dream seems to provide the basis of the autonomous-dream interpretation. Assuming the two embracing shots of the red-covered bed were not in the film: the dancing couples in the purple utopia would not be enough to let someone speak of the whole film as a dream representation. Rather, the opening images would be seen as "hallucinatory" or "fantastic." If the transition from the first to the second part of the film did not involve the awakening of Diane—if Betty did not "become" Diane through the act of waking up—then the two worlds of the film would be ontologically incompatible, but again, there would be no reason to assume that the whole film depicts a dream. Counterintuitive as it may seem, thus, the film-as-dream assumption appears to rest upon the bed as the opening and end marker of Diane's dream. It is not that opening and closing imagery undermine the plausibility of seeing the major part of the film as Diane's dream (Kreuzer 653), but vice versa, grasping the fact that Diane is dreaming roughly the first two hours of the film conditions the possibility of considering the whole film a dream representation. In other words, the "autonomous-dream interpretation" ("entire-film-as-dream") hinges on the "film-in-dream" interpretation.

Kreuzer argues that "the subjective shot of the bed accompanied by intense breathing sounds encourage[s] the interpretation of the whole film as a dream or a nightmare" (663; my translation)[13]—but why would we hear *someone* breath if the *film* is supposed to be dreaming, that is, if no dreaming character was intended? The point-of-view shot at the beginning would be sufficient to make clear that "the film" is about to start dreaming—an anthropomorphous perception that would evoke the idea of going to sleep *without* implying a human subject. The additional audible breathing, however, suggests that there is a character whose embodied perspective we share, even if we do not know yet whose body is breathing here. (In a way, thus, we are waiting for almost two hours for the acousmatic breathing sound to become de-acousmatized, i.e., to get an objective shot of the body whose perception we previously only knew from a first-person perspective.)

The fact that the elderly couple, that is, Diane's dream figures, materialize in her apartment at the end does not undermine the reality of Diane Selwyn (as Diane's awakening undermined the reality of Betty Elms), for Diane could merely be fantasizing about them (and possibly even her suicide). As Diane is looking at the blue key, Lynch cuts to an extreme close-up of her eye and flashes start to light up. Only after this, the elderly couple enters the apartment, so the extreme close-up may be seen as a marker of Diane's hallucination. Still, one cannot be certain which of these three possibilities is accurate: (1) Diane kills herself due to the elders' presence in the current reality (anti-realist reading); (2) Diane has a paranoid hallucination in which the elders haunt her, but she really kills herself; (3) Diane fantasizes about *both* the elders' appearance and her suicide. Her suicide is thus sketched as a merely *possible* ending to the story the film told—a possibility, however, that is contingent on the contracted killing of Camilla. If the whole film was Diane's death vision (Kreuzer 663, 665), then *why* would she kill herself? It seems that the minimal consensus of what can be said to "happen" in *Mulholland Drive* is an event that, ironically, we do not see, that is, Camilla's death.

What may contribute to the impression that *Mulholland Drive* depicts one single long dream is that it does not hierarchize Diane's dream self (Betty) and her waking self. There is a clear ontological division between the dream and the waking *world*, but it is not the case that the dream is "not real" in the psychological sense. What Betty experiences does not occur in the external world, true. But, similar to what I have observed in the previous chapters, the question who the protagonist is and has been is revealed at least as much by the dream as it is by the waking world. Precisely because the first two hours of the film are not "*just* a dream," but tell us something about who Diane *really* is, waking is not superior to dreaming when it comes to the question of Diane's psychological reality. It is not the case that, in that moment in which Diane wakes up, everything we have seen until now stops being true. Diane really *did* come to Hollywood wanting to be an actress and really *did* start an affair with the dark-haired Camilla (even if their names do not match). Rather than constituting two elements of a hierarchical relationship, waking and dreaming are depicted as two different modalities of existence revolving around the same core. They are two different expressions of her *Dasein* being tuned to love and professional success, as Boss's existential dream phenomenology would put it. It is only in their togetherness that they evoke the impression of a fully-fledged personality. Without the waking part of the film, Betty would seem rather one-dimensional and naive. Without the dream part, Diane would seem overly bitter and depressed. Thus, psychologically speaking, it is through the nonhierarchical, horizontal juxtaposition of Diane's waking and dream reality—Žižek says that *Mulholland Drive* (and *Lost Highway*) "posit the two dimensions, reality and fantasy, side by side" (*Pervert*, 01:12:27–01:12:33)—that her naive and her bitter side are integrated into a more complex image of a personality.

A second reason for the strong version of the film-as-dream reading may be gleaned from David Andrews's observation that "the second section has two divergent psychological purposes: both to imply a set of credible, naturalistic explanations for the dream's content and to reveal the mental deterioration of a mind from within that mind. That is, the second section must at once feel real and unreal, reliable and unreliable" (Andrews 30). Those who view the whole film as a dream tend to stress the second aspect that Andrews describes, having to do with Diane's psychotic perspective. However, what must not be overlooked in this is the possibility of an internal focalization of waking events. That is, the images in the waking part may be molded by Diane's perspective, but the events they refer to might have really happened nonetheless. The scene of the engagement party, for example, may be understood as the product of Diane's warped recollection of what *really* took place. Maybe it is only in Diane's memory that the blonde woman (who becomes Camilla in her dream) kisses her beloved Camilla, but it would be hasty to deduce from this that the party never happened. Perceptual unreliability does not necessarily imply dreaming but may suggest internal ocularization in the phenomenological form of an imaginative recollection of a real past event.[14]

Andrews questions the inevitability of the dream-in-film interpretation, arguing that "the word 'Lynchian' suggests a cinematic indeterminacy that defies monolithic explanation, naturalistic or supernatural, oneiric or psychogenic" (33). More specifically, he asks: "If the film is a function of Diane's mind, why, near the start of her dream, does the filmmaker so persistently depict Rita falling asleep, sleeping, and waking up? [. . .] [I]nterpreting these scenes as 'belonging' to Rita leads nowhere" (33). Against a part of this claim, I will try to show in section "'It is an Illusion,' i.e. This Is a Dream . . . " that the first scene at Winkie's Diner can be understood as a dream within a dream, with a specific psychological reason behind this structure. For other scenes such as Adam's meeting with the Castigliane brothers, however, the dream-within-a-dream reading does not seem plausible. Although equally interpretable as a dream marker (as before with Winkie's), the cut to the downtown office of Ryan Entertainment would have to be read as a *meanwhile* in order to remain consistent with the naturalistic dream-in-film interpretation. Notwithstanding the (im-)plausibility of the dream-within-a-dream structure, however, one could see the image of a sleeping Rita as a concealment implicitly referring to an *actually* sleeping Diane. The shift of attributes (sleeping Diane becomes sleeping Rita) would suit the shift of identity visible in Rita suspecting that *she* is Diane.[15] It appears that Diane's dream tries to—but ultimately cannot—avoid self-confrontation.

"Dream as Film" as the Bridge between "Dream in Film" and "Film as Dream"

Even if the film's beginning and end are seen as suggesting the possibility of an autonomous dream (Kreuzer 662), two things should be noted. First, this reading does not diminish the plausibility of assuming an ontological hierarchy between an initial (subordinate) dream part and a subsequent waking part. If it is assumed, for the sake of the argument, that Diane is a dream character in someone's dream as well (whose dream we do not know), then Betty could still be Diane's dream ego, that is, a dream ego in a dream of the second order. Second, the "(entire-)film-as-dream" hypothesis is not necessarily to be taken literally but might be seen as an allusion to the kinship between cinema and dream *that Lynch's film itself previously established* (in the first part of the film). Rather than resulting from inconsistent focalization (cf. Kreuzer 653), *Mulholland Drive*'s broader oneiricity may be due to a film/dream comparison that hinges upon the dream-in-film interpretation, combined with the self-reflexive awareness that *Mulholland Drive* is a film.

It is probably uncontroversial to say that, with Betty arriving in Los Angeles, countless cinematic tropes as well as references to film history and the film industry can be observed. Zina Giannopoulou, for example, calls *Mulholland Drive* "a film reflecting on its own historical and material conditions as a work of art" (6). Some examples: Betty in some ways echoes the cliché of a young, blonde, naive female character without much depth and rather simple motivations—a cliché that movies from the classical period in particular have established. Due to unnatural pauses between the turns and a slightly over-the-top sincerity, the dialogue between Betty and Irene at the airport has a staged quality, as does the moment where Betty thinks she lost her bags, but it is just the cab driver who already put them in his trunk and asks, "Where to?" without even considering that he should have asked Betty first whether it was okay to take her luggage (00:19:35). Thus, from the very beginning, Betty is depicted *as a movie character*, a Grace Kelly-type maybe: reflecting mass culture's beauty standard, and conceived of as rather "one-dimensional," as actress Naomi Watts suggests (Fuller). More specifically, her name references Betty Schaefer (Nancy Olson) from Billy Wilder's noir-classic and Lynch-favorite *Sunset Boulevard* (1950).[16] Young aspiring Hollywood screenwriter Betty Schaefer might have served as an inspiration for Diane's dream ego, the young aspiring Hollywood actress Betty (in addition to the intradiegetic explanation of Diane picking up the name "Betty" from the waitress's name tag at Winkie's).

Figures 7.7–7.8 The dark-haired woman's imaginary self-construction (00:25:19; 00:25:26).

The second character whose cinematic origins the film self-consciously puts on display is Rita, who chooses her name on the basis of iconic femme fatale Rita Hayworth in the lead role of *Gilda* (1946).[17] Lynch's point could not be any clearer here: the film shows us that it is aware of its own history. Furthermore, the way in which cinematographer Peter Deming composes the shot is telling. "Rita" does not simply read Hayworth's name by looking at the poster, but she sees the poster's reflection in a small mirror. At the same time, we see Rita's face reflected through a large mirror (see Figures 7.7 and 7.8). Movies, like mirrors, distort reality, this could mean. With the camera zooming in on the poster's mirror reflection, we join the "movie-like" deceptive look at reality both on the noematic level (the *Gilda* poster in the mirror) and on the noetic level: note how the markedly cinematic zoom in increasingly blurs the poster's mirror image (see Figures 7.7 and 7.8). In what could be understood as an allusion to Lacan's conception of the *mirror stage* in developmental psychology,[18] the dark-haired woman creates her identity through an encounter with the mirror image. The shot thus seems to imply that for both (dream) characters and viewers, movies create dreamlike states of illusion.

In addition to the characters, the aesthetics, narrative, and shooting locations also allude to film history and "the industry" throughout the first part of the film. Concerning the locations, the gate of Paramount Pictures that Betty passes through for her audition is not just a reference to the film industry in general but also to *Sunset Boulevard* (1950), in which it featured prominently.[19] Further, the courtyard of aunt Ruth's apartment recalls the exterior of Norma Desmond's mansion in Wilder's film. The recurring aerial shots of the Hollywood sign, Fisk's production design of Ruth's apartment recalling the interior of a 1950s apartment, the classical lighting and bright colors of the scenes, frequent cross-fadings—all of these elements play in form or content with conventions and symbols of cinema. Importantly, none of them do so in a way, though, that would disrupt the viewer's acceptance of and immersion in the fictional world. Concerning the narrative, Roger Ebert observes that "'Mulholland Drive' employs the conventions of film noir in a pure form. One useful definition of noirs is that they're about characters who have committed a crime or a sin, are immersed with guilt, and fear they're getting what they [d]eserve. Another is that they've done nothing wrong, but it nevertheless certainly appears as if they have."

What seems important to observe is where in the film these cinematic topoi are present and where they are not. Many of the conventional elements stressing the fiction film character of the first part have disappeared after Diane has woken up. The interior of her apartment does not recall the golden age of classical cinema anymore; the colors are rather bland and the contours have lost the shiny quality of the images showing Betty's arrival in Los Angeles. Extradiegetic film references have disappeared now. There is no Rita Hayworth-imitator among the characters, no *noir*-type suspense, and Betty's overly emphatic optimism has vanished, too. These aesthetic and conceptual changes do not, however, decrease the formal and stylistic self-awareness of the film. One of the major differences between the "Betty/Rita" reality and the "Diane/Camilla" reality concerns the way in which changes in time, space, and action are treated. When hard cuts marked spatiotemporal shifts in the first part, Lynch's approach was in accordance with a fundamental convention of cinematic language (even if the ambiguity of the scene at Winkie's as Rita's dream or as a parallel montage is quite idiosyncratic). The function of a noticeable cut to mark off sequences from each other is obvious: it enables the viewer to understand *where* and/or *when* something happens. The fluidity of spatiotemporal discontinuities of the second part has the opposite effect: when Diane made coffee and approaches the sofa, the camera closely follows her movement showing her bathrobe from behind (see Figures 7.9 and 7.10). As the bathrobe is leaving the frame to the left (see Figure 7.11), the camera continues its movement revealing the naked Camilla lying on the sofa (see Figure 7.12). In the reverse shot, a topless Diane jumps over the backrest and instead of a cup of coffee, she puts a glass of whiskey on the table (see Figures 7.13 and 7.14).

We are at an earlier point in time now, but the continuation of the camera movement—instead of a conventional ABA-cutting sequence[20]—concealed the temporal discontinuity, complicating orientation for the viewer.[21] Two distinct moments in time have just smoothly flowed into each other without notice. Similarly, when Diane is masturbating after Camilla broke up with her, the sound of a ringing phone blends this temporal plane with an earlier moment at which she receives

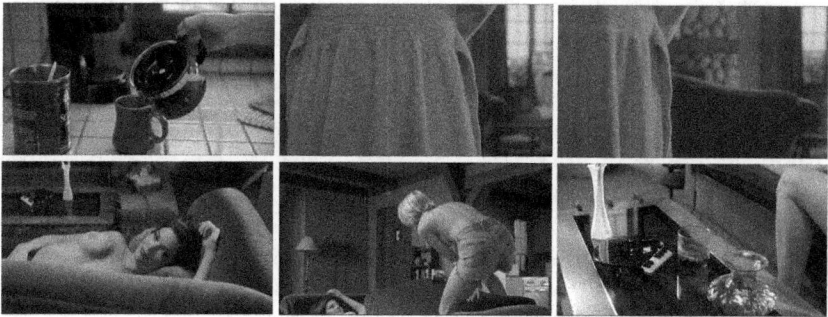

Figures 7.9–7.14 Continuity of movement concealing temporal discontinuity (02:01:37; 02:01:46; 02:01:47; 02:01:49; 02:01:50; 02:01:57).

Camilla's phone call. These cuts are completely associative. That is, Diane's experience of the present is stained by her painful memory of her past affair with Camilla: making coffee in her worn-off bathrobe, she yearningly remembers the eroticism of being with Camilla, which unfolded at the same spot where she is about to drink her coffee (by herself) now; hearing the ringing phone (which is never answered in the present) triggers her memory of when Camilla called to make sure Diane is really coming to her engagement party. Andrews speaks of Diane's nervousness "organizing the discontinuity editing of the second section" (31). Interestingly, what is frequently considered a characteristic element of both the nocturnal dream and its artistic representation—an associative technique (e.g., Kreuzer 56, 680)—is employed to mark Diane's fragmented perception of *reality* in Lynch's movie.

As one can see from this brief comparison, cinematic conventions in the representation of spatiotemporal discontinuities are confirmed in the first part and undermined in the second part of the film.[22] This raises the question: why, if not to suggest a kinship between the filmic medium and the dream, would these self-conscious film conventions and references occur in the first part of *Mulholland Drive*—interpretable as a dream—but not in the second?[23] It seems as if, by way of the dream-as-film hypothesis, the dream-in-film hypothesis (a dreaming Diane) gives an explanation for this difference.

Diane dreams in a specifically cinematic way because, like the dream, cinema immerses us in another reality. "Cinema is like a dream," *Mulholland Drive* seems to "argue," because watching a film is *like* dreaming, in that it gives us the illusion of a different reality as we are experiencing it. The film literalizes this metaphor by placing typically cinematic elements (on an aesthetic and story level) in the dream part of the film. On the one hand, these exposed cinematic elements signify the dream state because, like the physically impossible elements of a dream, they point to the irreality at the basis of what is experienced. Each of the self-reflexive elements thus reconfirms the opening marker of Diane going to sleep. At the same time, the cinematic tropes are reinterpreted as oneiric, given their occurrence in what we already accepted as Diane's dream. (In the latter case, the enclosing dream marker of Diane's red-covered bed acts as a signifier of the cinematic elements' oneiricity.)

To speak of "*re*-interpretation" here may seem appropriate in light of the film's idiosyncratic production history. *Mulholland Drive* was originally conceived of as the pilot of a TV series, which was rejected by the network ABC. An eighty-eight-minute TV movie that Lynch considers "embarrassing" was released in 1999 (Woods 214),[24] and more than a year later, a French production company gave the director the opportunity to make *Mulholland Drive* into a feature film. Eighteen additional pages of script were written and an additional fifty-nine minutes of footage were shot in 2000 to turn the project into the cinematic release of 2001. Interestingly, neither the "two-shot prologue" (Olson 527), that is, the dancers and the point-of-view shot of Diane going to bed, nor the scene of Diane's awakening is in the original screenplay. Apart from this, the plot of this screenplay follows pretty closely what we see in the first one and a half hours of the final cinematic release, with only a few deviations (notably, Lynch cut out the scene at Winkie's diner, "trying to please ABC" [Olson 530]). As indicated by the script, the pilot ended shortly after Betty and Rita found the corpse at the Sierra Bonita apartment.

Naturally, when comparing the pilot to the movie, the question as to the function of the dream marker arises. Why did Lynch add the two scenes of the red-covered bed with only minor deviations in the rest of the film? The answer may be obvious: through the enclosing dream marker, Lynch was able to give a sense of closure to a story that was originally conceived of as open-ended (as is the usual case with TV pilots). Had the pilot been accepted by ABC, the various storylines opened up probably would have continued, maintaining a certain degree of autonomy (like in *Twin Peaks*). Reinterpreting the pilot as a dream allowed Lynch to bundle the narrative threads, making everything that happened relevant to one character whose story could be told in the feature format.

The scene at the engagement party seems crucial in that regard. Here, Diane sees Luigi Castigliane, the blonde woman kissing Camilla, Coco, and the Cowboy—all of whom most likely would have had their storylines spanning over several episodes or even seasons of a *Mulholland Drive* series. Reworking the original material into the cinematic release from 2001, Lynch turned these characters into Diane's *day residue*, that is, people she met shortly before the dream and that assume certain roles in her unconscious due to the excruciating situation she met them in. That is, her unconscious recruits the serious-looking Castigliane and the Cowboy to reappear in her dream in order to oppress Adam (whom she hates the most right now because he is taking Camilla away from her). The blonde Camilla Rhodes from Diane's dream (Melissa George) might be thought of as what Freud calls a *mischperson* (*Traumdeutung* 324), that is, a dream character who combines aspects of several people, in this case aspects of Diane and Camilla (Laura Harring). First of all, the blonde woman (George) kisses Camilla (Harring) at the party such that it is plausible to assume that Diane *wants to be her* in this moment (she is still in love with Camilla). In Diane's dream, the blonde woman does not get to date Camilla, but she has the success that Diane has been longing for in vain. Thus, she can be seen as Betty's double. Assuming that Adam starts an affair with the blonde Camilla in Diane's dream, and that she *is* Betty's double, the dream gives another hint at the possibility that, like the real Camilla, Diane "could have had Adam," too. At the same time, the blonde woman "assumes" Camilla's name in the dream. Besides discrediting Camilla's acting skills, the name shift allows Diane to keep Camilla as her lover despite her professional success—to Diane, Camilla's professional success seems to be linked to her relationship with a famous director.

In transforming the pilot into the movie, Lynch must have performed a kind of backward dream interpretation: it is not that *I* had a dream whose meaning for my waking self has to be deduced through interpretation, revealing in what way dream elements relate to my pregiven identity. Making the pilot into the movie, Lynch must have asked himself: "What does the psyche of the person look like whose (compensatory) dream is the already-existing pilot?" (To compensate for Diane's nightmarish waking reality seems to be the major psychological function that the dream fulfills.) In the chronology of the production, thus, Lynch imagined a possible waking world *behind* the pilot after it was finished, a reality at its basis, constituting that which is compensated by what was already there. The dream functions as a mechanism expressing Lynch's *realist* interest in the fictional story he created through the pilot and allows him to go beyond that story, hence the dream's metafictionality. Through the dream, which introduces a dialectical principle to the story, he asks for the "real" elements that his original fiction suppressed, or (unknowingly) concealed. The dream realization not only introduces a second ontological level but also acts as the ultimate mechanism for reinterpretation inside the story, making visible Lynch's own reengagement with the pilot. "Rita" might not be an amnesic woman trying to recover her identity but the dream victim of her ex-lover who is (in reality) driven to despair by her rejection and thus wants to control her in the realm of imagination. Betty might not be the optimistic, naive aspiring actress but the idealization of a bitter murderer who is about to commit suicide.

What dawned as a hypothesis in my discussion of *Eraserhead* (1977), thus, is not only reaffirmed but also expanded here. Lynch uses the dream as a means for cinema to meet its own history, which in *Mulholland Drive* applies to both film history in general and its own production history in particular. If Lynch's film reflects on its own materiality (Giannopoulou 6), then the dream is what enables this reflection. In the dream part of *Mulholland Drive*, film is not a mere medium anymore, "conveying" a story through image and sound. Rather—or better: *on top of that*—it is a constant (visible and visual) act of self-reflection. Through the meta-medium of the dream (i.e., an exposed second medium within the first medium of film), the feature film *Mulholland Drive* reflects on what brought it into being, that is, the pilot, revealing it to be only a part of the story the feature wants to tell. Through the dream, *Mulholland Drive* thus displays an awareness of the contingency of the pilot's story and the means used to convey it. The cinematic conventions are not "absolute," in that, as the ontological split into dream and waking makes clear, Lynch exercises control over the way in which his film employs them. (As was shown, standard conventions of cinema are present in the dream part and absent in the waking part of the film. Without the dream revelation, it would not be possible to tell whether Lynch used these conventions deliberately.) The dream is *Mulholland Drive*'s meta-medium, in that it displays the film's self-awareness, allowing it to turn back on itself. The dream revelation turns the pilot's medial reality into a meta-medial possibility. Psychologically, this means that the dream restructures Diane's real experiences into a coherent, film-like love story. As I have shown, the dream reflects on Diane's experiences in a cinematically coded way, the *what* referring to the unrequited love and lack of success she experiences in Hollywood, the *how* involving codes from film history that are reinterpreted as oneiric.

The metaphorical dimension of the dream was already part of the original script. When Betty talks to Rita, she tells her how happy she is about being in this "dream place" now (Lynch, *Mulholland Drive (TV pilot)* 16); Los Angeles is described as the "City of Dreams" (9); as Betty gets to the Paramount Studios for her audition, "she stands for a moment staring at a dream" (72); arriving at her aunt's apartment, "Betty picks up her bags and enters, as if in a dream, through an ornate iron gate to a courtyard" (10). You could say that, through the transition from pilot to movie, which implied the translation of the dream metaphor into a psychological dream narrative, the *as if* in the original script's "as if in a dream" was deleted. The movie theme was equally present in the original script, as becomes clear through Betty convincing Rita about their amateur investigation: "Come on. It'll be just like in the movies. We'll pretend to be someone else" (42). What the feature film did in terms of the two preexisting themes was to link them, that is, to see not only "the movies" but also the dream as a form of "pretend[ing] to be someone else" (42).

All three ways of framing the story of *Mulholland Drive* seem essential to appreciate the interconnection of *film* and *dream* that Lynch's movie creates. Without regarding the first part as a dream (dream-in-film), one fails to recognize that *Mulholland Drive* does not only make a (self-reflexive) comparison between film and dream on the level of content but also on a formal level, by manifesting the metaphorical film/dream analogy as a concrete psychological dream, namely as a film-within-a-film, which enters into a dialogue with itself through the very marking of the dream. Thus, when I speak of "film as dream" in the context of *Mulholland Drive*, I refer to the second-level film, that is, the (dream-)film embedded within the film (weak version). Hence, due to its unusual production history, *Mulholland Drive* combines two fundamentally different approaches to filmic dream representation: "dream-in-film" and "film-as-dream." As I have tried to show, the connection between these two approaches is established through a third strategy, that is, "dream-as-film." Without considering the dream-as-film dimension, one not only fails to recognize the exposed cinematic style of Diane's dream, but one also ignores an approach that mediates between two interpretations of the film that initially seemed incompatible (i.e., "dream-in-film" and the strong version of film-as-dream).

Further, without considering the film-as-dream dimension of *Mulholland Drive*, one ignores both the production history of the project (most of the pilot was reinterpreted as a dream) and the weighting of dream time (117 minutes) in comparison to waking time (26 minutes). That is, most of the film depicts a dream. Overstraining this hypothesis, however, that is, seeing the entire film as an autonomous dream depiction (strong version), may raise more questions than it answers. Why, if Diane's current reality is a dream as well, does she kill herself in the end? She might not see her dream as a dream. But why would the film end here, without a third Naomi Watts character waking up in the moment of Diane's death? And what would this second-order dream (x dreaming of Diane dreaming of Betty) be motivated by? Considering the entire film an autonomous dream (strong version of "film-as-dream"), it would not be possible to say anything about *what happens* in *Mulholland Drive*. The film does not seem to be about the impossibility of telling a story (like Alain Resnais's *L'Année Dernière à Marienbad* [1961], for example), however—it does tell a story: someone is trying to make it in Hollywood while living through a tragic love story. Andrews calls the film "a profoundly sad meditation on how dreams of Hollywood success turn to dust—then to jealousy, murder, madness, escapist fantasy, and finally, suicide" (26).

Mulholland Drive's closing images, which have been read as undermining the hypothesis that Diane dreams the first part of the film and experiences the waking world in the second (cf. Kreuzer 653; Sinnerbrink "Cinematic Ideas"), could alternatively be understood as the film's way of indicating that the story it told does not *exclusively* belong to Diane Selwyn, but that others like her have had similar experiences in Hollywood. Almost as if the closing images came "from the city's point of view" (Rodley 268), it seems like Hollywood itself were summing up the story for us through a montage. Endowing its story with a certain degree of objectivity, *Mulholland Drive*'s ending implies that Hollywood is the entity generating the fears and goals that many, one of them being Diane Selwyn, become obsessed with. A negated facet of the—both metaphorical and literal—*dream factory* Hollywood is thus constituted by the "monsters it produces" (to allude to Francisco de Goya's famous etching *The Sleep of Reason Produces Monsters* [1799]) to keep itself running.[25] Although Norma Desmond from *Sunset Boulevard* does not kill herself in the end, her fate resembles that of Diane, in that both have fallen victim to the myth of Hollywood stardom. Lynch said that "*Sunset Boulevard* says so much about that Hollywood dream thing to me" (Rodley 272). *Sunset Boulevard* does not go as far as *Mulholland Drive* in making the Hollywood Dream psychologically manifest as a literal dream: although main character Joe Gillis wakes up from a "mixed-up dream" as he gets more and more entangled with Norma Desmond's life, there is no indication that he dreams any part of the story (*Sunset Boulevard* 00:27:00–00:27:02).[26] And yet, Lynch seems to follow Wilder's example when it comes to the devastating psychological effects of the Hollywood Dream on his main character. Diane resembles both Joe Gillis, who "always wanted" a pool (as a signifier of Hollywood success) and, in a darkly ironic scene, ends up floating lifelessly in it (01:43:32–01:43:36), and Norma Desmond of whom we are told in one of *Sunset Boulevard*'s final moments: "The dream she had clung to so desperately had enfolded her" (01:48:10–01:48:15), which perfectly describes Diane's fate as well.

Club Silencio—A Cinematic Reflection on the Bodily Nature of Film Viewing/Dreaming and on the Dreamlike Ontology of Film

To start off my discussion on Club Silencio, I would like to go back to the way in which the sequence is introduced. Rita speaks the words, "no hay banda" while being sound asleep (01:42:43–01:42:44), which raises the possibility that she already saw the Club Silencio performance in her dream. Even without considering the first part of *Mulholland Drive* a dream—Club Silencio occupying the crucial intermediary position leading from the dream world to the waking world—the sequence's connection to the dream is undeniable. As I just made clear by elaborating on the film's production history, however, the function of the dream in *Mulholland Drive* goes beyond simple prophecy. As a storytelling device, it presents the instrument that allows the movie to reflect and turn back on itself, on the story it tells (assigning new roles to almost every character involved), and on its own ontological nature as well as affective potential as a film. The latter two aspects are epitomized by the Club Silencio sequence. If

Mulholland Drive establishes an analogy between cinema and dream, then Club Silencio shows us what is at the heart of this analogy. A meditation on the reason why film viewing and dreaming could be considered similar, Club Silencio displays the mechanism responsible for our continuing acceptance of an—oneiric and filmic— unreality, despite our better knowledge.

"It [Cinema] Is an Illusion"—Viewer-Film Identification and Mediality

Not least against the backdrop of the first part of the film constructing itself as a cinematic entity, Club Silencio negotiates the relationship between viewer and film *as* Betty's relationship to the theatrical-musical performance on stage. I am the spectator of the film, *like* Betty is the spectator of the stage performance.[27] Like Betty, the film viewer knows that *it*, that is, the stage performance and, by extension, the filmic reality as a whole, *is an illusion*, as the Magician says. In the film experience, we are watching light being projected on a screen. Like the sounds that Betty and Rita hear, a film's images (and sounds) have been "recorded" and are now played for us. In this sense, they do not depict "reality," just like the sounds Betty hears are not real. Yet, Betty is strongly affected by the stage performance, both physiologically (her body starts shaking heavily when she hears the thunder) and emotionally (she starts crying over Del Rio's song). Through her visible reaction, and given that we tend to identify with her due to our common onlooker status, she prefigures a certain type of viewer response. One of the questions raised by this is why, despite our knowledge as to the illusory nature of what we are watching, we are affected by this appearance—a question that obviously transcends the boundaries of this particular sequence, in that it concerns a fundamental aspect of the film experience per se.

For Christian Metz, "the spectator of a [. . .] film no longer quite knows that he is at the cinema" (104). Following him, one might argue that the viewer's "dissociation of 'motoricity' from consciousness" (103) and lowered degree of wakefulness and awareness (107) are responsible for her acceptance of the "unreal" film scenario. Psychoanalyst-philosopher Slavoj Žižek tells us that the "paradox of cinema" is a "paradox of belief" (*Pervert*, 01:49:37–01:49:41). The cinematic experience does not revolve around a simple opposition of *belief–disbelief* in what happens on the screen, but it leads the viewer to believe "in a conditional mode" (01:49:47–01:49:49). That is, "I know very well that it's a fake, but nonetheless I *let* myself be emotionally affected" (01:49:49–01:49:54).

Arguably, Club Silencio conceptualizes viewer–film identification in a way that radically differs from Žižek's idea, in that he seems to make it an overly conscious endeavor based on active, rational decision-making ("I *let* myself be emotionally affected"). Instead, as I would suggest, the scene appears to agree with Sobchak's film phenomenology, according to which the relationship between viewer and film is to be thought of as a primarily bodily one. The Magician directly affects Betty's physical state: she starts shaking as he conjures up a thunder (see Figures 7.15 and 7.16).

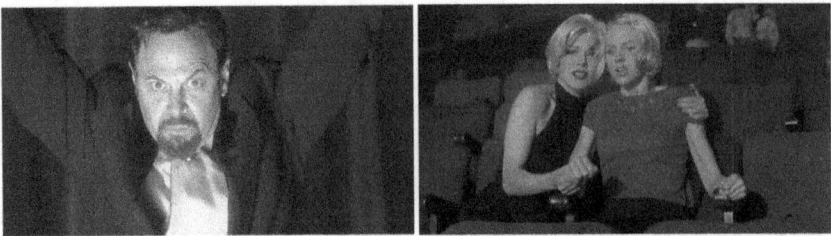

Figures 7.15–7.16 Betty's physiological reaction to the Magician conjuring up a thunder (01:47:37; 01:47:41).

The relationship of Betty (representing the film viewer) and the stage performance (representing the film world) is conceived of as physical rather than cognitive in nature and thus resonates with Shaviro's remark: "there is no structuring lack, no primordial division, but a continuity between the physiological and affective responses of my own body [. . .] and the bodies and images on screen" (255). Despite my knowledge as to their unreality, I am affected by the on-screen events because I pre-reflectively engage with the film world as a world that is of the same flesh as I am, because I, like the film itself, am able to commute perception into expression.[28] Betty's affectedness appears to be independent of her better knowledge because, at the pre-reflective stage of her viewing experience, higher-order categories like *real* and *illusory* do not apply. A connection between affectivity and dreaming may come to the fore at this point: the affective intensity of an experience increases the potential to evoke an oneiric effect because, like a nonlucid dream, it shifts our mode of experience from a reflective, distanced perspective toward the "close," pre-reflective, sensory involvement that is not yet differentiated into *real* and *unreal*.

Sobchak's account of film seems to provide an answer not only for how an affective response is possible in light of better knowledge but also explains why the viewer's reaction (potentially mirroring Betty's) might be so strong when the singer faints on stage. In Sobchak's view, we implicitly ascribe a certain corporeality to film. That is, we see a film as the expression of an embodied existence. *We are like the film* in that sense because we are embodied existences as well. In that moment in which Del Rio loses consciousness, it is not just that image and sound are disjunct all of a sudden, but the perception expressed by the scene is no longer readable as a *natural* one, as that of an embodied existence similar to myself. I cannot appropriate the scene as the expression of a natural perception because the film's act of viewing and its act of hearing (which normally cooperate) contradict each other. For Sobchak, "what we look at projected on the screen [. . .] addresses us as the expressed perception of an anonymous, yet present, 'other'" (*Address* 9). This "other" can no longer be understood as being "sensing and sentient" (Sobchak, *Address* 9) but becomes a necessarily *medial* other in that moment in which Del Rio faints and "her" voice keeps singing. Comparing the mediality evoked here to that of *Eraserhead*'s dream sequences, two aspects seem important. First, in *Eraserhead*, the medial character of Henry's dream was *represented* by the theater stage. It was grasped by pondering the question what a theater stage might stand for.[29] In *Mulholland Drive*'s Club Silencio, mediality *expresses* itself as a directly perceptible phenomenon of the film experience. It is grasped pre-reflectively by experiencing the scene. Second, Henry's dream implied medial aspects of the visible and medial aspects of the audible. Image and sound, as two separate, noncontradictory modalities of the film experience, both displayed medial characteristics. The mediality of Club Silencio, on the other hand, emerges from the *incompatibility* of image and sound, of motionlessness and co-movement.

Thinking back to the very beginning of *Mulholland Drive* for a moment, one might argue that the title screen already implies the mediality of the dream. Importantly, the title screen is already a part of Diane's dream, as it appears after we fade to black on the pillow. The medial otherness of the dream is expressed in the fact that the street sign—an object from everyday life (unambiguous; simple reference)—is integrated into a more complex frame of reference (ambiguous; complex reference). That is, the street sign of "Mulholland Dr." not only refers to a road in Los Angeles but also becomes the title of the film (see Figure 7.18). It is in the context of the film, and of the dream in particular, that an everyday object like a sign is able to take on a meaning that transcends its regular referentiality. More specifically, it is the ability of the filmic medium to select a part of the visible physical world as a *frame* and then place it at a certain moment in the succession of frames that allows for the "Mulholland Dr." sign to become the signifier of the film's title. Thus, at the risk of saying something trivial, it is the medial character of film (in its most fundamental functioning)—the very act of filmic depiction—that enables an object to enter into a more complex form of referentiality. (The nonmedial

Figures 7.17–7.19 Complex medial referentiality of title screen and opening credits (00:00:22; 00:02:41; 00:04:11).

physical world, in this perspective, is that which has *not* been selected.) Adding to this complexity, the title screen is also a medial reference, as it directly quotes the curb shot of *Sunset Boulevard*'s title screen (see Figure 7.17). Further, the credits are not merely paratextual: the letters reflect the limousine's headlights, like the "Mulholland Dr." sign did. The credits, normally not part of the diegesis (and thus *para*-textual), are affected by the limousine and thus "almost" become a part of the filmic text (see Figure 7.19).[30] However, as I have observed in regard to the cinematic tropes occurring throughout the first part, the medial character of *Mulholland Drive* is unlikely to break our suspension of disbelief. This changes in Club Silencio, where the dream's medial character imposes itself upon us. The exposed mediality of Club Silencio thus puts the subtle mediality of the first part of the film on display.

The fact that I feel a strong dissonance when Del Rio collapses shows that—even though I know that I am listening to a playback—I still try to reconcile image and sound. In Chion's account, we *audio-view* a film as a transsensory whole instead of processing the visual and auditory input separately (*Audio-Vision* 136).[31] Given my bodily rather than rational relationship to (the) film, it is impossible *not* to try to reconcile image and sound. More specifically, what I am unable to reconcile in regard to Club Silencio is the continuing movement of the *voice* as suggested aurally and the abrupt cessation of the visible articulatory movements (thought to be) at its basis, that is, the collapse of Rebekah Del Rio's body. Inherent in the scene is thus a paradox of movement (rather than Žižek's paradox of belief). A play between the execution and nonexecution of movement impulses, this paradox points to the double structure, the double corporeality to be more exact, at the heart of every film viewing *and* dreaming experience. To a large extent, the tension created through the scene builds on the viewer's ambivalent way of relating to the film world, which fluctuates between motionlessness and inner co-movement. As I have mentioned before, both the film viewer's and the dreamer's body is relatively motionless while experiencing a film or a dream. In the virtual world of the film or dream, on the other hand, there is always movement. A film depicts moving objects and people, "sees through" a moving camera, and shows a montage suggesting movement. In a dream, my dream ego is involved in a sensory-motor scenario, for which movement is indispensable (a dream composed of still images seems rather unlikely). This perceived movement causes an activation of the neural centers responsible for controlling and processing movement.

In Club Silencio, it is the movement of Del Rio's voice that, most likely through the activation of mirror neurons, causes the viewer's inner co-movement. This effect is particularly strong here due to the wide spectrum of tones she is singing in the chorus ("llorando por tu amor"). As a function of distinctive up-and-down movements in the melody, the increased affectivity may result from an intensified bodily response on the viewer's side. For these musical up-and-down movements, according to the theory of mirror neurons, are "reflected" in the viewer's speech organs' muscular activity necessary to produce these tones. Contributing to this bodily identification are both the crispness of her voice giving it a palpable quality and the extreme close-up of her face depicting the physiological "source" of what we hear. Perfectly lit, the shot reveals her lips, teeth, and tongue producing the sounds. The /r/ that is produced as an alveolar

Figures 7.20–7.21 Co-movement (immersion) and motionlessness (disruption) as the phenomenological manifestation of dreaming and waking experience (01:51:32; 01:51:51).

flap (the tip of the tongue touches the alveolar ridge, located just behind the teeth, very briefly) in "llorando" (see Figure 7.20), for example, is perfectly synchronized with the image, which is astonishing considering the fact that the song really *was* pre-recorded and then lip-synched during the shoot (Rodley 292). Indubitably, the disruptive effect of Del Rio's collapse is all the more intense in light of the previous strong bodily identification provoked by the scene's aesthetics stressing the material presence of the voice (see Figures 7.20–7.21).

To be concrete in regard to my analogy, the viewer's outer stillness (while watching the scene or dreaming) is evoked by Del Rio's collapsed and motionless body, while the viewer's inner co-movement is maintained by the continuing voice. The scene thus contains both aspects of the viewer's physiological identification with film, but it plays them out against each other. Thus, on a noetic level (referring to the act of consciousness), Del Rio's motionless body mirrors the viewer's body (while watching a film) and the sleeper's body (while dreaming). On the noematic level (referring to the object of consciousness), further, her motionless body evokes Metz's idea of cinema's imaginary status of the signifier. Distinguishing it from a theater play, which involves "real" people, real time, and real space, Metz says of the "cinematic screen" that

> what unfolds there may, as before, be more or less fictional, but the unfolding itself is fictive: the actor, the "décor," the words one hears are all absent, everything is recorded [. . .] it is the signifier itself, and as a whole, that is recorded, that is absence: a little rolled up perforated strip which "contains" vast landscapes, fixed battles, the melting of the ice on the River Neva, and whole life-times, and yet can be enclosed in the familiar round metal tin, of modest dimensions, dear proof that it does not "really" contain all that. (Metz, *Imaginary* 47)

In Metz's view, cinema is imaginary per definition because the signifier is absent. Sartre might say that cinema, like imaging consciousness, "posits its object as a nothingness" (11), "giv[ing it] as not being" (14). At the heart of film, there is "a nothingness," in that the actors and objects are not "really there"; their presence is merely evoked through the pre-recorded lights and shadows. To demonstrate the disruptive effect of disclosing the absence of the cinematic signifier, Lynch, ironically, recurs to another medium.

Theater seems to be the perfect choice because of the materiality of its signifier and its adherent impression of reality. As Metz observes, the actors in a play are of flesh and blood. A theater stage does not depict the image of actors and props; it rather involves physically present actors and objects. Doing justice to the amalgamation "movie theater," Club Silencio blends the theatrical, which claims the signifier's presence, with the cinematic, which implies the signifier's absence. As a result, Betty has a cinematic experience at the theater. Even though Del Rio is giving a stage performance, Betty experiences what (in Metz's view) defines the ontology of cinema, that is, the absence (and thus the imaginary status) of the signifier. In other words, cinema, by nature, presents a "something revolving around a nothing." It gives us "visibility without the presence of real things" (Wiesing 137). The same could be said of the dream, which only feigns material presence of its objects and people. Here, too, the signifier is absent. Dream signifiers are even more radically absent than cinematic signifiers, in that they have no material basis whatsoever. Unlike for film, there is no "metal tin" (cf. Metz, *Imaginary* 47) that could contain a dream image.

The significance of Metz's observation for the film experience in general might be negligible. The majority of films do not *show* the absence of the signifier. Instead, much of their immersive effect on the viewer builds on the impression of the signifier's physical presence. Film language has invented many techniques to conceal its fictitious nature (e.g., continuity editing) and thus create the impression of a material scenario. While watching a film, the spectator physiologically engages with what is depicted and, in that, behaves as if the signifier really were present—even more so while dreaming, where the dreamer interacts with a world that is physically present to him. It is only from the outside perspective that the signifier's absence, the immateriality of the film and dream world, is grasped. Rather than to the phenomenology of film, thus, Metz's claim speaks to the ontology of film. It concerns less the experiential perspective of the subject *from within* the film (or dream) than the reflective post hoc perspective *from outside* it.

In regard to *Mulholland Drive*, however, Metz's observation also resonates with the phenomenology of the scene (in addition to its ontology) because in Club Silencio, the viewer experiences the signifier as imaginary (even if she experiences the signifier's absence as a sensory presence, i.e., as a deeply unsettling bodily phenomenon). Still, it disregards that the prerequisite for the disruptive effect of Del Rio's collapse consists in our physiological engagement with what is depicted, that is, to some extent, we behave as if Del Rio really *were* present in that space where we are watching the movie. As I have shown, *from within* the dream or film, the theatrical serves to point to the material relationship between the experiencing subject (the viewer and Betty) and Del Rio. That is, it stresses the presence of the signifier (her vivid live singing), only to then reveal its absence (her collapse) in a second step. The contrast on which the scene's effect builds would fade if the spectator's relationship to the film were determined by her belief that the signifier is absent. If our reception behavior merely consisted in *knowing* that Del Rio is not present, then her collapse should not come as a shock but as a confirmation of what we already knew.

A strong emotional reaction on the viewers' part (if present) thus testifies to the primacy of our sensuous response to the scene (as opposed to a cognitive one), not only because bodily co-movement intensifies emotion but also because the Magician told us repeatedly that everything we hear is a tape recording. If our way of relating to film were solely cognitive, then we should not show an emotional reaction to the scene because we knew in advance about everything being a tape. The Magician, thus, functions to make sure that the viewer grasps the sensory-affective nature of her spectatorship. Chion's synchresis effect of cinema—that is, "the forging of an immediate and necessary relationship between what one sees and something one hears at the same time" (*Audio-Vision* 224)—is stronger than the words of the Magician, explaining that *it is an illusion* before. In that regard, the scene is a demonstration of the sensory power of cinema. Again, the words "it is an illusion" do not seem to diminish the affective response of the viewer. They do, however, express an awareness of cinema's capacity to affect the viewers' senses. The Magician, in that regard, personifies cinema itself, at least as *Mulholland Drive* conceptualizes it. Through the Magician, the film tells us that "it knows" of its sensory power before it demonstrates it. Club Silencio does not just *imply* the dominance of the senses over reason (as any shock scene in a horror movie does), but it consciously puts its ability for sensory affection on display by literally *staging* it. The scene is both a *reflection on* and a celebratory *demonstration of* the pre-reflective dimension of film and its ability to address the viewers' senses. This was not the case for Lynch's early short films, where dreams provided moments of sensory intensity as well (think of *The Alphabet*'s [1968] zoom in on the girl's mirror image as we hear her agitated inhale)—but, importantly, they did not *show* us their awareness to affect the viewers' senses.

"It Is an Illusion," i.e., This Is a Dream—The Sensory Knowledge of Diane's Unconscious

Club Silencio's self-reflexivity and viewer–film interaction aside for a moment, *knowledge* seems to be an interesting category in the context of Diane's psychology. For psychoanalyst Olga Cox Cameron, Diane's dream as a whole constitutes "a very specific form of not-knowing . . . a know that is simultaneously a refusal to know, a refusal to know that nonetheless knows." In her Freudian-Lacanian understanding, Diane's dream, and its "unknowing aspect" in particular, functions to evade the confrontation with her "traumatic grief," that is, the memory that she ordered Camilla's death (Cox Cameron). Fulfilling Diane's wish to sleep, her unconscious creates a story that is structured around the avoidance of an "impossible knowledge" (Cox Cameron). If this knowledge were acquired, a dream could not continue because the "fantasy structure" that supports it would collapse (Cox Cameron).[32] Cox Cameron argues that when aunt Ruth comes back to the apartment to look for her key—the object that signifies Camilla's death in the waking world—this comes "too close to breaking the circus of the dream" (Cox Cameron). To prevent a collapse, Diane's dream has Rita go into a dream about Winkie's. The dream within the dream thus serves to "distance even more and then render less real whatever it is you dream you are dreaming" (Cox Cameron).

Concerning the connection between the scene at Winkie's diner and the Club Silencio scene, Simon Riches observes that the former "symbolizes (in her [Diane's] dream reality) her own later moment of realization of Club Silencio" (41). What links Club Silencio to Winkie's on a formal level is that both sequences seem connected to a dreaming Rita, that is, they both raise the possibility of a dream within a dream. Their common theme is sensory intensity ruling over rational awareness. Dan could be said to *know* about the terrifying man's imminent appearance (at least he is able to verbalize his concern about the man's potential presence), but still faints when it happens. Even more clearly, Betty knows that she is listening to a tape-recording but is still strongly affected when Del Rio collapses on stage. Neither at Winkie's nor at Club Silencio does the reflective awareness in encountering an event protect Dan and Rita from an intensely felt experience. Further, in both cases, a dream event becomes "real" on a diegetically superior level: the *no hay banda* from Rita's dream is repeated by the Magician in Club Silencio, and the terrifying Bum from Dan's dream materializes behind Winkie's. While Rita's dream (a dream of the second order) becomes real on the level of Betty's and Rita's reality (i.e., Diane's first-order dream), Dan's dream (a dream of the third order) becomes real on the level of Rita's (second-order) dream (see Figure 7.22).

In Cox Cameron's understanding, thus, the dream-within-a-dream structure (i.e., Rita's dream within Diane's dream) functions as a modality of not-knowing. It is the expression that Diane's unconscious chooses in order to cope with the intolerable knowledge as to Camilla's death. By introducing a third-order dream—Dan tells us that he had a "dream about this place" in which he already saw the terrifying man (00:12:25–00:12:27)—Diane's unconscious makes sure that the hiring of Camilla's killer

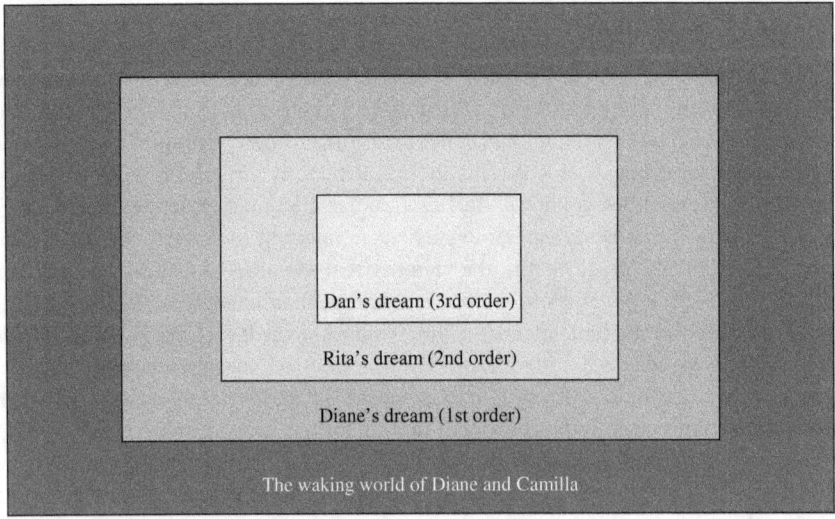

Figure 7.22 Possible dream layers in *Mulholland Drive*.

(which took place at Winkie's in the waking world) is sufficiently distanced in order for the dream to keep going. A second aspect serving the same goal would be the swapping of identities. If Diane saw herself instead of Dan in her dream, this would be "too close" to what really happened, and she might wake up. "Dan" (we do not learn his name in the waking world) is a person Diane randomly made eye contact with while she hired the killer at Winkie's. He was standing by the cash register in the waking world, in that same spot where his acquaintance Herb finds himself in both Dan's (third-order) dream and in Dan's reality (i.e., Rita's dream). Dan speaks of how scared he was in his dream and says that he became even more scared when he saw that Herb, standing by the register, was scared, too. Psychoanalysts would probably speak of a *displacement* of affect (*Affektverschiebung*) here: the fear that Dan projects on Herb in Rita's dream *is* (and originates from) the fear that Diane associates with "Dan" in the waking world. Similarly, Dan's encounter with the death-bringing man behind Winkie's is both the displaced rendition of Diane's encounter with Camilla's death—her question to the hitman, "What does it [the key] open?" (02:17:59–02:18:00), fades into an image of the man holding the blue box—and the foreshadowing of her own (possible) death because the terrifying Bum is part of the closing montage following Diane's suicide. His appearance thus seems metaphorically linked to both Camilla's and Diane's death.

As a function of Cox Cameron's "unknowing principle," the nesting of dream levels thus serves to distance a real event. The nesting is driven by a "refusal to know" (Cox Cameron). At the same time, however, the *becoming real* of higher-order dream events on lower-order dream levels (the appearance of the Bum and the Magician "repeating" the *no hay banda* from Rita's dream) points to the eventual failure of the avoidance of knowledge—hence Cox Cameron's talk of a "refusal to know *that still knows*." Club Silencio plays a pivotal role in that regard, since it forces the unknowing principle of Diane's unconscious—driving the plot of the film until now—to collapse, with the knowing aspect shining through what she experiences there. By exposing the illusion of the performance, Club Silencio points to the illusory nature of Betty's world. It is only able to do so because it contains knowledge as to the "reality behind [the illusion]" (Žižek, *Pervert* 01:47:27–01:47:30). That is, on *some* level, Betty's dream seems to be aware of its own dream status and of the functioning of her psyche's displacement. Yet this knowledge does not allow Diane to gain lucidity and control her dream. But neither does it lead Diane to wake up immediately. How can she "know and not know" at the same time that she is dreaming right now? In what sense can Diane be said to "know" that she is dreaming, if it does not imply a reflective awareness that would allow her to become lucid or to wake up immediately?

It could be argued that Diane's knowledge as to her dream state does not involve reflective awareness. Against this claim, one might object that the Magician's *it is an illusion* features prominently in Club Silencio. What could express the self-awareness of her dream state more clearly than these words? Granted, the Magician's words do seem to imply the dream's awareness of its being a dream, if *dream* is understood as the embodiment of *illusion*. Crucially, however, Betty only seems to grasp the meaning of these words when she *experiences* the illusion. That is, the ultimate truth about the illusory nature of Betty's world (and, by implication, of the American Dream) is communicated to her through the senses rather than through the mind. What was the case for the cinematic reflexivity of *it is an illusion* also rings true for the dream implications of these words: the reflective (and reflexive) dimension of the dream is pointed to only to be declared inferior to the sensory dimension. Introducing the reflective dimension before demonstrating its content, the scene introduces a dialectic between intentionality and sensation. While an intentional state (such as a belief, a wish, or an expectation) is directed to an object or semantic content, sensation is defined by its qualitative character, by what it is like to live through a certain experience (Beckermann 13–14). If semantic processing of *it is an illusion* were Betty's primary response, then her body should not be shaking in reaction to the illusory thunder conjured up by the Magician; her rational awareness would decrease the affective power of the performance to a minimum and she could lean back, knowing that what she is about to witness is just a trick. To the contrary, however, it is only through her bodily reactions (tenseness, shaking, crying) that she appears to grasp the illusory nature of both her world and her love for Camilla. Her body performatively materializes the meaning of *it is an illusion* by starting to shake: "there is no thunder" in the same sense that "there is no band," but Betty's body behaves in a way as if there were, thus confirming that *it is an illusion*. In phenomenological terms, *noema* (referring to the object of consciousness—"no hay *banda*") and *noesis* (referring to the act of consciousness—"*we hear* a band") are in contradiction. Without her body's shaking, *it is an illusion* might only refer to the stage performance as an isolated event to be observed from a distance. Her strong sensory involvement, however, shows Betty that it addresses her personally. Sensory involvement is what turns art into a lived experience as opposed to a distanced object that can be "possessed" by anyone. In this context, the dream is not only evoked as the experiential form of illusion but also as a maximally personal experience, in that it can only be experienced by the dreamer herself (only Betty's body is shaking).

Besides speaking to the repressed aspect of California's collective unconscious, a possible reason for why Lynch uses the Spanish translation of Ray Orbison's *Crying* is to make sure that Betty does not grasp the meaning of the song through a semantic processing of the lyrics—*and still "knows" what it is about*. It appears that the pain of a love relationship that has come to an end is already communicated through Del Rio's voice before word meanings come into play. Intuitively, Betty associates the lamenting quality inherent in the chorus' "llorando" with her relationship to Rita. Although Betty is unlikely to be able to *say* what the song is about, her intense crying while clutching Rita's hand indicates that she "carnally comprehends" the song (to use an expression by Sobchak, *Carnal Thoughts* 63). Isabella Van Elferen also understands the scene in terms of the body. To her, crying dissolves the boundaries of the body (outside and inside are blurred), and she connects this to the functioning of music per se, which "moves from outside to inside and back" (Van Elferen 184).

If, further, the *it is an illusion* of Club Silencio refers to the dream in general, then in this moment, it evokes Betty's and Rita's mutual love in particular. Betty's comprehension of the oneiricity of her world through the irreality of her relationship to Rita is of sensory rather than rational nature. Betty's (dream) senses *knew* before her (dream) mind that she has lost her love interest Camilla. While her experience might not allow her to consciously grasp it, she seems to feel her heart brokenness as a "potentiality" (Sobchak, *Carnal Thoughts* 63) of the song being performed on stage. The dream here does not only "symbolize" a real-life event (the loss of Camilla)[33] but also displays its tendency to dramatize real-life knowledge by translating it into a sensuously felt moment. Thus, there appear to be two modes of (self-)experience involved. Club Silencio implies a psychical movement by which a knowing, reflective self-experience (her memory of their love) is translated into a (merely) anticipatory, pre-reflective self-experience. According to Freud, "the thought content that has been transformed into a wish-fantasy becomes conscious *as a sensory perception*" (*Psychologie des Unbewußten* 186; my italicization and translation).[34] Club Silencio could be seen as an extension to Freud's observation because in this scene, it is not Diane's wish fantasy that becomes manifest as a sensory perception, but her knowledge as to the reality behind her dream.

It is only after the strong physiological responses of shaking and crying that Betty finds the blue box in her purse. Whether or not Pandora's box—a symbol for human beings' quest for knowledge—was on Lynch's mind, entering into the blue box signifies a transition from the knowledge-denying modality of experience of Betty's dream world to the "knowing" experience of Diane's waking world. That link between unknowing and knowing is provided by a "knowing through the senses," a knowing that has not yet solidified as awareness, that cannot be "refigured [. . .] into [. . . a] conscious thought" yet (Sobchak, *Carnal Thoughts* 63).[35] Through Club Silencio, cinema and dream are implied to be modalities of experience located *between* knowing and not knowing. This ambivalence characterizes both the viewer's cinematic experience and Diane's/Betty's dream experience. Neither Betty nor the film viewer can be said to "know" or "not know" that *it is an illusion*. In both cases, the narrative's gradual transition from the unknowing to the knowing experience is constituted by a carnal or sensory knowledge: a lived, pre-reflective, nonverbal, preconscious knowledge. Cinema and dream are thus characterized as privileged spaces to demonstrate the significance of this type of knowledge.

This knowledge seems to be irreducible to what philosophers call propositional knowledge (i.e., "knowledge that" it is a recording). The knowledge *that* there is no band by no means exhausts the knowledge gained through the experience of the band's (particularly Del Rio's) absence. Philosopher Frank Jackson's thought experiment in the article "Epiphenomenal Qualia" revolves around Mary—who is imprisoned in a black-and-white cell, knows all physical facts about color perception, and yet *learns something new* when she gets out and sees a red object for the first time (130). Similarly, Betty and the viewer appear to learn something new when Del Rio collapses on stage, something that was not in the words, "there is no band." We gain knowledge of the experience that concepts like *synchresis* and *schizophonia* attempt to describe[36] but ultimately cannot capture in its phenomenal "thickness." Club Silencio seems to tell us that both dreams and films matter for their ability to qualify the *what is like* of subjective experience (which seems to nullify the existence of propositional knowledge in comparison). Both phenomena can only be grasped once we attempt to understand them in their "-ing" forms rather than in their noun forms, that is, in their dynamic, procedural, and experiential character.

It seems crucial to note the narrative significance with which the sensuously intense moment of Del Rio's collapse is charged. Andrews suggests that "this is an art-for-art's-sake moment [. . .] renounc[ing] claims to narrative significance" (35). This ignores that Betty's tears performatively materialize the song's theme of crying over a lost love. Said theme applies perfectly to the story of Betty/Diane and Rita/Camilla. In regard to the overall narrative, the scene in Club Silencio only unfolds its potential if everything that has happened so far (except for the two-shot prologue) is interpreted as a dream that begins to collapse at the moment when Rebekah Del Rio collapses on stage. Only then does one see the narrative relevance of the scene, which is clearly related to its sensory-affective potential. The world we have accepted as the diegetic reality until now does not only turn out to be a dream at the moment when the cowboy says, "Hey little girl, time to wake up" (01:56:37–01:56:41), but already when the body of Del Rio collapses on stage while her voice persists (01:51:46–01:51:52). Club Silencio shows us on a purely affective level (because, as was pointed out, rationally, we "know" that everything is pre-recorded) what the story suggests only a moment later: that the world of Betty and Rita is an illusory dream world. When Del Rio's collapse exposes the illusion of the performance, she also exposes the illusory nature of Diane's film-like dream world as a whole. Thus, because the scope of the scene goes beyond Club Silencio, this is not a pure meta-reflection on cinema. Club Silencio not only builds on the dream-in-film interpretation, but it also gives another reason for it.

Not seeing the relevance of dreaming in regard to the transition between the Betty/Rita reality and the Diane/Camilla reality is to ignore the noetic aspect of the illusionary grasped in Club Silencio. That is, which mode of consciousness is responsible for the emergence of the illusionary? The American Dream, the previous cinematic reality, and Betty's identity prove to be illusionary in Club Silencio. In all three dimensions, the noetic aspect of the illusionary is the mode of dreaming. Diane *dreamt* Betty, or Betty "becomes" Diane by waking up; *Mulholland Drive* characterizes the language of cinema as inherently *dreamlike*; and the psychological basis of the American Dream is the activity of *dreaming*. If the first part were not the depiction of a dream, then Club Silencio's displaying of the deceptive nature of film would be unmotivated; it would be unrelated to the deceptive nature of the dream and thus independent of the place of the sequence in the story. But Club Silencio metaphorically anticipates on a self-reflexive level (i.e., seeing itself as an instance of *film*) what Betty is about to experience, that is, the deceptive nature of the current reality. Dreaming–waking is thus the story-level manifestation of the self-reflexive play with the ontology of cinema happening in Club Silencio.

This dynamic of dreaming–waking provides the model for immersion–disruption, which constitutes the possibility of *Mulholland Drive*'s illusory effect. The dynamic of dreaming and waking—of immersion and disruption—not only represents the narrative development of the film but also underlies the reception attitude prestructured by the film. In a condensed form, the viewer experiences the phenomenological principle underlying the entire film in the Club Silencio scene: immersion into a world that marks itself as fictitious from the outset (*Mulholland Drive*: the title and the opening credits introducing the film; Club Silencio: the Magician announcing the performance)—followed by a sensory-affective break that requires a reassessment of the situation (*Who is who? What happened?* etc.). "Once more before it is over," the dream must emphatically show its immersive potential, so to speak, before a completely different world—the waking world of Diane—emerges. Dreaming, in *Mulholland Drive*'s conceptualization, is a maximally immersive, waking up a maximally disruptive experience. "Silencio," once whispered by Rita out of her dream and again by the blue-haired woman at the very end of the film, fulfills a similar function in both cases (01:42:32–01:42:33 and 02:22:27–02:22:30). Diegetically, it causes Rita to wake up, leading her back into the "Betty-and-Rita" reality. The *silencio* at the end of the film brings the viewer back from the (metaphorically speaking) dreamlike world of the whole film to the waking world and, in this, acts as a precursor to the more explicit, fourth-wall breaking that Monica Bellucci performs toward the end of *Twin Peaks* (2017) by asking, *Who is the dreamer?* (cf. section "The Function of Gordon Cole's Dream . . . " in Chapter 5). Due to its occurrence at the very end of the film, this last *silencio* appears as explicitly self-reflexive, making the content-form paradox of saying "silencio" *out loud* a metaphor for *Mulholland Drive* as a whole. Thus, conceptualizing itself as "an ether borne of beauty" (Andrews 35), the film appears to become a presence revolving around an absence.

Conclusion

The "Twin Peak" of the Lynchian Oneiric

The present study set out from the observation that while the films of David Lynch are frequently identified by their "dreamlike qualities," these qualities tend to remain underspecified, particularly in terms of their experiential dimension. This is the first systematic book-length study exploring the nature of dream experience as it appears in the director's different phases and audiovisual formats. The earliest film analyzed here is *Absurd Encounter with Fear*, a mostly ignored short film from 1967, while the latest is the third season of *Twin Peaks*, an eighteen-hour television production from fifty years later. Over this period, Lynch has developed a cinematic aesthetics that is crucially shaped by the oneiric. "The oneiric," in the conception of this study, relies on four distinct but not mutually exclusive dimensions. The first one of them, which acted as the starting point for the present film analyses, is experience as it occurs in marked dreams. That is, it asked for the experiential nature of the dreams depicted in Lynch's films. In the second sense of the term, "oneiric" refers to experiences that are *like* experience in a marked dream; these experiences are dream*like* in the literal sense, with "dream" referring to a dream sequence. The third dimension is constituted by sequences that are "oneiric" in their attempt to imitate aspects of a sleeping person's nocturnal dream-experience; the sequences are literally dream*like*, with "dream" referring to the nonfictional night dream. And fourth, "oneiric" should include the way dream experience is conceptualized in and by Lynch's films. It is only at this point that, in addition to sequences evoking dream(-like) experiences, verbalizations *about* the dream come into play.

As the analyses have shown, a defining characteristic of the Lynchian oneiric can be pinned down to a certain double potential. That is, the oneiric as it appears in Lynch's films exhausts the full spectrum of the film experience between the poles of pre-reflective sensory address and reflective medialization. On the one hand, it constitutes a markedly sensory-perceptual mode of experience—both characters and viewers are frequently challenged in their perceptual patterns, while at the same time being immersed in the material dream scenario. On the other hand, the Lynchian oneiric provides a mode of both psychological and medial reflection. Not only the characters but the films themselves are inclined to "turn back" on themselves in a dream, exploring the preconditions, possibilities, and limitations of their own existence and ability to know the world. The oneiric in Lynch's films is thus of both phenomenological and philosophical interest. It should be noted that while the distinction between sensory and reflective oneiricity provides a useful conceptualization of the Lynchian film experience, these two categories are not always easy to separate. Their intertwinement is most noticeable in the aesthetics of Diane's dream in *Mulholland Drive* (2001). For the protagonist and the viewer of this film, the dream functions as a model for sensory immersion into another—medial—world. As the Club Silencio sequence emphatically demonstrates, however, the mediality of the dream is not grasped upon reflection but is *expressed* as a directly perceptible phenomenon of the film experience. It is grasped pre-reflectively by experiencing the moment in which singer Rebekah Del Rio collapses on stage while her voice keeps singing.

Pre-reflective Sensory Address

Concerning pre-reflective sensory address, it is worth coming back to the beginning of Lynch's career as a filmmaker. The section on Lynch's first short film *Absurd Encounter with Fear* (1967) discussed its oneiric potential in terms of two dimensions of the viewing experience. First, the film created a dreamlike state of immersion into an unfathomable scenario, mostly through the atmospheric quality of the soundtrack *Capriccio for Violin and Orchestra* (1967) by Krzysztof Penderecki. The film's diffuse atmosphere of threat, I have argued, was rooted in the viewer's inability to pick out individual elements of sense perception that she could direct her attention to. This sense of threat provided the basis for the viewer's acceptance of a totally unmotivated, alogical chain of events as causally necessary—similar to a nightmare whose events, while threatening from the within-dream perspective, stop making any sense in retrospect. The second aspect of the oneiric potential of *Absurd Encounter* was rooted in the blue man's look into the camera, which led him to drop to the ground, losing consciousness. The section revealed that, going beyond a mere shift concerning the fictional status of the events, this moment in the film provoked a kind of viewer involvement that is well known from dreaming. What this moment shared with the phenomenology of dreaming was the way in which I ambiguously relate to the film as a passive observer and an actively engaging participant, similar to when dreams provoke the dreamer's twofold involvement as observer (third-person perspective) and as agent (first-person perspective). *Absurd Encounter* conflated the observing and the participating modality of my spectatorship through the act of looking because through this act, I appeared to affect the event on the screen. That is, through a quick and unexpected zoom in, I fell under the illusion of causing the blue man's breakdown on the pre-reflective level of experiencing the film. The act of looking thus allowed me to "talk back" to the film through the primary sensory modality through which I have access to it.

If the oneiricity of *Absurd Encounter* hinged upon an *immersive* atmosphere, Lynch's second film, *The Alphabet* (1968), pointed to the *disruptive* end of the spectrum of the film experience. That is, to achieve its oneiric effect, it performed what has been called the "de-automatization of perception" in Russian Formalism. The girl's dream embodied a limited mode of both speech perception (muffled voice of the mother, general lack of semantics) and visual perception, what Laura Marks calls "seeing for the first time" (178). The visual style of Lynch's animation, strongly influenced by the paintings of Francis Bacon, allowed the film to explore the structural preconditions of seeing, thus becoming a kind of visual perception in the making. In terms of viewer–film interaction, the image that stood out was one of a human face turned upside down, with a fake nose attached to the chin and framed to the lower part of the face. The sensory-cognitive disruption of this shot was rooted in the viewer's difficulty to categorize the visual input—an effect that was amplified by our default-mode familiarity with human faces. As this dream image suggested, the Lynchian oneiric is shaped by the perceptual defamiliarization of the familiar.

It should not go without notice that Lynch's early short films contain no dialogue at all and hardly any words. If *The Alphabet* explicitly opposed a language-based approach to the world (symbolized by the alphabet), *The Grandmother* (1970) was a continuation of this impulse, in that the communication between the child protagonist and his title-giving grandmother unfolded on a purely tactile-acoustic level. The film, particularly the scene interpretable as a dream, prestructured a form of viewer perception for which Laura Marks coined the term *haptic visuality* (178). That is, when a seed grew into an unidentifiable object, the viewer was forced to explore what was in the frame by "visual palpation." Not recognizing the object as anything, the specific course of my saccadic movements was shaped by the way I imagined the object to feel like if I were to touch it (*canonical neurons* fire if the visible shape of an object has a certain *affordance* or *demand characteristics*; cf. Schönhammer, *Wahrnehmung* 144). At the same time, my saccadic movements were led by the boy's hands touching the object (*mirror neurons*). Because vision did not just reveal what the object was, its mastery over the other senses was undermined in Lynch's third short film. Due to this, it made sensual comprehension the primary mode of interaction with the on-screen scenario and broke with the principle of ambiguous sensation having to serve unequivocal narrative resolution (found in a myriad of films, e.g., in the first encounter with the dinosaur in Steven Spielberg's *Jurassic Park* [1993] or in the opening of Jane Campion's *The Piano* [1993]). A similar inclination toward materiality (rather than narrativity) could be seen in *The Grandmother*'s depiction of trauma. It was not just through the (narrative) sequence of events that the boy experienced a loss or trauma, as Lacanian readings have suggested. Even before Grandmother died in the cemetery, the boy, paradoxically, had a sensorial experience of loss, just by virtue of the fact that she had been materially present in his dream. The dream, in this sense, constituted the experiential order that let his trauma materially appear to his senses. It presentified desire (the desire to be loved) by translating it into a material "object" that the boy physically interacted with, allowing him the experience of absence through presence.

Concerning Lynch's first feature film *Eraserhead* (1977), I have argued that Henry's radiator acts as the nexus between waking reality and dream reality (ontologically), between the conscious and the unconscious (psychologically), and, on a phenomenological level, between two orders of experience that Jagna Brudzinska distinguished in her interpretation of Husserl. In the impressional-apperceptive order, the identity of people and objects is invariable. This is not the case in the phantasmatic-imaginary order, which is defined by the malleability of matter. The radiator was not just the gate to another world and marked the threshold of two layers of consciousness, it also introduced a different experiential order which was structured by material instability and frequent transformations and a general lack of spatiotemporal continuity. Interesting in regard to the distinction between these two orders of experience was the ambiguous role of sound in the movie. On the one hand, the change from the nonmusical sound textures of the waking world to the electronic organ music of the dream world reinforced the distinguishability of the impressional-apperceptive and the phantasmatic-imaginary order. The transformation of a nonmusical soundscape into music as Henry passes from waking to dreaming matched Brudzinska's characterization of the phantasmatic-imaginary as inherently medial. On the other hand, Lynch's use of sound *merged* the two orders of experience through the smoldering presence of a roaring sound throughout the film. At various transitions between waking and dreaming, the sound crescendoed, hinting at what Lynch called "a certain image of a bigger world" (Rodley 73). The chapter argued that "bigger world" refers to the respective other fictional level (to that of waking reality from the dream's perspective and to the dream reality from the waking perspective). Interestingly, Lynch's claim as to the shortcoming of the phenomenally given was translated into an immediately perceptible in the film experience *through sound*. On an acoustic level, this roaring sound thus constantly reminded the viewer of the respective other mode of experience, of the *other* within the *present*.

The roaring sound was seen as a manifestation of what Michel Chion's theory of film sound calls *ambient sound* (*Audio-Vision* 75). Watching and listening to a film, its ambient sound can be hard to distinguish from the sounds in the film viewer's physical environment, especially when it is slightly noisy. Like the phantasmatic-imaginary, then, any film's ambient sound as such can act as a (literally) "*polyphonic* intervention" (Brudzinska 64) into the viewer's auditory perception of her nonmedial environment. General film sound perception reflects what *Eraserhead* used the phenomenon for, that is, the merging of ontological levels (dream–waking and film–reality). That is, Lynch's first feature exploited the natural disposition of ambient sound for undermining the boundary between the film world and the real world in order to interlock the diegetic levels of dreaming and waking within the film. In other words, *Eraserhead* expressed the interlocking of fictional levels in the diegesis (dream–reality) as the merging between the film's ambient sound and the viewer's respective sound environment.

Reflective Medialization

The pole of reflective medialization, that is, the other end of the spectrum exploited by oneiric experiences in Lynch's films, becomes more palpable in light of the observations made about the development of oneiric self-reflexivity. The self-reflexivity of the Lynchian oneiric was first hinted at in *The Alphabet*, then concretized in *Eraserhead*, and later manifested its full potential in *Lost Highway*, *Mulholland Drive*, and *Twin Peaks* (2017). The four-minute short film *The Alphabet* depicted a girl's passage from waking to dreaming through the change from live action to animation. Dreaming was associated with the *process* of painting. The constantly evolving drawings not only corresponded to the malleability of the dream world itself, but for the viewer, this evoked an immediacy of experience that recreated the way in which the dream presented itself to the girl *while dreaming*. Film thus functioned at the service of imaginative vision, given the implication that the girl's act of viewing was creating the objects of her vision *through* her vision (rather than merely receiving sensory information from a pre-established outside world). As a form of "second-order" vision, the animation technique thus expressed the film's reflection on the otherness of visual perception in dreams.

If it was a *switch* to a second medium in *The Alphabet*, in *Eraserhead*, it was the spatial *incorporation* of a second world within the first that marked the transition from waking to dreaming. The theater stage behind the radiator introduced a second world and a second order of experience to the diegetic reality. The accessibility of this world was a function of Henry's state of consciousness. Although the stage already lit up inside his radiator while he was in a meditation-like state, he entered it only when he was dreaming. Twenty years later, the videotapes in *Lost Highway* displayed a formal resemblance to the stage in *Eraserhead*. Like the stage, the tapes acted as the element transforming the ordinary world of the story, while at the same time being embedded within it. Both second-order media contained the respective story's central element: with her dance performance on stage, the Lady in the Radiator led Henry to kill his baby; the tapes in *Lost Highway* provided the shocking revelation that Fred killed his wife. But unlike the stage in *Eraserhead*, the tapes in *Lost Highway* appeared to depict reality, particularly the third one showing Renée's murder. Building on the exposed mediality of the dream in *The Alphabet* and *Eraserhead*, however, Fred's dream was not to be viewed as independent from the tapes—that is, the medial element—either. The connection between his dream and the tapes was rooted in the fact that the tracking shot through the corridor was identical in both. After all, Fred's shock upon seeing the video footage, to a large extent, derived from this: he was not just scared because someone apparently invaded their home but because *he* was familiar with these exact images from his own dream. My chapter treated *Lost Highway* as a deconstructivist film in the tradition of Ingmar Bergman's *Persona* (1966). I proposed that the dream in *Lost Highway* (like in *Persona*) is of pivotal importance for the consistent deconstruction of the film's own world. Like Henry's dream, Fred's dream announced a second world to the story, but unlike in *Eraserhead*, it was not a second world *within* the first (the Lady existed "inside" the radiator) but *against* it. This second world, first manifested by the videotape footage and later by the plotline of Pete Dayton, was associated to, but never rendered reconcilable with, Fred's reality. The groundbreaking novelty of *Lost Highway*'s dream sequence in Lynch's oeuvre was that it introduced a second ontological layer to the story that was fundamentally in conflict with the first. Never before had a dream introduced a dialectic to the film that dismantled its own ontology (though one can see the anticipation of this function of the dream in the prologue of Lynch's previous *Twin Peaks: Fire Walk with Me* [1992]).

The dream in *Eraserhead* was a first hint at the connectedness of medial and psychological reflection. For one, it presented a mode of reflection on Henry's diurnal experience, particularly on his being a father. Further, the dream literally "staged" the film's self-consciousness through the illumination of a theater inside the radiator—light functioned as both a precondition for the cinematographic image and as a symbol for the emergence of (dream) consciousness. Zooming in on the development of medial reflection for a moment, the Red Room in *Twin Peaks* echoed the theatrical aesthetics of Henry's dream, but it let go of the self-reflexivity of *Eraserhead*'s light symbolism. Instead, Cooper's dream in the first season of the series marked its unreality by deviating from natural movement. That is, some (but not all) of the scene was recorded with actors moving and speaking backward. The scene as it appeared on the television screen had then been reversed again, the result being a defamiliarization effect that prevented the viewer from grasping oneiric time as either "flowing forward" or "flowing backward." A paradoxical movement characterized the otherness of dream time. *Lost Highway*, for one, expanded the proper temporality of Cooper's dream—the backward-burning cabin in the desert alluded to the backward-speaking occurring in the Red Room. More importantly, it connected the Red Room's proper temporality with the cinematic self-reflexivity that was first discernable in *Eraserhead*. While it does anticipate Renée's murder, the dream in *Lost Highway* was not merely prophetic, but it introduced a version of reality in which Fred killed Renée, which is logically irreconcilable with the version in which he did not. The logical paradox of the movie emerged by juxtaposing the beginning with the end. While in the opening, Fred *received* the intercom message "Dick Laurent is dead," Fred was the one *sending* that very same message in the closing sequence. The chapter on *Lost Highway* showed that the dream introduced a second world, which was incompatible with the first, as expressed by the circularity of the narrative. The film did not hierarchize the two diegetic planes but melted them together, thus becoming aporetic. Continuing *Eraserhead*'s oneiric reflection on film's poetic possibilities of representation and perception, *Lost Highway* suggested that it cannot represent truth. In this, the movie anticipated the role of the dream toward the end of *Twin Peaks* (2017), which deconstructed its own diegesis using a dream metaphor. When the clock of the Twin Peaks Sheriff's department froze in Part 17, Cooper's realization that "we live inside a dream" initiated a series of transformations of space and time that dissolved the diegetic reality of the series as viewers have come to know it.

But it was Gordon Cole's dream in Part 14 of *Twin Peaks* (2017) that displayed the intertwinement of dream and (both psychological and medial) reflection most clearly. Psychological reflection first: even if the oneiricity of the *Twin Peaks* universe was insurmountable in the end of the third season, Cole's dream, as a microstructure, had a special significance in providing him with the opportunity to grasp that oneiricity. His dream was the experiential mode of reflection, in the sense that it gave him the opportunity to question his most fundamental beliefs—not coincidentally, after the dream, Cole thought back to a moment from his past that had challenged his belief in reality (i.e., a scene featured in *Twin Peaks: Fire Walk with Me*). I have argued that *Twin Peaks* (2017) mirrors Johann Fichte's epistemological skepticism, which suggests that if life is a dream, thinking is the dream of that dream. Moreover, the connection between dream and reflection was even stronger in Lynch's series, given that reflection took the form of thinking about who the dreamer is. That is, out of all possible things she could say, Monica Bellucci's question as to the *dreamer* caused Cole's dream to enter a mode of reflection. In a dream within a dream (Cole's dream as part of the dream world of *Twin Peaks*), thus, the question concerning the identity of the dreamer triggered a profound form of self-reflection.

The meta-mediality (in addition to the psychology) of the reflection presented by Cole's dream has been shown to result from some of the choices made in its conception and way of shooting. For one, it was no coincidence that it is Gordon Cole—played by David Lynch himself—who had this dream. That is, asking him who the dreamer is, Bellucci alluded to Lynch being the creator of *Twin Peaks*. His double status was hinted at by the term "director," which applied to both the function of his fictional character Cole in regard to the FBI (he is the FBI *director*) and his function as the *director* of *Twin Peaks*. Further, Monica Bellucci played herself here. This in itself could have been seen as sufficient for the scene's metafictional spin: Bellucci might not only have spoken as a fictional character here when she said that "*we* are like the dreamer" but as her "real" self on behalf of the "real" audience of the series. This aspect became even clearer by considering the way the scene was shot. That is, with Bellucci asking who the dreamer is, the camera took the position of Cole such that she not only addressed him but also the viewer, speaking directly into the camera. While both Lynch-as-Cole and the viewer were invited to contemplate their identity, *Twin Peaks* conceptualized itself as a shared dream experience between its creator, actresses and actors, and viewers.

Before *Twin Peaks* (2017), *Mulholland Drive* also both reaffirmed and expanded the hypothesis concerning the meta-mediality of the dream that first imposed itself in the discussion of *Eraserhead*. In his movie from 2001, Lynch used the dream as a means for cinema to meet its own history, which, as has been shown, applied to both film history in general and to *Mulholland Drive*'s own production history in particular. That is, on the one hand, the first part of the movie, which is frequently interpreted as Diane's dream, alluded to film history and what is simply called "the industry" in Los Angeles in terms of its characters (Rita's femme fatale allure; the reference of "Betty" to Betty Schaefer from the noir-classic and Lynch-favorite *Sunset Boulevard* [1950]), aesthetics, narrative, and shooting locations. Many of the elements in the first part of the film played in form or content with conventions and symbols of cinema (e.g., the classical lighting, frequent cross-fadings, recurring aerial shots of the Hollywood sign, etc.). On the other hand, the dream played a crucial role in the production history of *Mulholland Drive*. Originally, *Mulholland Drive* had been conceived of as the pilot of a TV series, which was aired in 1999. After the network ABC had declined to produce an entire *Mulholland Drive* series, however, a French production company gave Lynch the opportunity to rework the pilot into the cinematic release from 2001. Presumably, the various narrative threads opened up in the original pilot would have continued in following episodes, had the show been picked up by ABC. Through the framing dream marker of the final feature film (at the beginning and after about two hours of the film), Lynch was able to give a sense of closure to the story of the pilot, which had previously been conceived of as open-ended. Lynch's reinterpretation of the original pilot as a dream went beyond pragmatism, though. That is, if *Mulholland*

Drive reflected on its own materiality and historicity (as had already been observed by Zina Giannopoulou), then the dream was what enabled this reflection. Film was not a mere medium anymore in the dream part of *Mulholland Drive*. In addition to conveying a story through image and sound, it was a constant (visible and visual) act of self-reflection. The dream, as a meta-medium (i.e., an exposed second medium within the first medium of film), was what allowed the feature film from 2001 to reflect on what had brought it into being, that is, the pilot (in a narrow sense) and the history of cinema (in a broader sense). Through the dream framing, the story and aesthetic means of the pilot became contingent to some extent, their absoluteness being undermined by the fact that the standard conventions and symbols of cinema were present in the first (dream) part and absent in the second (waking) part of the film. The dream has thus shown to turn the pilot's medial reality into meta-medial possibility. What had originally been thought of as Diane's "real experience" (from the pilot) was reworked into a coherent, film-like love story (in the feature film). In *Mulholland Drive*, the dream reflected on Diane's experience in a cinematically coded way, the *what* referring to the unrequited love and lack of success in Hollywood, the *how* involving codes from the history of cinema that the film reinterpreted as oneiric. As *Mulholland Drive* showed, thus, the psychological and the medial dimension of reflective oneiricity can be inseparable.

"Watch and Listen to the Dream of Time and Space"

Based on what this conclusion has recapped so far, an initial synthesizing observation could sound like this: following the temporal chronology of Lynch's films, there is a movement from a stress on materiality, sensory address, and "lower-order" physiological processes in the earlier films to a focus on "higher-order" processes, such as an increasing degree of self-reflexivity and dream layering, in more recent films. While Lynch's early depictions of the oneiric focus on the materiality of image and sound, his dream structures from the 1990s onward become increasingly complex and language plays an ever more important role. As the analysis chapters have shown, however, it is not the case that materiality is no longer an issue in Lynch's later dream depictions. The cognitive demand arising due to structural complexity does not substitute the pre-reflective dimension of the movies, but it exists *in addition* to it. Neither is it true that his early films are not "cognitively demanding" just because they are not as complex in terms of narrative structure. *The Alphabet*, for example, is not a film that is easy to understand just because its structure is not as complex as that of *Lost Highway* or *Mulholland Drive*. If there is a change in the way Lynch's films deal with the oneiric, it should not be framed as a linear unidirectional progression starting out from an exclusive interest in lower-order processes leading toward a focus on higher-order processes. That is, with the peak of narrative structural complexity in the third season *Twin Peaks* (2017), it is not the case that the sensory involvement of the viewer ceases to be of interest.

In fact, the discussion of the scenes at the room above the purple sea and at the Convenience Store suggested the exact opposite. Manipulating the natural flow of time, these scenes undermined the viewer's sensory-motor identification with characters and camera movement, providing intense moments of perceptual disruption. The scene at the purple sea, further, evoked the "double corporeality" of the nocturnal dream-experience: if it is one of the dream state's physiological characteristics for the dreamer to be "in" his sleeping body and "in" the dream world at the same time, then this double perspective can be evoked through the representation of movement *and* nonmovement. While the representation of inhibited movement (nonfluidity, repetition, backward flow, stretching) alluded to the dreamer's body being affected by sleep paralysis, Cooper's movement in the scene (which succeeded despite of the manipulations) alluded to the dreamer's identification with the agile virtual body of his dream ego, which is free to move about in the dream world. The recurring threatful knock in the scene heightened the tension between those two poles: biologically hardwired to escape potential danger, my impulse to *move away* was denied on several levels. First, Cooper, with whom I identified in the scene, did not escape—I was not granted the satisfaction of car chase sequences here. Second, I could not escape "in Cooper's place." Hence, my stillness while watching the scene was perceived as contributing to the inability to move depicted on screen. And most importantly, the recurrence of the knocking, combined with the inhibited movement suggested by the editing, significantly increased this feeling of having to move away while being unable to do so. Following Schönhammer's neurophysiological approach to the dream (cf. section "Neurophysiological Accounts" in Chapter 2), I know this feeling because I know what it is like to be temporarily paralyzed during sleep, with my brain interpreting the paralysis *as* a dream scenario that revolves around movement.

In *Twin Peaks* (2017), thus, the dream acts as both a mode of reflection on experience (Gordon Cole's "I saw myself from long ago" in his dream in Part 14) and as a matter of coming (back) to immediate perceptual experience. On the one hand, the series shows the meta-mediality of Lynch's dreams—that is, the dreams' tendency "to let appear an *other*" (cf. Brudzinska 60) in the film, which, as a medium, already lets appear an "other" by nature. On the other hand, it reconfirms what my discussion of *Absurd Encounter with Fear* revealed, that is, the fact that oneiricity may consist in a particular kind of immediate sensory viewer–film interaction, one that is easily overlooked if film is considered a mere object of vision and the viewer a merely passive observer. *Twin Peaks* (2017) might thus be called the "twin peak" of the Lynchian oneiric, given that it stands as the paradigmatic manifestation of Lynch's double interest in the dream. It is the dynamic interplay of reflective oneiricity (Bellucci's "We are like the dreamer who dreams, and then lives inside the dream. But who is the dreamer?" in Part 14) and sensory oneiricity (e.g., the room above the purple sea in Part 3) that has come to define Lynch's films at least since *Eraserhead*. *Mulholland Drive* displays the dynamism of these two forms of oneiricity most clearly, in that Club Silencio intermeshes sensory and reflective oneiricity in a single sequence. Negotiating the viewers' relationship to cinema *as* protagonist Betty's relationship to a musical performance on a theater stage, Club Silencio asks for the reason why we can be affected by performance, *knowing* that it is illusory. In comparison to Lynch's earlier work, something does change in Club Silencio. The sequence does not just *imply* the dominance of the senses over reason in the film experience, but it consciously puts its ability for sensory affection on display by literally *staging* it. Club Silencio simultaneously *reflects* on and *demonstrates* the pre-reflective dimension of film. This was not the case for Lynch's earlier films, where dreams provided moments of sensory intensity as well—but, importantly, they did not *show* us their awareness of their affective potential. The two poles of sensory address and reflective medialization are thus completely intermeshed in the sequence.

Generally speaking, the Lynchian oneiric tends to challenge solidified patterns of experience—early on, through the de-automatization of immediate sensory perception (*The Alphabet*, *The Grandmother*), later in terms of larger units of the film experience (*Lost Highway*, *Mulholland Drive*, and, most extremely, *Twin Peaks* [2017]). What goes along with the shift from early "local" to later "global" de-automatization is an increasingly palpable challenge to the respective film's own ontological make-up and the viewer's relationship to the film world. The increasingly complex diegetic worlds and our material relationship to them are both evoked and challenged through the dream. The transition from Cooper's dream in the first season of *Twin Peaks* (1990) to the prologue of *Twin Peaks: Fire Walk with Me* (1992) occupies a central position in this regard. While Cooper's dream from the first season is treated as a psychological phenomenon, the prologue of the movie from two years later conceptualizes the dream as an ontological phenomenon. The scene at the FBI headquarters in the film *Twin Peaks: Fire Walk with Me* questioned its own act of seeing by negotiating the ontology of the camera image. The reliability of video images was called into question, as Agent Cooper was simultaneously seen on the live image of the surveillance camera footage and in the room where he was watching that very footage. Seesslen referred to this as "the attempt to enable a pluralized vision within the same image" (136). The dreamlike perspective of the scene was to allow two contradictory perceptions to coexist in a single image without elevating one over the other, thus raising the question of the "safe ground" of the diegetic world. *Lost Highway* took up this idea—the title, in this context, was understood literally as evoking the absence of a material ground at the basis of the story. This idea was again associated with the dream in the movie (as was shown, the dream anticipated the composition and movement of the video camera footage). *Lost Highway* took the kind of self-questioning of *Fire Walk with Me* even further, however, by radically subverting the ontology of its own world—which remained intangible and existed only in images and sounds that (in the words of the new *Twin Peaks*) we "watch and listen to."

On a different note, the potential political value of the perceptual de-automatization constituted by the Lynchian oneiric is hardly deniable. In this, it seems important to stress the discrepancy between the political dimension *of* the film experience (for the viewers) and the lack thereof *inside* the stories (for the characters). That is, the de-automatization of perception (in the Šklovskijan sense; 15) provokes a "seeing anew" of what was thought to be known on the viewer's part. By *shocking* the viewer *into thought*, as the surrealists called it, the Lynchian oneiric presents an exercise in letting go of habitualized patterns of perception, a process whose effect is amplified by the preceding sensory immersion of the films. The *otherness* of oneiric experiences aims at a greater sense of perceptual and cognitive flexibility—the seed for any kind of political process. In letting the world appear strange again, the Lynchian oneiric does justice to the nature of film as a language that perpetually reinvents itself. James Monaco, for example, suggests that "[f]ilm speaks in neologisms" (183) and quotes Christian Metz: "When a 'language' does not already exist, [...] one must be something of an artist to speak it, however poorly. For to speak it is partly to invent it, whereas to speak the language of everyday is simply to use it" (Monaco 183).

An entirely different matter is the question of the *film characters*' capacity to act within and upon the dreams. Lynch's characters tend *not* to grasp the opportunity for change and reflection that some of the dreams present (e.g., Henry's dream in *Eraserhead*, Fred's dream in *Lost Highway*, and Cole's dream in *Twin Peaks* [2017]). They are depicted as victims rather than masters of their existential conditions, with "the past dictat[ing] the future" (as Part 17 of *Twin Peaks* [2017] puts it). In regard to the existential crises that Lynch's characters find themselves in, the dream might theoretically function as an escapist space providing relief from the burden of existence. In Lynch's dreams, to the contrary, the characters are directly confronted with the core of that burden: the girl's fear of the letters in *The Alphabet*; the boy's fear of loneliness in *The Grandmother*; Henry's fear of parental responsibility in *Eraserhead*; Fred's fear of marital infidelity in *Lost Highway*; and Diane's fear of romantic and professional failure in *Mulholland Drive*. The fact that the characters' capacities to act in dreams are limited is not so much because the dream is not granted this potential but rather because of the *kind of dreams* that Lynch's films represent. Many of the dreams present (more or less absurd) encounters with *fear*, that is, a type of dream that is inherently limiting rather than liberating. And even when the dreams do show escapist tendencies, these are always problematized and never uncritically celebrated. Lynch's films display a keen interest in that moment where reality breaks into fantasy. In *The Alphabet*, a nightmare confronts a young girl with her real fear of learning the letters after she fantasizes about an ideal naturalized evolution of the alphabet. After the boy in *The Grandmother* creates his ideal fantasy object, that is, the title-giving caring grandmother, a painful daydream forces him to realize that she does not exist. In *Lost Highway*, Fred's dream shows that his dissociative fugue (i.e., his escape into a fantasy world where he becomes Pete) cannot hide the fact that he killed his wife in real life. In *Mulholland Drive*, the dream stops when Diane's dream ego Betty finds the blue key in her purse; in Diane's waking reality, the key signals that the hitman she commissioned to kill her former lover Camilla finished the job. On the diegetic level, thus, Lynch's films display a rather *realist* interest in dreaming. Not conceiving of the dream as a pure "realm of possibility," they ask for its compensatory function, for the things inside the characters that the dream tries to—but eventually cannot—hide. So the dreams' lack of possibilities for the characters stands in contrast to the perceptual-cognitive flexibility demanded of the viewer. That is, Lynch's films combine a realist-psychological interest in the dream on the diegetic level with an aesthetic sense of possibility on the level of film–viewer interaction. It is the poetological rather than character level of Lynch's cinema that realizes the reflective potential of the dream.

Coming full circle, the movement that has progressively been emerging in this study is circular rather than linear. Becoming an increasingly complex higher-order phenomenon that structures the narrative, the Lynchian oneiric also lets the viewer "return"[1] to her senses. It displays an inherent fascination with the way in which we apprehend the material world and with the nature of film itself. *Twin Peaks* (2017) conceptualizes film as a sensory phenomenon without a world within which it is embedded. What *Persona* (1966) calls the "hopeless dream of being," to *Twin Peaks* becomes a "dream without a dreamer." In this context, the Log Lady's imperative to "watch and listen to the dream of time and space" (in *Twin Peaks*' [2017] Part 10) could be seen as evocative of the double nature of the film experience itself. On the one hand, *watch and listen* bespeaks the immediate sensory experience, the acts of consciousness through which we have access to film in the first place. *The dream of time and space*, on the other hand, expresses a reflection on the absence of a material world at the basis of both the nocturnal dream-experience and the film experience. The Log Lady thus unites the pre-reflective with the reflective dimension of the film experience, whose dynamic interplay creates much of the appeal of the Lynchian oneiric. On a theoretical note, this study started out from Vivian Sobchak and her application of Maurice Merleau-Ponty's philosophy, calling film "an expression of experience by experience" (*Address* 3). The Lynchian oneiric has emerged as both an expression *and a thematization* of experience by experience, as both immediate affection of the senses and mediated second-order reflection upon experience. Expressing and provoking sensory and reflective experience at the same time, the oneiric in the work of Lynch can only stand as an invitation to appreciate the experience of film to the fullest.

Notes

Introduction

1. Film critic Nicholas Lezard, for example, writes that "[i]f ever there was a director who put dreams on to the screen without trying to impose a coherent, readily graspable narrative order on them, it is David Lynch."
2. The *Oxford English Dictionary* is not alone in establishing a close connection between the Lynchian dreamlike, on the one hand, and the mysterious or the menacing, on the other. In the context of oneiric phenomena in Lynch's cinema, Roy Menarini, for example, writes that "i film si nutrono di visioni, profezie, apparizioni che non si sa mai a chi o a che cosa attribuire. Di qui, una sensazione diffusa di minaccia, che 'possiede' fantasticamente anche i luoghi apparentemente più sicuri, come la casa o la camera da letto" (Menarini 16). While the relationship between fear and the oneiric is not of central concern in this study, it will be discussed to some extent in the analysis chapters of *Absurd Encounter with Fear* (1967; cf. Chapter 3), *The Alphabet* (1968; cf. Chapter 3), *Twin Peaks* (2017; cf. section "Oneiricity and the Ambivalence of Sensory Motor Activation" in Chapter 5), and *Mulholland Drive* (2001; cf. sections "'Dream as Film' as the Bridge . . . " and "'It Is an Illusion,' That Is, This Is a Dream . . . " in Chapter 7).
3. Maurice Lahde's essay is titled "'We live inside a dream.' David Lynchs Filme als Traumerfahrungen" (95), which reflects the general validity the author claims in regard to the oneiricity of Lynch's cinema.
4. An even less informative view is that cinema in itself is dreamlike. Like a dream, many have argued, a film is experienced as a flow of images and sounds. Based on this modal resemblance, one might speak of the oneiric quality of film or, vice versa, of the film-like quality of dreaming. However, notwithstanding the difference in the source of the image flow (internal in the case of dreaming and external in the context of movies), there is no gain of insight into the relationship between film and dream through this mere juxtaposition. Every film is dreamlike in this minimal sense, just like every dream is film-like. I will take a closer look at the relationship between film and dream in Chapter 2.
5. Popper writes: "[A]llgemeine Wirklichkeitsaussagen [sind] nicht verifizierbar, sondern *nur falsifizierbar* [. . .] Anders ausgedrückt: Allgemeinen Wirklichkeitsaussagen kann, aufgrund wissenschaftlich zulässiger Begründungsmethoden, niemals ein positiver, wohl aber ein negativer Geltungswert zugeschrieben werden. Ihre methodische Überprüfung geschieht durch Falsifikationsversuche, also durch Deduktion vollentscheidbarer Prognosen [. . .] Als Abgrenzungskriterium kann das *Kriterium der Falsifizierbarkeit* verwendet werden: Nur solche Sätze sagen etwas über die Erfahrungswirklichkeit aus, die an ihr scheitern können" (Popper 10).
6. "Vermessen der [. . .] Erfahrungsspielräume" (Morsch 9–10).

7 Female and male possessive and personal pronouns are used "generically" throughout this book, that is, both include the respective other biological sex as well as any other gender categories not represented by this binary distinction.
8 "Ein filmischer Beitrag zur Medientheorie" (Michalsky 397).
9 "*Loslassen des leibhaftigen Selbst der Empfindung und zum Erscheinen-Lassen eines Anderen*" (Brudzinska 60).
10 As the section "The Dream between Metaphoricity and Literalness" in Chapter 3 will show, though the marking status of the boy's dream in *The Grandmother* (1970) is not without ambiguity, the film does combine the boy's symbolic passage into black with what may be read as a retroactive form of marking the dream.
11 A notable exception to the general scarcity of phenomenological studies on *any* director's oneiric potential is constituted by Simon Dickson's paper, "The Oneiric Film: Refocusing the Film-Dream Analogy from an Existential Phenomenological Perspective" and by Vlada Petrić's paper on "Tarkovsky's Dream Imagery."

Part I

1 Since the year 2000, at least forty monographs on Lynch's films have been published.
2 A notable exception, in this context, is Pierluigi Basso Fossali's study on Lynch, which devotes over thirty pages to the early short films. Even here, though, *Absurd Encounter with Fear* (1967) is not included in the analyses.

Chapter 1

1 See also Marshall McLuhan's characterization of phenomenology in light of his own media theory: "hinter jeder Situation [steckt] eine andere Situation [. . .], die durchschimmert. Und dieses Durchschimmern ist die Phänomenologie. Ich sage dazu einfach: 'Das Medium ist die Botschaft'—oder Figur und Grund. Der Grund scheint durch die Figur, oder die Figur durch den Grund. Beides kann vorkommen. Aber es ist dieser Vorgang der Lichtung, der das Phänomenologische ausmacht" (McLuhan qtd. in Fellmann 161).
2 "[P]hänomenologische Forschung [besteht] darin [. . .], das im Bewusstsein unmittelbar Gegebene theoriefrei zu beschreiben" (Fellmann 28).
3 Although the academic field of cultural studies has grown an increasing interest in the body in parallel to phenomenology, its underlying conception of the body is very different. Thomas Elsaesser and Malte Hagener speak of the "representation paradigm" of cultural studies (*Filmtheorie* 152), which is at odds with phenomenology's concern with direct lived-body experience. The body is not a symbol in phenomenology, even the conception of the *film's body* is not a metaphor for Sobchak; what she means by this, rather, is that film is an "empirical and functional subject-object" (Sobchak, *Address* 133). As Ferencz-Flatz and Hanich elaborate, "this is not to say that film is human—the viewing subject-object of the film merely has perceptual and expressive capacities that are *equivalent* to that of the viewer" (40). In their view, however, speaking of a literal "film body" is at odds with the phenomenological approach, given that it is a theoretical presupposition rather

than the result of a phenomenological description of experience (43). Ferencz-Flatz and Hanich thus see the potential of the idea of a *film's body* in its metaphorical meaning, that is, in conceiving of it as a "quasi-subject" with its own idiosyncratic qualities (43): "over and above an empathy with the body of characters, there might also be an empathy with the 'film's body' as a whole" (44).

4 When Sobchak speaks of "the address of our own vision" here, two meanings of "address" are intended. It refers to both the *film's act of addressing* our vision and to *that point from which* we expressively perceive the film (Sobchak, *Address* 25).

5 It should be stressed that "similar" does not mean "identical." There are differences between human and cinematographic vision. For example, a cinematographic image is *framed*—an aspect for which there is no equivalent in human visual perception. Further, human vision is binocular, that is, based on *two* retinal images, whereas cinematographic vision is monocular, with the camera producing a single image. Within that image, however, the fixation of a visible object by humans, a process shaped by the fusion of two images, can be closely imitated by the camera's selective focus.

6 "Da in einer phänomenologischen Logik der Ausdruck einer Erfahrung (im Film) nur in Form einer (weiteren) Erfahrung (des Filmzuschauers) ausgedrückt werden kann, lassen sich Film- und Zuschauererfahrung weder heuristisch noch hierarchisch auseinanderhalten" (Elsaesser and Hagener, *Filmtheorie* 150).

7 Even in empirical studies, however, properties of the measuring device are not separable from the measured information. No matter what method is applied to investigate a specific trait, the trait per se cannot be measured, which is why psychologists Donald Campbell and Donald Fiske introduced the broadly accepted concept of a "trait-method unit" (84). In their words: "In any given psychological measuring device, there are certain features or stimuli introduced specifically to represent the trait that it is intended to measure. There are other features which are characteristic of the method being employed, features which could also be present in efforts to measure other quite different traits. The test, or rating scale, or other device, almost inevitably elicits systematic variance in response due to both groups of features" (Campbell and Fiske 84).

8 This suggests an additional meaning of the term "film experience": our experience *with* films. That is, we watch a film differently depending on the films we have seen before. Our way of seeing a film is not only shaped by our way of seeing the (nonmedial) world but also by our past experience with movies. Obviously, the experience of one Lynch film changes depending on which of his other films one has seen.

9 "[Ä]sthetische Wahrnehmungsform, die im Körper verankert ist und die selbst zugleich im apparativen Dispositiv und in den Formen des menschlichen Ausdrucks verkörpert ist" (Morsch 8).

10 "[D]ie Phänomenologie [macht] nicht die Tatsachen, die bei einzelnen Menschen empirisch feststellbaren Einzelfälle intentionalen Erlebens und seiner Gegenständlichkeit zum Thema. Sie abstrahiert von den zufälligen, praktischen Bewußtseinsabläufen und Gegenständen und richtet ihren Blick auf die Wesensgesetze, die den Aufbau der Akte und der in ihnen erscheinenden Seinsregionen bestimmen" (Held 26).

11 As Merleau-Ponty suggests, "the empiricist philosopher [. . .] describes sensations and their substratum—as one might describe the fauna of a distant land—

without noticing that he himself also perceives, that he is a perceiving subject" (*Phenomenology* 214). In Christian Bermes's words: "Die Subjektivität und damit die Perspektivität des Wissenschaftlers wie auch des Menschen überhaupt wird ausgeschaltet, indem sie objektiviert wird" (Bermes 43).

12 While film phenomenology is not inherently feminist in the narrow sense, it is informed by an approach that values the individuality of lived-body experience over ideological constraints—an impulse that seems historically related to the feminist movement. Writing in the early 1990s, Sobchak elaborates: "[A]lthough what follows is not an overtly feminist work, it is written by a woman who has felt constrained by contemporary theoretical analysis, who wants to speak of more possibilities than either psychoanalytic or Marxist theory currently allows [. . .] [N]eo-Freudian psychoanalysis has not exhausted my experience, although it has often exhausted my patience. I refuse to be completely contained within its structures and described by its terms. Psychoanalysis is fine, perhaps, for disclosing the 'unconscious' of patriarchal texts and the power and constitutive nature of an experienced 'lack,' but it is not so fine for describing the pleasure and plenitude of an experience that includes—but is also in *excess* of—'sexual difference'" (Sobchak, *Address* xv).

13 In summing up Hans-Georg Gadamer's account, Terry Eagleton stresses the *historical* relativity of hermeneutics: "All interpretation is situational, shaped and constrained by the historically relative criteria of a particular culture; there is no possibility of knowing the literary text 'as it is'" (Eagleton 71).

14 "Einsicht, dass es gerade die Perspektive ist, die Erkenntnis ermöglicht" (Bermes 43).

15 This point in the film exemplifies the shift from what in Bill Nichols's terminology is called the "observational mode" to the "performative mode" of documentary film (*Documentary* 22). While the former shows "a direct engagement with the everyday life of subjects as observed by an unobtrusive camera," the latter "emphasizes the subjective and expressive aspect of the *filmmaker's own involvement* with the subject; it strives to heighten the audience's responsiveness to this involvement" (Nichols, *Documentary* 22; my italicization).

16 Held pointedly sums up the value of subjectivity in Husserl's phenomenological method: "Das objektiv Gültige, an sich Seiende ist uns gerade *in* seinem von den faktischen subjektiven Vollzügen unabhängigen Gehalt nur zugänglich durch den Rückbezug auf entsprechende subjekt-relative originäre Gegebenheitsweisen" (Held 21).

17 A problem with Sobchak's 1992 book *The Address of the Eye* is that it only rarely discusses particular films.

18 D'Aloia uses "visuomotor neurons" as an umbrella term for mirror neurons and canonical neurons (219). Mirror neurons fire when executing and observing *actions*; canonical neurons are activated when executing object-related actions and when observing an *object* with certain demand characteristics, for example, a door handle (see also Schönhammer, *Wahrnehmung* 144).

19 In a similar vein, Allan Hobson, despite a heavy focus on the neurobiology of dreaming, concludes his influential paper, "REM Sleep and Dreaming: Towards a Theory of Protoconsciousness," with this remark: "To the humanities in general, and to psychology and philosophy in particular, the new neuroscience of dream consciousness sends an appeal for more detailed attention to phenomenology that could help those disciplines without loss of their traditional and important adherence to meaning and to moral values" (Hobson 812).

20 Sobchak's 2005 paper "When the Ear Dreams: Dolby Digital and the Imagination of Sound" investigates film sound but focuses exclusively on Dolby Digital trailers.
21 Sobchak clarifies her view of the close connection between vision and consciousness in this passage: "In its expression of intentionality in existence and the world as a modality of perception, in its activity, its directedness, and its reversibility, vision echoes the intentional structure of consciousness. Or, rather, we could say more accurately that the intentional structure of consciousness echoes *within* our vision" (Sobchak, *Address* 94).
22 Interestingly, Merleau-Ponty, whose phenomenology is strongly influenced by the Gestalt psychology of Max Wertheimer, Wolfgang Köhler, and Kurt Koffka, transposes the idea of spontaneous, holistic perception of visual elements to the experience of music. In his words, "[t]he melody is not a sum of notes, since each note only counts by virtues of the function it serves in the whole, which is why the melody does not perceptibly change when transposed, that is, when all its notes are changed while their interrelationships and the structure of the whole remain the same" (Merleau-Ponty, "The Film" 334). Merleau-Ponty later speaks of "the melodic unity of film," by which he intends not only the "temporal *gestalt*" of film (rather conceiving of film as "a sum total of images") but also an acoustic *gestalt* (rather than seeing it as "a sum total of words or noises"; "The Film" 339–40).
23 Susanne Langer's approach, including her idea of the "presentational form" of both film and dream-experience, will be discussed in section "The Implicit Phenomenological Basis of the Film/Dream Analogy" in Chapter 2.

Chapter 2

1 Presumably, Sigmund Freud is at the basis of this conceptualization. He wrote that "an Stelle des inneren Anspruches, der ihn [den Schläfer] beschäftigen wollte, ist ein äußeres Erlebnis getreten, dessen Anspruch erledigt worden ist. Ein Traum ist also auch eine *Projektion*, eine Veräußerlichung eines inneren Vorganges" (Freud, *Psychologie des Unbewußten* 180).
2 "Wie künstlich und falsch erscheint an diesem unmittelbaren Traumereignis gemessen die übliche gedankliche Trennung einer solchen Zusammengehörigkeit in die zwei Stücke einer Aussenwelt und einer Innenwelt, in einem blossen aussenweltlichen Raumgegenstand, einen Zimmerraum einerseits und in irgendwelche darin unbeteiligt an ihm vorhandene, psychische Erlebnisse, Zustände und Verhaltensweisen des Menschen andererseits" (Boss 92).
3 Susan Sontag elaborates on the power dynamics of photography: "Photographs really are experience captured, and the camera is the ideal arm of consciousness in its acquisitive mood. To photograph is to appropriate the thing photographed. It means putting oneself into a certain relation to the world that feels like knowledge—and, therefore, like power" (Sontag 3–4).
4 Foucault writes that, in Freudian psychoanalysis, "[t]he imaginative plasticity of the dream is, for the meaning which comes to light in it, but the form of its contradictoriness. Nothing more. The image is exhausted in the multiplicity of meanings" (Foucault 34–5).

5 "*Die Gegenstände im Wie ihres Erscheinens* in zugeordneten Gegebenheitsweisen sind die 'Phänomene,' die 'Erscheinungen,' von denen die danach benannte 'Phänomenologie' handelt" (Held 16).
6 "[W]eil seine Technik in jedem einzelnen Moment die absolute (wenn auch nur empirische) Wirklichkeit dieses Moment ausdrückt, wird das Gelten der 'Möglichkeit' als einer der 'Wirklichkeit' entgegengesetzten Kategorie aufgehoben" (Lukács qtd. in Schneider 25).
7 "Alles ist wahr und wirklich, alles ist gleich wahr und gleich wirklich" (Lukács qtd. in Schneider 25).
8 "[D]ie der Beobachtung im strengen Sinne gar nicht zugängliche Ebene des Traums" (Schneider 25–6).
9 Chion explains that "the silent film may be called deaf insofar as it prevented us from hearing the real sounds of the story. It had no ears for the immediate aural space, the here and now of the action" (*Voice* 7).
10 "[D]as Werkzeug der Gesellschaft" (Von Hofmannsthal 142).
11 "Der Ersatz für die Träume" (Von Hofmansthal 141).
12 As Matthias Brütsch observes, the metaphor of the *dream factory* already came up almost twenty years earlier, proof of which is Ilja Ehrenburg's *Die Traumfabrik* from 1931 (cf. Brütsch 71).
13 "Die Schauspiele des Traums zählen zu den konstitutiven Merkmalen einer Ästhetik des Surrealen, die im Filmischen einen adäquaten Ort der Umsetzung findet, der jene surrealen Atmosphären und Wahrnehmungsformen am besten zu vermitteln vermag" (Lommel et al. 15). In a provocative style that is typical of the surrealist movement, Antonin Artaud wrote: "Si le cinéma n'est pas fait pour traduire les rêves ou tout ce qui dans la vie éveillée s'apparente au domaine des rêves, le cinéma n'existe pas" (Artaud qtd. in Brütsch 35).
14 "Der Traumzustand wurde so zu einem Modell, das die Realitätswahrnehmung bereichern, ja verändern sollte" (Brütsch 32).
15 Providing preliminary empirical evidence for the night dream's tendency toward synesthesia, Daniel Reznik et al. speak of "oneiric synesthesia" as a result of a "hyperassociative cognitive state following sleep" and suggest that "typically unidirectional neural pathways are omnidirectionally connected during sleep" (379).
16 Of particular importance is cinema's ability to induce states of hypnagogia and hypnosis. In Petrić's view, "the hypnagogic state of mind may be best induced by the illusion of physical penetration through space during film viewing; the hypnotic state of mind may be successfully achieved by an intensive perceptual concentration of the eyes upon objects which, as abstract graphic signs, change and move perpetually over a flat surface of the screen" (Petrić, "Film and Dreams" 13).
17 REM stands for "rapid eye movement" and describes sleep phases in which the muscles are paralyzed and dreams are more vivid and bizarre compared to NREM ("non-rapid eye movement") phases, whose dreams are more contemplative and are not accompanied by sleep paralysis.
18 "Die Bewegungslosigkeit der Zuschauer ist gewissermaßen die Bühne, auf der sich innere Mitbewegung mit dem körperlichen Geschehen auf der Leinwand entfaltet" (Schönhammer, "Traum und Film" 76).
19 For a paper that explores the phenomenology of cinema's capacity to induce actual states of daydreaming, see Hanich's "When Viewers Drift Off: A Brief Phenomenology of Cinematic Daydreaming" from 2019.

20 Martha Nochimson, on the contrary, suggests the fact that "we do have access to what Lynch thinks [. . .] must make all the difference" in terms of a scholar's methodological approach (31). This type of author-centered approach to film studies is questionable, since it is not the *director's* worldview that should determine the legitimacy of an approach but the potential of the approach to illuminate the work of art.
21 Drawing on Umberto Eco, Sobchak speaks of cinema's employment of "'lived modes' of perceptual and sensory experience (seeing, movement, and hearing the most dominant) as 'sign-vehicles' of representation" (*Carnal Thoughts* 74).
22 Francis Sparshott, just to give another example, argues that in a film, like in a dream, we "observe from a viewpoint at which we are not situated," such that we are "spectators participating without contact" (115–16).
23 Rotten Tomatoes user HorrorQueen S, for example, reviews *Inland Empire* (2006) like this: "Watching this is an experience. A very long movie that requires your full attention and an open mind. I needed to sit down and really think about how all of the scenes are connected to one another, but even before fully understanding I found it very enjoyable to watch. It is a weird, trippy ride for your senses and you'll come out of it feeling as though you watched something you will never encounter again. I also loved the subtle creepy vibe throughout. This was definitely a phenomenal film."
24 "[W]arum diese Filme den Zuschauer an Traumerfahrungen erinnern" (Lahde 95).
25 "[D]er implizite Leser [besitzt] keine reale Existenz; denn er verkörpert die Gesamtheit der Vororientierungen, die ein fiktionaler Text seinen möglichen Lesern als Rezeptionsbedingungen anbietet. Folglich ist der implizite Leser nicht in einem empirischen Substrat verankert, sondern in der Struktur der Texte selbst fundiert" (Iser 60).
26 "Rezeptionsvorgabe" (Schutte 181).
27 Eagleton's conclusion as to the status of meaning in the phenomenological approach to literature—"the meaning of a literary work is fixed once and for all: it is identical with whatever 'mental object' the author had in mind, or 'intended,' at the time of writing" (67)—seems hardly accurate in this light.
28 "[F]ormale Experimentierfreude" (Brütsch 235).
29 Whenever I speak of the *night dream* in this book, I am referring to the (hyphenated) *dream-experience* of an actual person, not the artistically crafted dream experienced by a fictional character.
30 For a phenomenological study of the night dream, see Murat Ates's 2023 book *Phänomenologie des Traums*.
31 A good place to start when it comes to this relationship would be Richard Askay's and Jensen Farquhar's 2006 monograph *Apprehending the Inaccessible: Freudian Psychoanalysis and Existential Phenomenology*.
32 "[B]i-valente Erfahrungsstruktur" (Brudzinska 59).
33 "Relation der Gleichrangigkeit und konstitutiven Gleichgewichtigkeit" (Brudzinska 59).
34 "[I]mpressional-apperzeptive [Wirkungsordnung]" (Brudzinska 59).
35 "Konstitution der Gegenstandsidentitäten [. . .] Kontrolle des Erfahrbaren" (Brudzinska 65).
36 "Einheitlichkeit und relative [. . .] Eindeutigkeit" (Brudzinska 65).
37 "[F]reie Verwandlungen" (Brudzinska 65).

38 "Verwandlungsordnung" (Brudzinska 65).
39 Siegfried Kracauer elaborates that "if they [films] are true to the medium, they will certainly not move from a preconceived idea down to the material world in order to implement that idea; conversely, they set out to explore physical data and, taking their cue from them, work their way up to some problem or belief. The cinema is materialistically minded; it proceeds from 'below' to 'above'" (Kracauer 309). The traditional arts, on the other hand, show a "top-down" movement; "they start with an idea to be projected into shapeless matter and not with the objects that constitute the physical world," which is why they amount to "an idealistic conception of the world," unlike cinema's "materialistic interpretation of the universe" (Kracauer 309). What we may note in this passage is Kracauer's departure from film reception rather than production. That is, a good deal of work in the pre-production process does consist in translating an abstract idea into material images. Watching a movie, however, the viewer derives (these) ideas from the material images—in a process that might also be called "inductive" in nature.
40 "[O]*riginäre Befähigung zum Loslassen des leibhaftigen Selbst der Empfindung und zum Erscheinen-Lassen eines Anderen*" (Brudzinska 60). One may also consider Ferdinand Fellmann's definition of *medium* in this context: "Ein Medium ist ein in sich geschlossenes syntaktisches System, das durch seine Strukturierung etwas *anderes* darstellt, als es selbst ist" (Fellmann 160; my italicization).
41 "[M]edialer Charakter [. . .] des Phantasmatischen" (Brudzinska 60); "[Das Phantasmatische hat] primär die Funktion, für etwas anderes zu gelten" (Husserl qtd. in Brudzinska 60).
42 The terms *noema* and *noesis* go back to Husserl and can be defined as the "*what* is experienced as experienced" (in the case of the former) and the "*mode* of its being experienced" (in the latter case; Ferencz-Flatz and Hanich 22).
43 "*Die Traumdeutung* [. . .] *ist die Via regia zur Kenntnis des Unbewußten im Seelenleben*" (Freud, *Traumdeutung* 595).
44 Cf. Medard Boss who writes: "Darum lässt sich auch das traumtheoretische Unterfangen durch nichts rechtfertigen, das die Dinge des Traumes zuerst zu blossen Abbildungen von 'realen' Gegenständen abwertet, nur um sie gleich darauf wieder mit um so mannigfaltigeren psychisch-symbolischen Projektionen aus des Traumsubjektes eigenem Unbewussten auszustatten. Wir müssen vielmehr die *Traumdinge ebenfalls als Dinge eigenen und vollen Dinggehaltes, die sie sind, und wie sie als unmittelbare Traumgegebenheiten erfahren werden, bestehen lassen*" (Boss 115; my italicization).
45 "Das bahnbrechend neue bei Freud war seine Erkenntnis [. . .], dass Versprecher Sinn ergeben, dass Träume, Delirien, Wahnvorstellungen und Halluzinationen Sinn ergeben [. . .] Die Gültigkeit dieser Entscheidung ist unabhängig von der Art des Sinns, den er entdeckt zu haben glaubte oder der Richtigkeit der Methoden, die er anwandte, um ihn zu ermitteln" (Castoriadis qtd. in Ates 81).
46 Cf. Ates: "Jede postfreudsche Trauminvestigation—dies gilt nicht nur für die Phänomenologie, sondern auch für die (an den Neurowissenschaften orientierte) empirisch-experimentelle Forschung in den Schlaflaboren—ist gewissermaßen eine Nutznießerin der Freudschen Vorarbeit. Denn sie alle befinden sich durch die von der Psychoanalyse ermöglichte Rehabilitierung des Traumphänomens, dass nämlich der Traum der Ausgrenzung entrissen und überhaupt wieder 'Gegenstand' theoretischer Untersuchungen werden konnte, in einer bereits begünstigten Ausgangssituation" (Ates 82).

47 For example, Lynch said that "*Sunset Boulevard* just has the greatest mood; you're immersed in it like a dream" (Marshall).
48 Cf. imdb.com/name/nm0000186/?ref_=ttfc_fc_wr1
49 A discursively constructed (in the Foucauldian sense) rather than essentialist conception of the dream(-like) is reflected in the systematic approach of this study: first of all, my point of orientation for the discussion of the oneiric is the dream marker. That is, what is dreamlike is, first and foremost, determined by the film. The film *suggests* the oneiricity of an experience by marking it as a dream such that nobody needs to "diagnose" the oneiricity from outside. Further, the films lead viewers to *describe* them as dreams or dreamlike experiences over and over again. In analogy to humor studies, where the analyst's job is to judge the humorousness (i.e., the potential to be perceived as funny; a binary category) of an utterance rather than its funniness (i.e., whether an utterance *is* funny; a gradual category), what I would like to elaborate on is the films' *potential* to create a dreamlike effect on their viewers rather than the question of whether or not they *are* dreamlike. What are the conditions responsible for this potential? The shift to the *potential* of creating oneiricity also reduces my subjective bias because I no longer have to agree on whether a scene is dreamlike in order to analyze it.
50 To be sure, even here, we talk about "the dream" *as it is reflected* in (phenomenological, psychological, and cinema) studies. We rely on the way it is "conceived of" (and thus "constructed" to some extent) in studies on it. We do not talk about *the* or *a* dream as it occurs, the "dream itself," first, because we have no direct means of access to it and, second, because any scientific discourse constructs its object of investigation to some extent (whether it is through the way a phenomenon is operationalized in experimental psychology or through the choice of a narratological as opposed to psychoanalytic approach to "the voice in narrative cinema," just to give two examples).

Chapter 3

1 This work is also known as *Six Figures Getting Sick* or as *Six Men Getting Sick (Six Times)*.
2 The film is missing in Rodley's filmography, for example (295–306).
3 As previous chapters have shown, critics as well as wider audiences frequently attribute dreamlike qualities to Lynch's cinema in general, which is most prominently exemplified by the *Oxford English Dictionary*'s recent definition of the term "Lynchian" as referring to a "dreamlike quality of mystery or menace" ("Lynchian").
4 Lynch uses Penderecki's music again in "Part 8: Gotta Light?" of *Twin Peaks* (2017; cf. section "The Convenience Store" in Chapter 5).
5 Further contrasts evoked are the unnatural appearance of the characters in a natural environment; the expected threat of sexual assault versus the relative harmlessness (albeit strangeness) of his actual behavior; the "over-the-top" expressivity of the music versus the sobriety of a corn field's appearance.
6 As clarified in Part I, first-person descriptions are not thought of as referring to my (exclusively) individual experience but are chosen when a scene provokes subjective

involvement to the extent of constituting a structural aspect of the film's aesthetics. The first person (plural or singular), however, does not intend to represent *all* viewing experiences but refers to a *possible* response prestructured by the film—one that will ideally resonate with some readers and viewers.

7   Schönhammer gives as an example the overwhelming blend of visual and auditory stimuli of a city, which makes it impossible to focus on a single one of them, hence the "fuzziness" of our attention (*Wahrnehmung* 293).

8   Hobson assumes that "[t]he absence of three wake-state modulators and the persistence of dopamine release" are at the basis of the dreamer's lack of self-reflective awareness (810).

9   Cf. Arthur Schopenhauer, claiming that "im Traum [behauptet] das Gesetz der Kausalität sein Recht [. . .], nur daß ihm oft ein unmöglicher Stoff untergeschoben wird" (81).

10 As mentioned before, I use female and male possessive and personal pronouns "generically" throughout this book, that is, both pronouns include the respective other biological sex as well as any other gender categories not represented by this binary distinction.

11 In this regard, *Absurd Encounter* may be seen as anticipating the negotiation of ethical dimensions of the gaze that *Blue Velvet* (1986) and *Inland Empire* (2006) deal with in great depth.

12 To be precise, I should add that the viewer's initial discomfort is achieved through the blue man approaching the camera/viewer (00:00:08–00:00:35), which may be seen as implying our bodily presence in the scenario. As he passes by us (00:00:36–00:00:38), the viewer's presence is denied, or at least ignored, only to be suddenly reaffirmed in the end (00:01:47–00:01:49). Playing with the viewer's vague suspicion, first denying it only to then verify it for the sake of shock, is a structure frequently exploited by horror films. On a different note, it should be mentioned that, unlike in the following chapters, time codes refer to a version of *Absurd Encounter* uploaded on YouTube, as the film has not been released on any DVD or Blu-ray. Unless indicated otherwise, time codes refer to the film that is under discussion in the respective chapter.

13 "Filme, die als Endmarkierung einen Blick in die Kamera einsetzen, heben die innerdiegetische Grenze zwischen Traum und Realität somit dadurch hervor, dass sie eine andere Grenze—diejenige zwischen Fiktion und Wirklichkeit, zwischen Diegese und Zuschauerraum—kurzzeitig berühren oder gar überschreiten" (Brütsch 136).

14 Evan Thompson describes the difference between the two perspectives while dreaming like this: "Fleeing while being chased is a common dream theme. When you feel your pursuer at your back and see him coming as you look over your shoulder, you're experiencing what's happening from the first-person perspective. When you're watching the chase from above and you see yourself running away, you're experiencing the chase from the third-person perspective. These perspectives can also shift back and forth as you dream" (E. Thompson 129).

15 Arguably, there are two more images in the film that occupy this unclear ontological status, both highly symbolic: (1) the girl recognizing herself in the mirror (00:03:44–00:03:45) and (2) the film's final moment showing the girl vomiting blood (00:04:28–00:04:37).

16 The style of this surface is similar to that of Lynch's painting from the same year, *Man Throwing Up* (1968).

17 Slavoj Žižek explains that "the *objet petit a* is not what we desire, what we are after, but, rather, that which sets our desire in motion, in the sense of the formal frame which confers consistency on our desire: desire is, of course, metonymical; it shifts from one object to another, through all these displacements, however, desire nonetheless retains a minimum of formal consistency, a set of phantasmic features which, when they are encountered in a positive object, make us desire this object—*objet petit a* as the cause of desire is nothing other than this formal frame of consistency" (Žižek, *The Plague* 39).

18 "Sprengung der 'Haut der Dinge' . . . um zu zeigen, wie Dinge zu Dingen und Welt zu Welt wird" (Zechner 74).

19 "Automatismus der Wahrnehmung" (Šklovskij 15).

20 "[D]ie beim Zuschauer ausgelöste Irritation findet eine Entsprechung in der vorübergehenden Verwirrung des Träumers, der sich in der Wachwelt erst wieder zurechtfinden muss" (Brütsch 136).

21 Concerning the sound effects of *The Alphabet*, David Hughes observes that "[a]ccording to legend, Lynch tried to record the effects himself, using a rented Uher tape recorder; the machine was broken, however, resulting in a certain distortion of sound that Lynch, true to form, loved" (9).

22 "[V]erlorene Echos des Urknalls, der das Universum selber hervorbrachte" (Žižek qtd. in Heiland 154).

23 "[D]as unidentifizierbare Klangobjekt, ein Geräusch oder Sound, ohne Bezug, oder Ort" (Heiland 149).

24 "Sehen ohne unmittelbares Erkennen" (Zechner 76). She uses this formulation in her discussion of Merleau-Ponty's writings on the paintings of Paul Cézanne.

25 *Blue Velvet* (1986), *Twin Peaks* (1990–1), and *Mulholland Drive* (2001) explore the theme of horror lurking beneath a serene surface.

26 Brütsch speaks of "sequenzimmanente Markierungsformen" (152). Rather than clearly marking them as dreams, the frequent references to sleeping throughout the scenes playing out between the boy and the Grandmother allude to the possibility of interpreting the Grandmother as the boy's dream character.

27 Lynch considers this final scene "a kind of failure" (Rodley 47), not because it too easily hints at the Grandmother's existence in the boy's dream but for aesthetic reasons—"I should have made another [pod] and then put it on his head" (Rodley 47). His wish to put it on his *head* suggests the boy's mind as the originator of the pod.

28 Three further elements supporting the interpretation of Grandmother existing in a dream shall not go unnoticed: (1) the seeds have already been placed in the room and are stored in a large labeled bag. It appears that the dream, as an "automatized function of the human mind," is only waiting to *offer* the fulfillment of the boy's wish. (2) The upstairs room's edges are painted with white chalk. A possible reference to Francis Bacon's "cage," this may suggest the immateriality, hence the imaginary nature of the attic's space. (3) Much to the boy's shock, his parents chase after him when he is about to visit Grandmother one time. After he fantasizes about killing his parents, the boy arrives in the upstairs room without the parents tailing him. The implication could be that the upstairs "room" is really the boy's dream space and can only be visited by him alone. After all, the only person interacting with the Grandmother is the boy.

29 "Interne Fokalisierung" (Kuhn 123–4).

30 "Verwandlungsordnung"; "Teleologie der [. . .] Wunscherfüllung" (Brudszinska 65).

31 Beautifully, this is hinted at by the camera appearing to "emerge" from the back of his head right after we first see him in his room.
32 "Estremamente 'materico'" (Menarini 91).
33 Canonical neurons are activated when executing object-related actions and when observing the *object*. Mirror neurons are activated when executing and observing *actions* (Schönhammer, *Wahrnehmung* 144).
34 The scene can be found at youtube.com/watch?v=22Ju9XYdT8A.
35 According to Schönhammer, playful—that is, nonpurposeful—movement is quintessential for the emergence of dream and meditative states (*Wahrnehmung* 172).
36 "Kurt Lewin coined the term *Aufforderungscharakter*" based on the observation that "[t]he postbox 'invites' the mailing of a letter, the handle 'wants to be grasped,' and things 'tell us what to do with them'" (Gibson 138). James J. Gibson, in his *Ecological Approach to Visual Perception*, spoke of an object's *affordance* in this context: "The concept of affordance is derived from these concepts of valence, invitation and demand but with a crucial difference. The affordance of something does *not change* as the need of the observer changes" (Gibson 138–9).
37 As Daniele Dottorini observes, the body functions as both a concrete living organism and an abstract linguistic sign in the film (83). In this regard, it is interesting to observe how the *material body is abstracted* through the make-up and the boy's suit and the *animated bodies are concretized* through screams and other "textural" sounds such as the emission of foam in the opening.
38 The causal reciprocity of the concrete and the abstract is reinforced on the acoustic level through the copresence of synthetic and organic sounds.
39 "punti ciechi. Ecco allora che alla focalizzazione sugli interstizi spaziali si associa la presenza di intervalli temporali impercepiti" (Basso Fossali 48).

Chapter 4

1 Stanley Kubrick's *2001: A Space Odyssey* (1968) represents the absence of sound in outer space "realistically" in that sense.
2 Michel Chion uses the neologism "synchresis" for "the spontaneous and irresistible weld produced between a particular auditory phenomenon and visual phenomenon when they occur at the same time" (*Audio-Vision* 63).
3 Thomas Elsaesser's and Malte Hagener's way of putting it—sound asking "Where?," with the image answering "Here" (*Filmtheorie* 174)—manifests the classical cinema's hierarchy between image and sound, with the former dominating the latter.
4 This phenomenon is also important in *Eraserhead*, when Henry awakes in his bed but is still dreaming (00:53:08), as well as in *Twin Peaks: Fire Walk with Me* (1992).
5 Publishing his *Interpretation of Dreams* at the turn of the nineteenth to the twentieth century, Freud comments that the two formulations are used to an equal extent at that time (*Traumdeutung* 63).
6 "Spielleiter" (Kaul and Palmier 41).
7 "Mit äußerster Kraft versucht er erfolglos, die funkensprühende (Erzähl-)Maschine zu stoppen" (Kaul and Palmier 41).
8 To be exact, there is a continuity error: he stepped into the puddle with his right foot (00:07:54) but takes off his left shoe and sock (00:13:30–00:13:45).

9   For a critical documentary on the history and politics of Transcendental Meditation and Lynch's involvement in the organization, see David Sieveking's *David Wants to Fly* (2010).
10 What E. Thompson might be referring to in his interpretation is this passage from the Brhadānyaka Upanishad: "This is how he dreams. He takes materials from the entire world and, taking them apart on his own and then on his own putting them together, he dreams with his own radiance, with his own light. In that place this person becomes his own light. In that place there are no carriages, there are no tandems, and there are no roads; but he creates for himself carriages, tandems, and roads" (Olivelle 59).
11 Lynch quotes this version of the Upanishads in his 2006 book *Catching the Big Fish*.
12 In the same vein, Jousse writes: "*Eraserhead* takes its place in that class of film able to directly connect the subconscious mind of its maker with the subconscious mind of its viewers" (Jousse 15).
13 "Die Traumarbeit zwingt uns eine unbewußte psychische Tätigkeit anzunehmen, welche umfassender und bedeutsamer ist als die uns bekannte mit Bewußtsein verbundene" (Freud, *Anwendungen* 36).
14 "[L]atente Traumgedanken"; "manifeste[r] Trauminhalt" (Freud, *Traumdeutung* 284).
15 "Die *Nullokularisierung*, wenn das, was die VEI [visuelle Erzählinstanz] zeigt, an keine der Figuren gebunden ist, wie im sogenannten *nobody's shot*" (Kuhn 128).
16 "[. . .] was eine Figur weiß *und* wahrnimmt" (Kuhn 140).
17 "[Q]uasi-gegenwärtiges phantasmatisches *Re-Präsentationsbewusstsein*" (Brudzinska 63).
18 "Unsere psychische Topik [. . .] bezieht sich auf Regionen des seelischen Apparats, wo immer sie im Körper gelegen sein mögen" (Freud, *Psychologie des Unbewußten* 133).
19 "Der Kern des *Ubw* besteht aus Triebrepräsentanzen, die ihre Besetzung abführen wollen, also aus Wunschregungen" (Freud, *Psychologie des Unbewußten* 145).
20 In this light, it is interesting that the dreams in *Eraserhead* contain almost no dialogue.
21 A second aspect that should not go unnoticed is that decapitation, in Freudian psychoanalysis, symbolizes a man's fear of castration (*Traumdeutung* 358). "He loses his head" would mean that he "fails" at sex with his neighbor. Through censorship, the dream translates this unconscious fear into a digestible form. McGowan's interpretation, for example, builds upon Lacan's conception of castration understood not as "a literal event but [as] the metaphorical process that produces the desiring subject" (*Impossible* 40).
22 Arguably, a film that dramatizes Freud's dream conception quite accurately is Georg Wilhelm Pabst's *Geheimnisse einer Seele* (1926). Here, repressed memories from the protagonist's childhood are triggered by recent experience—the combination of an unconscious and a preconscious wish produces the dream.
23 Martin Heidegger writes: "Freud postuliert für die bewußten menschlichen Phänomene die Lückenlosigkeit in der Erklärbarkeit, d.h. die Kontinuität von Kausalzusammenhängen. Weil es solche 'im Bewusstsein' nicht gibt, muß er 'das Unbewußte' erfinden, in dem es die Lückenlosigkeit von Kausalzusammenhängen geben muß. Das Postulat ist die durchgängige Erklärbarkeit des Seelischen [. . .] Dieses Postulat ist nicht aus den seelischen Erscheinungen selbst genommen, sondern ist das Postulat der neuzeitlichen Naturwissenschaft" (Heidegger 260).

24 The unconscious is used as an explanatory element in season one of *The Sinner* (2017), for example. Here the gradual uncovering of the protagonist's initially repressed "unconscious" experience is the crucial compositional principle in the narrative structure. As the story progresses, her actions become more and more logical in light of her traumatic, repressed experience in the past.

25 "[E]in [...] stimmige[r] Ausdruck der Lebenssituation des Träumenden" (Gehring 200).

26 "Erleben eines latenten Inhalts durch einen manifesten Inhalt hindurch" (Merleau-Ponty, *Vorlesungen* 80).

27 "Die wahrgenommenen Phänomene müssen in unserer Auffassung gegen die nur angenommenen Strebungen zurücktreten" (Freud, "Fehlleistungen" 62).

28 Lynch frequently compares films to dreams when they are particularly immersive to him. He said, for example: "I think I might have screened *Sunset Boulevard* by Billy Wilder early on for the crew before we started shooting *Eraserhead*. *Sunset Boulevard* just has the greatest mood; you're immersed in it like a dream," adding that "[t]he Hollywood he describes in the film probably never existed, but he makes us believe it did, and he immerses us in it, like a dream" (Marshall).

29 "Zwei Ordnungen der Erfahrung [,] [...] die *impressional-apperzeptive* und die *phantasmatisch-imaginäre*" (Brudzinska 58–9).

30 The aspect of the head/brain as the producer of the dream imagery is reminiscent of *The Grandmother*, where the dream is self-reflexively marked by the painting of a brain-like structure, that is, the organ responsible for dreaming (cf. section "The Dream between Metaphoricity and Literalness" in Chapter 3).

31 Given that the intentional state of a "death wish" does not exist—there is no such state as "*being* dead," "I" cannot think "myself" as "non-existent"—it is questionable whether this expression makes sense. That is, if "wish" implies the presence of a wish's subject in regard to the *time* of its (potential) fulfillment, it is a contradictory expression. If it is equivalent to "x has a wish to kill himself" or "x is suicidal," it is not. *Eraserhead*'s decapitation sequence, rather than "containing Henry's death wish," creates a scenario in which *he* transforms into *world*, in which he is deprived of the possibility to act in the world. The dream, thus, depicts the dissolution of his world relationship.

32 Jousse, for example, writes that "ultimately *Eraserhead* is the story of a birth, a beginning and a metamorphosis" (15).

33 According to Lahde, the paradoxical relationship between Henry and his environment mirrors the dreamer's relationship to the dream environment: they both cause and are at the center of their respective world, yet they are "helplessly exposed to it" (Lahde 105; my translation).

34 For Sobchak, the reversible structure of cinema consists in the image's ambiguity of presenting both an act of seeing (a "viewing view as the experience of consciousness") and an array of seen objects forming a world (a "viewed view as the consciousness of experience"; *Address* 22).

35 "Das Unbewusste lässt sich begreifen [...] als dasjenige, was zwar den Rahmen impressional-apperzeptiver Gegebenheit sprengt, sich jedoch gleichzeitig unmittelbar als quasi-gegenwärtiges phantasmatisches *Re-Präsentationsbewusstsein* realisiert: in der Traumerfahrung, im Symptom, in der Fehlleistung [...] Das Unbewusste als Phantasmatisch-Imaginäres ist aber auch ständig mit dem Impressional-Apperzeptiven verzahnt, und zwar als durchaus polyphone *Intervention* in die Wahrnehmung, als phantasmatische *Einschreibung* bei protentionalen Weckungen" (Brudzinska 63–4).

36 "[E]rfahrungstheoretischer Sinn" (Brudzinska 55).
37 "Manifestation einer *anderen Anwesenheit*" (Brudzinska 63).
38 "Anti-Phänomen" (Brudszinska 63).
39 "Absenz, Lücke oder Bruch des bewusstseinsmäßigen Verlaufs"; "Entgleisung oder Mangel der Erfahrung" (Brudzinska 62).
40 "Rahmen impressional-apperzeptiver Gegebenheit" (Brudzinska 63).
41 "*[O]riginäre Befähigung zum Loslassen des leibhaftigen Selbst der Empfindung und zum Erscheinen-Lassen eines Anderen*" (Brudzinska 60).
42 "[M]ediale[r] Charakter des Phantasmatisch-Imaginären" (Brudzinska 60).
43 "[Das Phantasmatische hat] primär die Funktion, für etwas anderes zu gelten" (Husserl qtd. in Brudzinska 60).
44 In Chion's terminology, the music in this case provides an example for "acousmatic sound" that is never "de-acousmatized," that is, sound whose source is not revealed in the course of the scene (*Audio-Vision* 72). In Lynch and Frost's terminology, the "music [is] *in* the air," as The Man from Another Place (Michael J. Anderson) puts it in Cooper's dream in *Twin Peaks* ("Episode 2: Zen, or the Skill to Catch a Killer" 00:40:40–00:44:40). Further similarities between the theater stage in *Eraserhead* and the "Red Room" in *Twin Peaks* are constituted by the geometrical black-and-white floor design, the curtains, and the "magical" (dis-)appearance of characters.
45 The development of the Dolby technology in the mid-1970s was invaluable for this effect. Spatial orientation in the movie theater dispersed (Elsaesser and Hagener, *Filmtheorie* 178) such that the film's prior "localization on the screen" was undermined. With the arrival of Dolby, film became an increasingly spatial experience. *Eraserhead* builds on this: Lynch's "room tone" not only does not have a source in the diegesis, but it is also in itself an "impossible" artifact. Through the way in which it was designed, it is a purely technological product with no equivalent in natural perception. What we hear exposes its character of being fabricated. It cannot be produced by any natural environment. In this, it may be compared to a multiply exposed image in how several input sources are overlayed (in production) and appear as simultaneously present (in reception); *Eraserhead* neither ascribes the sound to the image or the visually represented world as its originator nor is the sound completely "outside of" that world.
46 "[P]olyphone *Intervention*" (Brudzinska 64).
47 Compared to the previous Upanishad-inspired reading, Brudzinska's understanding of the unconscious gives an alternative reason for why the dream *world* is generally accessible in the waking world. Since the dream is understood as the prototypical manifestation of the phantasmatic-imaginary, and the latter constitutes a "polyphonic intervention into perception" (Brudzinska 64), it is always potentially present. The theater stage, in that sense, manifests the unconscious as *another* presence. The transitions reveal a fundamental point of conflict between the two approaches: according to Brudzinska's approach, when Henry starts (day-)dreaming, a second order of experience emerges, as if he *diverted* from an original path of direct apperception; in an Upanishad-inspired interpretation, Henry gets to his dream world through the *narrowing* of awareness; it is not another, second form of consciousness but a more subtle spectrum of that same one "wave" of consciousness (which is always there) becoming visible.

48 It should be noted that Husserl's own view on dreaming is very different from Brudzinska's. He considers dreaming a form of perception, not as a phantasmatic experience (Ates 76–7).

49 "[D]ie tatsächliche Handlung *in* dieser Szene [ist] dem absurden Bild *von* dieser Szene unterzuordnen" (Schmidt 45).

50 "[I]hre Orte und ihre Zeiten [entstehen] sozusagen nur aus reiner filmischer Sprache" (Seesslen 32).

51 "[W]ahrhafte[r] Ort"; "wahrhafte Zeit"; "Lesbarkeit" (Seesslen 32).

52 Lynch uses dialogue for the first time in *Eraserhead*. In his own words, "you could see dialogue as kind of a sound effect or a musical effect" (Rodley 72). For Merleau-Ponty, "language is comparable to music in the way that it remains tied to its material embodiment; each language is a distinct and ultimately untranslatable manner of 'singing the world,' of extracting and expressing the 'emotional essence' of our surroundings and relationships" (Toadvine; cf. Merleau-Ponty, *Perception* 193). Lynch and Merleau-Ponty, each in their own way, rebel against language concealing its inherent expressiveness due to its capacity for signification.

53 Recalling Kant's concept of *aesthetic ideas*, Sinnerbrink calls "cinematic thinking" a "non-conceptual or affective thinking in images that resists cognitive closure or theoretical subsumption" (139).

54 Using an expression by Merleau-Ponty, Sobchak calls film "an expression of experience by experience" (*Address* 36). Inclined to describe the dream in the same way, one should consider that dreams are spontaneous, unplanned, and exclusive to the dreamer in their immediate experiential form, whereas films are carefully constructed, planned, and intersubjectively accessible.

Chapter 5

1 In line with the naming in the 2016 Blu-ray version of seasons one and two, and the 2017 Blu-ray version of season three, "*Episode* x" refers to episodes of the first two seasons of *Twin Peaks* (1990–1) while "*Part* x" refers to episodes of the third season of *Twin Peaks* (2017) in this book. The pilot, further, was not included in the numbering of episodes such that "Episode 2" is actually the third episode of season one, "Episode 3" is the fourth episode, and so on.

2 The sequence was originally made for the alternate ending of the European version of the pilot (in case the series did not get picked up by any European network). Here, it is not marked as Cooper's dream but introduced as happening "25 years later" ("Alternate international pilot" 01:46:43–01:52:44).

3 Just as an example for the impact of the dream sequence on popular culture, one may think of *The Simpsons*' tribute in "Who Shot Mr. Burns? (Part 2)" (00:13:12–00:13:50), where Chief Wiggum (Hank Azaria) and Lisa Simpson (Yeardley Smith) replace Agent Cooper and Laura Palmer.

4 This may be related to the fact that American English does not allow [ɪ] to precede a second vowel in diphthongs (British English does, e.g., in "beer" [bɪə(r)]). Also, we tend not to be aware of the centralized allophonic variant of /i/, particularly because the distinction between [i] and [ɪ] is not represented in writing.

5 In Husserl's *Phenomenology of Inner Time-Consciousness*, Erleben is distinguished from Erlebnis. The former involves "living through" an experience in a pre-reflective sense, whereas the latter makes the experience an *object of* consciousness (Zahavi 330).
6 "Ästhetische Eigenzeiten werden als exponierte und wahrnehmbare Formen komplexer Zeitgestaltung, -modellierung und -reflexion verstanden"; "[Sie] formieren Vergangenheit, Gegenwart und Zukunft anders, als sie in der linearen Zeit erscheinen" (Gamper and Hühn 23–4).
7 "'Zeit' tritt ästhetisch in nicht-semantischen Qualitäten hervor, wenn sie Präsenz-Effekte im Unterschied zu Sinn-Effekten erzeugt, etwa als Rhythmus, Takt, Stimmung, Tempo, Dauer, Reim, Atem, Körper-Performanz und bewegtes Bild" (Gamper and Hühn 17).
8 The character has two names because, in the series' mythology, the evil spirit Mike possesses its human "host" Phillip Gerard.
9 In Lynch's words, in the Red Room, "there's no problem with time. And anything can happen. It's a free zone, completely unpredictable and therefore pretty exciting but also scary" (Rodley 19).
10 The emergence of the theater stage in *Eraserhead* could also be seen as related to the sensation of warmth, since it appears inside Henry's radiator.
11 Further similarities concerning the set design of the Red Room in *Twin Peaks* and the theater stage inside the radiator in *Eraserhead* are obvious: the geometrically black-and-white-shaped floor and the curtains. Another link in the production of the two dream sequences is that Lynch first experimented with the technique of phonetic reversal when preparing a scene for *Eraserhead*'s pencil factory. The scene was never shot, though (Rodley 165–7).
12 Building on Gamper and Hühn's terminology, you might speak of "Eigen(t)raumzeitlichkeit" in German.
13 Concerning the "literary form of the fragment" in German Romanticism, Petra Gehring writes: "Bezüge zum Traum liegen auf der Hand, sofern das Fragment—kurz, unverbunden, auf wenige Bilder beschränkt und wie ein Splitter auf eine allenfalls aufblitzende mögliche Welt-in-sich zurückverweisend—in formaler Hinsicht eine ganze Anzahl traumähnlicher Merkmale zeigt" (*Traum und Wirklichkeit* 115).
14 This interpretation is discussed in the context of other readings of the film in Chapter 7.
15 For example, Reddit user inkswamp writes this: "My theory is that some (if not all) of the Roadhouse scenes are actually dreams, where we're following a number of dreamers who are living inside their dreams. Like many dreams, these don't seem connected to the reality that we know and seem to be populated by people we've never heard of, transient figures who seem very important during the dream but are absolutely irrelevant outside of it."
16 In an act of protest, Audrey "chained herself to the Twin Peaks savings and loan vault" in Episode 29 (00:23:51). After an explosion of a bomb in said place, the episode leaves open what happened to Audrey.
17 Deleuze argues that in the time-image—and in the *implied dream* in particular (he gets this notion from Michel Deviller)—"it is no longer the character who reacts to the optical-sound situation, it is a movement of world which supplements the faltering movement of the character" (59).
18 Michael J. Anderson, who played the Arm in the first two seasons and in the *Twin Peaks* film, declined to appear in season three.

19 The writings of occultist Kenneth Grant and his idea of a "Mauve Zone" possibly inspired Lynch's and Frost's (he uses other concepts of Grant in *The Secret History of Twin Peaks*) conception of the place: "The place of transition between the conceptual and reified universe on the one hand and the void reality of the noumenal universe on the other hand, Grant designates as the Mauve Zone and relates it to the symbolism of the swamp [. . .] In order to reach the true reality, one needs to enter knowingly into the state of deep sleep which functions as the principal gateway to this state" (Djurdjevic 99).

20 In this regard, this sequence anticipates the negotiation of the reality status of camera footage in Lynch's succeeding film *Lost Highway* (1997; see section "Mediality and/as Dissociation" in Chapter 6).

21 In philosophical terms, this could be understood as a reflection of George Berkeley's principle *esse est percipi* ("to be is to be perceived").

22 "Es handelt sich [. . .] um den Versuch, ein mehrfaches Sehen im gleichen Bild zu ermöglichen" (Seesslen 136).

23 A multiperspectival approach to the image can be found in Bacon's paintings, too. In Lynch's filmography, this approach anticipates one of the central themes of the identity trilogy (*Lost Highway*, *Mulholland Drive*, and *Inland Empire*), where the question for the characters' identity is inextricably linked to an exploration of the ontological status of the film image (video in *Lost Highway*, digital video in *Inland Empire*) and of performance (*Mulholland Drive*).

24 It is the same noise we hear in "Part 1: My Log Has a Message for You," where the Fireman tells Cooper to "listen to the sounds" (00:04:05–00:04:38).

25 Already in Part 2, the scene was repeated (00:15:25–00:15:50 *and* 00:22:25–00:22:50).

26 In Part 1, the Fireman told Cooper to "remember 430"—indicating the number of miles on the odometer as Cooper and Diane cross dimensions—as well as to remember "Richard and Linda" (00:05:10–00:05:26).

27 In this regard, the ending comes full circle with the very beginning of season three where the Fireman told Cooper that "it is in our house now" ("Part 1" 00:04:42–00:04:48).

28 This interpretation recalls the Log Lady's introduction to Episode 14: "A poem as lovely as a tree. . . . As the night wind blows, the boughs move to and fro; the rustling, the magic rustling that brings on the dark dream. *The dream of suffering and pain*; pain for the victim, pain for the inflictor of pain—*a circle of pain, a circle of suffering*. . . . Woe to ones who behold the pale horse" (my italicization; 00:00:10–00:00:47).

29 Anastasia Kozyreva speaks of an "affective past" (as distinguished from a "remembered past") "which is present as an affective horizon and as a sphere of sedimentation and forgetfulness [. . .] [T]he past has no other reality which could be attributed to it besides affective reality, relative to one's impressional present" (215).

30 Chion's notion of the *screaming point* seems fitting in that regard: "Usually where a filmmaker constructs a good story full of complications in order to draw things out to a screaming point, he makes sure to show how the screaming point can escape the very person orchestrating it in the story [. . .] [I]t is clear that the man is but the organizer of the spectacle, the producer of this extravaganza, but that the screaming point ultimately is beyond him, just as it is beyond the woman who issues it as the medium [. . .] The screaming point is where speech is suddenly extinct, a black hole, the exit of being" (Chion, *Voice* 79).

31 After directing "Episode 14: Lonely Souls," Lynch went off to shoot his film *Wild at Heart* (1990), only coming back to the set of *Twin Peaks* toward the end of the second season. He returns as Gordon Cole in Episode 25 and directed the second season's finale, Episode 29.
32 The popularity of the first season was enormous. Allegedly, Soviet leader Gorbachev called President Bush enquiring about who killed Laura Palmer (Quinn).
33 Right from the start, *Twin Peaks* (1990–1) placed itself within the tradition of the mystery genre, as the Log Lady's introduction to the pilot shows: "Welcome to Twin Peaks. My name is Margaret Lanterman. I live in Twin Peaks. I am known as the Log Lady. There is a story behind that. There are many stories in Twin Peaks. Some of them are sad, some funny. Some of them are stories of madness, of violence. Some are ordinary. Yet they all have about them *a sense of mystery*—the mystery of life" (my italicization; "Pilot" 00:00:10–00:00:45). Menarini, for example, sees *mystery* as one of the most important "concepts" of Lynch's films (15).
34 In *Catching the Big Fish*, Lynch gives a different source for his Upanishad quote— Shearer's and Russell's 1978 translation *The Upanishads*—which does not contain the passage he quotes, though.
35 For a study that explores the spatial basis of conceptualizations of *time*, see Lera Boroditsky's "Metaphoric Structuring: Understanding Time through Spatial Metaphors" (2000).
36 The idea of *seeing oneself* in a dream was already discernible in *The Alphabet* (1968; cf. section "Materiality and Symbolism" in Chapter 3) and, for example, in one of Lynch's lithographs from 2011 entitled, *It was at night when the hands reached out and gathered the clouds from the eyes and I saw myself*.
37 The original passage in Fichte's *Bestimmung des Menschen* reads: "Es ist kein Seyn.—Ich selbst weiss überhaupt nicht, und bin nicht. Bilder sind: sie sind das Einzige, was da ist, und sie wissen von sich, nach Weise der Bilder:—Bilder, die vorüberschweben, ohne daß etwas sey, dem sie vorüberschweben; die durch Bilder von den Bildern zusammenhängen, Bilder, ohne etwas in ihnen Abgebildetes, ohne Bedeutung und Zweck. Ich selbst bin eins dieser Bilder; ja ich bin selbst dies nicht, sondern nur ein verworrenes Bild von den Bildern.—Alle Realität verwandelt sich in einen wunderbaren *Traum, ohne ein Leben, von welchem geträumt wird, und ohne einen Geist, dem da träumt*; in einen Traum, der in einem Traume von sich selbst zusammenhängt. Das Anschauenist der Traum; das Denken,—die Quelle alles Seyns und aller Realität, die ich mir einbilde, meines Seins, meiner Kraft, meiner Zwecke,—ist der Traum von jenem Traume" (Fichte 65–66; my italicization).
38 "Nicht Dinge 'an sich,' sondern nur die konsistenten Strukturen unserer subjektiven Erkenntnisvermögen geben uns die Welt" (Gehring, *Traum und Wirklichkeit* 114).
39 "[W]ir [können] überhaupt nur in der Form von Bildern Wissen haben" (Gehring, *Traum und Wirklichkeit* 114).
40 The spider-dreamer passage in the *Eternal Stories from the Upanishads* continues like this: "Having created the creation, the Creator entered into it" (Egenes and Reddy 71).
41 In the context of *Lost Highway* (1997), to name an example, one may think of Žižek's rather far-fetched conclusion that "[t]he temporal loop that structures Lost Highway is [. . .] the very loop of the psychoanalytic treatment in which, after a long detour, we return to our starting point from another perspective" (*Ridiculous* 17). It remains unclear on what level Žižek's claim is to be understood. Is Fred "cured" through the self-encounter at the end of the film, similar to a patient who has undergone

therapy? To what end did Lynch make a film that symbolizes the structure of the psychoanalytic process?

42 According to actress and Lynch's longtime collaborator Laura Dern, after Lynch won an honorary Oscar in 2019, he said, "we're just lucky [. . .] I mean, they're not our ideas. We're just lucky if we catch them" (Sharf). Lynch has often expressed that he thinks of his artistic process as a mere channeling of ideas. In the words of Terrence Rafferty, "Lynch speaks of ideas as if they were things entirely outside him, [. . .] the way a devout Christian speaks of grace." Lynch's and Rafferty's remarks recall Terry Eagleton's comment on Frank Leavis's notion of art: "Art [. . .] is not to be seen as the expression of an individual subject: the subject is just the place or medium where the truth of the world speaks itself" (64). This dynamic, that is, the relative passivity of the artist, seems to inform the way Lynch refuses to identify his *Twin Peaks* character as the sole dreamer (in the sense of an originator) in Part 14. Inhabiting the dream world of *Twin Peaks* is conceived of as an experience shared between the viewer and its personified author.

Chapter 6

1 Cf. Haneke's *Caché* (2005), which uses the same premise to set up its story.
2 The production company CIBY-2000 promoted the film as "a psychogenic fugue." Lynch only became aware of the concept after the responsible publicist told him about it. Lynch said that "it sounds like such a beautiful thing—'psychogenic fugue.' It has music and it has a certain *force* and dreamlike quality. I think it's beautiful, even if it didn't mean anything" (Rodley 239). Lynch himself described the film like this: "A 21st Century Noir Horror Film. A graphic investigation into parallel identity crises. A world where time is dangerously out of control. A terrifying ride down the lost highway" (Hughes 224).
3 The memory aspect is considered central to the phenomenon, to the extent that, in the fifth edition of the *Diagnostic and Statistical Manual of Mental Disorders* (DSM-5), the fugue state is regarded as "a specifier of dissociative amnesia rather than a separate diagnosis" (APA, *DSM-5* 812).
4 "Alice personifiziert somit das Nachtseitige und sexuell Ausschweifende von Renee" (Kaul and Palmier 94).
5 Similarly, Minuz writes: "Alice rivela in fondo ciò che Renee aveva tenuto nascosto a Fred, raccontando la storia che la lega al losco giro di Andy e Mr Eddy" (Minuz 95).
6 Despite a pledge with Lynch not to do so, Gifford explains the film like this: "Fred Madison creates this counter world and goes into it, because the crime he has committed is so terrible that he can't face it. This fugue state allows him to create a fantasy world, but within this fantasy world, the same problems occur. In other words, he's no better at maintaining this relationship, dealing with or controlling this woman, than he was in his real life. The woman isn't who he thinks she is, really, so all the so-called facts of his known life with Renee pop up again in Alice Wakefield" (cf. Hughes 214–15).
7 "[D]as Gefühl sich selbst—keine andere, zweite Persönlichkeit—von außen zu beobachten" (D. Langer 88).

8   The DSM lists hallucinations and delusions, among others, as "defining features of schizophrenia" (APA, *DSM-5* 58).
9   The DSM suggests that "[d]issociative fugue is [. . .] common in dissociative identity disorder" (APA, *DSM-5* 291).
10 "Unfähigkeit [. . .], verschiedene Aspekte der Identität, des Gedächtnisses und des Bewußtseins zu integrieren" (Saß qtd. in D. Langer 88).
11 The DSM elaborates: "Dissociative disorders are characterized by a disruption of and/or discontinuity in the normal integration of consciousness, memory, identity, emotion, perception, body representation, motor control, and behavior. Dissociative symptoms can potentially disrupt every area of psychological functioning" (APA, *DSM-5* 291).
12 Concerning the difficulty to separate between schizophrenia and dissociative identity disorder (formerly called "multiple personality disorder"), it has been observed that "patients with DID endorsed 8 of the 11 [. . .] first-rank symptoms that had been considered indicative of schizophrenia," that is, "voices arguing, voices commenting on one's action, influences playing on the body, thought withdrawal, thought insertion, made impulses, made feelings, and made volitional acts" (Howell 150). Further, "presence of psychotic symptoms" is listed among the DSM's examples of "other specified dissociative disorder[s]" (APA, *DSM-5* 292). However, Elisabeth Howell observes that "[i]n DID, rather than as indications of schizophrenia, the hallucinated voices and the made actions are understood as due to the activities of a dissociative identity. The psychotic person is more likely to attach a delusional explanation, such as 'The CIA has implanted a chip in my brain.' [. . .] [T]he person with DID—as opposed to someone who is psychotic—often has the ability to be in two states of mind at once" (Howell 6). For Andrew Brook, schizophrenia is a "disorder in which unified consciousness appears to have shattered" (210), whereas in dissociative identity disorder, unified consciousness "appears to have split" without shattering (212). In his characterization of the so-called "coconscious variety of DID," however, "one will experience what the alter(s) say(s) and do (does) from the standpoint of observing the saying and doings (even though one recognizes them to be a part of oneself), not from the standpoint of doing them" (Brook 223–24), which again resembles D. Langer's description of schizophrenia.
13 Kaul and Palmier speak of the mysterious videotapes as the "Kernidee zu dem Film" (90).
14 "Ein filmischer Beitrag zur Medientheorie" (Michalsky 397).
15 "Gerade im Bezug auf den Traum gilt es, Erlebnis und Erzählung dieses Erlebnisses [. . .] auseinanderzuhalten" (Brütsch 393).
16 Warren Buckland observes that it is impossible to tell whether or when Fred stopped recounting the dream. On the one hand, we have "returned to Fred and Renee in bed, the place where Fred began narrating the dream," on the other, there is no continuity between the two embracing shots because Fred and Renée are now both asleep, with Fred about to wake up (Buckland 58).
17 Arguably, associating a face with identity does not involve symbolism. It is not a *convention* to represent identity by means of the face; it is anchored in human perception. We identify a person by their face. The face directly indicates the identity of a person without a "translation" into a convention-based sign.
18 "[D]ie Haut als symbolische Fläche zwischen Selbst und Welt" (Elsaesser and Hagener, *Filmtheorie* 140).

19. "Wie könnten wir sagen, der Film 'handele' von einem schizophrenen Mörder, wenn er sich doch so offensichtlich selbst von Schizophrenie infizieren läßt" (Seesslen 172).
20. "Lynch [beschränkt] sich keineswegs auf die Darstellung von Wahnsinnigen und ihres Verhältnisses zur (normalen) Umwelt [. . .] Die Regeln des Wahnsinns greifen vielmehr auch auf die formale Gestaltung der Filme über" (D. Langer 69). D. Langer compares Lynch's artistic approach to insanity to Gilles Deleuze's and Félix Guattari's philosophical approach to insanity in *Anti-Oedipus: Capitalism and Schizophrenia* (D. Langer 71). Both Lynch's works and that of Deleuze and Guattari "contain" insanity rather than merely "dealing with" it (D. Langer 71).
21. "Dostojewski-Ebene"; "die innere Schilderung einer Auflösung von Person, Perspektive und Wahrnehmung" (Seesslen 171).
22. "Gleichsetzung von 'innen' und 'außen'" (D. Langer 89).
23. To give a counterexample, the resolution of David Fincher's *Fight Club* (1999) ultimately creates an objective external perspective according to which Tyler Durden is the protagonist's alter. Unlike in *Lost Highway*, the surveillance camera footage is undoubtedly of an authenticating nature: it shows us what *really* happened.
24. "Gefühl [. . .], als ob ihm [dem Zuschauer] der Boden unter den Füßen weggezogen würde" (Sellmann 252).
25. In Kaul and Palmier's view, too, the film's broader oneiricity results from the irrationality of the scenario, which is exemplified by the transformation of Fred into Pete: "Die Logik einer solchen Verwandlung ist irrational wie die eines Traumes, und das Verschieben von Bedeutungen und Identitäten gehört zur Traumlogik. Es wird eine alptraumhaft geheimnisvolle Welt in *Lost Highway* erzeugt, ohne dass die Verwandlung und deren Folgen als Traum Freds (oder gar Petes) zu deuten wären. Die Identitätsverdoppelungen lassen sich also als Folge des fantastischen Moments der Metamorphose erklären" (Kaul and Palmier 94).
26. "[U]nbewohnbare Bilder, [. . .] denen es vor sich selber graut" (Seesslen 156).
27. "[U]n enigmatico rapporto di riversibilità, uno sdoppiamento della stessa scena in due sguardi" (Minuz 96).
28. Although this scene is not marked as a dream, this "splitting" may be interesting in light of Elisabeth Howell's observation that the same dream being dreamt from different perspectives is a common experience for people with dissociative identity disorder (241).
29. "Der Status der Bilder ist höchst prekär in diesem Film, der auf der einen Seite seinen Protagonisten Fred allein durch Videoaufnahmen zum Mörder seiner Frau erklärt, ihn damit sogar zum Tod durch den elektrischen Stuhl verurteilt, und der auf der anderen Seite die Beweiskraft seiner Bilder durch das Außerkraftsetzen seiner Erzähllogik selbst unterläuft" (Michalsky 400).
30. For Vera Schröder, the "surrealistic character" of *Lost Highway* is the result of a "feeling of unease": "Das Gefühl des Unbehagens und der Unruhe, etwas nicht zu begreifen oder sofort zu verstehen, verleiht diesem Film seinen surrealistischen Charakter" (Schröder 313).
31. "Eine beobachtende Instanz [. . .] ist in dieses Haus gedrungen, das zugleich eine symbiotische Gemeinschaft mit dem Mann hat. 'Es' nimmt wahr, was Fred nicht wahrnehmen kann" (Seesslen 171).
32. "Questo sogno viene ora interamente oggettivato nel doppio regime delle immagini del racconto (Renee cerca Fred chiamandolo per nome dopo che questi sembra

scomparso nel buio del corridoio [. . .]) e nelle immagini delle riprese video che ci mostrano la scena dell'omicidio, lì dove il sogno si interrompeva bruscamente [. . .] Dunque il regime onirico coincide qui con il regime narrativo, ma soprattutto viene meno il circuito che separava le immagini video e il film, annullando così quella sorta di oggettività 'allestita,' messa in atto da Fred stesso" (Minuz 100).

33 To be more precise, Minuz does observe the perceptual indistinguishability of "internal" and "external," but instead of relating it to the dream, he discusses it in terms of the Möbius strip-like structure of the story as a whole (100–1).

34 McGowan, for example, holds that "Lynch maintains a separation between the world of social reality (i.e, the realm of desire) and that of fantasy" ("Finding Ourselves" 52).

35 Rodley is not alone with this musical conception of "psychogenic fugue," as shown by this passage in Kaul's and Palmier's book: "Die Parallelen verweisen auf die Identität Freds mit Pete und geben der Struktur des Geschehens tatsächlich einen fugenartigen Charakter, aber nur im musikalischen Sinne, insofern Freds Thema durch Petes 'Stimme' versetzt vorgetragen wird, um am Schluss wieder in Freds 'Stimme' überzugehen. Es handelt sich also um Fugenkunst auf der Ebene der Filmstruktur, nicht um die psychogene Fuge einer Filmfigur" (Kaul and Palmier 92–3).

36 According to Freud, "[t]he part which is later taken on by the superego is played to begin with by an external power, by parental authority" (qtd. in McGowan, "Finding Ourselves" 58).

37 "[L]'autore dei video" (Minuz 95).

38 "In *Lost Highway* geht es [. . .] auch um einen Diskurs über die Formen der Wahrnehmung" (Seesslen 168).

39 "Wie kann man dieses radikal fremde Unding denn überhaupt [. . .] in eine Realität hineindenken? Das wäre die Frage vor jeder psychologischen Frage, die man am Traum noch festmachen könnte" (Gehring, "Existentielle Psychologie" 00:56:18–00:56:31).

Chapter 7

1 Just to be clear, Camilla Rhodes is not played by Melissa George in the second part of the film but by Laura Elena Harring.

2 Her character's name is not mentioned in the second part. The credits list only Melissa George as playing Camilla Rhodes, though.

3 More drastically even, the Club Silencio scene arguably implies that Diane's dream "blames" Camilla for her own death. After all, they only visit Club Silencio because Rita has the impulse to go there (due to her dream), and it is here that Betty finds the blue box (i.e., the representation of Camilla's murder) in her purse. In this regard, it should not be ignored that it is Rita who opens the blue box, which suggests that in Diane's dream world, Camilla killed herself.

4 *Conceptual metaphor* is understood in the sense of George Lakoff's and Mark Johnson's *Metaphors We Live By* (1980).

5 For a documentary that captures American celebrity cult in post-1990s America, see Lauren Greenfield's already-mentioned *Generation Wealth* (2018).

6. In Merleau-Ponty's account, external influences on the individual, he speaks of "the significance of nature and history that I am," are not delimiting but enabling factors of one's freedom (*Phenomenology* 482).
7. "[E]ine gleichberechtigte Parallelität der präsentierten fiktionalen Welten" (Laas 277).
8. "[U]mfassender und allgemeine[r] Traumzustand" (Kreuzer 662).
9. "[A]utonome Traumdarstellung" (Kreuzer 662).
10. For a detailed segmentation of the entire film into sequences, see Basso Fossali (446–55).
11. Kreuzer's (654) claim as to the external focalization of the shot of the Hollywood sign, for example, does not seem mandatory: an aerial shot of the sign has become iconic in popular culture such that its occurrence in Diane's dream could result from her psyche's internalization of a medial representation of the sign.
12. Arguably, the opening shot thematizes *seeing* (the bodies of the dancing couples) and *not seeing* (their black silhouettes). In a Gestalt-psychological reading, one could argue that the criterion of difference upon which seeing is based, that is, the ability to distinguish *figure* from *ground*, is reduced here. By multiplying the dancing couples and reducing them to their outlines, the shot implies a kind of seeing that problematizes its own perceptual capacity.
13. "[D]ie subjektive Kameraeinstellung auf das Bett, die von intensiven Atemgeräuschen begleitet ist, eröffne[t] die Interpretation des gesamten Films als Traum oder auch Alptraum" (Kreuzer 663).
14. Similarly, the moving legs of the chicken that Henry is cutting up in *Eraserhead* (1977) should not lead to the view that the dinner at the X's house never took place (see section "The Emergence of (Dream) Consciousness" in Chapter 4).
15. Later in the film, this is complemented by Rita's identity beginning to melt away. As Betty and Rita are getting closer to each other, they are slowly merging into one: Diane's unconscious is beginning to become aware that Rita (in the way she appears in the first part of the film) is a figment of Diane's imagination, which is why Rita chooses to wear a blonde wig. One of Betty's/Diane's features carries over to Rita, marking her as a product of Diane's mind. In this, Rita's loss of identity may be read as Diane's unconscious processing the fact that Camilla is dead—in the dream, too, Camilla gradually dissolves. Further, Camilla's death might also be seen as the reason for Betty's vanishing into thin air in the last moments of the dream. Just like Camilla "disappears" in the waking world, Betty disappears as they get back to Ruth's apartment after Club Silencio.
16. In *Twin Peaks* (1990–1; 2017), "Norma," the name of the owner of the Double R Diner, may have been inspired by *Sunset Boulevard*'s Norma Desmond. More explicitly, "Part 15" reveals Wilder's film to be the source of FBI director Gordon Cole's (not coincidentally played by David Lynch) name by having a scene from the classic play on Dougie Jones's TV.
17. Besides the "dangerous attractiveness" of both characters and the general *noir*-type atmosphere, there are two lines in *Gilda* that seem to resonate with *Mulholland Drive* in particular. First, after Gilda's (Rita Hayworth) husband has been avoiding her for a while, she confronts him, saying, "I thought you were an *amnesia* victim or something" (*Gilda* 01:26:16–01:26:19). In a later scene, when Gilda performs on stage, she sings about how "when we're together, I'm in a *dream world* of sweet delight" (*Gilda* 01:30:17–01:30:28).

18. In Lacan's conception, the child's ego is formed through the identification with their own mirror image. As Anthony Wilden puts it, "through his perception of the image of another human being, the child discovers a form (*Gestalt*), a corporeal unity, which is lacking to him at this particular stage of his development [. . .] [T]his primordial experience is symptomatic of what makes the *moi* an Imaginary construct. The ego is an *Idealich*, another self, and the *stade du miroir* is the source of all later identification" (Wilden qtd. in Sobchak, *Address* 108–9). Since the "direct object (the Self There) becomes identified with the visible Other (the Mother) who also appears in the mirror," Lacan speaks of a *méconnaissance*, "a deceptive knowledge" at the heart of ego formation (Sobchak, *Address* 109). The mirror scene in *Mulholland Drive* may thus be seen as alluding to the deceptive and imaginary aspect of identity per se.
19. Lynch complained about not being able to show the whole gate, saying that "Paramount won't let you show their logo any more. You can only show the bit of the gate below it. It's one of their rules and I think it's a really stupid rule. But the car that you see in that shot in Mulholland Drive is the actual Sunset Boulevard car" (Rodley 273).
20. For an example of this structure, one may think of Henry's first two encounters with the stage inside the radiator in *Eraserhead* (1977).
21. Another example for the concealment of a temporal shift through the continuation of movement would be the cut between the announcement of Camilla's and Adam's engagement and the commissioning of Camilla's murder at Winkie's. About to hear the words that shatter the last glimpse of hope for a common future with Camilla, Diane abruptly turns away in disgust. She continues "that" movement at Winkie's, where the clinking sound of dishes catches her attention.
22. Paradoxically, this may also constitute a further reason for confusing the dream part with the waking part: we accept the first two hours of the film as a filmic reality because it largely corresponds to a set of classical editing conventions, that is, a "norm" that we have learned from our experience with films. Given that the oneiric is inherently linked to defamiliarization (e.g., Engel, "Poetics" 39), anything that deviates from that norm—that is, the "Diane/Camilla" reality of the film—could thus be seen as a dream.
23. Andrews identifies a psychological function at the basis of the aesthetic differences between the two parts, but he does not address the explicitly reflexive dimension of the dynamic: "in the second section, Diane's conscious memory darkens her past, making it more hateful, more sordid, than is naturalistically probable, just as in the first, Diane's unconscious memory makes her dream life shinier than is naturalistically possible" (Andrews 31).
24. Cf. imdb.com/title/tt1619856/?ref_=nv_sr_srsg_3.
25. Interestingly enough, Powdermaker's study *Hollywood. The Dream Factory* appeared in 1950—in the same year as *Sunset Boulevard*.
26. Peculiar (though not "oneiric" per se) is the film's impossible narrative perspective: Gillis dies at the end of the film and yet his voice-over tells the story.
27. Another hint at the intended meta-reflexivity of the scene is provided by Olson's recollection of the cast-and-crew screening of *Mulholland Drive*. Before the movie started, Lynch briefly addressed the audience, "assum[ing] the attitude of a performance artist" (Olson 525): "He switched on the [audio cassette] recorder, and we heard an orchestra play a fanfare, then he turned off the machine. A beat of silence, then he said, 'Good evening.' Then the machine on (fanfare), off, 'Welcome

to the cast and crew screening of,' machine fanfare on, off, 'Mulholland Drive,' more recorded fanfare on, off, 'Thank you all for being here.' As Lynch quickly left the stage and took his seat next to Mary the crowd laughed and applauded their clever master of ceremonies as though they'd just witnessed a comedy club routine" (Olson 525).

28 Concerning cinema's ability to commute perception into expression, Sobchak elaborates: "The film actualizes and realizes its ability to localize, unify (or 'center') the 'invisible' intrasubjective exchange or commutation between the perception of the camera and the expression of the projector. As well, it makes this exchange visible and intersubjectively available to others in the expression of its perception—in the visible commutation between the perceptive language of its expressive being (the pre-reflective inflection of its 'viewing view' as the experience of consciousness) and the expressive being of its perceptive language (the reflection of its 'viewed view' as the consciousness of experience)" (Sobchak, *Address* 22).

29 In terms of the story, the theater stage acts as a refuge to Henry, opening up another place where he can be happy (at least initially). In *Mulholland Drive*, the stage in Club Silencio serves the opposite narrative function, in that Del Rio's performance shatters the illusion of a happy, exciting, and successful life.

30 In contrast to this, the pre-prologue credits ("A Film by David Lynch," 00:00:32) do not show this light effect, as the limousine has not appeared yet.

31 Chion elaborates: "A film's aural elements are not received as an autonomous unit. They are immediately analyzed and distributed in the spectator's perceptual apparatus according to the relation each bears to what the spectator sees at the time" (Chion, *Voice* 3).

32 An interesting moment, in this regard, occurs when Betty "sees herself" at the Sierra Bonita apartment but does not recognize the corpse (credited as Lyssie Powell) as herself. Unlike in *The Alphabet*, thus, where the dream collapses as a result of the girl recognizing the dream figure as herself, the dream can continue here (even if the image duplicates Betty and Rita, hinting at the oneiric doubling of identities at play). What psychoanalysts would call "censorship" manifests itself as (Betty's) "seeing without immediate recognition" here (Zechner 76).

33 Interestingly, the film's central symbolism of the blue key—signifying Camilla's death—does not emerge due to the dream but is already part of the waking world.

34 "Die Vollendung des Traumvorganges liegt darin, daß der regressiv verwandelte, zu einer Wunschphantasie umgearbeitete Gedankeninhalt als sinnliche Wahrnehmung bewußt wird" (Freud, *Psychologie des Unbewußten* 186).

35 Philosophers of mind might argue that Betty displays "phenomenal consciousness"— there is "something it's like" for her to be in this state—but that she lacks "access consciousness," which would require the ability to report or describe what it is that one is conscious of (cf. E. Thompson 7).

36 Concerning the latter concept, composer R. Murray Schafer has argued that "the invention of electronic equipment for the transmission and storage of sound" has allowed us to "split the sound from the makers of the sound. This dissociation I call schizophonia, and if I use a word close in sound to schizophrenia it is because I want very much to suggest to you the same sense of aberration and drama that this word evokes, for the developments of which we are speaking have had profound effects on our lives" (Murray 43).

Conclusion

1 The third season of *Twin Peaks* (2017) is also known as *Twin Peaks: The Return*, which is usually understood as referring to the story of Cooper's "return" to the town of Twin Peaks and to the "return" of the television series *Twin Peaks* after twenty-five years.

Works Cited

"Alternate International Pilot." *Special Features, Twin Peaks: Das ganze Geheimnis*, Paramount Universal Pictures (Blu-ray), 2016.
American Psychiatric Association (APA). *Diagnostic and Statistical Manual of Mental Disorders. Text Revision.* 4th ed., American Psychiatric Publishing, 2000.
American Psychiatric Association (APA). *Diagnostic and Statistical Manual of Mental Disorders.* 5th ed., American Psychiatric Publishing, 2013.
Andrews, David. "An Oneiric Fugue: The Various Logics of *Mulholland Drive*." *Journal of Film and Video*, vol. 56, no. 1, 2004, pp. 25–40.
L'Année Dernière à Marienbad. 1961. Directed by Alain Resnais, performances by Delphine Seyrig, Giorgio Albertazzi, and Sacha Piteoff, StudioCanal (Blu-ray), 2009.
Annie Hall. 1977. Directed by Woody Allen, Metro-Goldwyn-Mayer Studios (DVD: "Der Stadtneurotiker"), 2009.
Askay, Richard, and Jensen Farquhar. *Apprehending the Inaccessible. Freudian Psychoanalysis and Existential Phenomenology.* Northwestern University Press, 2006.
Ates, Murat. *Phänomenologie des Traums.* Hamburg, Meiner, 2023.
Badalamenti, Angelo. "Dance of the Dream Man." *Music from Twin Peaks*, Warner Bros. Records, 1990.
Badalamenti, Angelo. "Jitterbug." *Mulholland Drive*. 2001. *Spotify*, open.spotify.com/track/3DOWayQ0qjXiAjVrK4ePM2?si=9d214264d7834c37. Accessed Mar. 15, 2021.
Basso Fossali, Pierluigi. *Interpretazione tra mondi. Il pensiero figurale di David Lynch.* 2nd ed., Pisa, Edizioni ETS, 2008.
Baudry, Jean. "The Apparatus." *Apparatus*, edited by Theresa Hak Kyung Cha, Tanam Press, 1981, pp. 41–62.
Bazin, André. *What Is Cinema? Volume II.* Translated by Hugh Gray, University of California Press, 2004.
Beckermann, Ansgar. *Analytische Einführung in die Philosophie des Geistes.* 3rd ed., Berlin, Walter de Gruyter, 2008.
Bergman, Ingmar. *Persona.* 1966. Performances by Liv Ullmann and Bibi Andersson, Arthaus (Blu-ray), 2014.
Bermes, Christian. *Maurice Merleau-Ponty zur Einführung.* 3rd ed., Hamburg, Junius Verlag, 2012.
Bernet, Rudolf. "Unconscious Consciousness in Husserl and Freud." *Phenomenology and the Cognitive Sciences*, vol. 1, no. 3, 2002, pp. 327–51.
Binswanger, Ludwig. "Dream and Existence." *Dream and Existence*, edited by Keith Hoeller, translated by Forrest Williams and Jacob Needleman, Humanities Press, 1993, pp. 81–105.
Booker, T., and the M.G.s. "Green Onions." *Green Onions.* 1962. *Spotify*, open.spotify.com/track/4fQMGlCawbTkH9yPPZ49kP?si=9060d384f13c4edf. Accessed Mar. 15, 2021.
Boroditsky, Lera. "Metaphoric Structuring: Understanding Time through Spatial Metaphors." *Cognition*, vol. 75, no. 1, 2000, pp. 1–28.

Boss, Medard. *Der Traum und seine Auslegung*. München, Kindler, 1974.
Bowie, David. "I'm Deranged." *1. Outside*. 1995. *Spotify*, open.spotify.com/album/0pUursv GUAgcDiEqYlnZ0q?highlight=spotify:track:71EAUWoX6EjdJ2AmBKSB7N. Accessed Mar. 15, 2021.
Bradshaw, Peter et al. "The World's 40 Best Directors." *The Guardian*, Nov. 14, 2003, theguardian.com/film/2003/nov/14/1. Accessed Jan. 6, 2021.
Brook, Andrew. "Disorders of Unified Consciousness: Brain Bisection and Dissociative Identity Disorder." *Disturbed Consciousness: New Essays on Psychopathology and Theories of Consciousness*, edited by Rocco J. Gennaro, MIT Press, 2015, pp. 209–25.
Brudzinska, Jagna. "Die phänomenologische Erfahrung und die Frage nach dem Unbewussten. Überlegungen im Anschluss an Husserl und Freud." *Interdisziplinäre Perspektiven der Phänomenologie*, edited by Dieter Lohmar and Dirk Fonfara, Springer, 2006, pp. 54–71.
Brütsch, Matthias. *Traumbühne Kino. Der Traum als filmtheoretische Metapher und narratives Motiv*. Marburg, Schüren, 2011.
Buckland, Warren. "Making Sense of *Lost Highway*." *Puzzle Films: Complex Storytelling in Contemporary Cinema*, edited by Warren Buckland, Blackwell Publishing, 2009, pp. 42–61.
Bulkeley, Kelly. "The Dream Logic of *Twin Peaks*." *Fan Phenomena: Twin Peaks*, edited by Marisa C. Hayes and Franck Boulegue, University of Chicago Press, 2013, pp. 66–73.
Bulkeley, Kelly. "Dreaming and the Cinema of David Lynch." *Dreaming*, vol. 13, no. 1, 2003, pp. 49–60.
Caché. Directed by Michael Haneke, France 3 Cinéma, 2005.
Campbell, Donald T., and Donald W. Fiske. "Convergent and Discriminant Validation by the Multitrait-multimethod Matrix." *Psychological Bulletin*, vol. 56, no. 2, 1959, pp. 81–105.
Carroll, Lewis. *Alice's Adventures in Wonderland*. Puffin Classics, 2015.
Carroll, Noël. *Mystifying Movies*. Columbia University Press, 1988.
Castoriadis, Cornelius. *Figures of the Thinkable*. Stanford University Press, 2007.
Chateau, Dominique. "The Film That Dreams – About David Lynch's TWIN PEAKS Season 3." *Stories: Screen Narrative in the Digital Era*, edited by Ian Christie and Annie van den Oever, Amsterdam University Press, 2018, pp. 119–41.
Un Chien Andalou. Directed by Luis Buñuel, 1929.
Chion, Michel. *Audio-Vision: Sound on Screen*. Edited and translated by Claudia Gorbman, Columbia University Press, 1994.
Chion, Michel. *David Lynch*. Translated by Robert Julian, 2nd ed., British Film Institute, 2006.
Chion, Michel. *The Voice in Cinema*. Translated by Claudia Gorbman, Columbia University Press, 1999.
Cousins, Mark, director. "1939–1952: The Devastation of War and a New Movie Language." *The Story of Film: An Odyssey*, written and narrated by Mark Cousins, Hopscotch Films, 2011.
Cox Cameron, Olga. "Dream Logic in Mulholland Drive." Freud/Lynch: Behind the Curtain, Freud Museum London, The Rio Cinema, 2018.
Cruz, Gilbert. "David Lynch on Michael Jackson and that Crazy Frog from 'Twin Peaks.'" *The New York Times*, Jul. 13, 2018, nytimes.com/2018/06/13/arts/television/david-lynch-room-to-dream.html. Accessed Feb. 5, 2020.

D'Aloia, Adriano. "The Intangible Ground – A Neurophenomenology of the Film Experience." *NECSUS. European Journal of Media Studies*, vol. 1, no. 2, 2012, pp. 219–39. doi: 10.5117/NECSUS2012.2.DALO.

"David Lynch – Plume of Desire." *Modem*, 2 May 2016, modemonline.com/modem-mag/article/3676-france--paris-david-lynch---plume-of-desir. Accessed Feb. 19, 2020.

"David Lynch Interview from 1979." *YouTube*, uploaded by filmvilag, Jul. 9, 2013, youtube.com/watch?v=l3WFOPWbG8I. Accessed Oct. 15, 2019.

"David Lynch Presents the History of Surrealist Film." *Open Culture*, Oct. 11, 2013, openculture.com/2013/10/david-lynch-presents-the-history-of-surrealist-film-1987.html. Accessed Nov. 30, 2019.

Deleuze, Gilles. *Cinema II: The Time-Image*. Translated by Hugh Tomlinson and Robert Galeta, 5th ed., University of Minnesota Press, 1997.

Deren, Maya. "Meshes of the Afternoon." 1943. *Wikimedia*, wikimedia.org/wikipedia/commons/2/2f/Meshes_of_the_Afternoon_%281943%29.webm. Accessed Mar. 15, 2021.

Desta, Yohana. "David Lynch Still Hates Season 2 of *Twin Peaks* More than You." *Vanity Fair*, May 19, 2017, vanityfair.com/hollywood/2017/05/david-lynch-twin-peaks-season-two#. Accessed Jan. 10, 2020.

Dickson, Simon. "The Oneiric Film: Refocusing the Film-Dream Analogy from an Existential Phenomenological Perspective." *Academia*, academia.edu/18049918/The_Oneiric_Film_Refocusing_the_Film_Dream_Analogy_from_an_Existential_Phenomenological_Perspective. Accessed Mar. 3, 2021.

Djurdjevic, Gordan. *India and the Occult: The Influence of South Asian Spirituality on Modern Western Occultism*. Palgrave Macmillan, 2014.

Dottorini, Daniele. *David Lynch – Il cinema del sentire*. Recco, Le Mani, 2004.

Downing, Lisa. "George Berkeley." *Stanford Encyclopedia of Philosophy*, Jan. 19, 2011, plato.stanford.edu/archives/spr2013/entries/berkeley/. Accessed Mar. 8, 2021.

Drivet, Leandro. "Genesis and Profanation of the Other World: The Interpretation of Dreams." *The International Journal of Psychoanalysis*, vol. 98, no. 6, 2017, pp. 1669–97. doi: 10.1111/1745-8315.12661. Accessed May 29, 2020.

Eagleton, Terry. *Literary Theory: An Introduction*. Blackwell, 1983.

Ebert, Roger. "A Twisted Road through a Landscape of Dreams." *rogerebert.com*, Nov. 11, 2012, rogerebert.com/reviews/great-movie-mulholland-dr-2001. Accessed Jun. 3, 2020.

Eberwein, Robert T. *Film and the Dream Screen – A Sleep and a Forgetting*. Princeton University Press, 1984.

L'Eclisse. Directed by Michelangelo Antonioni, Cineriz, 1962.

Eco, Umberto. *A Theory of Semiotics*. Indiana University Press, 1976.

Elsaesser, Thomas, and Malte Hagener. *Film Theory: An Introduction through the Senses*. 2nd ed., Routledge, 2015.

Elsaesser, Thomas, and Malte Hagener. *Filmtheorie zur Einführung*. Hamburg, Junius Verlag, 2017.

Egenes, Thomas, and Kumuda Reddy. *Eternal Stories from the Upanishads*. New Delhi, Smriti Books, 2002.

Engel, Manfred. "Towards a Poetics of Dream Narration." *Writing the Dream. Écrire le rêve*, edited by Bernard Dieterle and Manfred Engel, Königshausen & Neumann, 2017, pp. 19–44.

Engel, Manfred. "Traum und Malerei." Doctoral colloquium, RTG "European Dream-Cultures," Dec. 19, 2018, Saarland University, Saarbrücken. Lecture.

Ewins, Michael. "The Stars Turn and a Time Presents Itself." *Sight & Sound*, vol. 28, no. 1, 2018, pp. 33–6.

Fellmann, Ferdinand. *Phänomenologie zur Einführung*. Hamburg, Junius Verlag, 2012.

Ferencz-Flatz, Christian, and Julian Hanich. "What is Film Phenomenology?" *Studia Phaenomenologica*, vol. 16, no. 1, 2016, pp. 11–61.

Fichte, Johann Gottlieb. *Die Bestimmung des Menschen*. 4th ed., Berlin, CreateSpace Independent Publishing Platform, 2016.

Fincher, David, director. *Fight Club*. 20th Century Fox, 1999.

Foucault, Michel. "Dream, Imagination and Existence." *Dream and Existence*, edited by Keith Hoeller, translated by Forrest Williams and Jacob Needleman, *Review of Existential Psychology & Psychiatry*, vol. 14, no. 1, 1985, pp. 29–78.

Frank, Caroline, and Markus Schleich. "Einleitung – Twin Peaks, die Rückkehr. Woher und wohin?" *Mysterium Twin Peaks. Zeichen – Welten – Referenzen*, edited by Caroline Frank and Markus Schleich, Wiesbaden, Springer VS, 2020, pp. 3–21.

Freud, Sigmund. "Die Fehlleistungen." *Gesammelte Werke XI*, edited by Anna Freud, E. Bibring, W. Hoffer, E. Kris and O. Isakower, 5th ed., Frankfurt (M), S. Fischer Verlag, 1969, pp. 5–76.

Freud, Sigmund. *Die Traumdeutung*. 2nd ed., Frankfurt (M), Fischer Taschenbuch Verlag, 2010.

Freud, Sigmund. "The Question of Lay Analysis." *The Standard Edition of the Complete Psychological Works of Sigmund Freud, Volume XX (1925–1926): An Autobiographical Study, Inhibitions, Symptoms and Anxiety, The Question of Lay Analysis and Other Works*, translated by James Strachey, London, Hogarth Press, 1991, pp. 177–258.

Freud, Sigmund. *Studienausgabe Band III: Psychologie des Unbewußten*. Edited by Alexander Mitscherlich, Angela Richards, and James Strachey, 9th ed., Frankfurt (M), S. Fischer Verlag, 2001.

Freud, Sigmund. *Werkausgabe in zwei Bänden. Band 2: Anwendungen der Psychoanalyse*, Edited by Anna Freud and Ilse Grubrich-Simitis, Frankfurt (M), S. Fischer Verlag, 1978.

"Freud/Lynch: Behind the Curtain – Conference Trailer." *YouTube*, uploaded by Freud Museum London, Apr. 23, 2018, youtube.com/watch?v=1YDzQvmNyPM. Accessed Oct. 22, 2019.

Frost, Mark. *Twin Peaks: The Final Dossier*. Macmillan USA, 2017.

Fuller, Graham. "Naomi Watts: Three Continents Later, An Outsider Actress Finds Her Place." *Interview Magazine*, 2001, lynchnet.com/mdrive/interview.html. Accessed Jun. 3, 2020.

Funny Games. Directed by Michael Haneke, Österreichischer Rundfunk, 1997.

Gamper, Michael, and Helmut Hühn. *Was sind Ästhetische Eigenzeiten?* Hannover, Wehrhahn, 2014.

Geheimnisse einer Seele. Directed by Georg W. Pabst, Ufa, 1926.

Gehring, Petra. "#12. existentielle Psychologie. Binswanger. Foucault." *philosophie. podcast. serie I. Traum*. 2006. *iTunes*, itunes.apple.com/de/podcast/philosophie-podcast-serie-i-traum/id254819580?mt=2. Accessed Mar. 15, 2021.

Gehring, Petra. *Traum und Wirklichkeit. Zur Geschichte einer Unterscheidung*. Frankfurt (M), Campus Verlag, 2008.

Generation Wealth. 2018. Directed by Lauren Greenfield. *Prime Video*, amazon.de/Generation-Wealth-Lauren-Greenfield/dp/B089XYKRDK/ref=sr_1_2?__mk_de_DE=%C3%85M%C3%85%C5%BD%C3%95%C3%91&dchild=1&keywords=generation+wealth&qid=1614849586&sr=8-2. Accessed Mar. 4, 2021.

Giannopoulou, Zina. "Introduction." *Mulholland Drive*, edited by Zina Giannopoulou, Routledge, 2013, pp. 1–7.
Gibson, James J. *The Ecological Approach to Visual Perception*. London, Lawrence Erlbaum Associates, 1986.
"Gilda." Directed by Charles Vidor, Columbia, 1946. *Internet Archive*, Jul. 3, 2014, archive.org/details/Gilda. Accessed Jun. 4, 2020.
Gorbman, Claudia. *Unheard Melodies: Narrative Film Music*. BFI Publishing, 1987.
De Goya, Francisco. "The Sleep of Reason Produces Monsters." *Google Arts & Culture*. 1799, artsandculture.google.com/asset/the-sleep-of-reason-produces-monsters-francisco-de-goya-y-lucientes/XgG3AE0s3xlYCw. Accessed Mar. 15, 2021.
Granat, Zbigniew. "Sonoristics, Sonorism." *Grove Music Online*, oxfordmusiconline.com/grovemusic/abstract/10.1093/gmo/9781561592630.001.0001/omo-9781561592630-e-0002061689?rskey=v8oVcJ&result=1#omo-9781561592630-e-0002061689-div1-0002061698. Accessed Mar. 5, 2019.
Grandville, Jean-Jacques. *Premier rêve. – Crime et expiation*. 1847. *Dark Classics*, darkclassics.blogspot.com/2011/04/jean-ignace-isidore-gerard-first-dream.html. Accessed Oct. 10, 2019.
Grandville, Jean-Jacques. *Second rêve. – Une promenade dans le ciel*. 1847. *Dark Classics*, darkclassics.blogspot.com/2011/04/jean-ignace-isidore-gerard-second-reve.html. Accessed Oct. 10, 2019.
Hanich, Julian. "When Viewers Drift Off: A Brief Phenomenology of Cinematic Daydreaming." *The Structures of the Film Experience by Jean-Pierre Meunier*, edited by Julian Hanich and Daniel Fairfax, Amsterdam University Press, 2017, pp. 336–52.
Haraway, Donna. "Situated Knowledges: The Science Question in Feminism and the Privilege of Partial Perspective." *Feminist Studies*, vol. 14, no. 3, 1988, pp. 575–99.
Haubner, Steffen. "Eraserhead." *Filme der 70er*, edited by Jürgen Müller and Philipp Bühler, Taschen, 2017, pp. 512–19.
Heidegger, Martin. *Zollikoner Seminare*. Edited by Medard Boss, Frankfurt (M), Klostermann, 1987.
Heiland, Konrad. *Der Soundtrack unserer Träume. Filmmusik und Psychoanalyse*. Gießen, Psychosozial-Verlag, 2013.
Held, Klaus. "Einleitung." *Die phänomenologische Methode. Ausgewählte Texte I*, edited by Klaus Held, Reclam, 1985, pp. 5–51.
Hobson, J. Allan. "REM Sleep and Dreaming: Towards a Theory of Protoconsciousness." *Nature*, vol. 10, no. 11, 2009, pp. 803–13. doi: 10.1038/nrn2716. Accessed Oct. 13, 2020.
HorrorQueen, S. "Review of *Inland Empire*, by David Lynch." *Rotten Tomatoes*, Mar. 27, 2018, rottentomatoes.com/m/inland_empire/reviews?type=user. Accessed Sep. 1, 2020.
Howell, Elisabeth F. *Understanding and Treating Dissociative Identity Disorder. A Relational Approach*. Routledge, 2011.
Hughes, David. *The Complete Lynch*. Virgin Books, 2001.
Husserl, Edmund. *Phantasie, Bildbewusstsein, Erinnerung. Zur Phänomenologie der anschaulichen Vergegenwärtigungen. Texte aus dem Nachlass (1898–1925)*. Edited by Eduard Marbach, The Hague, Martinus Nijhoff Publishers, 1980.
Inception. Directed by Christopher Nolan, Warner Bros. Pictures, 2010.
Inkswamp. "What's with the Roadhouse?" *Reddit*, Aug. 5, 2018, reddit.com/r/twinpeaks/comments/94s9vn/all_whats_with_the_roadhouse/. Accessed Jan. 23, 2020.
Iser, Wolfgang. *Der Akt des Lesens*. München, Wilhelm Fink, 1984.

Jackson, Frank C. "Epiphenomenal Qualia." *The Philosophical Quarterly*, vol. 32, no. 127, 1982, pp. 127–36.

Jost, Francois. *L'oeil caméra: Entre film et roman*. 2nd ed., Lyon, Presses Universitaires de Lyon, 1987.

Jousse, Thierry. *Masters of Cinema: David Lynch*. Cahiers du Cinéma, 2010.

Jurassic Park. Directed by Steven Spielberg, Amblin Entertainment, 1993.

Kaul, Susanne, and Jean-Pierre Palmier. *David Lynch. Einführung in seine Filme und Filmästhetik*. München, Wilhelm Fink, 2011.

Kozyreva, Anastasia. "Non-representational Approaches to the Unconscious in the Phenomenology of Husserl and Merleau-Ponty." *Phenomenology and the Cognitive Sciences*, vol. 17, no. 1, 2018, pp. 199–224. doi: 10.1007/s11097-016-9492-9. Accessed Nov. 18, 2019.

Kracauer, Siegfried. *Theory of Film. The Redemption of Physical Reality*. Princeton University Press, 1997.

Kreuzer, Stefanie. *Traum und Erzählen in Literatur, Film und Kunst*. München, Wilhelm Fink, 2014.

Kuhn, Annette, and Guy Westwell. *Oxford Dictionary of Film Studies*. Oxford University Press, 2012.

Kuhn, Markus. *Filmnarratologie. Ein erzähltheoretisches Analysemodell*. Berlin, De Gruyter, 2011.

Laass, Eva. "Krieg der Welten in Lynchville. *Mulholland Drive* und die Anwendungsmöglichkeiten und -grenzen des Konzepts narrativer UnZuverlässigkeit." *"Camera Doesn't Lie." Spielarten erzählerischer Unzuverlässigkeit im Film*, edited by Jörg Helbig, Trier, WVT, 2006, pp. 251–81.

Lahde, Maurice. "'We Live Inside a Dream.' David Lynchs Filme als Traumerfahrungen." *"A Strange World." Das Universum des David Lynch*, edited by Eckhard Pabst, München, Ludwig, 1998, pp. 95–110.

Lakoff, George and Mark Johnson. *Metaphors We Live By*. University of Chicago Press, 1980.

Langer, Daniela. "Die Wahrheit des Wahnsinns. Zum Verhältnis von Identität, Wahnsinn und Gesellschaft in den Filmen David Lynchs." *"A Strange World." Das Universum des David Lynch*, edited by Eckhard Pabst, München, Ludwig, 1998, pp. 69–94.

Langer, Susanne K. *Feeling and Form. A Theory of Art*. Charles Scribner's Sons, 1953.

Leigh, Danny. "Eraserhead: The True Story behind David Lynch's Surreal Shocker." *The Guardian*, Mar. 22, 2017, theguardian.com/film/2017/mar/22/david-lynch-eraserhead. Accessed Nov. 21, 2019.

Lezard, Nicholas. "David Lynch: Director of Dreams." *The Guardian*, Feb. 17, 2012, theguardian.com/film/2012/feb/17/david-lynch-film-director-dreams. Accessed Feb. 10, 2021.

Lommel, Michael et al. *Surrealismus und Film*. Bielefeld, transcript, 2008.

"Lose Your Head." *The Cambridge Dictionary*, dictionary.cambridge.org/dictionary/english/lose-your-head. Accessed Oct. 30, 2019.

Lynch, David. *Catching the Big Fish. Meditation, Consciousness, and Creativity*. Penguin Books, 2007.

Lynch, David. *Mulholland Drive (TV-pilot)*. 1999, Dec. 12, 2018, *Indie Film Hustle*, sellingyourscreenplay.com/wp-content/uploads/screenplay/scripts/Mulholland-Drive.pdf. Accessed Jun. 5, 2020.

Lynch, David, director. "The Alphabet." 1968. *Eraserhead*, performances by Peggy Lynch and Robert Chadwick, Arthaus (Blu-ray), 2018.

Lynch, David, director. *Blue Velvet*. 1986. Performances by Kyle MacLachlan and Laura Dern, MGM (Blu-ray), 2011.

Lynch, David, director. "David Lynch - Absurd Encounter with Fear (1967)." *YouTube*, uploaded by Opio do Trivial, Oct. 22, 2014, youtube.com/watch?v=qDqN9-VD9dM. Accessed Mar. 14, 2019.

Lynch, David, director. *The Elephant Man*. Paramount Pictures, 1980.

Lynch, David, director. *Eraserhead*. 1977. Performances by Jack Nance, Laurel Near, Jack Fisk, Charlotte Stewart, Jeanne Bates, and Allen Joseph, Arthaus (Blu-ray), 2018.

Lynch, David, director. "The Grandmother." 1970. *Eraserhead*, performances by Richard White, Dorothy McGinnis, Virginia Maitland, and Robert Chadwick, Arthaus (Blu-ray), 2018.

Lynch, David, director. *Inland Empire*. 2006. Performances by Laura Dern, Harry Dean Stanton, and Justin Theroux, Concorde Home Entertainment (Blu-ray), 2011.

Lynch, David, director. *Lady Blue Shanghai*. Performances by Marion Cotillard and Emily Stofle, Christian Dior SE, 2010.

Lynch, David, director. *Lost Highway*. 1997. Performances by Bill Pullman, Patricia Arquette, and Balthazar Getty, Concorde Home Entertainment (Blu-ray), 2011.

Lynch, David, director. *Mulholland Drive*. 2001. Performances by Naomi Watts, Laura Harring, and Justin Theroux, Concorde Home Entertainment (Blu-ray), 2011.

Lynch, David, director. "Six Men Getting Sick." 1966. *Eraserhead*, Arthaus (Blu-ray), 2018.

Lynch, David, director. *The Straight Story*. 1999. Performances by Richard Farnsworth, Sissy Spacek, and Harry Dean Stanton, Arthaus (Blu-ray), 2017.

Lynch, David, director. "Twin Peaks: Fire Walk with Me." 1992. *Twin Peaks: Das ganze Geheimnis*, performances by Sheryl Lee, Kyle MacLachlan, Ray Wise, and David Bowie, Paramount Universal Pictures (Blu-ray), 2016.

Lynch, David, painter. *Man Throwing Up*. 1968, Rodger LaPelle and Christine McGinnis. *David Lynch: Someone is in My House*, by David Lynch et al., Prestel, 2018, p. 139.

Lynch, David, painter. *Sick Man With Elephantine Arm*. 1968, Rodger LaPelle and Christine McGinnis. *David Lynch: Someone is in My House*, by David Lynch et al., Prestel, 2018, p. 137.

Lynch, David, painter. *Woman With Tree Branch*. 1968, Rodger LaPelle and Christine McGinnis. *David Lynch: Someone is in My House*, by David Lynch et al., Prestel, 2018, p. 136.

Lynch, David, and Mark Frost, creators. "Twin Peaks." 1990–91. *Twin Peaks: Das ganze Geheimnis*, performances by Sheryl Lee and Kyle MacLachlan, Paramount Universal Pictures (Blu-ray), 2016.

Lynch, David, and Mark Frost, creators. *Twin Peaks. A Limited Event Series*. 2017. Performances by Kyle MacLachlan, Sheryl Lee, David Lynch, and Monica Bellucci, Paramount Universal Pictures (Blu-ray), 2018.

Lynch, David, and Kristine McKenna. *Room to Dream*, Canongate Books, 2018. Audible, https://www.amazon.com/arya/webplayer?asin=B079F4DXVC&ref=adbl_typ_cloudplayer_dt&useRelativeUrl=true&fetchNewPlayQueue=true&contentDeliveryType=MultiPartBook. Accessed Feb. 26, 2023.

, "Lynchian."*Oxford English Dictionary*, oed.com/view/Entry/69513711. Accessed Mar. 13, 2019.

Magritte, René. *La Saignée*. 1939. *Museum Boijmans*, boijmans.nl/en/collection/artworks/4234/la-saignee. Accessed Oct. 14, 2019.

"Making-of *Mulholland Drive*." Special Features, *Mulholland Drive*, Concorde Home Entertainment (Blu-ray), 2011.

Marks, Laura. *The Skin of the Film: Intercultural Cinema, Embodiment, and the Senses*. Duke University Press, 2000.

Marshall, Colin. "David Lynch Lists His Favorite Films & Directors, Including Fellini, Wilder, Tati & Hitchcock." *Open Culture*, Sept. 18, 2013, openculture.com/2013/09/david-lynch-on-his-favorite-directors-including-fellini-wilder-tati-and-hitchcock.html. Accessed Nov. 4, 2019.

McCloskey, Michael. "Spatial Representation in Mind and Brain." *The Handbook of Cognitive Neuropsychology: What Deficits Reveal about the Human Mind*, edited by Brenda Rapp, Psychology Press, 2001, pp. 101–32.

McGowan, Todd. "Finding Ourselves on a 'Lost Highway': David Lynch's Lesson in Fantasy." *Cinema Journal*, vol. 39, no. 2, 2000, pp. 51–73.

McGowan, Todd. *The Impossible David Lynch*. Columbia University Press, 2008.

McGowan, Todd. "Lost on Mulholland Drive: Navigating David Lynch's Panegyric to Hollywood." *Cinema Journal*, vol. 43, no. 2, 2004, pp. 67–89.

McGowan, Todd. "Lynch on the Run: The Proximity of Trauma in the Short Film." *Compact Cinematics*, Bloomsbury, 2017, pp. 45–54.

McKenna, Kristine. "Painting is a Place." *David Lynch. Someone is in My House*, Prestel, 2018, pp. 11–19.

Menarini, Roy. *Il Cinema di David Lynch*. Alessandria, Falsopiano, 2002.

Merleau-Ponty, Maurice. "The Film and the New Psychology." *The Robot in the Garden: Telerobotics and Telepistemology in the Age of the Internet*, MIT Press, 2000, pp. 332–46.

Merleau-Ponty, Maurice. *Phenomenology of Perception*. Translated by Donald A. Landes, Routledge, 2012.

Merleau-Ponty, Maurice. *Vorlesungen I*. Translated by Alexandre Métraux, Berlin, De Gruyter, 2010.

Metz, Christian. *Psychoanalysis and Cinema: The Imaginary Signifier*. Macmillan, 1985.

Michalsky, Tanja. "David Lynch: *Lost Highway*. Ein filmischer Beitrag zur Medientheorie." *Das bewegte Bild: Film und Kunst*, edited by Thomas Hensel, Klaus Krüger, and Tanja Michalsky, München, Wilhelm Fink, 2006, pp. 397–418.

Michelson, Annette. "Toward Snow." *Artforum*, vol. 9, no. 10, 1971, pp. 30–7.

Mildly Amusing Channel. Comment on "Twin Peaks - Cooper and The Eyeless Woman." *YouTube*, uploaded by Mario Carlos Rodríguez Canto, May 26, 2017, youtube.com/watch?v=HEkdR5-8Kss. Accessed Oct. 23, 2019.

Minuz, Andrea. "Lost Highway." *David Lynch*, edited by Paolo Bertetto, Venezia, Marsilio, 2008, pp. 90–109.

The Mirror. Directed by Andrei Tarkovsky, Mosfilm, 1975.

Monaco, James. *How to Read a Film: Movies, Media, and Beyond*. 4th ed., Oxford University Press, 2009.

Morin, Edgar. *The Cinema, or the Imaginary Man*. Translated by Lorraine Mortimer, University of Minnesota Press, 2005.

Morsch, Thomas. *Medienästhetik des Films. Verkörperte Wahrnehmung und ästhetische Erfahrung im Kino*. München, Wilhelm Fink, 2011.

Morrey, Douglas. "Bodies that Matter." *Film-Philosophy*, vol. 10, no. 2, 2006, pp. 11–22.

Murch, Walter. "Foreword." *Audio-Vision*, edited and translated by Claudia Gorbman, Columbia University Press, 1994, pp. vii–xxiv.
Mutz, Julian, and Amir-Homayoun Javadi. "Exploring the Neural Correlates of Dream Phenomenology and Altered States of Consciousness during Sleep." *Neuroscience of Consciousness*, vol. 2017, no. 1, 2017, pp. 1–12. doi: 10.1093/nc/nix009. Accessed May 29, 2020.
Nochimson, Martha. *David Lynch Swerves: Uncertainty from Lost Highway to Inland Empire*. University of Texas Press, 2013.
Nichols, Bill. *Introduction to Documentary*. 3rd ed., Indiana University Press, 2017.
Nichols, Bill. *Maya Deren and the American Avant-Garde*. University of California Press, 2001.
Oever, Annie van den. "The Prominence of Grotesque Figures in Visual Culture Today: Rethinking the Ontological Status of the (Moving) Image from the Perspective of the Grotesque." *Image & Text*, vol. 2011, no. 18, 2011, pp. 100–23.
Olivelle, Patrick. *Upanisads*. Oxford World's Classics, 2008.
Olson, Greg. *David Lynch: Beautiful Dark*. Scarecrow Press, 2008.
Once Upon a Time in the West. Directed by Sergio Leone, Paramount Pictures, 1968.
Pattison, George. *Kierkegaard: The Aesthetic and the Religious*. Palgrave Macmillan, 1992.
Penderecki, Krzysztof. "Capriccio for Violin and Orchestra," 1967. *Spotify*, open.spotify.com/track/4TUvDUoDAkZaKoLM34AyFM. Accessed Mar. 13, 2019.
Petrić, Vlada. "Film and Dreams: A Theoretical-Historical Survey." *Film and Dreams*, edited by Vlada Petrić, South Salem, 1980, pp. 1–48.
Petrić, Vlada. "Tarkovsky's Dream Imagery." *Film Quarterly*, vol. 43, no. 2, 1989–90, pp. 28–34.
The Piano. Directed by Jane Campion, Jan Chapman Productions CiBy 2000, 1993.
Popper, Karl R. *Die beiden Grundprobleme der Erkenntnistheorie. Aufgrund von Manuskripten aus den Jahren 1930–1933*. Edited by Troels Eggers Hansen, 3rd ed., Tübingen, Mohr Siebeck, 2010.
Powdermaker, Hortense. *Hollywood, the Dream Factory*. Boston, Little, Brown and Company, 1950.
"Primary Process/Secondary Process." *International Dictionary of Psychoanalysis*, encyclopedia.com/psychology/dictionaries-thesauruses-pictures-and-press-releases/primary-processsecondary-process. Accessed Mar. 11, 2019.
Quinn, Allison. "'Twin Peaks' Fan Gorbachev Asked Bush Who Killed Laura Palmer." *The Moscow Times*, Nov. 18, 2014, themoscowtimes.com/2014/11/18/twin-peaks-fan-gorbachev-asked-bush-who-killed-laura-palmer-a41488. Accessed Feb. 17, 2020.
Rafferty, Terrence. "In a Weird Way, David Lynch Makes Sense." *lynchnet*, Mar. 10, 2002, lynchnet.com/articles/nytimes2002.html. Accessed Feb. 19, 2020.
Rammstein. "Rammstein." *Lost Highway*. 1997. *Spotify*, open.spotify.com/track/7Kl8hfSH4uG9nEFTkA5CNG?si=953c218887e14b6f. Accessed Mar. 15, 2021.
Rascaroli, Laura. "Oneiric Metaphor in Film Theory." *Kinema: A Journal for Film and Audiovisual Media*, Nov. 20, 2002, openjournals.uwaterloo.ca/index.php/kinema/article/view/982. Accessed Mar. 3, 2021.
Rear Window. Directed by Alfred Hitchcock, Paramount Pictures, 1954.
Redon, Odilon. "Germination." *Dans le rêve*. 1879. *MoMA*, moma.org/collection/works/192449. Accessed Oct. 10, 2019.
Redon, Odilon. "Limbes." *Dans le rêve*. 1879. *MoMA*, moma.org/collection/works/192451. Accessed Oct. 10, 2019.

Reed, Lou. "This Magic Moment." *Lost Highway*. 1997. *Spotify*, open.spotify.com/album/77PY9VYriArqduEpkD2Ues?highlight=spotify:track:5C4sfjPfsnAEYHgxnxQTjf. Accessed Mar. 15, 2021.

Reed, Ryan. "The Last Word on 'Twin Peaks' by David Lynch's Co-creator Mark Frost." *salon*, Nov. 7, 2017, salon.com/2017/11/07/the-last-word-on-twin-peaks-by-david-lynchs-co-creator-mark-frost/. Accessed Nov. 19, 2019.

Reznik, Daniel et al. "Oneiric Synesthesia: Preliminary Evidence for the Occurrence of Synesthetic-Like Experiences during Sleep-Inertia." *Psychology of Consciousness: Theory, Research, and Practice*, vol. 5, no. 4, 2018, pp. 374–83. doi: 10.1037/cns0000160.

Reznor, Trent. "Driver Down." *Lost Highway*. 2017. *Spotify*, open.spotify.com/track/1gQLcsENUSq2PbK2BFKTa4?si=15a6bdf5f5d444d8. Accessed Mar. 15, 2021.

Riches, Simon. "Intuition and Investigation into another Place: The Epistemological Role of Dreaming in *Twin Peaks* and Beyond." *The Philosophy of David Lynch*, edited by William J. Devlin and Shai Biderman, University Press of Kentucky, 2011, pp. 25–43.

Riddoch, M. Jane and Glyn W. Humphreys. "Object Recognition." *The Handbook of Cognitive Neuropsychology: What Deficits Reveal about the Human Mind*, edited by Brenda Rapp, Psychology Press, 2001, pp. 45–74.

Rodley, Chris. *Lynch on Lynch*. 2nd ed., Faber and Faber Inc., 2005.

Sampino Mattarelli, Riccardo. *David Lynch Sound Designer*. Falconara Marittima, Edizioni Crac, 2014.

Sanna, Antonio. "Entering the World of *Twin Peaks*." *Critical Essays on Twin Peaks: The Return*, edited by Antonio Sanna, Palgrave Macmillan, 2019, pp. 3–21.

Sartre, Jean-Paul. *The Imaginary – A Phenomenological Psychology of the Imagination*. Translated by Jonathan Webber, Routledge, 2004.

Schafer, R. Murray. *The New Soundscape: A Handbook for the Modern Music Teacher*. Berandol Music Limited, 1969.

Schmidt, Oliver. *Leben in gestörten Welten. Der filmische Raum in David Lynchs Eraserhead, Blue Velvet, Lost Highway und Inland Empire*. Stuttgart, ibidem, 2008.

Schneider, Irmela. "Filmwahrnehmung und Traum. Ein theoriegeschichtlicher Streifzug." *Träumungen. Traumerzählung in Film und Literatur*, edited by Bernard Dieterle, St. Augustin, Gardez, 1998, pp. 23–46.

Schönhammer, Rainer. *Einführung in die Wahrnehmungspsychologie: Sinne, Körper, Bewegung*. 2nd ed., Stuttgart, UTB, 2013.

Schönhammer, Rainer. "Traum und Film – Die besondere Beziehung der 'Siebten Kunst' zu unwillkürlichen mentalen Bildern." *PsyDok*, 2007, hdl.handle.net/20.500.11780/3613. Accessed Nov. 11, 2019.

Schopenhauer, Arthur. *Über die vierfache Wurzel des Satzes vom zureichenden Grunde: Eine philosophische Abhandlung*. Berlin, Contumax, 2016.

Schröder, Till. "Akustische Dimensionen – Funktion und Wirkung des Filmtons in *Twin Peaks*." *Mysterium Twin Peaks. Zeichen – Welten – Referenzen*, edited by Caroline Frank and Markus Schleich, Wiesbaden, SpringerVS, 2020, pp. 73–87.

Schröder, Vera. "David Lynchs *Lost Highway* als surrealistischer Film." *Surrealismus und Film. Von Fellini bis Lynch*, edited by Michael Lommel, Isabel Maurer Queipo, and Volker Roloff, Bielefeld, transcript, pp. 301–14.

Schutte, Jürgen. *Einführung in die Literaturinterpretation*. 5th ed., Weimar, J. B. Metzler, 2005.

Seesslen, Georg. *David Lynch und seine Filme*. Marburg, Schüren, 2000.

Sellmann, Michael. "*Hollywoods moderner* film noir." *Tendenzen, Motive, Ästhetik*. Würzburg, Königshausen & Neumann, 2001.
Sharf, Zack. "Laura Dern Reveals What David Lynch Really Thought About Winning An Oscar." *Indiewire*, Dec. 2, 2019, indiewire.com/2019/12/laura-dern-david-lynch-oscar-reaction-1202193559/. Accessed Feb. 19, 2020.
Shaviro, Steven. *The Cinematic Body*. University of Minnesota Press, 1993.
Shearer, Alistair, and Peter Russell, translators. *The Upanishads*. HarperCollins, 1978.
Sieveking, David, director. *David Wants to Fly*. Lichtblick Film, 2010.
Simonds, Derek, creator. *The Sinner*. Midnight Choir Inc. and Universal Content Productions, 2017.
Sinnerbrink, Robert. "Cinematic Ideas: David Lynch's 'Mulholland Drive.'" *Film-Philosophy*, vol. 9, no. 34, 2005, film-philosophy.com/vol9-2005/n34sinnerbrink. Accessed May 29, 2020.
Sinnerbrink, Robert. *New Philosophies of Film: Thinking Images*. Continuum, 2011.
Sinnerbrink, Robert. "Review: Everything You Always Wanted to Know About Lynch But Were Afraid to Ask Lacan." *South Atlantic Review*, vol. 72, no. 4, 2007, pp. 128–32.
Šklovskij, Viktor. "Die Kunst als Verfahren." *Russischer Formalismus. Texte zur allgemeinen Literaturtheorie und zur Theorie der Prosa*, edited by Jurij Striedter, München, W. Fink, 1969, pp. 3–35.
Sobchak, Vivian. *The Address of the Eye: A Phenomenology of Film Experience*. Princeton University Press, 1992.
Sobchak, Vivian. *Carnal Thoughts. Embodiment and Moving Image Culture*. University of California Press, 2004.
Sobchak, Vivian. "Phenomenology." *The Routledge Companion to Philosophy and Film*, edited by Paisley Livingstone and Carl Platinga, Routledge, 2009, pp. 435–45.
Sobchak, Vivian. "When the Ear Dreams: Dolby Digital and the Imagination of Sound." *Film Quarterly*, vol. 58, no. 4, 2005, pp. 2–15.
Sontag, Susan. *On Photography*. Penguin Books, 2008.
Sparshott, Francis E. "Vision and Dream in the Cinema." *Philosophical Exchange*, vol. 2, no. 1, 1971, pp. 111–22.
Stow, Percy, and Cecil Hepworth, directors. "Alice in Wonderland (1903) - Lewis Carroll | BFI National Archive." *YouTube*, uploaded by BFI, Feb. 25, 2010, youtube.com/watch?v=zeIXfdogJbA. Accessed Oct. 10, 2019.
Sunset Boulevard. 1950. Directed by Billy Wilder, performances by Gloria Swanson, William Holden, and Nancy Olson, Paramount Universal Pictures (Blu-ray), 2017.
Taylor, Paul. "Eraserhead." *Queen's Film Theatre Winter Programme*, Nov. 1979, pp. 10–11.
This Mortal Coil. "Song to the Siren." *Lilliput*. 1992. *Spotify*, open.spotify.com/track/0bM3fUvaZHBFUXyFNjCx1R?si=d2bd167469c34946. Accessed Mar. 15, 2021.
Thomas, Kerstin. "Dreaming in Pictures – Picturing the Dream. Oneiric Strategies in 19th and 20th Century Art." Symposium Mediating the Dream / Les genres et médias du rêve, Aug. 29, 2018, Saarland University, Conference Presentation.
Thompson, Evan. *Waking, Dreaming, Being: Self and Consciousness in Neuroscience, Meditation, and Philosophy*. Columbia University Press, 2017.
Thompson, Peter. "Margaret Thatcher: A new illusion." *Perception*, vol. 9, no. 4, 1980, pp. 483–4.
Thorne, John. *The Essential Wrapped in Plastic: Pathways to Twin Peaks*. John/Thorne, 2016.

Toadvine, Ted. "Maurice Merleau-Ponty." *Stanford Encyclopedia of Philosophy*, Sep. 14, 2016, plato.stanford.edu/entries/merleau-ponty/. Accessed Feb. 15, 2019.

2001: A Space Odyssey. Directed by Stanley Kubrick, Metro-Goldwyn-Mayer, 1968.

Van Elferen, Isabella. "Dream Timbre: Notes on Lynchian Sound Design." *Music, Sound and Filmmakers: Sonic Style in Cinema*, edited by James Wierzbecki, Routledge, 2012, pp. 175–88.

Von Hofmannsthal, Hugo. "Der Ersatz für die Träume." *Gesammelte Werke. Reden und Aufsätze II. 1914–1924*, edited by Bernd Schoeller and Rudolf Hirsch, 2nd ed., Frankfurt (M), S. Fischer Verlag, pp. 141–6.

"Who Shot Mr. Burns? (Part 2)." *The Simpsons*, directed by Wes Archer, performances by Hank Azaria and Yeardley Smith, Twentieth Century Fox, 2006.

Wiesing, Lambert. *The Philosophy of Perception: Phenomenology and Image Theory*. Translated by Nancy Ann Roth, Bloomsbury, 2014.

Woods, Paul A. *Weirdsville USA: The Obsessive Universe of David Lynch*. Plexus Publishing, 2000.

Yacavone, Daniel. *Film Worlds: A Philosophical Aesthetics of Cinema*. Columbia University Press, 2014.

Zahavi, Dan. "Inner (time-)Consciousness." *On Time -ime iousnesstp://example. cHusserlian Phenomenology of Time*, edited by Dieter Lohmar and Ichiro Yamaguchi, Springer, 2010, pp. 319–39.

Zechner, Anke. *Die Sinne im Kino. Eine Theorie der Filmwahrnehmung*. Frankfurt (M), Stroemfeld, 2013.

Zippel, Nicola. "Dreaming Consciousness: A Contribution from Phenomenology." *Rivista internazionale di filosofia e psicologia*, vol. 7, no. 2, 2016, pp. 180–201. doi: 10.4453/rifp.2016.0019. Accessed Mar. 11, 2019.

Žižek, Slavoj. *The Art of the Ridiculous Sublime: On David Lynch's Lost Highway*. Seattle, Walter Chapin Simpson Center for the Humanities, 2002.

Žižek, Slavoj. *The Plague of Fantasies*. Verso, 1997.

Žižek, Slavoj, presenter. *The Pervert's Guide to Cinema*. Directed by Sophie Fiennes, Filmedition Suhrkamp, 2016.

Zoller Seitz, Matt. "The Best Show on TV Is *Twin Peaks: The Return*." *Vulture*, Jul. 6, 2017, vulture.com/2017/07/vulture-tv-awards-best-show-twin-peaks-the-return.html. Accessed Jan. 22, 2020.

Index

abstraction   61, 63, 84, 111
Absurd Encounter with Fear   5, 6, 8–9, 43, 49–53, 59, 62, 77, 88, 120, 210–11, 218
act of viewing   15, 16, 54, 55, 129–30, 152, 198, 214
aesthetics   1, 3, 4, 9, 10, 14, 17, 18, 26, 29, 36, 37, 42, 45, 58, 71, 76, 79, 93, 110, 113, 128, 141, 142, 149, 158, 159, 166–8, 173, 190–2, 201, 210, 211, 215–17, 220
  cine-aesthetic   163
  proper time   114–15, 133
affectivity   2, 14, 21, 22, 27–9, 39, 71, 74, 142–4, 159, 163–4, 196, 198, 200
afference   75
alienation   30, 48, 62, 77, 115, 126, 133, 143
The Alphabet   5–7, 9, 26, 34, 53–64, 70, 77, 105, 111, 113, 138, 147
ambiguity   3, 37, 51–3, 63, 67, 74, 86, 88–90, 102, 162, 163, 165, 191, 199, 211–13
animation   9, 53–5, 64, 65, 77–81, 84, 111, 166, 212–14
Annie Hall   52
Arquette, Patricia   153, 156, 158, 159
atmosphere   1, 9, 49–51, 55, 73, 126, 127, 137, 174, 211
audiovision   21, 22, 33, 34, 44, 73, 91, 130, 132–4, 200, 203
awakening   58, 59, 85, 87, 97, 105, 131, 135, 148, 151, 160, 161, 163, 166, 168, 177, 178, 185–7, 192, 205, 208, 209

Bacon, Francis   58, 65, 67, 212
Badalamenti, Angelo   117, 137, 174, 175
Basso Fossali, Pierluigi   3, 78, 85, 133
Bellucci, Monica   6, 36, 144–52, 209, 216, 218

Bergman, Ingmar   4, 214
Binswanger, Ludwig   103, 106, 143
black   65–7, 80, 90
  and white   136, 140, 144, 146, 149, 207
Blue Velvet   43
body   13, 16, 17, 23, 27, 31–2, 34, 39, 52, 56–8, 60, 63, 65, 69, 71, 74–6, 91, 92, 95–6, 100, 103, 113, 117, 123, 125–7, 134, 183, 187, 197, 198, 200, 201, 206, 208, 218, *see also* double corporeality
  lived   8, 17, 34, 73, 130
Boss, Medard   23, 41, 188
Brudzinska, Jagna   3, 38, 39, 70, 100, 104, 106, 107, 109, 112, 167, 168, 212, 213, 218
Brütsch, Matthias   26, 32, 37, 41, 52, 59, 90, 160
Buñuel, Luis   4, 26, 35

Cardwell, Herbert   87
Chion, Michel   3, 21, 22, 26, 61, 63, 108, 117, 133
consciousness   8, 9, 13, 16, 17, 20, 27, 28, 34, 38–9, 44, 50, 51, 61, 68, 69, 91–8, 100, 105–7, 109–11, 113, 145, 159, 164, 166, 186, 197, 201, 206, 208, 213–15, 221

Dalí, Salvador   26, 41
deconstructivism   10, 45, 124, 139, 161, 172, 173, 214, 215
defamiliarization   62, 67, 114, 212, 215
Deleuze, Gilles   122–3, 128, 134
demand characteristics   74, 212
Deming, Peter   190
Deren, Maya   123, 164
desire   7, 42, 51, 56, 74, 78, 79, 84, 126, 143, 182, 185, 212
Dickson, Simon   29, 31, 32

Index

diegesis 45, 52, 93, 97, 111, 118, 122, 132, 133, 135, 142–3, 162, 170, 173, 200, 213, 215
disruption 2, 6, 7, 30, 132–4, 173, 201, 208, 212, 218
dissociative identity disorder 159, 166, 167
double corporeality 126–8, 200, 217
dream, *see also* oneiric
  American 6, 43, 180–5, 205, 208
  conceptualization 5, 6, 11, 24–5, 34, 39, 148, 152, 164, 172, 180–5, 203, 209, 210, 216, 219, 221
  dreamlike experience 5, 10, 26, 143, 150, 179
  as an existential state 7, 13, 29, 39, 42, 56, 60, 66, 103, 104, 106, 138, 142–4, 148, 188, 220
  experience 2–6, 9, 10, 13, 14, 24, 27, 33, 37, 39–41, 45, 62, 69, 85, 95, 97, 104, 110, 111, 114, 151, 159, 160, 183, 207, 210, 216
  layer(s) 173, 204, 214, 217
  lucid 24, 28, 67, 91, 137, 138
  marked 4, 5, 9, 25, 26, 29, 44, 45, 143, 144, 148, 210
  metaphor 1, 28, 45, 124, 150, 151, 173, 185, 192, 195, 215
  neurophysiology 30–2, 127, 145, 218
  nocturnal dream-experience 5–7, 25, 45, 49, 67, 77, 91, 104, 111, 112, 120, 122, 126, 148, 168, 192, 210, 218
  and phenomenology 2, 11, 23, 24, 29, 34, 37–42, 104, 107, 152, 188, 211
  and psychoanalysis 11, 24, 25, 37–42, 76, 100, 102–4, 106, 203, 205
  symbolism 42, 43, 56, 58–63, 66–9, 87–95, 100, 103, 104, 108, 111, 119–20, 144, 145, 173, 182, 184, 204, 207, 212, 215
  temporality 9, 87, 108, 114, 115, 118, 120–2, 126, 128, 133, 142, 173, 215
  world 23, 32, 54, 55, 62, 87, 91, 94–7, 104, 109, 110, 126, 127, 135, 145, 146, 148, 151, 168, 196, 202, 207, 208, 213, 214, 216, 218
Dune 43

efference 32, 75, 127
Elmes, Frederick 87
emotion 24, 35, 36, 50, 51, 56, 69, 73, 103, 117, 121, 126, 138, 143, 162, 163, 203
Eraserhead 5, 34, 35, 43, 82–112
experience
  experiential order 10, 77, 79, 105, 168, 173, 212
  expression of 16, 17, 145, 221
  immediacy of 2, 7–9, 13, 21, 27, 34, 62, 99, 104, 107–9, 160, 163, 168, 171, 185, 203, 213, 214, 218, 219, 221
  lived 14, 206 (*see also* lived body)
  spatial 20, 21, 23, 27, 30, 31, 53, 58, 60, 66, 67, 76–7, 80, 85, 87, 88, 95, 97, 108, 110, 116–18, 121, 123, 125, 127, 130, 134, 145, 146, 161, 165, 168, 201, 202, 214, 215
  temporal 9, 24, 45, 63, 108, 113–15, 118, 120, 121, 123–7, 133, 142, 144, 146, 160, 162, 166, 168, 173, 180, 184, 191, 215, 218, 221

fear 7, 50, 53, 56, 60–2, 102, 126, 138, 168, 182, 196, 205, 220
Fichte, Johann Gottlieb 146–8, 152, 168, 215
figure/ground 9, 50, 63
film
  experience 4, 6, 14–28, 32, 35, 38, 42, 49, 51, 53, 98, 109, 130, 139, 141, 142, 152, 162, 171, 197, 199, 202, 210, 211, 213, 219, 221
  film/dream analogy 25–8, 32–3, 35, 151, 195
  history 1, 11, 52, 55, 90, 189, 190, 194, 216
  phenomenology 4, 11, 13–20, 23, 33, 36, 197
first-person perspective 15, 20, 52, 187, 211
Fisk, Jack 49, 88, 190
Foucault, Michel 13, 23, 24, 40, 41, 103, 104, 148–9
fourth wall 36, 52, 150, 209

Freud, Sigmund   37–42, 50, 79, 98–104, 106, 163, 184, 193, 207, *see also* dream, and psychoanalysis
Funny Games   138

Gehring, Petra   103, 147, 152, 172
Generation Wealth   18
Gilda   175, 190
The Grandmother   5, 8–9, 34, 43, 64–81, 84, 88, 90, 92, 126, 138, 160, 212, 219, 220
Greenfield, Lauren   18

hallucination   40, 60, 79, 90, 156, 170, 186, 187
Haneke, Michael   138
haptic visuality   5, 72, 212
Hitchcock, Alfred   73, 75, 120
Hobson, Allan   50–1, 67, 161, 166
Hollywood   26, 41, 137, 181–5, 188, 190, 194–6, 217
horror   56, 61, 64, 113, 203
Husserl, Edmund   13, 36, 38, 68, 81, 90, 103, 107, 110, 212

identity   6, 38, 42, 60, 74, 105–7, 142, 146, 148–51, 158–73
imagination   28, 55, 66, 68, 80, 90, 97, 100, 103, 106, 109, 122, 149, 158, 194
immersion   2, 7, 42, 68, 80, 95, 104, 111, 116, 117, 143, 144, 168, 190, 192, 201, 202, 208–11, 220
impressional-apperceptive   38, 105, 107, 109, 110, 212, 213
Inception   105
indeterminacy   34, 57, 115, 125, 142–4, 161, 188
Inland Empire   43, 121, 144
integrability   60, 104, 110, 159, 163, 166, 168, 188
intentionality   16, 20, 68, 99, 100, 107, 206
  act   21, 22
  noema and noesis   38–9, 58, 133, 190, 201, 206
  operative   22
introspection   19–20

Jurassic Park   74, 125, 212

Kant, Immanuel   147
knowledge   18, 20, 22, 37, 39, 42, 79, 94, 106, 147, 152, 198, 203
  carnal   29, 72
  denial of   3, 37, 72, 142
  oneiric   29, 30, 32
  propositional   72–3, 207
  sensory   203–9
  situated   18
Kracauer, Siegfried   8, 38, 71

Lacan, Jacques   7, 40, 42, 56, 78, 79, 190, 203, 212
Langer, Susanne   22, 27
language   1, 14, 15, 22, 26, 56, 99, 104, 110, 113, 191, 202, 208, 212, 217, 220
L'Eclisse   141
Lost Highway   2–7, 9, 37, 41, 43, 44, 95, 138, 153–73, 188, 213–15, 217, 219, 220
Lynchian   1–2, 4, 6–8, 11–13, 19, 25, 33, 35–7, 42, 43, 188, 210, 212, 213, 218–21

McGowan, Todd   7, 40, 41, 78–80, 170, 183
MacLachlan, Kyle   113, 123, 148
Marks, Laura   5, 57, 72, 211, 212
materiality   32, 58–62, 70–7, 79, 103, 194, 202, 212, 217
mediality   2, 9, 38, 84, 108, 110–12, 133, 164–73, 197–203, 211, 214, 216, 218
meditation   22, 33, 34, 92–4, 97, 98, 109, 214
Merleau-Ponty, Maurice   14, 17, 21–4, 34, 41, 53, 57, 60, 73, 104, 161, 185, 221
Meshes of the Afternoon   164
Metz, Christian
The Mirror   91
mirror neurons   20, 50, 117, 200, 212
mood, *see* atmosphere
movement   15, 20, 32, 49–51, 53, 58, 77, 78, 95, 113, 115, 118, 133, 173, 199, 215, 218
  camera   30–1, 138, 165, 172, 191, 218
  image   123, 133–4

inhibited   75–6, 126–8, 200, 218
inner co-   31, 58, 200–1, 203
musical   55, 117, 200
paradoxical   114, 173, 200, 215
saccadic   72, 212
Mulholland Drive   3–6, 8, 10, 28, 32, 37, 43, 121, 138, 166, 174–209, 211, 213, 216–20
music   50, 51, 62, 83, 84, 91, 108–9, 116–20, 122, 133, 137, 170, 197, 200, 206, 213, 218
mystery   1, 102, 113, 144, 158, 159, 162

objectivity   16, 20, 125, 129, 165, 168, 169, 196
  feminist   18
objet petit a   56
ocularcentrism   20
Once Upon a Time in the West   80
oneiric, *see also* dream
  film   8, 11, 12, 25, 29, 33
  four dimensions   5–6, 10, 25
  Lynchian   2, 4, 6–8, 11, 12, 19, 25, 26, 33–7, 42, 43, 210, 212, 213, 218–21
ontology   24, 54, 67, 68, 77, 87, 91, 95, 97, 105, 108, 109, 129, 140, 152, 161, 162, 164, 169, 172, 173, 180, 184, 186, 187, 189, 194, 212–14, 219
  ambiguity   3, 37, 67, 143
  disruption   130, 133, 134, 173
  of film   15, 35, 133, 134, 145, 149, 151, 196–203, 208, 219
  and psychology   9, 146, 148, 170, 171, 219
other(ness)   3, 9, 15, 16, 38, 53–5, 58, 78, 104, 106–10, 114, 115, 120, 166–8, 173, 198, 199, 213–15, 218, 220

painting   49, 53, 54, 57, 58, 65, 67, 69, 87, 113, 117, 161, 212, 214
Penderecki, Krzysztof   49, 211
perception   2, 4, 9, 18–20, 24–6, 31, 37, 39, 45, 50, 51, 54, 60, 62, 63, 70, 71, 77, 87, 88, 91, 92, 99, 106, 107, 111, 114, 115, 117, 118, 121, 130, 133, 145, 147, 160–2, 164, 165, 167, 168, 171, 184, 187, 192, 207, 211, 212, 214, 215
  auditory   20–2, 108–9, 213

de-automatization   2, 7, 55–8, 163, 211, 219
  embodied   3, 109, 187, 198
  and expression   4, 13–15, 17, 19, 198
Persona   214, 221
Petrić, Vlada   28, 30–2, 42, 52–3, 120, 126
phantasmatic-imaginary   38, 77, 104–7, 109, 110, 212–13
phenomenology   3, 8, 11, 12, 16, 17, 19, 24, 28, 34, 107, 202
  of dreaming   2, 29, 37–42, 52, 70, 104–5, 211 (*see also* dream, and phenomenology)
  existential   14, 39, 104, 149, 188
  of film   4, 13–15, 19, 23, 33, 36, 152, 197
  neurophenomenology   19–20
photography   24, 31, 54
The Piano   74, 212
pixilation   77–8
point of audition   21
point of view   21, 99, 100, 165, 168, 192, 196
pre-reflective experience   2, 3, 7, 8, 18, 19, 30, 33, 34, 37, 39, 49–53, 74, 152, 198, 203, 207, 210, 211, 217, 219, 221
projection   15, 23–4, 64, 169
proper time, *see* dream, temporality
psychoanalysis, *see* dream, and psychoanalysis
psychoanalytic film theory   3, 7, 25, 27, 41–2, 76, 197
psychosis   70, 159, 161–2, 169, 171, 188

reality   25, 26, 28, 30, 35, 45, 50, 52, 64, 68, 70, 78–81, 95, 97, 105, 109, 113, 124, 129, 130, 134, 136, 138–45, 147, 148, 152, 158–65, 167, 169–73, 181, 183–5, 187, 188, 190, 192–4, 197, 202, 205, 207, 208, 213, 217, 220
Rear Window   73
reflexivity   18, 129, 139, 151, 169–73, 203, 206, 213, 215, 217
REM sleep   31–2, 127

retroactive mode   29–30, 69–70, 122
Rodley, Chris   1, 6, 35, 50, 53, 58, 64, 65, 69, 73, 98, 109, 117, 122, 143, 158, 162, 170, 196, 201, 213

Schönhammer, Rainer   28, 31–2, 50, 58, 73, 75, 127, 212
second-order seeing   9, 54, 166, 214
self   3, 16, 23–4, 27, 38–9, 79, 94, 95, 101, 105–7, 149, 161, 166, 171, 186, 187, 193, 207
sensory experience   2, 7, 39, 221
sensory-motor activation   30–2, 42, 75, 91, 123–8, 133–4, 200, 218
Sinnerbrink, Robert   2, 3, 41–2, 183, 195–6
sleep paralysis   32, 76, 127, 218
Sobchak, Vivian   4, 8, 13–17, 20, 24, 29, 33, 34, 38, 40, 54, 71–4, 114, 115, 125, 130, 141, 145, 152, 197–8, 206–7, 221
sound   3, 21, 22, 31, 56, 61–2, 72–3, 87, 91, 108–9, 123, 133, 198–200, 213, *see also* auditory perception
  acousmatic   61–2, 117
  ambient   22, 108, 213
  soundscape   22, 108, 111, 133, 138, 154, 155, 213
spectator   7, 14–16, 19, 21, 27–9, 42, 53, 197, 202–3, 211, *see also* viewer
Spellbound   120
Spielberg, Steven   74, 125, 212
subjectivity   15–21, 35, 66, 168
Sunset Boulevard   174, 189, 190, 196, 200, 216

surrealism   26–7, 41, 167, 219
synesthesia   9, 27, 111

Tarkovsky, Andrei   4, 33, 91
temporality, *see* dream, temporality
Thompson, Evan   20, 22, 27, 34, 40, 52, 67, 91–7, 145, 186
time-image   122–3, 128, 134
trauma   56, 78–9, 89, 132, 138–40, 212
Twin Peaks   3–9, 28, 32, 36, 37, 43–5, 95, 113–52, 172, 173, 193, 209, 210, 213–21

Un Chien Andalou   26
uncanniness   1, 61, 164
unconscious   18, 40, 42, 92, 96, 115, 122, 181, 183–5, 193, 203–6, 212
  experience   97–110
  Freudian   28, 39, 79, 88, 98–104
  phenomenologization   106–10
viewer   3, 14–17, 19, 20, 25, 27–33, 35, 36, *see also* spectator
viewer–film relationship   2, 9, 36, 42, 49, 51–3, 77, 197–203, 218, 220

Watts, Naomi   174, 178, 180, 189, 195
wish   28, 38, 40, 69, 70, 79, 100–2, 106, 170, 183, 184, 203, 206, 207

Yacavone, Daniel   17, 22, 163

Zechner, Anke   57, 62, 161
Žižek, Slavoj   3, 41, 44, 61, 158, 188, 197, 200, 205